PHYSIOGRAPHIC PROVINCES OF THE NORTHEAST

D1261433

SCALE IN MILES
10 0 10 20 30 40 50

St. Lawrence Valley Province and Champlain Lowland Section

Adirondack Province

Mohawk Section

Hudson Lowland Section

New England (Upland) Province

Northern Piedmont Lowland Section

Coastal Plain Province

White Mountain Section

Seaboard Lowland Section

THE ARCHAEOLOGY
OF
NEW YORK STATE

WILLIAM A. RITCHIE

THE
ARCHAEOLOGY
OF
NEW YORK STATE

REVISED EDITION

PUBLISHED FOR THE AMERICAN MUSEUM OF NATURAL HISTORY

THE NATURAL HISTORY PRESS, GARDEN CITY, NEW YORK

27408

CONTENTS

LIST OF ILLUSTRATIONS

Figures

Plates

PREFACE
to the Second, Revised Edition

The first draft of this book reported on archaeological researches in the New York State area to 1964. Site excavations conducted during the subsequent four years have added some significant new data, chiefly of a quantitative nature, which both clarify and enlarge the record of aboriginal life as described in the first edition, in 1965. Most of the new work was done by the New York State Museum and Science Service, but substantial additions to the Iroquoian segment of prehistory in the state have been made by other institutions, in Buffalo (White, 1967), Rochester (Hayes, 1967), and Syracuse (Tuck, 1967). There have also been amateur contributions, as noted below. Field work for a part of each season between 1964 and 1967 by the writer on Martha's Vineyard, Massachusetts, has illuminated some aspects of coastal ecology and adaptation and, furthermore, resulted in the formulation of a radiocarbon-dated outline of prehistory for southern New England, correlative in part with the similarly dated culture sequence in New York (Ritchie, 1969).

In this preface I shall present a summary of the salient new data. Necessary revisions of the original text have also been made. These, however, comprise only small changes and the modification of Figures 1

and 2. Since illustration of the new materials would, for the most part, simply duplicate the published artifact forms, no additional plates have been added.

While our excavations of the last few years in New York have involved some sites referable to each of the six stages of prehistoric cultural development, the most important contributions have pertained to the Paleo-Indian and Archaic segments. In the first category, the exploration of the West Athens Hill site (Cox. 7) takes first rank.

The West Athens Hill Site
(Cox. 7)

This unique, quarry-workshop-habitation station, the largest known Paleo-Indian site in New York State, was discovered and reported by R. Arthur Johnson of Albany, following bulldozer clearing of a rocky knoll, three miles west of the Hudson River, in Greene County (Figure 2, site number 7). This and an adjacent knoll, rises from a long ridge of Normanskill shale containing veins of gray to green, high grade flint, much utilized by all prehistoric Indians of the area. The finding of a fluted point led to a preliminary investigation by Robert E.

Funk of the Science Service staff and the writer, followed by major excavations conducted by the former in 1966.

Most of the evidence was found in a broad, shallow depression between the knolls, a sheltered area, apparently the principal habitation locus. The occupation was concentrated in an area measuring about thirty by sixty feet. The physical stratigraphy consisted of three soil layers, namely, stratum 1, a dark brown humic zone, four to six inches thick, which contained most of the Early Hunter artifacts, all of the scanty Late Archaic and Woodland remains, and a great amount of flint debitage; stratum 2A, a light brown, silty soil, zero to six inches thick, with much debitage and the remainder of the most ancient implements; and stratum 2B, a few inches of sterile, yellow-brown, sandy soil, with small, angular, shale fragments, investing the uneven bedrock.

More than 1400 artifacts and most of the chipping debris are referable to the Paleo-Indian people of the Clovis tradition. Briefly, the inventory, similar to that from the Potts site (Plates 6–10), is as follows: twenty-four fluted points, whole, fragmentary, or in process; about 200 bifacially worked pieces, including ovate knives and blanks or preforms for such knives and for fluted points; ninety-six simple end scrapers, mainly trianguloid in outline, a few with weak graving spurs at one end of the working edge; approximately 220 side scrapers and knives, based on broad, flat flakes retouched along one and sometimes two edges, the majority somewhat arbitrarily considered scrapers because of the greater thickness and steeper beveling of the working edge; and a very large number of variously retouched and utilized flakes and cores. Some of this material suggests that its intensive study will eventuate in the recognition of as yet undefined new tool forms for this early culture.

While by far the bulk of the chipped stone artifacts were derived from the local flint outcrops, a small remainder made of exotic flints is present, comprising Pennsylvania jasper, Ohio Upper Mercer flint and western New York Onondaga flint. This fact may indicate regions in which these nomadic people had sojourned prior to their entry into the Hudson Valley.

As befits a quarry-workshop locus, pebble hammerstones, of simple, unpitted form, abounded. Of unusual interest are several flat, sandstone abraders showing fine line wear, perhaps from sharpening awls or grinding the lower edges of the fluted points.

No trace of bone remained and no hearths, postmolds or other features rewarded careful search. The pattern of artifact distribution, however, possibly revealed the location of small hut sites. A definite clustering of artifacts was evident forming in most cases arcs or semicircles averaging eight feet in diameter, suggesting hearth-centered activities. The same range of artifacts occurred in each cluster, namely, hammerstones, blanks, end scrapers, side scrapers, knives and sometimes fluted points.

The West Athens Hill assemblage compares very closely with that from the other early Paleo-Indian sites in the Northeast, mentioned or described in this book, but it differs from all in being the only quarry-workshop of this early period so far discovered.

The Kings Road Site
(Cox. 25-4)

A small but instructive component of the Clovis tradition, the Kings Road site

(Cox. 25-4), was discovered in October 1966 by Thomas P. Weinman. It is situated on a very low rise, near a small swale, in an area of gently rolling clay bottom land between low hills and steep ridges of Normanskill shale, approximately two miles west of the Hudson River in Greene County (Figure 2, site number 8).

The occupied area, as indicated by the distribution of artifacts and a small quantity of chipping debris, is a rough oval measuring fifty by eighty feet. A total of 150 square feet have thus far been excavated by Thomas and Paul Weinman, with some assistance from Robert E. Funk. All material has been found in the brown, plowed topsoil, extending to a maximum of fourteen inches over the sterile, compact, yellow clay subsoil.

As of January 1968, 351 artifacts have been found by surface hunting and by excavation. These fully conform with recognized types and comprise the following categories: three fragmentary finished fluted points and portions of four others in process, plus a preform or blank; forty-seven end scrapers, of which fourteen have from one to three small graving spurs; sixty-seven side scrapers; three spoke-shave scrapers; forty-three flake knives; nineteen biface tools, probably knives; and about 150 other items, including fragments of bifaces in process, retouched flakes and utilized flakes and cores. There are also two possible anvilstones.

Of special interest is the high percentage of exotic flints on this component which utilized chiefly the local Normanskill flint. Approximately 10 per cent of the total collection of tools was imported into the eastern New York area from regions to the west, south and north. Recognizably Ohio stone is Flint Ridge chalcedony and Upper Mercer blue-black flint; the western variety

of Onondaga flint may have come from western New York or adjacent Ontario; eastern Pennsylvania is represented by red, brown and yellow jasper; upper New York by Fort Ann flint, and adjacent New England probably by maroon jasper. These facts, which can be widely duplicated on Paleo-Indian sites in New York and elsewhere in the Northeast, suggest, probably, considerable mobility by the small bands of Early Hunters, and they assist in indicating the directions of their movements, and perhaps of their contacts or associations with other small groups. A north-south route of movement also suggests a seasonal shift of the New York occupants, most likely in response to migratory game herds, quite possibly of the caribou.

The Port Mobil Site

A probable Paleo-Indian component, the Port Mobil site, was discovered in the spring of 1967 on southern Staten Island, by Joseph Bodnar of nearby Charleston, who kindly reported it and lent his specimens for study to the writer. It is situated on high ground, approximately twenty to forty feet above sea level, sloping down to the Arthur Kill, distant about 1000 feet to the southwest (Figure 2, site number 9). Additional site data were received from Professor Bert Salwen of New York University, who awaits permission from the Mobil Oil Company to conduct excavations at the site.

As the area has been extensively disturbed by bulldozing and other activities, most of the site has probably been destroyed. The artifacts were found on the surface of the scraped and eroding slope and in earth pushed up around the storage tanks.

Besides the Paleo-Indian remains, a fair

quantity of later material has been found, including a few plain, grit-tempered potsherds.

All of the artifacts attributable to the Paleo-Indian component are of small size by comparison with those from such other New York State components as Potts (Ritchie, 1965, p. 22) and West Athens Hill. Typologically, however, they closely conform to the recognized categories of the Clovis tradition in the East. With few exceptions, the specimens are chipped from a tan or yellow jasper, some of it identifiable with eastern Pennsylvania sources. Several pieces exhibit a chalky consistency believed to be due to weathering. The five exceptions are made of eastern New York Normanskill flint.

The inventory of implements to date (January, 1968) is as follows: two intact fluted points, three broken fluted points, and three such points broken in manufacture. All are short, one may have been repointed, another has prominent outflaring ears like the Cumberland variety. Basal and lateral grinding are absent on the finished points. There are fifteen end scrapers; seven side scrapers; two spokeshave scrapers, one very small; nine flake knives; two graving tools, one bipointed; and one biface knife with broken base.

About 500 yards south of this site, on the tidal beach of the Arthur Kill, Mr. Bodnar, his son, nephews and other people have picked up, as they were eroded from along the swampy shore line, the following artifacts of Paleo-Indian typology: six fluted points, whole or fragmentary, of jasper, New York State and exotic flints; a large, convergent side scraper of brown flint; two side scrapers of Normanskill flint; one specimen each of flake knife, single and double spokeshave scraper; one utilized flake for a side scraper with concave edge. The

material of these specimens is yellow jasper, except as specified, and there appears to be a definite relationship between the two well separated components.

The Vergennes Phase

Supplementary data on several phases of the Archaic stage in the New York area have recently been acquired. For the earliest or Vergennes phase our previous knowledge was drawn very largely from the KI site, in Vermont, described on page 85. Further information on this key site was obtained through the writer's excavations there in 1966 which has been added to the text on page 85.

During the course of an archaeological reconnaissance in the eastern Adirondack area in 1967, I learned of the destruction by sand removal of what appears to have been an even larger component of the Vergennes phase, the first major site of this culture recorded for New York, situated in the Champlain Valley near the mouth of the Little Ausable River in Clinton County. The site had occupied a sand terrace about twenty-five feet above the river which from just above this point to its mouth is a deadwater stream, largely surrounded by marsh, an environmental setting now known to have been favored by the people of the Vergennes culture.

Nothing remained of the site when it was visited by me, but according to my informants, Richard Passino of Keeseville and Noah Carte of Peru, who have the collections from this component, the artifacts occurred in reddish sand under the heavily pine forested, black duff layer. No bones, hearths or other features were noted, although burned stones and chipping debris, chiefly quartzite, were present.

The combined collection from this site,

which represents only a part of its content, as much was lost in sand removal, is rich in artifacts of ground slate, comprising at least fifteen ulus, six with ridged top, and fragments of several others; thirty ground slate points or stemmed knives and many fragments, of several forms, but chiefly barbed with serrated tang. There are also twelve plummets, some very well made, with plain, grooved or knobbed top; four gouges, representing two styles, a shallow, short form and a long, narrow, deeply grooved variety; four large, rather crude, mostly thin celts; two unfinished plano-convex adzes; three choppers; numerous pebble hammerstones; whetstones; and rough rod-shaped stone artifacts of unknown use, like those from the KI site. Of much importance are two atlatl weights, a lunate specimen completely pecked out and partially perforated from both sides of the centrum by means of a solid core drill, and half of a finished specimen of trapezoidal form.

Projectile points predominate, as usual, with the Otter Creek type constituting the great majority. As at KI, most of these are of gray quartzite, with smaller representations of flint and argillite. Again, as at KI, the Otter Creek type point had a minor association with other recognized Laurentian forms, including the Vosburg type and wide side-notched and stemmed forms. Other chipped implements from the Bridge site comprised ovate and trianguloid knives, and drills with Otter Creek type base. The total series constitutes an impressive confirmation of the known or suspected Vergennes complex and virtually duplicates, although far richer in ground slates and plummets, the KI series, illustrated on Plates 26 through 28, both in typology and materials.

The Vergennes culture is apparently present on a major, undated site on Alumette Island in the Ottawa River, Province of Quebec, excavated by Clyde Kennedy, who in 1966 showed me his material in Ottawa. The large series of artifacts includes Otter Creek points, most of them smaller than Vermont and New York specimens; ground slate ulus, some with ridged back; holed bannerstones of trapezoidal or short-winged form; stone gouges; and many copper tools, such as socketed spears, toggle spears, spears with tangs and spurs, spuds, fishhooks, gorges, awls and knives. Bone-work was fortunately preserved on this site and included multiple unilaterally barbed points with angular barbs, eyed needles and ground beaver incisors.

Small Stemmed Point Cultures

An important breakthrough in the Late Archaic of eastern New York and southern New England came as the result of simultaneous discoveries in these two areas in 1964 of apparently related complexes characterized by the use of small stemmed points usually made of quartz. In the central Hudson Valley Funk excavated the Sylvan Lake Rockshelter and defined the Sylvan Lake complex (Funk, 1965). On Martha's Vineyard, Massachusetts, the writer excavated the Hornblower II site and defined the Squibnocket complex (Ritchie, 1965a; 1969).

The key station for the Sylvan Lake complex, located thirteen miles southeast of Poughkeepsie in Dutchess County, is an unusual rockshelter, measuring approximately twenty-seven feet wide by fifteen feet deep by five feet high. Three strata were discerned, stratum 1, a ten inch layer of mixed rubble, brown soil and refuse containing a small number of artifacts of Late and Middle Woodland occupations;

stratum 2, a twenty to thirty-seven inch thick deposit of compact, tan-colored, silt-like sediment, the main relic-bearing member; and stratum 3, a mixture of coarse rock rubble and gray soil, six to eighteen inches thick, overlying massive rocks, apparently covering the bedrock. The small series of fourteen projectile points from stratum 3 comprises untyped forms, a few of which bear some similarities to the Otter Creek and Brewerton Eared Notched types. These were associated with several non-diagnostic artifacts.

The upper levels of stratum 2 yielded a few projectile points of the Susquehanna tradition intermixed with a larger number of point forms relating to the middle levels of the site where the concentrated materials of the Sylvan Lake complex were found. The basal levels of stratum 2 were assigned by Funk to the Vosburg phase, as mentioned on page 84.

Several important radiocarbon dates have been obtained on charcoal from the various levels of this site. The oldest date thus far determined for a site in New York, 4610 B.C.±100 (Y-1655), applies to the base of stratum 2. From stratum 3 a younger date of 4030 B.C.±120 (I-2599) was derived. The Vosburg horizon near the base of stratum 2 yielded a date of 2780 B.C.±80 (Y-1535), the Sylvan Lake horizon, near the center of the same stratum, was dated at 2210 B.C.±140 (Y-1536).

The Sylvan Lake complex is characterized chiefly by the dominance of small stemmed points, for the most part of quartz. Funk has grouped his approximately 200 specimens of this kind into a new category of Sylvan Stemmed points, which on analysis can be separated into several intergrading varieties comprising Bare Island, Wading River (see below), and Lamoka-like forms. A small, thick, side-notched point form, the Sylvan Side-notched type, accompanied the stemmed forms at all levels, and there was a small remainder of unclassified stemmed or side-notched points, some resembling Normanskill and Brewerton Laurentian types.

Associated traits of the complex comprise side scrapers, ovate knives, expanded base drills, crude choppers, notched atlatl weights, pebble hammerstones, and antler tine flakers.

Of the several other sites in eastern and southern New York assignable to the Sylvan Lake complex on the basis of artifact trait similarity, the largest and most important is the Wading River site, excavated by the writer in north-central Long Island in 1956 (Ritchie, 1959, pp. 78–88) (Figure 4, site number 14). The narrow, stemmed, white quartz point which predominated on this shell midden site is the same point form which was most abundant in the Sylvan Lake Rockshelter and on Martha's Vineyard, Massachusetts, where recent excavations by the writer have resulted in his definition of the Squibnocket complex (page xix). Because it was first found by excavation as part of a definite, although unnamed assemblage, at the Wading River site, the writer has now formally described this distinctive "small stemmed point" as the Wading River type (Ritchie, 1965a; 1969). It is one of a variety of narrow-bladed, straight stemmed points of small to medium size, and is not to be confused with the stemmed variety of the Lamoka type, with its thick, unfinished base (Ritchie, 1961, pp. 29–30), or the prevailingly larger Bare Island type which it most closely resembles (ibid., pp. 14–15). Prior to the recent discoveries at Sylvan Lake Rockshelter and on Martha's Vineyard, the small stemmed points of eastern and southern New York were for the most part placed in the category of Lamoka-like and Bare Island points (Ritchie, 1958).

Beyond doubt, the Wading River type point was a shared trait of a number of probably mutually interrelated hunting complexes of Late Archaic times, widely distributed throughout eastern and southern New York and southern New England, two of which, the Sylvan Lake and the Squibnocket, have been radiocarbon-dated around 2200 B.C. The former has already been described (page xx); the contemporaneous Squibnocket complex was discovered and described by the writer at the same time in eastern Massachusetts. The evidence for it came from the excavation in 1964 and 1966, respectively, of two stratified, shell midden sites on Martha's Vineyard, namely, the Hornblower II site on Squibnocket Pond, town of Gay Head and the Vincent site in Vineyard Haven, town of Tisbury (Ritchie, 1969). On both stations the basic stratum, number 4, pertained to the Laurentian tradition and at Hornblower II this level was carbon-14 dated at 2270 B.C.±160 years (Y-1530). No datable charcoal was found in this horizon at the Vincent site.

Stratum 3, immediately overlying stratum 4 at both sites, produced the artifacts and features of the Squibnocket complex, and one radiocarbon date was obtained from a hearth in this stratum at the Hornblower II site. This date of 2190 B.C.±100 years (Y-1529) is the same as that for the Sylvan Lake complex in eastern New York (page xx).

At the Vincent site especially, the distributional evidence strongly suggests some temporal overlap of the Laurentian and Squibnocket complexes, and I believe that the latter, with a quartz pebble industry, represents a movement of new people and

culture into the Northeast, which assimilated and submerged the resident groups of Laurentian antecedents, whose older region of dispersion lay to the north in the St. Lawrence Valley. The Squibnocket complex probably formed part of a still undefined narrow point tradition with connections in the Middle Atlantic area, which occurs throughout the coastal plain and the major river valleys, principally the Susquehanna, Hudson and Connecticut (page 143). The Kent-Hally site on Bare Island in the lower Susquehanna apparently pertains to this cultural tradition (Kinsey, 1959), as do numerous components known from this and the other named valleys. The evidence suggests, furthermore, that cultures of this tradition became the dominant Late Archaic manifestations of the eastern and southern New York and southern New England region, beginning around 2200 B.C., and that they constituted the native cultures there with which the cultures of the Susquehanna tradition, diffusing from the same Middle Atlantic region, were to interact, beginning some 700 years later. Evidence in support of this hypothesis was found by Funk in the upper levels of stratum 2 at the Sylvan Lake site (Funk, 1965, 1966), and by the writer in stratum 2 of the Hornblower II site, stratum 3A of the Vincent site, and stratum 3 of the Peterson site (Ritchie, 1969).

To the Squibnocket complex as currently known from our Martha's Vineyard excavations belong the following artifact traits: projectile points of three types; namely, Wading River, its probable derivative, the Squibnocket Stemmed, and the Squibnocket Triangle,[1] nearly all of quartz; the trianguloid and retouched flake knife; plummet; notched atlatl weight; chopper; unpitted

[1] These three newly defined point types are formally described in Ritchie, 1969.

pebble hammerstone; probably graphite and hematite paintstones; the cylindrical pestle and plano-convex adz. In bone and antler there are polished splinter awls, and probably the barbed bone point, conical antler projectile point, cylindrical antler flaker and deer ulna awl.

The artifact congeries, which is very similar to that of the obviously related and coeval Sylvan Lake complex, seems to reflect a primary emphasis on hunting, probably with the javelin or short spear thrown by an atlatl. Large numbers of animal bones, chiefly of the deer, support this assumption. At the Martha's Vineyard sites seal remains showed that hunting was not confined to land mammals but included inshore and perhaps offshore hunting. Some probable fishing gear—plummets and the barbed bone point—attest to another kind of food from the sea, and large quantities of shellfish, principally hard clam, further demonstrate the coastal adaptation of the Squibnocket people. (See full account in Ritchie, 1969).

The Hickory Hill Marsh Site

A little new and significant information relating to the Transitional stage has recently come to light through the chance discovery of a small, productive, apparently single component site of the Frost Island phase, which is discussed on page 156. What is known as the Hickory Hill Marsh site was uncovered when a very low rise in the Montezuma Marsh was being leveled by bulldozer in 1965 by the New York State Conservation Department. The site lies well out in the marsh off the southern end of Howland Island, dominated here by a high drumlin called Hickory Hill. The elevation is something less than ten feet below the 380 foot contour, along which the major sites of all ages in this area lie

(page 38), and the site could have been occupied only during a perod of drought sufficient to substantially lower the water level of the great marsh. If we may judge the time of occupation by the single radiocarbon date for the Frost Island component at the O'Neil site, only about six miles to the east, this hunting and fishing camp in the fen was inhabited around 1250 B.C. (page 157).

The foreman in charge of the work, George Gage, carefully collected the material as it was uncovered and brought it to the New York State Museum for identification.

The collection comprises over fifty Susquehanna Broad points, exhibiting all the usual variations in blade size and breadth, of local flint with one exception, a rhyolite point; six large semilozenge-shaped knives (resembling figures 16, 21 of Plate 51); an ovate knife; a strike-a-light made from a broken projectile point; two drills with Susquehanna Broad type bases; two rude celts; several large steatite potsherds; and six fragmentary bone and antler artifacts, the first such implements reported from a site of this culture. These important specimens are identifiable as a polished bone splinter awl; two slender, multiple, unilaterally barbed, bone points; a single, unilaterally barbed, antler point with linehole; and a perforated antler tine section of unknown use. Deer bones and burned rock fragments occurred with the artifacts in the fine brown peat which rests upon a marl foundation formed when this area constituted the final remnant of glacial Lake Iroquois (page 97).

New Sites of the Meadowood Phase

Two recently excavated sites of Early Woodland provenience are of unusual interest since both are habitation components of the Meadowood phase, previously known chiefly from burial loci (page 180). The first excavated and smaller camp site, Nahrwold No. 2 (Shr. 51-4), was explored by the writer in 1965 on the Arthur G. Nahrwold farm just south of Middleburg, Schoharie County, New York. It was found during the exploration of the much larger Nahrwold No. 1 site, further referred to below, and occupied about a quarter acre of a high sand terrace bordering the flood plain of Schoharie Creek.

Artifacts found on the surface by Harold Zoch of Middleburg, who reported the site, pertained to Early Woodland and Archaic occupations and a more intensive investigation of the earlier component, conducted by the writer in 1966, will be reported elsewhere.

Beneath an eight inch plow zone the soil consisted of compact, homogeneous, tan-colored, sandy loam, free of natural stones. From plow-line to twenty-four inches, the site was heavily productive of flint rejectage, chiefly the large flat flakes and spalls characteristic of the Meadowood flint knappers. Both regional Onondaga and Mohawk Valley Little Falls flints were present, the latter in small amounts. Quarry blanks, cache blades, projectile points, simple and stemmed end scrapers, hammerstones and unworked quartz crystals were the principal items found, either scattered through the sand or in concentrated areas, some of which appear to have been pits with obliterated outlines. Fire-broken stones were sparingly present in random fashion or in small concentrations obviously representing hearths, one of which yielded charcoal, radiocarbon-dated at 760 B.C. ±80 years (Y-1651), a date which fits nicely within the established range for this culture (Figure 1). Potsherds, all of Vinette 1 type, were of rare occurrence, but fortunately both a sherd and a Meadowood type point were found in association with the dated feature. No bone had been preserved in the mildly acid soil (pH 6.5) save small calcined fragments, some recognizable as deer remains.

Although smaller, this site resembles the Riverhaven No. 2 component of the Meadowood culture, located at the extreme western end of the state (page 190), in producing an inordinate quantity of flint debitage, suggesting primary use as a workshop component to which quarry blanks were transported from regional quarry centers for manufacture into the thin "cache" or "mortuary" blades characteristic of this phase (pages 181, 198).

The Scaccia Site
(Cda. 17-3)

The much larger Scaccia site (Cda. 17-3) lies a mile south of Cuylerville, Livingston County, New York, on a lobe or spur comprising about three-fourths of an acre, jutting eastward from the high terrace composed of glacio-fluvial sands and gravels, bordering the flood plain of the Genesee River. Little Beards Creek flows thirty feet below the site along the base of the terrace. It was reported to the New York State Museum and Science Service in 1965 by Charles F. Wray of West Rush, who, with his associates, Albert Hoffman and Donald Cameron, had already excavated seventy-five pits (Wray, 1965), and it was further explored the following summer by a Science Service party under Robert E. Funk.

This was a multicomponent site, both the surface and some of the pits yielding artifacts of Lamoka and Laurentian provenience. One burial with a blocked-end tube and an Adena stemmed point of exotic flint was found in 1965 and a fine birdstone of truncated or bust type, probably derived from a plowed-out grave, was a surface find in 1966. These items show use of the site during the Middlesex phase, which may have overlapped the Meadowood occupation (Figure 1).

The Science Service excavations disclosed fifty-three additional pits and hearths. Most of the larger pits found on this site seem to have been storage features in which refuse was later disposed of. They contained varying quantities of dark soil, charcoal, flint chipping debris, fire broken stones; lost or discarded artifacts, whole or broken; animal bones and carbonized vegetal remains, none of cultigens. Most of the smaller, basin-shaped depressions held burned stones, charcoal and some ashes, and had fire-reddened walls indicative of hearths.

The faunal remains have been studied and reported on by John E. Guilday of Carnegie Museum and will be discussed in full in the site report. As usual, the white-tailed deer was the principal source of animal food, but the list includes the gray squirrel, woodchuck, muskrat, beaver, porcupine, rabbit or hare, dog, raccoon, black bear, turkey, blue or snow goose, unidentified species of duck, snapping turtle, Blanding's turtle, bullfrog, catfish and sucker.

The carbonized plant vestiges have been identified by Dr. Richard A. Yarnell of Emory University as hickory nut shells, acorn meats, a grape seed and, perhaps, a *Viburnum* seed.

The artifact inventory corresponds in most respects with that described elsewhere in this book for the Meadowood phase. It is important to emphasize that the pottery, all of Vinette 1 type, consisting of forty-six rim sherds and 662 body and base pieces, was well distributed throughout the site and was an unequivocal and

important trait of the Meadowood culture. The projectile points are of the Meadowood type, with two variants, to be described in the site report; there are several forms of drills, all characteristic of the Meadowood phase; a few end scrapers and strike-a-lights; together with pebble hammerstones, anvilstones, mullers, celts, plano-convex adzes, a bar type birdstone in process, fragmentary gorgets and a crescentic slate pendant. The fortunate preservation of bone permitted the recovery of awls made from rough or polished splinters of long bone and the deer ulna, a bird bone whistle with three perforations, a single-barbed bone harpoon with line-hole, a bone gorge, and antler flaking tools, all apparently referable to the Meadowood component.

Another radiocarbon date for the Meadowood culture was obtained at this site. The sample of clean charcoal was taken from Feature 19, a large pit in which it was associated with 147 Vinette 1 sherds and other items referable to this phase. The date of 870 B.C. $\pm$ 60 years (Y-1651) is, next to that for the Oberlander No. 2 site, the oldest yet determined for a Meadowood site, and it accords well with the artifact evidence (Figure 1).

The Roundtop Site
(Apl. 1)

Two major sites of the Late Woodland stage were excavated by the writer between 1964 and 1966, resulting in some substantial contributions, including carbon-14 dates, to prior knowledge of the early and late Owasco and early Iroquois cultures.

The large and important Roundtop site at Endicott, Broome County, New York, was explored in August, 1964, soon after it was reported by Murray Shapiro of Endicott. The site lies on a terrace between fifteen and twenty feet above the north shore of the Susquehanna River, at the edge of a steep knoll, 260 feet high, which gives its name to the site.

Prior to our excavations, Mr. Shapiro and associates Michael Laccetti and Dr. Philip Collella, had dug well over 100 pits and other features, acquiring large collections of pottery and stone implements. These were kindly made available for study and Mr. Shapiro's collection was generously donated to the New York State Museum.

With a small party of graduate student assistants, the writer excavated 5000 square feet of the site, re-exposing many of the previously dug pits and adding twenty-five new features, comprising large storage pits, smaller pits apparently used for cooking, and beds of fire-broken stones, of a kind often found on such sites, probably for roasting game (page 280). Our work also exposed a very large number of post molds, including the patterns of two complete and perfectly defined oblong houses of longhouse type, with rounded ends. A central door opening occurred at either end of both houses. The larger of the overlapping floor plans measured ninety-two feet in length by twenty-two feet in width, the smaller, seventy-nine by twenty-five feet. These features resemble other house floors on Owasco sites, notably the Maxon-Derby site of about the same age and stage of Owasco cultural development (page 281 and Figure 9).

At the request of the State University of New York at Binghamton, the remainder of the site at the conclusion of our excavations was relinquished for field school use, under the supervision of Assistant Professor William Lipe. The writer's final report on the site will incorporate all available data.

The large collection of typically early Owasco artifacts, especially pottery, from the Roundtop site, will be analyzed and described in the report referred to. More than half of the pottery series pertains to the Carpenter Brook Cord-on-Cord type, with herringbone, plat and linear corded-punctate designs executed with corded-stick or paddle edge over a completely cord-malleated surface (Ritchie and Mac-Neish, 1949, p. 108). As elsewhere discussed, this is the prevailing ceramic treatment in the Carpenter Brook phase (page 292). Levanna Cord-on-Cord, another early Owasco type, accounts for some thirty per cent of the remainder, with other early Owasco varieties present in minor amounts (Ritchie and MacNeish, 1949, p. 110). In some of the pits, typical sherds of the Clemson's Island culture of the Susquehanna Valley in Pennsylvania were intermixed with Owasco types, thus providing further evidence for the writer's statement of intercultural connections (pages 273, 274).

Of primary importance was the discovery by the Science Service party on the Roundtop site of carbonized plant remains constituting the earliest radiocarbon-dated evidence for cultigens in New York State. The material came from Feature 35, a large, deep U-shaped pit, sixty-two inches in diameter and forty-six inches deep, with unequivocal charcoal and ceramic associations. The radiocarbon date of A.D. 1070± 60 years (Y-1534) is the earliest so far obtained for an Owasco site.

The plant specimens were identified by Dr. Richard A. Yarnell of Emory University as corn cob fragments and kernels of typical "Northern Flint" variety, bean cotyledons (*Phaseolus vulgaris*), squash seeds, (probably *Cucurbita pepo*), "squash" seed (probably *Cucurbita pepo*, var. *ovifera*, the egg gourd or yellow flowering gourd), hawthorn seeds and fruits (*Crataegus*), plum seeds and fruit (probably *Prunus americana*), acorn meats, butternut shells (*Juglans cinerea* L.) and walnut shells (*Juglans nigra* L.). (Letter of June 28, 1967).

Dr. Paul C. Manglesdorf of the Botanical Museum of Harvard University, identified a sample of the corn cobs and kernels as "an eight-rowed flint corn." (Letter of April 8, 1965).

The Nahrwold No. 1 Site
(Shr. 51-4)

A large, heavily occupied village site of the Late Woodland stage on the Arthur G. Nahrwold farm, less than a mile south of Middleburg, Schoharie County, New York, has been previously mentioned as the locus of recent excavations. The Nahrwold No. 1 site, reported by Harold Zoch of Middleburg, partially overlaps the much earlier Nahrwold No. 2 site (page xxiii) on the same broad sandy terrace, rising approximately twenty-five feet above the flood plain of Schoharie Creek, which flows one-fifth of a mile to the west. During the month of August, 1965 and 1966, 18,600 square feet of the site were fully exposed to the compact sandy loam subsoil level by the writer with four student and several volunteer assistants, members of the Van Epps-Hartley Chapter, New York State Archeological Association.

The Nahrwold No. 1 site was an open town of about two acres. No palisade lines could be found despite careful search. It had been intensively occupied from late Castle Creek Owasco times through much of the succeeding Oak Hill phase of early Iroquois culture (page 302). According to the radiocarbon dates from charcoal taken out of pits with associated potsherds, the minimum period over which this site was inhabited, probably not continuously, was approximately 150 years, or from A.D. 1310 ±95 years (I-2399), for the late Castle Creek phase, to A.D. 1450±80 years (Y-1650) for the late Oak Hill phase (Figure 1).

Two hundred fifty-eight features and thousands of post molds were exposed. The plethora of post molds has created a confusing picture, indicative of overlying house patterns, traceable in part as the typical oblong, round-ended, communal longhouses, which we have found to characterize the Owasco and early Iroquois cultures (pages 281, 307).

The numerous features, many intersecting, comprised chiefly food storage pits of medium to large size, like those described for the Owasco culture on page 280, and a small number (about ten per cent) of smaller cooking pits, containing hearths. Two human burials and two dog burials were also found.

The artifact series is typical for the cultures represented; pottery greatly predominates, as usual on sites of this kind. Carbonized corn occurred in some of the pits. Animal bones, especially those of the deer, were abundant. The site will be described in some detail in a later report.

INTRODUCTION

This volume integrates into a single synoptic account the main events of the long and involved story of human prehistory in the State of New York and its environs. The archaeological data, old and new, are presented from a historical-developmental viewpoint, as indicated in the contents. Also, insofar as available evidence permits, each cultural unit is described, more or less systematically, according to the following outline of organization: discovery and naming; spatial, ecological and chronological setting; physical characteristics of related people; subsistence economy and the means and methods involved; housing and settlement pattern; dress and ornament; artifact technology; transportation; trade relationships; warfare; aesthetic and recreational activities; social and political organization; mortuary customs; and religio-magical and ceremonial activities. The non-material aspects of the culture included in this outline are, of course, the most difficult to reconstruct, and must be inferred from such other aspects as the subsistence, settlement pattern and mortuary data, and from analogies with historic tribal groups of the same general area. The difficulties, shortcomings and dangers inherent in this method are referred to in later sections of the work, and no claims are made to more than hypothetical and exiguous results with these portions of the synthesis.

Although the writer has drawn upon the whole of his research experience, recounted in much detail in numerous site reports and other accounts to which the reader is referred in the course of the narrative, this is no twice-told tale. For in addition to making available for the first time information on recently discovered archaeological sites and cultures, earlier published material has been rescrutinized in order to extract if possible such inferences as seem pertinent and valid to this fresh, anthropological approach.

The emphasis has thus been shifted from a primary concern with taxonomy, chronology, culture content and relationships, to the examination of whole cultures, within the relatively narrow limits afforded by their archaeological survivals. This has been called the "conjunctive" method in archaeological research (Taylor, 1948), and it has never *fully* been achieved anywhere, to my knowledge, certainly not in the present volume, which suffers from the usual limitations imposed upon archaeological interpretations and reconstructions by the prevailingly sparse and fragmentary data. This is especially true in a region of poor preservation of organic substances because of climatic conditions and site situations. There are also the hazards of long settlement and consequent destruction by white civilization, including the depredations of relic collectors.

In a prior major general synthesis for the same area (Ritchie, 1944), the chronology was wholly relative, constructed from stratigraphy and seriation, for the most part, and the total time estimate, in harmony with then prevailing ultraconservative opinion, was limited to some sixteen centuries. The discovery, and application since 1950, of the radiocarbon method of dating, by Willard F. Libby (Libby, 1955), has suffused a new vitality into the study of prehistory, opening remote vistas into the past. As a result, the period encompassed in the current resynthesis spans approximately eight thousand years from the Paleo-Indian hunters to the protohistoric tribes at the dawn of the seventeenth century. The last forty-five hundred years of this chronology in our area is supported by carbon-14 determinations, the earlier portion by extrapolation from similarly dated remains elsewhere in the United States (Figure 1).

In addition to the radiocarbon chronology, the present work departs from prior syntheses (Ritchie, 1938, 1944, 1951) in the drastic modification of the classificatory system employed in the historical ordering of the data. The Midwestern Taxonomic Method formerly used is herein largely abandoned, because of a much fuller body of material, both regional and comparative, and the growing realization that the older system lacks the necessary flexibility for the realistic orientation of what seems to be a complex of cultural continuums, undergoing, through time, large and small changes.

Rather than again attempt the imposition of a more or less rigid paradigm upon such protean materials, the writer has elected to adopt most of the recommendations of Willey and Phillips with regard to establishing archaeological units and their integration (Willey and Phillips, 1958, pp. 21–48). The reader may find helpful the following definitions and explanations of the taxonomic terminology to be found in the text and in the cultural sequence chart, Figure 1.

Site and Component. These are terms of general usage in the same sense as in the Midwestern classificatory system (McKern, 1939, p. 308). A site is a restricted area of occupation by one or more groups; a component is the single expression of culture at a site, which, if but once inhabited, is a single-component site, and if occupied by two or more different groups, a multicomponent site or station.

Phase. As formulated by Willey and Phillips (1958, pp. 22–24) and used in the current context, a phase carries essentially the same meaning as a "focus" in the Midwestern Taxonomic system (McKern, 1939, p. 308), the term formerly used by the writer. The phase may be defined as a recurring complex of distinctive archaeological traits, sufficiently different from any other complex to suggest that it represents the product of a single cultural group, pertaining to a limited territory and to a relatively brief period of time.

Culture. In this work the trite and ambiguous term "culture" is the rough equivalent of the term "aspect" in the Midwestern taxonomy (McKern, 1939, p. 308) and as employed by the writer in prior syntheses. As herein used, culture stands for the particular strain of social heredity of a group of individuals larger than that represented by the phase, and united by the sharing of a common tradition or traditions.

Tradition. A cultural tradition is most

simply defined as a custom, concept or trait, or a combination of such units, with persistence in time. A tradition has the social sanction of the group that observes it, for whom it represents propriety from one generation to another. Thus a tradition may give form or character to one or more aspects of the culture, and this fact may be reflected in archaeologically preserved traits or artifacts.

Horizon and Horizon Style. The spatial distribution of like cultural traits and assemblages on approximately the same time level is called an archaeological horizon. The related concept of the horizon style refers to a specific art style, artifact type, burial mode or other trait which has spread rapidly over a broad geographic range. While the horizon is an integrative unit serving to unify related phases of culture, the primary value of the horizon style is the temporal correlation of otherwise unlike and widely separated cultures (Willey and Phillips, 1958, pp. 31–33).

Stage. Reference is thus made to cultural developments within broad and somewhat arbitrarily delimited economic and technological boundaries, with their material artifactual associations. Chiefly for consistency and the avoidance of introducing confusing new terminology, the current scheme conforms to that in general usage in eastern United States archaeology. This would seem to have clearer applicability to the historical-developmental sequences over most of this area than other more descriptive nomenclatures, admirably suited as these seem to be to areas of higher New World civilizations.

It is extremely important to emphasize the essential distinction between the concept of stage and that of chronological period. The stage is free of temporal and spatial limitations. Nevertheless, cultural development requires a time dimension (Willey and Phillips, 1958, pp. 64–66). Now, because of the radiocarbon dating technique, it has been possible to establish an approximate chronological framework for the local sequences which together compose the developmental stages of our archaeological history (see Figure 1).

When the researches summarized in this volume were begun by the writer in 1925, existing archaeological knowledge of New York State was almost wholly derived from excavations of unequal quality and very limited scope on a few "Iroquoian" and "Algonkian" sites, chiefly in the coastal region, and the emphasis of that period was almost wholly upon content. The first attempted synthesis proposed a sixfold classification into an Algonkian period, with three divisions, an Eskimo-like culture, a Mound-builder occupation and an Iroquois occupation of New York (Parker, 1922, pp. 46–130). The limited points of agreement with this largely theoretical system, as disclosed by field work accomplished up to 1942, are explained elsewhere (Ritchie, 1944, pp. 2–11), following an earlier attempt, using the Midwestern Taxonomic Method, at correlation with the same scheme (Ritchie, 1936a, p. 4).

In 1937 the writer made a large-scale effort to describe and classify the aboriginal cultures of New York in a thesis, which was greatly abridged and published the following year (Ritchie, 1938). This was elaborated in his syntheses of 1944 and 1951, already referred to. Comparison of the sequence charts of these three works with Figure 1 clearly shows the growth and changes effected by the expanding field research of the last three decades. It is not presumed or implied that no further important additions or modifications of the current scheme are possible or even proba-

A CULTURE SEQUENCE AND CHRONOLOGY OF NEW YORK STATE

STAGE: WOODLAND (Late / Middle / Early)

Western Subarea

Culture or Tradition	Phase	Component & C14 Dates
IROQUOIS	Eaton	Newton-Hopper, Buffum Street, Eaton
	Shelby	Shelby, Fort Hill
	Long	Nursery, Long
	Oakfield	Oakfield A.D.1509±50 (M-651)
POINT PENINSULA	Hunter's Home	Portage A.D.1000±75 (M-H63)
HOPEWELLIAN	Squawkie Hill	Poland Center, Canadea, Killbuck, Vandalia, Lewiston A.D.160±80 (Y-1276)
ADENA		

Central Subarea

Culture or Tradition	Phase	Component & C14 Dates
IROQUOIS	Chance	Christopher
	Oak Hill	Hummel, Kelso A.D.1390±100 (Y-380), Howlett Hill A.D.1390±60(Y-1489), Furnace Brook A.D.1300±60 (Y-1817)
	Castle Creek	Chamberlain A.D.1290±60(Y-199), Bainbridge, Castle Creek A.D.1435±200(M-179), A.D.1196±200(M-493)
	Canandaigua	O'Neil 4 A.D.1160±80 (Y-1278), A.D.1150±80 (Y-1275), Bates A.D.1298±200(M-762), A.D.1196±100 (T-425), Goloth A.D.1125±100 (T-425), Sackett A.D.1130±150 (M-1076), Lakeside (Emerson) Park
OWASCO	Carpenter Brook	Wickham 3, Levanna, St. Helena, Maxon-Derby A.D.1100±100 (Y-1173), A.D.1100±150 (M-1077), Jack's Reef #2, Carpenter Brook, Roundtop A.D.1070±60 (Y-1534)
	Hunter's Home	White A.D.905±250 (M-176), Kipp Island #4, Bluff Point, Hunters Home
POINT PENINSULA	Kipp Island	Plum Point, Wickham 2 A.D.740±100 (Y-1172), Durkee, Menard Bridge #1, Felix, Jack's Reef #1, Kipp Island #3 A.D.630±100(Y-1379)
HOPEWELLIAN	Squawkie Hill	Kipp Island #2 A.D.310±100(Y-1378), Rector, Sea Breeze, Geneseo, Squawkie Hill
POINT PENINSULA	Canoe Point	O'Neil 3 A.D.240 (Y-1277), Wickham 1, Vinette 2
ADENA	Middlesex	Kipp Island #1, Walsh, Cuylerville, Amber, Vine Valley

Northern Subarea

Culture or Tradition	Phase	Component & C14 Dates
IROQUOIS		Durfee, Pine Hill, Washburn
		Calkins
OWASCO		Pillar Point
POINT PENINSULA	Kipp Island	Long Point, Point Peninsula
POINT PENINSULA	Canoe Point	Grindstone Island
ADENA	Middlesex	Long Sault Island

Eastern Subarea

Culture or Tradition	Phase	Component & C14 Dates
		Wagner's Hollow, Martin
IROQUOIS	Garoga	Smith, Clock, Cayadutta, Garoga
		Otstungo
	Chance	Getman A.D.1398±50 (M-763), Deowongo Island, Kingston, Chance
	Oak Hill	Oak Hill #7 A.D.1337±50 (M-185), Weaver Lake, Nahrwold #1 A.D.1450±80(Y-1650)
	Castle Creek	Menands Bridge, Nahrwold #1 A.D.1350±95 (I-2399)
OWASCO	Canandaigua	Snell A.D.1156 ±200 (M-492)
	Carpenter Brook	Enders, Talbot, Hilltop
	Hunter's Home	Willow Tree A.D.955 ±250 (M-177), Parsoni, Turnbull
POINT PENINSULA	Kipp Island / Burnt Hill	Weiman 4, Kipp Island(?) A.D.700 ±100(Y-1382), Westheimer
ADENA	Middlesex	East Branch, Toll-Clute, Palatine Bridge

Southern Subarea

Culture or Tradition	Phase	Component & C14 Dates
	Shantok	Fort Corchaug, Pantigo
WINDSOR	Niantic	Old Field B, Niantic Point (Conn.)
EAST RIVER	Clasons Point	Milo, Helicker's Cave, Finch Rock House, Clasons Point
WINDSOR	Sebonac	Sook Hides
EAST RIVER	Bowmans Brook	Grantville B, Wilkins, Bowmans Brook
WINDSOR	Sebonac	Wells, Old Field A, Aquebogue, Sebonac
WINDSOR	Clearview	Manhasset Rock, Clearview, Throgs Neck
WINDSOR	North Beach	Matinecock Point, North Beach, Pelham Boulder
ADENA	Middlesex	Denning Point

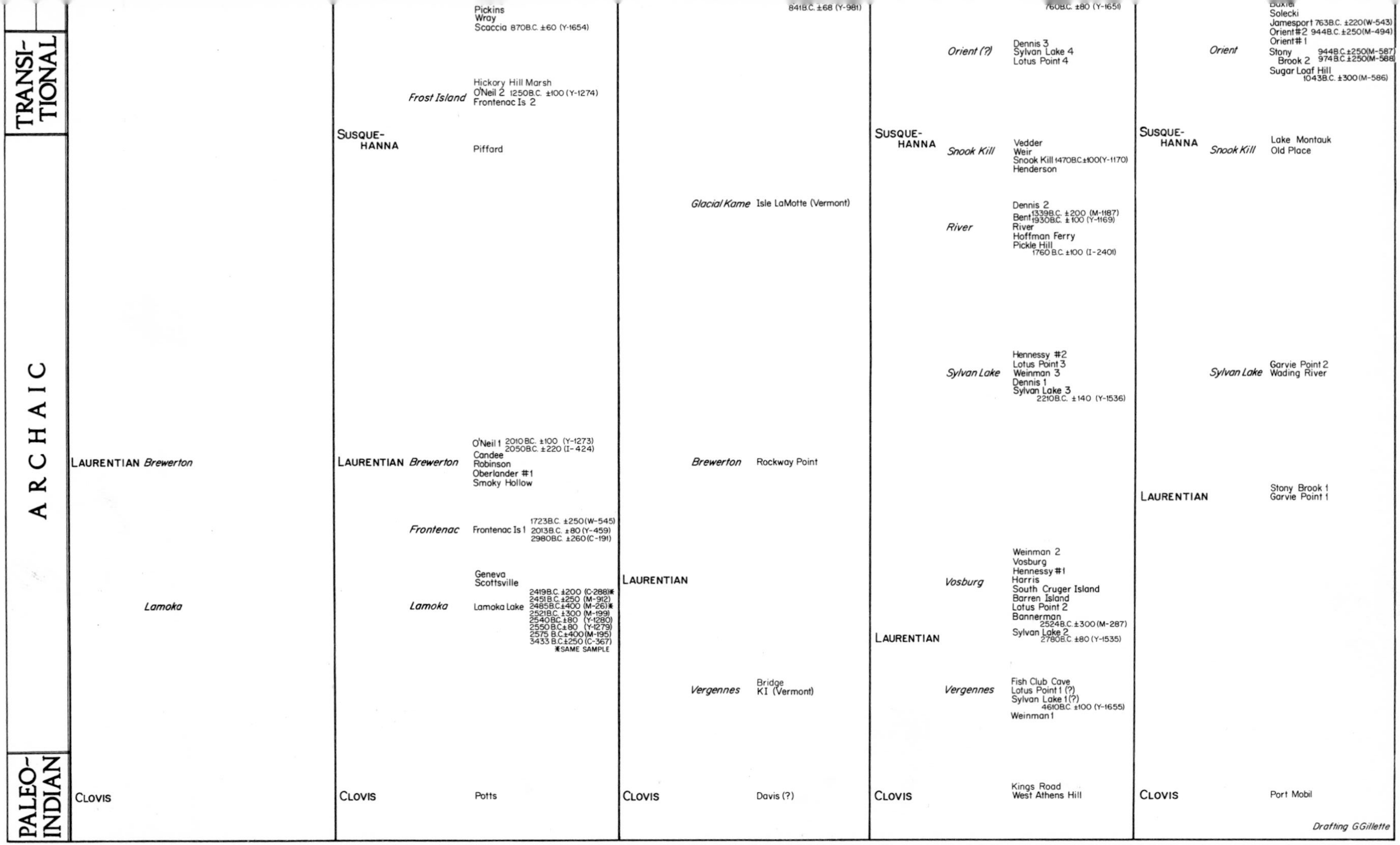

Figure 1 Culture sequence and chronology of New York State.

TRANSI-TIONAL

ARCHAIC

PALEO-INDIAN

Column (far right / top dates):

Bowle
Solecki
Jameson 1763B.C. ±220(W-543)
Orient #2 944B.C. ±250(M-494)
Orient #1
Stony 944B.C. ±250(M-587)
Brook 2 974B.C. ±250(M-586)
Sugar Loaf Hill
1043B.C. ±300(M-586)

Orient

Lake Montauk
Old Place

SUSQUE-HANNA *Snook Kill*

Sylvan Lake Garvie Point 2
Wading River

LAURENTIAN

Stony Brook 1
Garvie Point 1

CLOVIS Port Mobil

761B.C. ±80 (Y-651)

Orient (?)

Dennis 3
Sylvan Lake 4
Lotus Point 4

SUSQUE-HANNA *Snook Kill*

Vedder
Weir
Snook Kill 1470B.C.±100(Y-1170)
Henderson

River

Dennis 2
Bent 1930B.C. ±200 (M-1187)
River 1930B.C. ±100 (Y-169)
Hoffman Ferry
Pickle Hill 1760 B.C. ±100 (I-2401)

Sylvan Lake

Hennessy #2
Lotus Point 3
Wenman 3
Dennis 1
Sylvan Lake 3 2250B.C. ±140 (Y-1536)

Vosburg

Wenman 2
Vosburg
Hennessy #1
Harris
South Cruger Island
Barren Island
Lotus Point 2
Bannerman
Sylvan Lake 2 2524B.C.±300(M-287)
2780B.C. ±80 (Y-1535)

LAURENTIAN

Vergennes

Fish Club Cave
Lotus Point 1 (?)
Sylvan Lake 1 (?) 4610B.C.±100 (Y-1655)
Wenman 1

CLOVIS

Kings Road
West Athens Hill

841B.C. ±68 (Y-981)

Glacial/Kame Isle LaMotte (Vermont)

Brewerton Rockway Point

LAURENTIAN

Vergennes Bridge
K1 (Vermont)

CLOVIS Davis (?)

SUSQUE-HANNA

Frost Island

Pickins
Wray
Scaccia 870B.C. ±60 (Y-1654)

Hickory Hill Marsh
O'Neil 2 1250B.C. ±100 (Y-1274)
Frontenac Is 2

Brewerton Pifford

LAURENTIAN *Brewerton*

Frontenac

O'Neil 1 2010B.C. ±100 (Y-1273)
2050B.C. ±220 (I-424)
Condee
Robinson
Oberlander #1
Smoky Hollow

Frontenac Is 1 1723B.C. ±250(W-545)
2003B.C. ±80(Y-459)
2980B.C. ±260(C-191)

Lamoka

Geneva
Scottsville

Lamoka Lake 2499B.C. ±200 (C-286)*
2451B.C. ±200 (M-912)
2485B.C. ±400 (M-261)*
2520B.C. ±300 (M-199)
2640B.C. ±180 (Y-1280)
2556 B.C. ±80 (Y-279)
2575 B.C. ±400(M-915)
3433 B.C.±250 (C-367)
*SAME SAMPLE

CLOVIS Potts

Bottom band (wide left):

SUSQUE-HANNA

LAURENTIAN *Brewerton*

Lamoka

CLOVIS

NOTE: Arabic numerals indicate components on a stratified site.   Horizontally separated components on a stratified site.   Culture phases are numbered from bottom to top.   Revised to Feb 1968 by Wm A. Ritchie

ble. Therefore the present offering may best be regarded as only another step forward in refinement and interpretation of the prehistoric archaeology of New York State.

Reference to the cultural-succession chart (Figure 1), and to the map of New York State showing the distribution of the archaeological sites described or mentioned in the text (see Figure 4), reveals a somewhat arbitrary geographical subdivision of the state into five subareas, in each of which the prehistoric course of events appears to have been more consistent than was the case between any two separate sections. The degree of parallel development between subareas was, expectedly, closest on the basis of drainage and topographical relationships. Thus western and central New York, and eastern and southern New York, respectively, stand in closest paired agreement. The eastern area in turn exhibits some measure of continuity with western New England, the southern section with southern New England but especially with eastern New Jersey and eastern Pennsylvania. The northern subarea, farthest removed spatially and culturally, exhibits close ties with southern Ontario and Quebec and western Vermont. The western section links with northwestern Pennsylvania and more remotely with the upper Ohio Valley, also predictably with the Niagara Peninsula of Ontario.

There is a demonstrable broad correlation of the subareas with the principal watersheds of the state, viz., the western with the Allegheny River and Lake Erie, the central with Lake Ontario and the Susquehanna River system, the eastern with the Delaware and Hudson rivers, the northern with the St. Lawrence River and its tributaries, the southern with the tidewater and

coastal area. As will be seen in the course of this study, cultural influences, and probably population movements, were intrinsically related to these water routes within and beyond the confines of New York.

While the subareas trespass upon the boundaries of the physiographic provinces, demarcated on the endpaper map, some rough agreement is indicated by the following facts: the western and central subareas include parts of the Great Lakes Section of the Central Lowland Province and the Glaciated Allegheny Plateau Section (a small piece of the Unglaciated Allegheny Plateau Section is included in the western subarea). The eastern subarea lies mainly within the Mohawk-Hudson-Champlain Lowland sections, rimmed on the west by the Catskill Mountain and Glaciated Allegheny Plateau sections and the Adirondack Province, on the east by the long, rugged folds of the Taconic and Green Mountain sections of the New England uplands. Hence the eastern subarea is well isolated from central New York, except through the narrow Mohawk Valley, and from eastern New England, a situation strongly registered in the archaeological remains.

Parenthetically, these several, almost continuous, mountain and highland barriers, besides shutting out ready communication with the west and east, afforded in themselves very limited resources to food collectors and even less to food producers. The forest covers were probably then as now principally conifers, and the soils were stony and unproductive. Hunters and food collectors largely confined themselves to the deciduous or mixed deciduous and coniferous forests, which provided the mast foods sustaining deer, turkey and associated fauna, and their predators. Groups with a diversified economy which included hoe tillage also required lighter, more fertile soils workable with primitive agricultural tools.

There may possibly be still another, non-material factor contributing to the obviously sparse and sporadic inhabitation of the mountain areas, where only occasional small winter (?) camp sites have so far been identified. According to Speck, "The fear of evil consequence resulting from the ascent of high mountains is general to Algonkian tribes of the Northeast." This is because their "concept of the earth seems linked in some imaginative fashion with that of the mountain. The latter is venerated apparently through its association with the idea of its being the abode of a spirit-force" (Speck, 1935, p. 58). This prevalent ideology may have its ancient roots extending deep into Archaic times in the Northeast.

The northern subarea comprises essentially the St. Lawrence Valley Province and contiguous Champlain Lowland Section, north and east respectively of the vast barrier mass of the Adirondack Mountains. Finally, the southern subarea consists almost entirely of the Long Island Section of the Coastal Plain Province, having numerous floral and faunal relationships with the Middle Atlantic region.

In summarizing the accomplishments of his long labors, the writer is acutely aware of his debt to many other persons standing in various relationships to him, from site owners, who have almost without exception granted freely and cordially the necessary permission to explore on their lands, to professional colleagues and amateur archaeologists, who have with like generosity shared with him their data and ideas. To all of these his sense of gratitude is deep and sincere. Specific acknowledgments will be given in their proper context throughout the book.

Particular appreciation is hereby expressed to the many loyal, enthusiastic and able field assistants, some unpaid volunteers, most of them undergraduate and graduate students from a considerable roster of colleges and universities throughout the country, who have shared with me the joys and sorrows of search and discovery. Perhaps it is pertinent, for the emphasis it brings to the validity of the story unfolded in the pages which follow, to mention the writer's constant and detailed participation in, as well as his direction of, the field work upon which most of this account rests. This on-the-spot attention at all times has permitted observations and interpretations of a firsthand character, not possible, I believe, in more remote relationships with field parties under indirect supervision.

I wish also to express my strong sense of obligation to the following individuals and institutions who have provided grants in aid of my research; Mr. Eli Lilly and the Indiana Historical Society, Mr. Ward Melville of New York City, the Viking Fund (Wenner-Gren Foundation for Anthropological Research), the American Philosophical Society (Grants No. 1049 and No. 3014, Penrose Fund) and the National Science Foundation (Grants 2598, GS-1177 and 22101). My thanks are also extended to the New York State Education Department, which generously awarded me a Professional Development Leave of six months' duration for the purpose of writing this book. For permission to rephotograph materials in their collections, to reproduce some of their negatives, representing in large part my field photographs of the period up to 1949, and for other courtesies, I thank the Rochester Museum of Arts and Sciences. Since that date, my work has been under the auspices of the New York State Museum and Science Service, to which are credited most of the illustrations not otherwise attributed. Finally, for help with such tedious tasks as proofreading and the preparation of the Index, I am indebted to my wife, Beatrice.

THE ARCHAEOLOGY
OF
NEW YORK STATE

I The Earliest Occupants—
Paleo-Indian Hunters
(c. 8000 B.C.)

The history of human habitation in New York State and the Northeast began with the haphazard and unrestricted wanderings of tiny groups of hunters equipped with a small inventory of chipped-stone tools which included, as the principal item of identification, the fluted javelin head or spear point of Clovis or generalized Clovis form (Plate 1). The physical appearance of these people is still unknown, no skeletal remains definitely attributable to them having as yet been found. They were part of a widely diffused and extremely scanty population, chiefly traceable by a surface distribution of their distinctive weapon point over a considerable portion of North America, with fainter traces extending into Mexico and Central America. Similar faint traces penetrate northward from the Canadian prairies into Alaska, where the trail is lost. No fluted points are known from Siberia or elsewhere in the Old World. Hence it is believed that, although the Early Hunters were related to a population which spread into North America via a land bridge at the Bering Strait during the latter part of the Wisconsin glacial age of the Late Pleistocene epoch, the Clovis fluted point was a New World invention (Krieger, 1954, pp. 274–75). It is alleged to have possessed a peculiar and still un- determined advantage in the killing of big game animals, chiefly proboscidians.

In the Southern High Plains, adjacent Rocky Mountain foothills, Colorado Plateau and portions of the now desert basin area of New Mexico and Arizona, Clovis fluted points have been discovered in direct association with the bones of the mammoth, Columbian elephant, mastodon, bison, horse and other late glacial period mammals, at "kill sites," buried in deposits indicative of moist and cool climatic conditions (Wormington, 1957). Hearth charcoal from certain of these sites radiocarbon dates the time of occupation between approximately 10,000 and 9000 B.C. At some sites the Clovis or Llano culture horizon is overlaid by geological deposits pertaining to an arid and presumably warm interval, which was succeeded by a second cool, moist climatic episode, recorded in humic soils which have yielded the fossil remains of an extinct species of bison (*Bison antiquus antiquus*) and fluted points of the Folsom form. These are usually smaller, thinner and better chipped than their presumed ancestral Clovis prototypes, and they seem to have been a specialized type for hunting the large bison of the period. Carbon-14 dates place the Folsom period between about 9000 and 8000 B.C., but some overlapping of

1

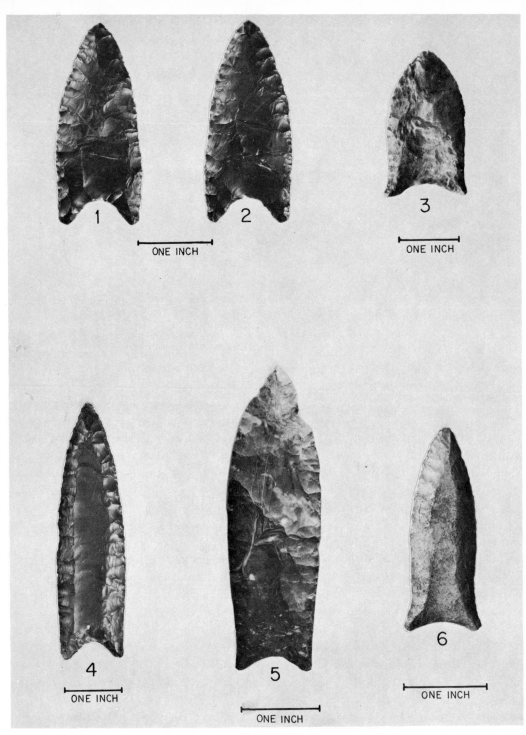

ONE INCH

ONE INCH

ONE INCH

ONE INCH

ONE INCH

PLATE 1 Varieties of fluted points from New York. 1, 2 Clovis type, Flint Mine Hill, Coxsackie, Greene Co.; 3 modified Clovis, Pipes Neck Creek, Greenport, Long Island; 4 Clovis type, Town of Van Buren, Onondaga Co.; 5 modified Clovis, Seneca River near Mosquito Point, Cayuga Co.; 6 Cumberland-like point, near Bouckville, Madison Co. 1, 2 collection of James Burggraf, Samsonville, N.Y.; 3 Roy Latham, Orient, N.Y.; 4 the New York State Museum; 5 Gordon C. DeAngelo, Oran, N.Y.; 6 Foster Disinger, Binghamton, N.Y.

Clovis and Folsom cultures is indicated by the evidence.

In the eastern United States (i.e., east of the Mississippi River) the true Folsom type of fluted point has not been recorded; although "Folsomoid" forms occur which can be readily intergraded with the Clovis related series. It is therefore improbable that Folsom bison hunters ever inhabited this portion of the United States. Here in the East, also, no "kill sites" have yet been uncovered. In fact, nothing is currently known about the faunal and floral associations with the period of the Paleo-Indian in this entire area, nor can the time of this occupation be established with the reliability of the data from the Southwest. However, inferences based upon the geochronology of the Great Lakes region suggest a near contemporaneity for the Clovis hunters both west and east of the Mississippi.

The evidence for Early Man in the Northeast consists chiefly of the scatter of fluted points, a few small probable camp sites, such as the Davis and Port Mobil sites in New York and the Wapanucket No. 8 component in Massachusetts (Figure 2, sites number 4, 6, 9), and several definite and larger components mentioned below. It points clearly to a sparse, highly mobile population of very small groups, perhaps bands consisting of a score or so of individuals related by blood or marriage. These little bands ranged freely far and wide over a vast, unoccupied, virgin country, whose appearance, climatic conditions and other attributes will be discussed later on. It is probable that this pattern of free wandering, similar to that of Paleolithic times in the Old World, was uniquely confined to the Paleo-Indian period in our area, and was conditioned by a vast unexplored territory, a scanty population, and a primary, although probably not exclusive,

dependence upon migratory game animals, whose local availability chiefly determined the hunters' temporary limits of sojourn.

A seasonal or periodic return to a camp site with unusual advantages, or perhaps the incipience of a restricted wandering-community pattern, in which territorial interest by a particular band was beginning to be manifested, is suggested by the presence in the eastern United States of less than a dozen, and in the Northeast of some seven definite habitation components indicative of either a larger than usual local group or, more likely, a repeatedly inhabited encampment by a small body of people. Such sites in or immediately adjacent to the Northeast are Shoop in southeastern Pennsylvania (Witthoft, 1952); Reagen in northwestern Vermont (Ritchie, 1953); Bull Brook in northeastern Massachusetts (Byers, 1954, 1955, 1956); Debert in Nova Scotia (page 7); the recently investigated, smaller Potts site in north-central New York, described below (page 22) and the lately excavated West Athens Hill and Kings Road sites in the Hudson Valley (pages xv, xvi). (Figure 2, sites number 1–3, 5, 7, 8). Occasional references only will be made to the three first mentioned sites, since they have been well described in the readily available literature cited.

Artifacts

On all of the definite and probable camp sites, fluted points occur as part of a quite consistent complex of exclusively chipped stone implements. Except for the weapon points, these may be classified as cutting, scraping and boring tools, indicative of industries in wood, bone and leather, no vestige of which has been preserved. The uniformity of this tool complex reflects the

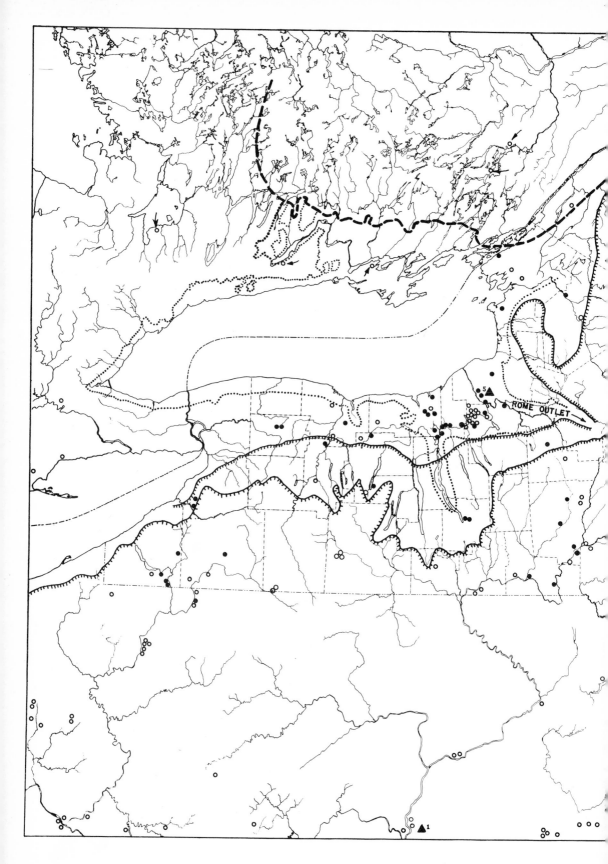

ROME OUTLET

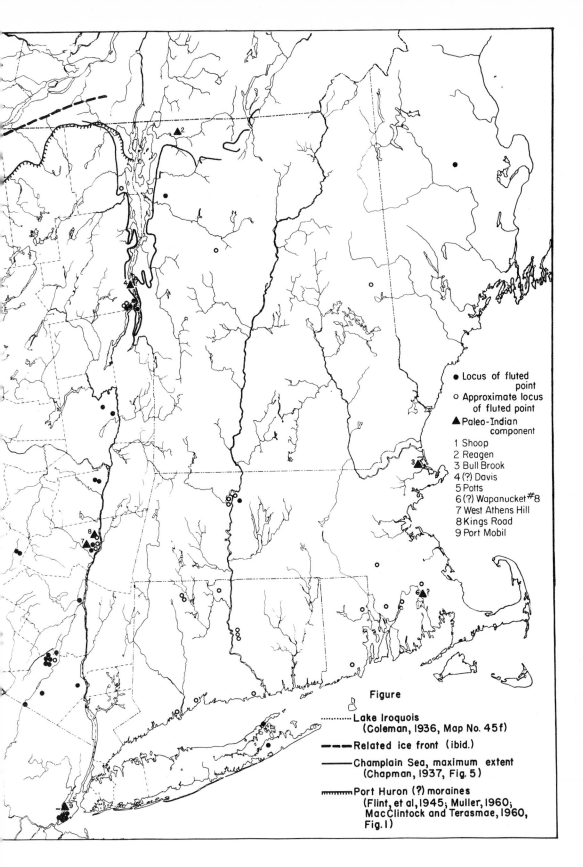

Figure 2   Distribution of Paleo-Indian components and fluted points in the Northeast in relation to Port Huron (?) moraines, Lake Iroquois and the Champlain Sea.

weapon-point category, and although there exist some regional typological differences in all the traits, which also suggests time depth for the culture as a whole, the tool complex may be generally described as a very limited assemblage of end scrapers, side scrapers, knives, borers and gravers, made by marginally retouching flakes which have been detached from cores, and because one broad face has been left plain or unmodified, they are designated as uniface tools. On the Reagen, Potts and West Athens Hill sites, some of the knife forms were chipped on both faces (bifacially), like the fluted points, and the same bifacial treatment was accorded a specialized tool called a twist drill, which is unique to the Bull Brook site.

The general uniformity of the Paleo-Indian artifact complex wherever it occurs suggests the relatively rapid dissemination of the hunters, with small groups probably budding off as a population increase took place in some region, causing pressure on the local food supply. It also suggests a strong traditional reserve combined with long isolation and the lack of dissimilar cultural contacts which could diffuse new ideas to disturb the status quo.

As already mentioned, however, some probably significant typological differences do exist within the Paleo-Indian assemblage as a whole. Thus, five or six general form categories can be recognized in fluted points of eastern North America, including the Northeast. The major form is the Clovis or Clovis Fluted. These are large (about two or five inches in length), lanceolate points, having parallel, slightly excurvate edges and concave base which, like the lower edges, is usually ground smooth, and channeled or fluted faces (Plate 1, Figures 1, 2, 4). The fluting extends for varying distances on either face from base to tip,

and is sometimes multiple ("Enterline" fluting; Witthoft, 1952, pp. 482–83) (Plate 1, Figure 1). The range in shape, size and quality of workmanship in these points is considerable and some examples can best be described as "generalized" Clovis points. A variant of the Clovis type has a slight constriction just above the base (Plate 1, Figures 3, 5). A slender type with marked constriction near the base and prominent flaring "ears" is known as the Cumberland point, and is found only in the eastern United States. In the Northeast only a few such points have been found, but an attenuated variety of the Cumberland form is more numerous (Plate 1, Figure 6). Finally, the fluted pentagonal point, noted especially for the Reagen site in Vermont and the Williamson site in Dinwiddie County, Virginia (McCary, 1951), may prove to be a later modification of the Clovis point, which it closely resembles except for its pentagonoid outline. There are other traits at the Reagen site which strongly suggest that it belongs late in the Paleo-Indian period of the Northeast.

The materials of fluted points vary extensively, but they are usually of high-grade silicious stone, seemingly carefully selected for chipping qualities. Commonly the material is exotic to the region where the point was found, a fact which has furnished some useful clues to the movements of these early hunters, as well as testifying to the nomadism of their lives. In the Northeast a combination of fluted-point materials, distribution of these weapons, and the few actual or probable camp sites leads to some very definite conclusions regarding the movements into and within the area of the first inhabitants. The factor of distribution also sheds some light on the time at which this entry occurred, as will be shown later.

Distribution

Despite the wide latitude of fluted points indicative of extensive exploration and open territory, the distributional pattern signifies preference for certain kinds of terrain, as well as for particular locales. A predilection for well-elevated situations is attested by a majority of the determinable find-spots of fluted points in New York and by the locations of most known Paleo-Indian components in the Northeast. In central and southwestern New York, however, over 30 per cent of all fluted points have been found on and about the margins of low swampy ground formerly occupied by lakes. In subsequent times these same places were strongly attractive to Archaic and other cultural groups. For about 12 per cent of additional specimens the locus may be described as only slightly or moderately elevated (a few to about ten feet) above the general surrounding level, while for nearly half of the specimens data of this kind are unobtainable because the exact provenience of many of the specimens studied in museums and private collections is unknown. They were collected prior to 1926, when the temporal provenience of the fluted style of point was first recognized, following its discovery at Folsom, New Mexico.

Like most of his successors, the Paleo-Indian shared a decided choice for main waterways. The thin scatter of fluted points in the Northeast follows the principal river systems, and the evidence demonstrates that the primary movements had originated to the south and southwest of the area. A trail of fluted points ascends along the Ohio and Allegheny rivers into southwestern New York; another follows the Susquehanna and Delaware systems from Pennsylvania into central New York; while yet another leads northward through the Hudson Valley. The Long Island Sound coastline of southern New England, continuous with the then possibly much broader Atlantic Coastal Plain, appears to have provided a fourth route from which entry was effected into river valleys such as the Connecticut, and farther north along the coast. The distribution diminishes rapidly north of Massachusetts, only a few points having been recorded to date beyond the latitude of Bull Brook (Figure 2) at Mount Desert Island, Maine, and Quaco Head, St. John, New Brunswick. A very important site has, however, recently been excavated at Debert, Nova Scotia (Byers, 1966). It is interesting to observe that the Shoop site is located on well-elevated terrain along a small tributary of the Susquehanna; the Reagen site is high above the Missisquoi River, flowing into the northern end of Lake Champlain, which is closely related by the Lake George connection, along which fluted points occur, to the Hudson Valley route; while the Bull Brook component occupies a glacial kame along a salt marsh, readily accessible from the postulated coastal approach. Most of the new Paleo-Indian components in New York described below are also located on high ground now or formerly accessible by water.

Large, fertile valleys, their environs and the coastal plain supported the heaviest populations of food animals and the aboriginal men who fed upon them in later prehistoric and early historic times, and there is little doubt of a similar ecological relationship in a still more remote past. This probably best explains the absence or extreme scarcity of fluted points and subsequent cultural remains from large regions like the Adirondack and Catskill mountains and the rugged, folded mountain and ridge country separating New England from New York east of the Hudson-Champlain lowland.

However, it is obvious that the Early Hunters penetrated inland from the major river valleys, following smaller tributary streams into the rough uplands seldom used by later Archaic peoples. While the occasional discovery of a fluted point in a remote mountain valley or terrace may connote only the place of death of a large game mammal, struck many miles away and lost to the hunter, enough instances of this kind in Pennsylvania and New York lead also to the supposition just outlined.

Materials and Movements

Mention has been made that the often exotic materials constituting fluted points provide a clue to original provenience and therefore to the movements of their makers. It is significant that points of identifiable Pennsylvania jasper (yellow, brown and red) occur sporadically to the north of the chief quarry centers in Lehigh, Bucks, and Berks counties, Pennsylvania, appearing most commonly along the courses of the Delaware, Susquehanna, Hudson and Wallkill rivers. A thinner line leads eastward, following the New England coast and apparently terminating at Bull Brook. There is also a sprinkling of such points along the Genesee, Seneca and Oneida rivers, while a single specimen from the shore of the St. Lawrence at Cedar Point, Jefferson County, is of this material. The native eastern New York gray, greenish-gray, and green Deepkill flint, with major quarries and workshop sites near Coxsackie, Greene County; and green, red, black and gray, sometimes color-banded, Normanskill flint of the same area, comprise the majority of

points from the Hudson, eastern Mohawk, Lake George and lower Champlain valleys, and have been recognized at Shoop and probably at Bull Brook (Wray, 1948). A few fluted points from central, northern, western and southwestern New York are of Upper Mercer flint from east-central or southeastern Ohio, or of Flint Ridge, Licking County, Ohio, chalcedony. However, the majority of fluted points from this part of New York and from adjacent northwestern Pennsylvania, and a small percentage of those from Ohio (Prufer and Baby, 1963, p. 45) are fashioned from gray, blue-gray, and mottled gray and tan, high-quality Onondaga flint. This is obtainable, with local variation in color and markings that provide useful clues to the approximate district of derivation and geological formation, in a broad band of outcrops across central New York, from the Niagara Peninsula of Ontario to near the Hudson Valley, and then ranging south-southwestward into New Jersey and Pennsylvania to the Tri-State district. A large prehistoric quarry and workshop center for the western New York Onondaga variety has recently been discovered at Divers or Spirit Lake, north of Batavia, Genesee County, New York, by Richard L. McCarthy of Lockport, New York. Like the Coxsackie quarries of eastern New York, point types of all ages from Paleo-Indian to late prehistoric have been found there. The majority of the Shoop-site artifacts are described as of deeply weathered mottled Onondaga flint, characteristic of western New York and southern Ontario exposures. Minor representations of Little Falls whitish flint, Leray black flint, pale gray Beekmantown flint, and other New York State varieties have been definitely or tentatively recognized in fluted points usually found close to potential sources of supply.

On the other hand, for a majority of the artifacts from the Reagen and Bull Brook sites, the sources of the materials are unknown and non-local. All these facts taken together indicate that the fluted-point people entered various regions of the Northeast by following major river courses. They came equipped with hunting gear and flaked tools of simple character, identified as yet on only a few sites in the area, which were fashioned from high-grade flints or other lithic materials foreign, insofar as known, either to the area as a whole or to the particular region of occurrence. The subsequent explorations of these hunters discovered local supplies of good-quality flints on which they later came to depend. Whatever else they had of a perishable nature, such as wooden tools, basketry and skin articles, has returned ages ago with their makers to dust, and at least in the Northeast it is most improbable that conditions propitious for the preservation of any such remains existed.

The relatively considerable amount of Pennsylvania jasper found in New York State, together with the pattern of its distribution, leads one to suspect that Paleo-Indian people may have been resident in eastern Pennsylvania, the obvious source of this jasper, and in the region of the Shoop site, until climatic and other conditions to the north became more favorable. Since tools and weapons made of eastern and western varieties of New York flints appear in some numbers in Pennslyvania, it is likely that there were seasonal movements back and forth along the river routes.

Antiquity, Geology and Ecology

This problem leads us into a more detailed consideration of the period of Paleo-Indian occupation of the Northeast. In the Upper Great Lakes area the surface distribution of fluted points (no components have yet been identified) in relation to such radiocarbon-dated geological features as glacial moraines, old lake beds, and fossil beach lines of these glacial and postglacial bodies of water has led some archaeologists to conclude that Paleo-Indians were in this region of the eastern United States during the period from about 11,000 to 6500 B.C., a time of abundance of mastodons, and of comparable antiquity to the related Clovis hunters of the West. Although direct evidence is lacking, it has been assumed that fluted-point-tipped spears were employed here in the killing of these elephant-like animals (Mason, 1958, 1960, 1961; Quimby, 1958, 1960). This is analogous to their known use at the Clovis, Naco and Lehner sites in New Mexico and Arizona. This proposition seems reasonable, but it is nevertheless difficult to understand why, considering the truly large number of proboscidian remains discovered in the eastern United States, and even in New York State, not one single reliable instance is recorded of associated evidences of man. This may be explained in part by the fact that only a relatively few such skeletons were carefully excavated; the majority were accidentally found and dug out by earth-moving machinery and reported too late to allow adequate observations of this kind.

The most promising section of New York State in which to search for this kind of evidence is probably the Wallkill River and tributary Dwaarkill valleys, and the broad old lake bed known as the "Black Dirt Area," drained by the Wallkill, in Orange County. As indicated on the maps, Figures 2 and 3, mastodon and mammoth skeletons and fluted points are relatively abundant in this locality.

9

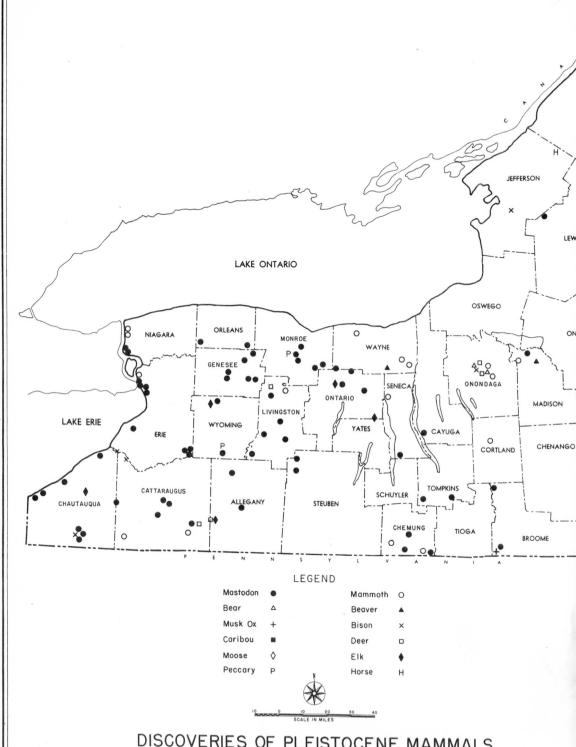

LEGEND

Mastodon	●	Mammoth	○
Bear	△	Beaver	▲
Musk Ox	+	Bison	×
Caribou	■	Deer	□
Moose	◇	Elk	◆
Peccary	P	Horse	H

SCALE IN MILES

DISCOVERIES OF PLEISTOCENE MAMMALS
IN NEW YORK STATE

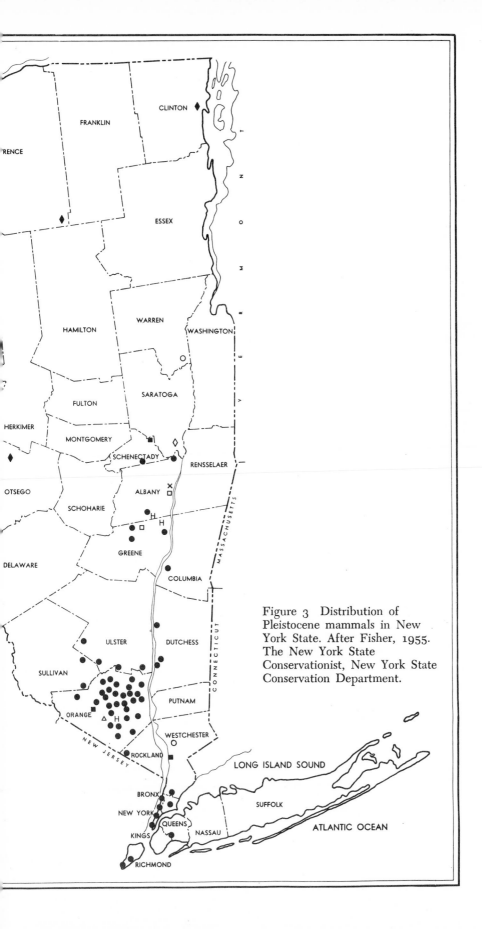

Figure 3 Distribution of Pleistocene mammals in New York State. After Fisher, 1955. The New York State Conservationist, New York State Conservation Department.

In an earlier work (Ritchie, 1957) the writer based his postulate of a minimum antiquity of about 5000 B.C. for the Paleo-Indian in the Northeast on the then prevailing geological dating of postglacial Lake Iroquois and the subsequent Champlain Sea. He was able to correlate the distribution of approximately half of the known fluted points from New York State with the shore lines of these lakes. He specifically stated that this estimate was contingent upon the validity of the current geochronology and that there was the possibility of greater antiquity for similar remains immediately south of these and their respective contemporary water barriers (ibid., pp. 15–17). Subsequent modifications of geological opinion for the age of both these features require a drastic downward revision of this dating, in closer harmony with the radiocarbon assays for Clovis in the Southwest and Early Man estimates in the Upper Great Lakes region (Mason, 1960). There are also now carbon-14 dates for the Paleo-Indian sites in the Northeast at Bull Brook, Massachusetts and Debert, Nova Scotia.

No clear picture of the geochronology of the Northeast has, however, yet emerged. Correlations between proglacial and postglacial lake stages and glacial moraines in the Upper and Lower Great Lakes areas have not been satisactorily effected. Most importantly, the correlatives in the Ontario basin of the Port Huron (Mankato) and Valders moraines are still under debate. The following outline of late glacial history in the New York State area is therefore tentative.

Although six or seven substages of the last or Wisconsin glacial age of the Pleistocene period are recognized (Hough, 1958, p. 94), the archaeological history of the Northeast can, in all probability, be encompassed within the upper third, certainly within the upper half of the Wisconsin (Figure 2). Our brief summary therefore begins with the Late Cary substage or stadial, having a minimum radiocarbon date from a bog near Corry, Pennsylvania, nine miles north of the terminal moraine, of around 12,000 B.C. (Droste, et al., 1959). During the Cary maximum, at least 14,000 B.C., most of the Northeast was under a thick ice mantle and inaccessible to man. There is no doubt, however, of man's residence in North America at, and probably long before, this time. Clovis hunters were very likely present in the western, especially the southwestern, United States, and probably in the Southeast as well. They may even have ranged as far north as southern Pennsylvania, below the limits of the Cary ice. The period of occupation of the Shoop site near Harrisburg is unknown.

Evidence has not yet been found in New York State of a warmer or interstadial interval between the Cary and Port Huron (formerly called Mankato) glacial substages. Indeed, existing data point to a more or less continuous ice withdrawal throughout the whole of Wisconsin time in this area, with temporary halts and slight readvances, of a single major ice sheet. Although the matter is currently a problem for further research, a number of geologists now believe that the Lake Escarpment moraines in western New York and the Valley Heads moraines of the central part of the state constitute a complex marking the approximate maximum stand of the Port Huron ice margin (Muller, 1957, 1957a, 1960, and by conversation of November 20, 1961). Northward lies a system of recessional moraines that includes the recently identified Fort Covington moraine (MacClintock and Terasmae, 1960).

Paleo-Indian penetration of the area at

this time, around 10,500 B.C., would have been confined to southern New York and south-southeastward, where fluted points have been found along waterways and in some instances on high outwash terraces, as shown in Figure 2.

Studies of fossil tree pollens obtained from core borings of lake and bog sediments within the glaciated region indicate a cold and wet climatic association with the Port Huron stage, and a vegetation cover with spruce and fir dominance in the forests, which may have been separated from the ice front by a narrow belt of park-tundra (Potzger and Otto, 1943; Deevey, 1943, 1951; Martin, 1958; Terasmae, 1959, 1960; Beetham and Niering, 1961). This tundra zone apparently consisted of isolated clumps of spruce and fir, with scattered herbaceous growth (grasses, sedges, willows, etc.) between them. If man were present here at this period he would have had available as game animals the mastodon, mammoth, barren-ground caribou, giant beaver, elk, deer and many smaller mammals. Remains of all the enumerated species have been found in Pleistocene deposits in New York State and elsewhere in the Northeast (Hartnagel and Bishop, 1922; Hay, 1923; Potzger, 1951; Fisher, 1955) (Figure 3). A unique apparent association of man and one of these animals is the recent discovery of a Cumberland-like point in the lowest level of the Dutchess Quarry Cave in Orange County, New York, which also yielded bones, teeth and antler fragments of the caribou (*Rangifer tarandus*) (Guilday, n.d.).

Evidence is accumulating to show that Lake Iroquois began as a proglacial lake developed in front of the recessional Port Huron ice, after the latter had wasted back to an indeterminate position in or north of the Ontario basin (Karrow, Clark and

Terasmae, 1961, p. 666; Coleman, 1936, pp. 26–29). Through a channel at Rome, this water body drained eastward into Lake Albany in the eastern Mohawk and Hudson valleys (Fairchild, 1909, 1928; Coleman, 1936) (Figure 2). Several radiocarbon dates place this event at around 10,000 B.C. One of these dates was obtained on a black spruce log from laminated silt and clay deposits of the Lake Iroquois beach overlying glacial till, unearthed during engineering excavations at Lewiston, New York (W-883, 12,080±300 B.P. or 10,120 B.C. ±300 years; Rubin and Berthold, 1961, p. 86).

According to Professor Ernest H. Muller of Syracuse University, "the proglacial lake sequence at Lewiston was not interrupted by glacial readvance later than 12,000 years ago," i.e., subsequent to the Port Huron (Mankato) stadial (by correspondence of December 6, 1960). Elsewhere (Muller, 1960, p. 29) he calls attention to a date of 12,000±300 B.P., or c. 10,000 B.C. (W-507, Rubin and Alexander, 1960, p. 134) on a spruce log from marly silt overlying outwash gravel near a mastodon site in the southeastern corner of Erie County, New York, as providing a minimum age for the recession of the Port Huron sheet from this position. Rapid recession of the ice border is indicated by an 11,410±410 B.P. date (c. 9454 B.C.) (Y-460, Deevey, Gralenski and Hoffren, 1959, p. 147) for spruce wood found with the King Ferry, Cayuga County, New York, mastodon, some thirty miles north of the Valley Heads moraines, now believed to denote the maximum advance in central New York of the Port Huron ice. Another mastodon, dated one thousand years later (10,450±400 B.P. or 8489 B.C.±400 years, W-1038) was excavated in 1959, near Byron, Genesee County, about twenty-eight miles north of the King

Ferry locus, but some eighty miles to the west. The site lies north of the Batavia moraine, believed to be of Port Huron age, and south of the Lake Iroquois strand line. Despite careful excavation by the Buffalo Museum of Science, no trace of the association of man was discovered (Heubusch, 1959, p. 9).

Recent researches at the west end of Lake Ontario have produced a carbon-14 age of 11,510±240 B.P. or 9550 B.C. (Y-691) for wood from a fossiliferous silt-and-clay layer between Port Huron till and Lake Iroquois beach gravel at Hamilton, Ontario, showing that the beginning of Lake Iroquois must lie close to 10,000 B.C. (Karrow, Clark and Terasmae, 1961).

The strong strand line of Lake Iroquois (Figure 2) proves that this body of water had a relatively long existence, and the recent Canadian radiocarbon dates suggest a life span of around fifteen hundred years (ibid., pp. 665–66). Data from Hamilton, Ontario, further indicate that a low-water stage, with cold-water fossils, followed the draining of Lake Iroquois sometime prior to 8000 B.C. when its outlet channel, formerly at Rome, was shifted to a lower level in the St. Lawrence Valley, after the Port Huron ice had melted back from Covey Pass, Quebec (MacClintock and Terasmae, 1960; Karrow, Clark and Terasmae, 1961). This short-lived low-water stage in the Ontario basin, intervening between lakes Iroquois and Ontario, has variously been referred to as the Gilbert Gulf (Fairchild, 1928, pp. 159–65) and Lake Frontenac (Hough, 1958, p. 202). According to the most recent estimates, Lake Ontario began before 8000 B.C., not as an arm of the Champlain Sea, next to be referred to, but as a fresh-water body at a higher elevation than the marine-inundated St. Lawrence Valley (Karrow, Clark and Terasmae, 1961, p. 665).

Following the waning of the Port Huron ice sheet from upper New York State and adjacent Quebec, the glacially depressed land mass of the St. Lawrence lowland was invaded by a eustatic marine transgression known as the Champlain Sea, whose existence is currently estimated at between 6000 and 9000 B.C., at which time the sea level is thought to have been from thirty to one hundred feet lower than at present (Fairbridge, 1960; Terasmae, 1959; Karrow, Clark and Terasmae, 1961). The approximate limits of this cold-water sea, as determined from the extent of clays and sands containing fossil pelecypod shells (*Saxicava*, *Mocoma* and *Balanus*) is shown in Figure 2. The very recent acceptance of the radiocarbon dates on these shells (between *c.* 8000 and 9000 B.C.) places the maximum age of the Champlain Sea some four thousand years earlier than was formerly believed. The validity of the earlier shell dates was questioned because it was generally considered that older carbonates carried in solution by sea water might have been incorporated into the shell structure of the animals, resulting in older than actual ages on the carbon-14 assays. (See discussion in Ritchie, 1957, p. 16; and Mason, 1960, pp. 371–72.) However, subsequent tests seem to have clarified the problem (MacClintock and Terasmae, 1960, p. 239). This being the case, it would now appear that the fluted points found in the upper Lake George and lower Lake Champlain region may have been left by hunters along the Champlain Sea strand as long ago as 6000 to 9000 B.C. (Figure 2). The possibility was earlier considered by the writer (1957, p. 17) that the Reagen site in Vermont, situated on marine dune sand covering the flank of a hill overlooking the Missisquoi River from an elevation of some three hundred feet, or five hundred feet above modern sea level, might represent a near-shore camp site, repeatedly visited during a waning stage of the Champlain Sea. The same possibility may apply to the Davis material, found near Crown Point, New York, at a lower elevation, which would have been submerged by the marine embayment at its maximum extent (Figure 2 and page 19).

The Champlain Sea episode seems in part to have been contemporaneous with the Two Creeks Interstadial, a warmer but by present standards still cool and moist interval between the Port Huron and Valders glacial substages, radiocarbon-dated with considerable exactitude between about 10,000 and 9500 B.C. At this period dense forests of spruce, fir and jack pine, with some intermixture of tamarack, cedar, oak, birch and other trees, covered the area south of the Great Lakes as well as some undetermined portion of the Northeast lying below the residual glacial ice. These forests were the home of most of the above enumerated Pleistocene fauna.

A dated mastodon find already referred to is of this period. It occurred in a small boggy depression on the Myles Colgan farm near King Ferry, Cayuga County, New York. Among the marl-embedded bones of this animal were black-spruce cones and wood; the latter was radiocarbon-dated at 11,410±410 years ago (Y-460, Deevey, Gralenski and Hoffren, 1959, p. 147) or about 9454 B.C. Pollen profiles taken in this bog and in the immediate vicinity showed the dominance here as in the Upper Great Lakes area of spruce-pine forests during the Two Creeks interval (Cox, 1959, pp. 14–15, 23, 27–28).

Around 9500 B.C. the Two Creeks period was terminated by another advance of the ice, the Valders, the last important glacial episode of the Wisconsin age. This event is extremely well dated by radiocarbon analysis of a fossil forest of spruce, pine and birch trees, broken and buried by the Valders ice, near Manitowoc, Wisconsin. In the Northeast the extent of the Valders ice has still to be determined, but it is now generally believed that the terminal moraines lie north of the Ontario basin and the St. Lawrence River. Hence this glacial stadial never directly involved New York State and New England (Mason, 1960; Karrow, Clark and Terasmae, 1961). For still debatable reasons the mastodon and other Pleistocene fauna declined, apparently rather rapidly, during the Valders glacial span, to extinction by or soon after the close of the period. Whether the predations of Paleo-Indian hunters hastened or materially contributed to this extinction is a moot question.

Climatic conditions in the Northeast remained cold and bleak for a long time following the Valders maximum, as attested by the pollen profiles. There seems even to have occurred a final weak ice advance, the Cochrane, in lower Canada, around 6000 B.C., recorded by the local bog sediments in the growth of dense stands of spruce and balsam fir. The period of some three thousand years between the Valders and Cochrane is known as the Late Glacial. It appears to have marked the beginning in the Northeast of geophysical conditions approximating those of the present, except probably for a somewhat lower than modern sea level (Fairbridge, 1958, 1960a).

As already suggested, Paleo-Indian hunters may have frequented the shores of the Champlain Sea in pre-Valders, Valders and early post-Valders time. During the latter period it is believed that isostatic upward movements of the land, in its recovery from the depressing weight of glacial ice, proceeded faster than the eustatic rise of sea level, resulting from the return to the oceans of the melt water of the decaying glaciers. The net result lifted the St. Lawrence lowland and Ontario basin to somewhere near their present levels, thus terminating the Champlain Sea transgression.

The presence of Paleo-Indian hunters of the Clovis tradition in the Northeast during the latter part of the Valders glacial substage in the Great Lakes region has recently been confirmed by the excavation of the remarkable Debert site in north-central Nova Scotia. An average date of 8635 B.C.±47 years has been obtained for this site on thirteen radiocarbon-dated charcoal samples from hearths in association with artifacts (Byers, 1966).

The less reliable date of around 7000 B.C. for the Bull Brook, Massachusetts, site was formerly the only radiocarbon determination for a Paleo-Indian site in the eastern United States. This date, the average of three samples, was derived from scattered charcoal granules recovered from the artifact-bearing horizon of the site, without any direct association with human artifacts (Byers, 1959b).

Around 7000 B.C. climatic conditions in the Northeast were moderating and becoming more arid. In consequence, the arboreal dominance was shifting from jack pine, fir, spruce and birch, to white and red pine, with an increasing proportion of broad-leaved hardwoods, chiefly oak and beech. Although this broad hypsithermal interval, which persisted until approximately 1000 B.C., was in general warmer than the present, it included alternate phases of thermal maxima and cooler episodes, which are reflected in the pollen spectra, illustrating alterations in the forest cover over a wide area of the country (Deevey and Flint, 1957; Terasmae, 1960; Beetham and Niering, 1961; Sears, 1963). These changing forest conditions will be discussed in some detail in later parts of this book.

The Late Paleo-Indian Stage

Early in the postglacial period, Paleo-Indian hunters may have left the Northeast for parts unknown, or they may simply have dwindled in number from an already scanty maximum to a few remnant bands. Something of this kind seems indicated by the Reagen site in Vermont, where the undated culture complex suggests a late modification of the Paleo-Indian of the Clovis tradition, presumably in response to a changing ecological setting more like that of the present, from which the large Pleistocene game animals had disappeared (Ritchie, 1953). The prevailingly smaller and lighter projectile points of the Reagen assemblage hint at the pursuit of lesser mammals, such as the deer and elk. Incidentally, the discovery at the earlier Bull Brook site of calcined long-bone fragments, "possibly of a deer" (Byers, 1955, p. 274), strongly suggests that the diet of the Clovis hunter in the Northeast was by no means confined to proboscidians and other big game, but probably included a wide range of food animals of all available kinds and species.

At the Reagen site, in addition to the variant styles of fluted point mentioned earlier (page 6), unfluted trianguloid, lanceolate, and even a few very weakly stemmed forms, of small size, were found. Some of these are slightly reminiscent of subsequent Archaic points of the same area, others, especially the unfluted Clovis-like and lanceolate specimens, may reflect the faint influence into the Northeast of elements of the Plano tradition. This Paleo-Indian tradition in the western United States apparently overlapped with the fluted-point tradition in some sections, but in the main succeeded it both there and in the Upper Great Lakes area (Mason,

1961). The large category of Plano and unfluted Paleo-Indian points includes the Plainview, Meserve, Milnesand, Midland, Scottsbluff, Eden, Angostura, Agate Basin, Browns Valley, Hell Gap, and other lanceolate types, characterized in general by parallel or ribbon flaking of a high order of excellence (Wormington, 1957; Mason, 1962, p. 231; Agogino, 1963). These various point styles are principally associated in the western United States with sundry extinct species of bison, culminating in the modern *Bison bison*. In the Upper Great Lakes area, certain of these later Paleo-Indian types, viz., Plainview, Eden, Scottsbluff, Browns Valley and perhaps others, have been reported, chiefly as surface finds, in association with fossil beaches and water planes of glacial and postglacial lakes, but never with faunal remains (Quimby, 1960; Mason, 1961).

In the Northeast, evidence for the presence of man with a Plano tradition is slender but probably unequivocal. The writer has from time to time seen in private collections, or himself discovered, projectile points, usually fragmentary, showing the characteristic collateral flaking and certain other features described for Eden points. For example, Plate 2 illustrates both faces of such a point, clipped from a deeply patinated greenish-gray flint with darker streaks, a surface find between Newfield and Newmarket, Rockingham County, New Hampshire.

More convincing testimony has recently come to light through the excavations made between 1956 and 1961 by George N. Gogo of Summerstown, Ontario, on Thompson's Island in the St. Lawrence River near Cornwall, Ontario, Canada. This small, narrow island, less than a mile long, was deeply submerged by the waters of the Champlain Sea (page 14), and the points to be described came from elevations of

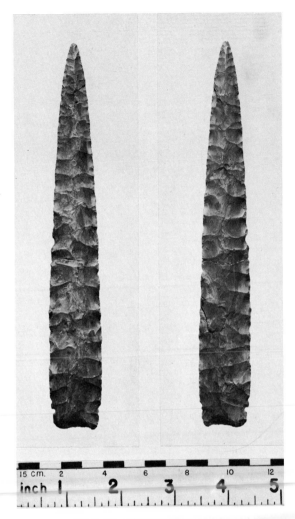

PLATE 2 Probable Plano point, Rockingham Co., N.H. Collection of Homer Folger, Troy, N.Y.

four feet or less above the present river level, and at various places on the island, all within thirty feet of the modern shore line. In every case they lay in the sandy-clay subsoil, at depths of from four to twelve inches below the contact of the subsoil and the dark humus layer. No other artifacts occurred in the subsoil, but Archaic and Woodland types of points and some pottery came from the humus cover,

17

PLATE 3   Probable Plano points, Thompson's Island, Ontario. Collection of George N. Gogo, Summerstown, Ontario.

which varies in thickness from four to twenty inches over the island.

While in Ottawa, the writer learned of this discovery through the courtesy of James V. Wright of the National Museum of Canada, and applied to Mr. Gogo for

data, the loan of the specimens, and permission to publish the finding, all of which was generously granted. On Plate 3 may be seen the seven fragmentary specimens that comprise the finds to April 1962. All are made of unpatinated gray-brown or seal-brown flint of unknown origin. They are exceedingly thin, beautifully flaked in the collateral technique, and have straight or slightly convex bases with slight evidence of wear or grinding.

On being sent these photographs for her opinion, Dr. Marie Wormington of the Denver Museum of Natural History commented as follows: "I am extremely interested in the picture of the points which you sent. They are utterly unlike Plainview points, which are much shorter, much broader, and have concave bases. The general proportions are much like those of Eden points, and the type of flaking is that found on many Edens and on Agate Basin points. I should strongly suspect that they are of Paleo-Indian age." (Letter of May 25, 1962.)

Continuity with, or connections between, late Paleo-Indian and Archaic in the Northeast have not as yet been demonstrated, although this is suggested by some of the material at the Reagen site in Vermont (page 16). Elsewhere in the eastern United States, however, Early Archaic complexes were already beginning to emerge, as shown by the radiocarbon dates of 6000 B.C. or older from lower levels of such sites as Research Cave, Jakie Rockshelter and Graham Cave, Missouri; Modoc Rockshelter and the Ferry site in Illinois; and Russell Cave, Alabama. The immediate antecedents of these assemblages are not yet clearly traceable to Paleo-Indian foundations, although individual point-style sequences are demonstrable, e.g., Meserve prototypes for the Dalton point of the early Southeast Archaic. Probably the best existing continuity is the North Carolina Piedmont sequence of Joffre Coe (1964), recently studied by the writer at Chapel Hill through the courtesy of Dr. Coe. From a possible Clovis fluted predecessor, Coe has established, through stratigraphic excavations in several sites along the Yadkin River, an apparently partly developmental progression from the Hardaway blade through the Hardaway-Dalton and Hardaway Side-Notched varieties of an estimated age of 7000 B.C., to the Palmer types (c. 6500 B.C.), the Kirk series (c. 6000 B.C.), the Stanly (c. 5000 B.C.), and finally the Savannah River form of c. 1500 B.C.

Before leaving this general discussion of the Paleo-Indian hunters of the Northeast, new data will be recorded which have been gathered by the writer since his last synthesis of similar material (Ritchie, 1957). These include additional discoveries of fluted points either as isolated surface finds or in association with other characteristic artifacts of Paleo-Indian typology in apparent components, which include the first so far known in New York State. Added surface finds of fluted points bring the total number to 124 now on record, and plotted on the map, Figure 2, which may be compared with Figure 1 in Ritchie, 1957. The six new components embrace the Davis, Potts, West Athens Hill, Kings Road and Port Mobil sites in New York, and the Wapanucket No. 8 component in eastern Massachusetts, excavated by members of the Massachusetts Archaeological Society under the direction of Maurice Robbins (Robbins and Agogino, 1964).

The Davis Site
(Tda. 2-1)

This probable small camp site of the Paleo-Indian period, the first such component to be identified in New York State, came to the writer's attention in the fall of 1958 during his examination of the collection of Earl Davis, who had found the ma-

19

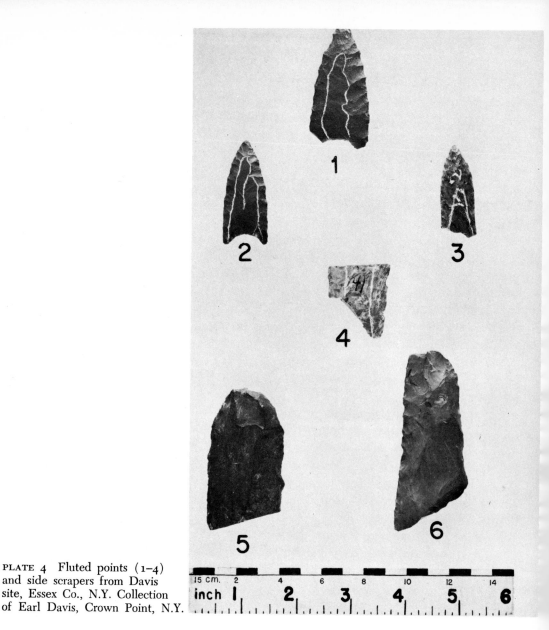

terial described below, and also archaeological specimens of Archaic cultures, on his farm, located about one and three-quarters miles north of Crown Point Village, Essex County. The area of discovery lies within the limits of the Champlain Sea, on a marine clay terrace 120 feet above the present level of Lake Champlain and some 150 yards inland from the steep rock embankment which here forms the lake shore (Figure 2, component number 4).

The Paleo-Indian relics were discovered by Mr. Davis on the surface of his garden and apple orchard, adjacent on the south to the farm buildings. Through his courtesy the site was twice visited by the writer, and the Early Man material illustrated on Plate 4 was borrowed for photographing and recording for publication. Later, Mr. Davis located in his collection five additional specimens bearing his catalogue notation for this component. These have been seen, and drawn, but not photographed, and will be included in the description which follows.

This little group of ten artifacts was collected over an area of approximately one third of an acre, where also was found a small quantity of flakes matching the artifact materials, a few fire-shattered rocks, and three large projectile points of characteristic Archaic (Laurentian) forms. Other specimens of this later occupation, including a ground slate knife, gouges, adzes, etc., came from elsewhere on the farm.

It is possible that the Paleo-Indian component extends beyond the area mentioned. Except for the small garden plot, the ground is heavily turfed and rarely plowed, and random test pitting by the writer revealed nothing. A further search will be made when the land is again under cultivation.

Besides the discoveries on his own land, Mr. Davis found a fluted point of yellow jasper, shown on Plate 4, Figure 2, half a mile southeast at Porters Marsh. It lay on beach gravel, near the water's edge, several hundred feet from the lake-shore embankment, but it exhibits no trace of water erosion. Nothing further was found there on my visit with Mr. Davis, and its occurrence on the beach is a mystery.

The form, two of the dimensions (the thickness is three sixteenths of an inch), the nature of the multiple fluting, and the good workmanship of this point, which is almost certainly fashioned of southeastern Pennsylvania jasper, are depicted in the illustration. The base and lower edges are, as usual, smoothly ground.

The artifact assemblage from the Davis site includes five fluted points, not one of which is absolutely whole. All seem to have been of the parallel-sided variety and all are rather crudely made, with only slight basal and lateral grinding. Three of the specimens are pictured on Plate 4, Figures 1, 3, 4; the fourth very closely resembles Figure 3, both in size and shape. It is, however, more nearly complete, with one ear present. The fifth point is represented only by a medial section, three-quarters of an inch long, fluted on one face, the opposite side being carefully chipped to produce an even convex surface which was not channeled.

Four of the five points have been manufactured from Beekmantown flint, which is striped and mottled in various tones of gray. It is of much interest to observe that this local material could have been derived from the Davis farm, at a locality only one tenth of a mile north of the site of discovery. Here, close to the escarpment edge overlooking the lake, Mr. Davis showed the writer a cluster of shallow pits, obviously quarry holes, made in the Beekmantown limestone, and nearly filled with stone rejectage and woods debris. The surrounding surface was littered with workshop debitage, among which were found hammerstones and point discards of broad triangular form characteristic of the Late Woodland horizon.

More thorough search and excavations here might reveal some Paleo-Indian traces. Ready sources of the Beekmantown flint, however, occur throughout this area.

The one fluted point of exotic material, a maroon-colored jasper-like stone, is shown as Figure 1 of Plate 4. The material has been described as "a deadringer for taconite from the Mesabi Iron Range of Upper Michigan" by Roger Borst, Curator of Geology, New York State Museum and Science Service.

Four scraping tools, and a small red "jasper" flake with slightly retouched edge, complete the Davis-site inventory. Two of the former are illustrated on Plate 4 as Figures 5 and 6. Figure 5 may be described as a combined side and end scraper of maroon-colored stone, like the point, Figure 1, just described. Obviously, the fluted point and scraper traveled together from some unknown, and probably distant, source to the Davis site. This tool is seven sixteenths of an inch in maximum thickness, prismatic in cross section, and made on a thick flake. The edge on one side is steeply retouched, less so on the other.

Figure 6 of the same plate is a side scraper of greenish-gray flint, probably Normanskill flint from eastern New York, since the upper surface is characteristically weathered light gray. It is seven sixteenths of an inch in its greatest thickness, planoconvex in cross section, and was made from a thick flake or spall. The broader, lower end exhibits recent shattering, possibly by fire.

The third, unillustrated scraper, is a thick biface tool of slightly weathered local Beekmantown, or possibly regional Fort Ann flint, coarsely chipped over both faces. It measures three inches in length, half an inch in thickness, and has a steeply beveled scraping edge chipped at one end.

Finally, there is a simple, small (one inch long), uniface, plano-convex end scraper, of unweathered Beekmantown flint which is of questionable association with the Paleo-Indian complex. It could well belong with the three Laurentian points, already stated to have been found in the same garden patch.

It would seem that a tiny group of hunters, coming from afar, had sojourned at the Davis site, possibly when it was on or close to the Champlain Sea shore. Having discovered local exposures of the good-quality Beekmantown flint, they then and there worked this material into fluted points.

Somehow, the jasper point from nearby Porters Marsh may have been a relic of this group, despite the wide disparity in its place of discovery, which suggests entirely modern conditions of lake level and topography at the time of its deposition.

The Potts Site
(Flt. 4-4)

The first major component of the Paleo-Indian stage of culture to be discovered and reported in the State of New York is located on the Caleb H. Potts farm, Lot 49, Schroeppel Township, one and a half miles west of the village of Pennellville, Oswego County (Figure 2, component number 5). The site occupies an indeterminate area of the western end of a glacial drumlin at an elevation of approximately twenty feet above the surrounding country (Plate 5). It overlooks to the east the swampy valley of Sixmile Creek, a southeastward-flowing tributary of the Oswego River, which it joins, after flowing through Peter Scott Swamp, the northern margin of which is only two miles from the site. This district lies well within the confines of Late Pleistocene, proglacial Lake Iroquois (Figure 2), and according to current geological estimates might have been habitable after about 8000 B.C. (page 14). At this time, however, and doubtless for a considerable period thereafter, the whole area of the former lake bed would have been extremely marshy. Even today the extensive vestiges of this vast fenland are clearly visible in the low-lying portions between the glacial drumlins and eskers which characterize the whole region.

Over many years while working his land, especially the garden plot of approximately a quarter of an acre on a fairly level terrace-like portion of the drumlin just south

PLATE 5   The Potts Paleo-Indian site, Oswego Co., N.Y. Looking north.

of the farmhouse, Mr. Potts collected the flint artifacts which came to the surface in plowing. This material was acquired by Mr. Herbert K. Brown of Fulton, who subsequently found several additional artifacts in the garden, including the large Clovis point fragment shown on Plate 6, Figure 2. Two end scrapers (Plate 7, Figures 1, 18) were also found here by Brown's companion, Charles Jerred, also of Fulton. In November 1962, soon after receiving the report of these discoveries from Mr. Brown, the writer and Robert E. Funk of the State Science Service Anthropological Survey visited the site with Mr. Brown and made a number of unproductive test pits in vari-

ous parts of the ridge. Further exploratory work by the writer and a field crew in 1963, both on the higher western part of the drumlin and in the garden area, also failed to discover any artifacts.

Through the courtesy of Messrs. Brown and Jerred the site and its artifacts, which have generously been donated to the New York State Museum, have been made the subject of a more detailed account to be published elsewhere (Ritchie and Funk, n.d.), hence the brevity of the following description of the artifacts, the first known assemblage of Paleo-Indian implements from a New York site. They are fully illustrated on Plates 6–10.

PLATE 6 Fluted points (1, 2) and fragmentary knives from the Potts site, Oswego Co., N.Y.

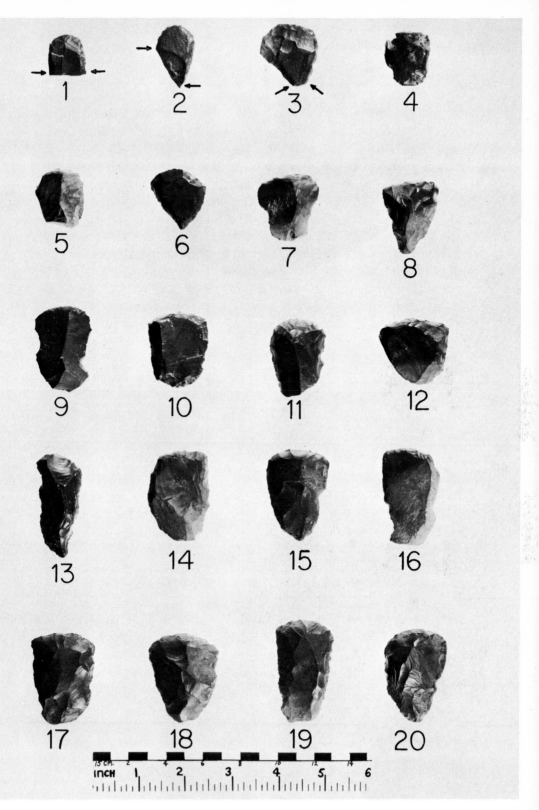

PLATE 7 End scrapers from the Potts site, Oswego Co., N.Y.

The sixty-eight artifacts have been analyzed into the following eight generally recognized categories of weapons and tools:

Projectile points. Only two specimens have so far been found, both of Clovis type, one small, with parallel sides which, like the base, have been rubbed smooth (Plate 6, Figure 1); the other a fragment with basal grinding showing damage by fire (Plate 6, Figure 2), which reconstructed on paper gives a probable original length of ninety-three millimeters and a breadth of thirty-nine millimeters.

Simple end scrapers. These objects, twenty-six in number, comprise 38 per cent of the total artifacts and are illustrated on Plates 7 and 10.

One specimen has a weak graving spur at each end of the primary scraping edge (Plate 10, Figure 1), while four are similarly modified at front or sides (Figures 2–5).

Side scrapers. These twenty-two specimens account for 32 per cent of the total artifacts. They are uniface tools, made from generally thick, broad flakes or spalls, with a few large, crude flake scars which have served to more or less flatten the upper surface. All are marginally retouched to moderate steepness along one or both sides, as shown on Plates 8 and 9.

Small, narrow side scrapers. The two examples of these somewhat drill-shaped tools seem to warrant a separate category from the artifacts just described, mainly because they are based on small, narrow flakes, chipped to a blunt point at one end (Plate 9, Figures 4, 5). The sides are steeply retouched, and the lower face is flat and unworked. The expanded oval base of Figure 5 is thinned by upper-surface chipping; the truncated base of Figure 4 appears to represent an accidental fracture. This specimen is eight millimeters thick, twice that of Figure 5.

Knives from retouched flake. The collection contains seven artifacts (10 per cent of total) which have been tentatively identified as knives, because of the thinness of the flake and flatness of the bevel on the retouched edge or edges (Plate 10, Figures 7–14).

Knives, lanceolate or ovate. These bifacially-chipped artifacts number seven (10 per cent of total), and include no entire specimen but apparently both tip and basal sections (Plate 6, Figures 3–8). A poor quality of collateral flaking is exhibited by Figures 3, 5, 6 and 8.

Scraper knife. A single tool, based on a thick, roughly rectangular flake, with rude bifacial chipping, and three slightly beveled, retouched, scraping or cutting edges, seems equally well adapted for scraping or cutting (Plate 6, Figure 9).

Spokeshave graver. Plate 10, Figure 6, portrays the only example of this type found on the site. A nearly flat, thick (eight millimeters) flake has been steeply chipped (ninety degrees) on two concave edges, and less steeply (about forty-five degrees) on one slightly convex edge (see arrows on illustration). The juncture of the incurvate edges forms a large graving point or beak showing tiny, delicate flake scars on the tip.

Material. Without exception the pieces identified as Paleo-Indian are chipped from a variegated, mostly dark, gray or gray-and-tan, lustrous, high-grade flint, with bluish mottlings. Several geologists were unable to identify the probable source of the stone, but Michael Ozol, then a graduate student in geology at Rensselaer Polytechnic Institute, currently preparing a dissertation on the Onondaga cherts, pointed out the similarities between the artifacts and samples of middle-formation Onondaga flint from western New York. This flint is characteristically different from

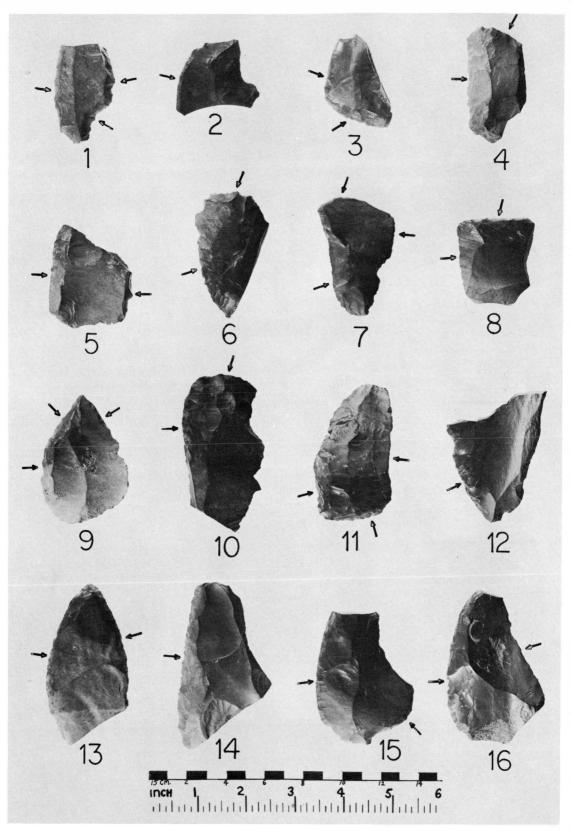

PLATE 8   Side scrapers from the Potts site, Oswego Co., N.Y.

PLATE 9 Side scrapers from the Potts site, Oswego Co., N.Y.

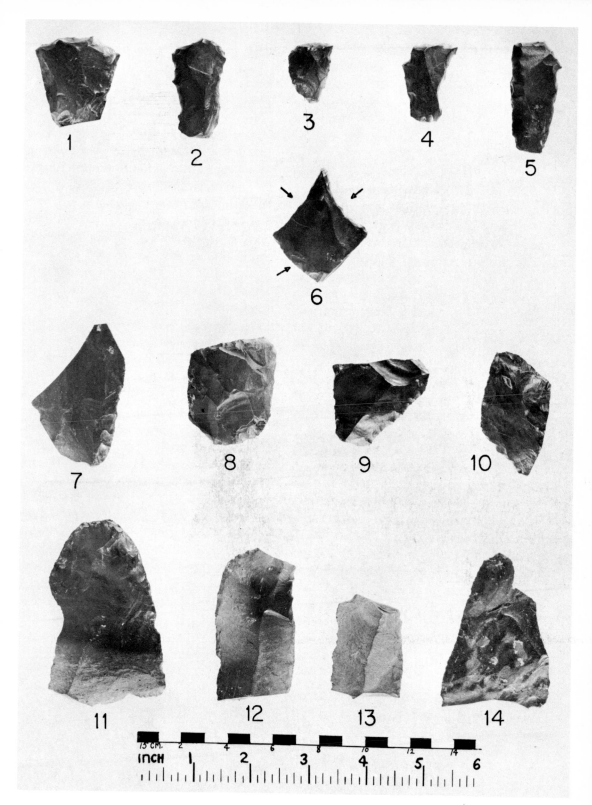

PLATE 10 Spurred end scrapers (1–5), spokeshave graver (6) and flake knives (7–14) from the Potts site, Oswego Co., N.Y.

that of the upper formation of Onondaga of the same area, which is prevailingly of lighter colored grays, also mottled, and heavily marked with tan and brown areas (Wray, 1948, pp. 40–41).

Comparisons with Paleo-Indian sites in the Northeast. The short fluted point with parallel sides and multiple channeling from the Potts site has counterparts at Shoop and Bull Brook, but not at the Reagen site; the large fragmentary point apparently is not matched at any of these sites.

End scrapers from all four sites are very similar. At Shoop and Bull Brook examples with corner graving spurs on the working edge seem more common than at Potts; they are absent at Reagen.

The broad, flat, "ear-shaped" side scraper and the more irregular forms occur on all four of the sites; the so-called "Enterline" variety (Plate 9, Figures 1–3) is common at Shoop and Bull Brook, but not at Reagen; the small, narrow side scraper (Plate 9, Figures 4, 5) is listed for Bull Brook and Shoop. Uniface gravers, common at Bull Brook, are present at Shoop, but not at Potts or Reagen.

The spokeshave graver (Plate 10, Figure 6) from Potts has its closest representation in four specimens of a smaller and more delicate variety from Reagen. The same site also produced a good double-spoke-shave scraper. No tools of these kinds were reported from the Shoop and Bull Brook sites.

Retouched flake knives of the kind described were shared by all four Paleo-Indian sites in the Northeast, but the bifacial ovate form is not listed for Bull Brook. Single-shouldered knives are known only from the Reagen site, where were also uniquely present pentagonoid and lanceolate pentagonoid points, some fluted; and talc pendants. At Bull Brook a peculiar artifact form called a "twist drill" had its sole representation.

In the collections at these four Early Hunter sites there were very few tools based on true blades struck from prepared cores, contrary to assertions in the Shoop site report, the large majority being modified from broad flakes.

Shoop site flint workers used predominantly western New York Onondaga flint, with minor quantites of eastern Pennsylvania jasper, Flint Ridge, Ohio, chalcedony, and Deepkill and Normanskill flints from eastern New York. All sources of Reagen materials, except for a few pieces of recognized Vermont stones, remain unknown. Much Bull Brook material is also unidentified, although a few specimens seem to have been manufactured from eastern New York flints and Pennsylvania jasper.

II   The Archaic or Hunting, Fishing, Gathering Stage

(*c.* 4500–1300 B.C.)

The Archaic, as a term to denote an early level of culture based on hunting, fishing and gathering of wild vegetable foods, and lacking pottery, the smoking pipe and agriculture, was first applied by the writer to the Lamoka culture following his excavations at the Lamoka Lake site (Ritchie, 1932; Willey and Phillips, 1958, p. 104). The traits singled out as especially diagnostic of the Lamoka complex were the chopper, narrow-bladed projectile point, beveled adz, and a class of antler pendant or pendant-like artifacts. Following excavations on two other sites of the Lamoka phase, a full trait list was published, and to the list of traits *not* found in the Archaic were added steatite vessels, copper and shell artifacts, the barbed harpoon, gorget, bannerstone, grooved ax, gouge and birdstone (Ritchie, 1936, p. 18). The writer's discovery in 1937 of the Brewerton phase and its subsequent inclusion in the Archaic stage, expanded, but did not essentially modify, the concept of the Archaic as an early stage in the developmental culture sequence of New York. Copper tools, the barbed bone point, bannerstone and gouge were, however, added to the list of Archaic possessions (pages 79–80).

Since the early 1940s the scope of the Archaic has gradually been broadened to include complexes lacking ground stone implements and some containing tubular pipes and even simple pottery, while its span has assumed continent-wide proportions. Moreover, following the introduction of the radiocarbon-dating technique in 1950, the temporal limits of the Archaic have been extended to overlap with the preceding Paleo-Indian stage of culture in various parts of the United States (Willey and Phillips, 1958, pp. 111–14), although so far not in the Northeast. Because of these facts it is difficult to render at this time a clear-cut definition for the Archaic. In the more restricted sense employed by the writer in 1944, ". . . the archaic level as a whole shows (a) a large variety and numerical abundance of chipped stone types; (b) the lack of all the so-called problematical group of polished stone artifacts, except the bannerstone of several simple forms; (c) a considerable typological range in and large number of bone tools; (d) the prevalence of copper tools and the total lack of copper ornaments; (e) the general absence of shell artifacts; (f) the complete dearth of pipes; (g) the want of pottery, except in perhaps the closing phase; (h) the non-existence of agricultural traces; and (i) the large variety of burial practices, generally not involving mortuary offerings" (Ritchie, 1944, pp. 319–20).

Cultures of the Archaic stage in the

Northeast area give evidence of mobility, small-band organization, and simple social structuring. Most of the sites are small, and lack traces of substantial dwellings, fortifications, storage pits, and even graves. Important exceptions to all these generalizations exist, however, and will be remarked upon in appropriate contexts. The Archaic here, as in most areas, was primarily forest-adapted at all times. Far from uniform, the northeastern Archaic, like its counterparts in the Southeast and upper Mississippi Valley, displays a surprising variety in the details of its content, reflecting in part local ecological adaptations, and probably also the inherent dissimilarities of the several historically diverse traditions involved in its composition, as well as the varying interactions which took place between cultures within, and to a lesser extent, outside, the area.

This variety, although less well marked among the manifestations of the Laurentian Archaic, imparts a distinct regional flavor from area to area, with a noticeable tendency for distinctive complexes to be related to major drainage areas, suggesting territorial distributions of tribal (?) units, analogous with the historic picture of tribal arrangement in the Northeast, although not of course directly corresponding thereto.

The subsistence basis characteristic of the Archaic cultural stage in the Northeast is correlated with the ecological milieu of late postglacial times in that area, or from approximately 4500 to 1300 B.C. This period corresponds to the Late Archaic as now measured against the total known Archaic time scale for the eastern United States, which goes back to nearly 8000 B.C. at Modoc Rock Shelter in southern Illinois (Fowler, 1959); around 7700 B.C. at Graham Cave, Missouri (Logan, 1952); and to approximately 6000 B.C. at Russell Cave, Alabama (Miller, 1957). The radiocarbon-dated span for the northeastern Archaic encompasses the latter portion of the warm and dry hypsithermal interval, and apparently all of the warm, moist climatic episodes which followed, and which are believed to have considerably surpassed the present in average warmth. The vegetational cover included mixed hardwoods—oaks, hickory, chestnut, beech, elm—with some conifers—spruce, hemlock and pine. The fauna, still extant in the area, included the white-tailed deer, moose, black bear, beaver and turkey, as the animals of most importance to man. To this oak-chestnut, deer-turkey biome one of the earliest radiocarbon-dated Archaic cultures of the Northeast, the Lamoka phase, was well adjusted.

Although current radiocarbon datings place certain other manifestations in the Northeast as far back as, or even earlier than, the Lamoka (pages xx, 84, 91), it seems doubtful that valid evidence has so far been advanced in this area for an early phase of the Archaic, not to mention a possible pre-Archaic, such as the Early Macon, Old Quartz and Dairy Field assemblages of Georgia and South Carolina (Kelly, 1938; Caldwell, 1954, pp. 37–39; 1958, pp. 8–10). Byers' speculations concerning the possibility of "extremely Early Archaic" complexes in New England and Pennsylvania (Byers, 1959a, p. 240) do not seem to me thoroughly convincing. In the first place, his "Kelley Phase" of Occupation 1 at the Ellsworth, Maine, sequence, which was not distinguished as a separate complex at the time of excavation (ibid., p. 247), remains a unique and very limited assemblage of, in the main, indistinctive artifact forms. It is not clear what constitutes the typological difference between its main items, the large scrapers (ibid., p. 247, Figures 4, 1–6), and the unillustrated "large scrapers consisting of spalls with no re-touch, but with worn edges," from the succeeding Occupation 2 (ibid., p. 244).

I am also unconvinced of the asserted stylistic differences among the materials from the loam, junction, and till at the E. D. Prey site, near East Killingly, Connecticut (ibid., pp. 240, 247, 249 and Figure 2).

Perhaps the best evidence for an Early Archaic complex in the Northeast comes from the De Turk site near Neversink Station, Berks County, southeastern Pennsylvania (Witthoft, 1954, p. 40; 1959, pp. 83–85). The material from this station, seen by the writer in February 1962 through the courtesy of Mr. Witthoft, is all surface-derived, and is a boulder-extracted quartzite industry comprising large, lanceolate blades of medium thickness, with straight or convex bases; beveled scrapers from re-touched spalls, often with reversed beveling; thick spall knives; and heavy core choppers, resembling early forms in Coe's Piedmont sequence in North Carolina. Very little ground stone occurred on the site, two specimens only, of what look to be rude adz blades. Witthoft estimates this complex may be eight thousand to nine thousand years old.

On the other hand, evidence has been accumulating in recent years, especially in eastern New York, for a number of late manifestations of the Archaic stage which fall in the period between approximately 2200 B.C. and the beginning of the Transitional stage, signalized by the introduction of stone pots and finally by Vinette 1 pottery, around 1000 B.C. Reference is here made especially to the Sylvan Lake, River and Snook Kill phases, described below. The Snook Kill was closely followed by the Transitional Frost Island phase, another newly defined cultural phase, whose strong-est expression occurs in central New York, which it penetrated from eastern Pennsylvania via the Susquehanna River system. This and the Orient phase of Long Island are the best known of the Transitional cultures in New York.

In a real sense, however, the Archaic stage of culture in the Northeast did not terminate with the introduction of pottery. It has indeed persisted into modern times in Labrador, in the life way of the Montagnais and Naskapi (Speck, 1935). These tribes, and some of the probably longer areally established Wabanaki group of forest-dwelling Algonkians south of the lower St. Lawrence (Speck, 1926, 1940), probably lived, until recently, rather like their Archaic predecessors of the general northeastern area, and efforts have been made in the following descriptions of the specific cultures to illuminate certain phases of antiquity by reference to ethnohistorical data. The circuitous character of this approach appears, however, in the following caveat by Grahame Clark: "Existing peoples can only be used as sources for reconstructing the lives of prehistoric peoples with extreme caution and within well-defined limits, since one is otherwise in danger of assuming what one is after all trying to discover." (Clark, 1957, p. 172.)

The seminomadic life attested for the northern tribes is thus strongly indicated by the archaeological criteria of the Archaic. The type of community patterning known as restricted wandering evidently prevailed. Under this system, group movements took place within well-defined territorial limits, often following a seasonal round, similar to that of the modern Mistassini Indians of south-central Quebec (Rogers and Rogers, 1959, pp. 131–38). This manner of life is well suited to a hunter-fisher folk with "sparse, scattered or seasonally available food resources," whose exploitation requires considerable mobility. Usually there is little storable surplus, although meat, fish, shellfish, berries and certain other wild vegetable foods may be dried (or smoked, in the case of the animal foods), while acorns and other seeds are readily hoardable in pits, probably bark-lined and roofed, such as are found on Lamoka sites in New York.

The community members, usually numbering around one hundred, constitute a band composed primarily of nuclear or extended family groups which may separate at certain seasons, as for fall and winter hunting and trapping, and reassemble at other times, as at a good fishing ground in spring and summer. The band itself is the major social unit holding the territory, and it may nominally be led by a chief having advisory rather than coercive power. He may indeed be a shaman who heads his group through his control of magical puissance. The group may be a loosely knit body, in flux through the departure at will of any of its members or the attachment of friendly individuals or families. There is generally a sharing of the available food supply; individual status differences are minimal and based upon ability; there is little personal property and its inheritance is unimportant. Hunting and curing magic are the main expressions of religion (Beardsley, et al., 1956, pp. 136–37).

Most Archaic sites appear to reflect this kind of community patterning. Thin refuse or, as usual, none at all, is indicative of a short stay and a small population. Between seasonal or intermittent visits most of the organic refuse would disappear through decay or scavenging by foxes, porcupines, mice and other animals. Sometimes the purpose of a site can be determined from the specialized tools found there, but even on obvious fishing stations, hunting gear,

food-grinding devices and general-purpose tools are usually found.

Some of the larger Archaic sites described in this report seem to testify to a semisedentary residency conforming apparently to a central-based wandering community pattern, in which the group spends a major part of each year at a settlement or "central base," to which it may or may not return again (Beardsley, et al., 1956, pp. 138–39). Here there is a stable and ample food supply of some kind, such as the fish and acorns at Lamoka Lake, or the fish and waterfowl at Brewerton and Frontenac Island. The relatively long concentration of the assembled band members at one locus builds up a sufficient refuse mantle or midden to hold over to the succeeding year, when a new increment of ashes, charcoal, animal bones, vegetable remains, artifacts, and sand and gravel floor spreads (a very important item, rarely ever observed and recorded; see pages 74, 96) is laid down. Thus, in time, several feet of debris may accumulate. This is precisely what we seem to see at the major sites mentioned, and while it is virtually impossible to isolate the individual annual levels, some insight into cultural changes through stylistic modifications or adoptions of new traits can be obtained through careful dissection of these midden deposits.

On such sites evidences of housing may be found, and graves often occur, usually randomly placed in the refuse rather than in any regular cemetery.

Rare among the Archaic stations of the Northeast, in respect to the evidence they have produced of a settlement pattern illustrative apparently of the central-based wandering community type, are the Lamoka and Wapanucket No. 6 sites, the former described below (page 74), the latter located on a high sand terrace above the north shore of Assowompsett Pond, in

Middleboro Township, Plymouth County, Massachusetts. Excavated by the Cohannet Chapter, Massachusetts Archaeological Society, between 1956 and 1959, under the direction of Maurice Robbins, the Wapanucket No. 6 site produced a cluster of seven closely grouped circular house floors, arranged roughly in two parallel arcs (Robbins, 1960). Six of these features ranged from thirty to forty-five feet in diameter; one, considered a probable ceremonial structure, measured sixty-six feet across. All were outlined by post molds, paired for the most part, averaging two and a half inches in diameter and about eleven inches in depth.

A peculiarity of these houses, which were probably covered with sheets of bark, was an overlapping doorway passage, or short protected entrance corridor, which faced away from the prevailing wind direction. Hearths and pits were present, but without any consistent arrangement, inside the floor outlines.

The large Wapanucket No. 6 lodges were doubtless not for the accommodation of single biological family units, but rather for extended family groups, numbering perhaps fifteen to twenty people, related by blood and marriage, per house. Robbins (1960, p. 79) has estimated a total village population of approximately one hundred persons.

The Wapanucket No. 6 site, attributed to the Late Archaic period because of its artifact inventory, which comprised a variety of projectile-point forms, the ground stone ulu of two styles, perforated bannerstone, plummet, gouge, grooved sinker, and less-diagnostic articles, has been radiocarbon-dated, both by hearth and crematory charcoal from burials, at respectively, 2292 B.C.±300 years (M-764, Crane and Griffin, 1959, pp. 184–85), and 2341 B.C.± 250 years (M-969, Crane and Griffin, 1961,

p. 117). This date of around 2300 B.C. is consistent with that of the late Brewerton phase in central New York (page 91) and somewhat later than the related, but poorly defined Vosburg phase in eastern New York (page 84), both of the Laurentian tradition, to which also I would attribute the principal cultural assemblage at the Wapanucket No. 6 site. Radiocarbon dates for the Lamoka phase are consistently around 2500 B.C.

There are few pure or closed Archaic sites in the Northeast, or apparently elsewhere, hence the difficulty of determining what artifacts, and sometimes features, belong together in a single complex representing the material culture of a particular group of people. Deep stratigraphic sequences, like those found, for example, along the Yadkin River of the North Carolina Piedmont (Coe, 1964), seem not to exist in our area, although some stratigraphy, or at least typological differentiation, can often be obtained, as will be shown in the site discussions which follow (Cf. Bullen, 1949, pp. 9, 32–33, 78–79; Ritchie, 1958, pp. 25–34).

The principal reason accounting for this situation is to be found in the fact that habitation loci, usually repeatedly used, perhaps for generations, by the same cultural group,[1] generally proved attractive to successive groups, separated by no great intervals of time. Hence artifacts of different complexes and periods became inter-

[1] Speck remarks on this custom among the Penobscot of Maine as follows: "At fairly regular intervals in ascending the Penobscot or other large rivers, are signs and sites of over-night camping stations where parties have been accustomed for generations to halt. These are usually awesome, scenic spots, high and dry, overlooking considerable stretches of water. They may be discerned by the much-used fireplaces, camp debris, and grassy plots indicating the well-worn landing places. Signs and signals are occasionally seen at these stations, left by previous occupants." (Speck, 1940, p. 78.)

mixed, even in aboriginal times, prior to the advent of that great mixer, the plow. The writer has seen, through the courtesy of Mr. and Mrs. Otto R. Burger of New York City, tent frames and smoking racks of the present Tête de Boulé of the Lake Kempt and Lake Manowan region of the upper St. Maurice River in Quebec, situated on the same points of land where ancient camp spots occur, as marked by stone fireplaces devoid of embers but with associated stone implements (Burger, 1953). Similar fireplaces with charcoal and rusted tin cans were observed only a few feet removed from some of these.

THE LAMOKA PHASE

The Lamoka culture became known through the excavations of the Rochester Museum, begun by the writer in 1925, on the large Lamoka Lake site, Tyrone Township, Schuyler County (Figure 4, site number 1), where in investigations conducted with very limited assistance and between crops, rich finds were made of stone, bone and antler artifacts, features of various kinds, refuse of animal and vegetable foods, and a small number of human burials (Ritchie, 1932). Confirmatory data were obtained in 1935 and 1936 from two smaller sites, both having refuse and a surviving bone content, viz., the Geneva site, Seneca County, and the Scottsville or Woodchuck Hill site, Monroe County, both since destroyed for road ballast (Figure 4, sites number 2, 3) (Ritchie, 1936). Significant cultural, and especially skeletal, materials pertaining to the Lamoka people and their relationship to other groups were recovered in 1939 and 1940 at Frontenac Island in Cayuga Lake, Cayuga County (Ritchie, 1944, pp. 268–92; 1945). These four sites constitute the essential basis for the following description of the Lamoka culture.

Additional but minor data have been gathered from a large number of small camp sites, on a few of which occur plow-deep patches of black dirt, evidently refuse from which all osseous matter has decayed, leaving only scanty, usually surface-strewn stone relics, chiefly hammerstones, anvils, and the characteristic Lamoka-type point and beveled adz, artifacts with unknown context prior to the discoveries at Lamoka Lake. Typical of this group of camp sites are the Lawson, and Ross and Di Santo components in central New York (Figure 4, sites number 4, 5; Plate 11).

Persistent and intensive search for another Lamoka component of sufficient size to produce data, especially on the settlement pattern, has been unrewarded, and the uniqueness of the Lamoka Lake site is now more than ever likely. Unfortunately, since the publication on this site was issued, it has become the center of amateur activities of an indiscriminate and scientifically fruitless character. Brief reinvestigations by the writer in 1958 and 1962, however, proved very useful and further work may be undertaken there.

The major cultural manifestation at the Lamoka Lake site was at first attributed to an Archaic Algonkian group in a vain effort to correlate this completely new complex with the hypothetical first period of Algonkian occupation of Parker (Parker, 1922, p. 48). Following the adoption of the McKern or Midwestern Taxonomic Method of classification in 1935 (McKern, 1939), the complex was described as the Lamoka Focus of the Archaic Pattern, and the traits and characteristics of the culture, based upon the three sites excavated to that time, were enumerated (Ritchie, 1936; cf. 1944, pp. 292–310, 387–94).

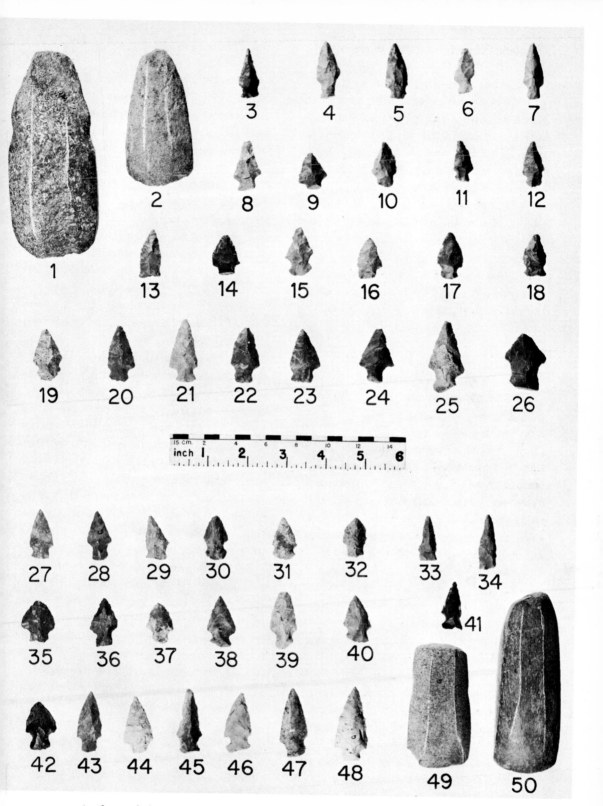

PLATE 11 Artifacts of the Lamoka phase from the Lawson site, Seneca Co. (1–26), and Ross and Di Santo site, Wayne Co. (27–50). 1, 2, 49, 50 beveled adzes, others projectile points of Lamoka type. Collection of Harold Secor, Savannah, N.Y.

Currently, the writer continues to regard the Lamoka culture as a discrete and distinctive entity, among the earliest radiocarbon-dated Archaic assemblage yet revealed by the long and detailed investigations in the New York State area. The product of a particular physical group, its origins are still shrouded in mystery, its destiny only broadly illuminated. It has, however, survived the critics' early doubts of an Archaic stage of aboriginal culture in the eastern United States and it has since been amply shown to have been but one of many such cultures.

Geographical and Ecological Setting

The Lamoka is peculiarly a New York State culture, with a minor extension westward into the Ontario Peninsula and a stronger one to the south in north-central and northeastern Pennsylvania, especially in Potter County and along the Susquehanna River. The heartland embraces the Genesee country and eastward across the Finger Lakes to Oneida Lake. The peripheral area, where the culture occurs thinly, is wider, extending slightly into the eastern portion of the state. Within this broader range are found scattered surface traces consisting of some part of the stone industry, chiefly the Lamoka-type projectile point, indicative of small, temporary camps. Test excavations on a number of these, even on the rare examples which retain traces of refuse, have failed to uncover post molds or pits, and only very occasionally a hearth marked by burned stones and soil. The distribution of the culture in terms of its most diagnostic single trait, what I have termed the beveled adz (Plate 18, Figures 13, 16, 17), a tool not known to characterize any other complex, follows closely the pattern given (Figure 5). Single

specimens within or beyond the remote fringes may best be considered strays, probably picked up elsewhere and transported by later Indians.

The chief differences between the map, Figure 5, and earlier published versions (Ritchie, 1936, p. 21; 1944, p. 297) is the apparent absence of the Lamoka from north of Lake Ontario. Reconnaissances by Canadian investigators and by the writer in this part of Canada have failed to locate definite traces of the culture in this area.

Within the territory of its occurrence, the Lamoka culture is almost entirely restricted to the immediate vicinity of lakes and streams, especially the smaller lakes and shallower portions of larger ones, medium-sized to large rivers, and large marshes. Very rarely Lamoka camp sites are found on small streams and big springs, from one-quarter mile to about a mile back from navigable and fishable waters. The Piffard site, Livingston County, New York (Figure 4, site number 26), and the Hagerman site near Asylum, Bradford County, Pennsylvania, are among the best examples of such components.

It is of interest to note that in all cases the site situation is clearly related to present topographical conditions and water planes. Beyond doubt, the geographical conditions, as well as the flora and fauna, have changed very little since Lamoka times, nearly five thousand years ago. Lamoka sites, for example, are on the same level and obvious beach line as Owasco and Iroquois sites, scattered at points of vantage along the 380-foot contour bordering the great Montezuma Marsh, and the Lamoka and Frontenac Island sites afford further instances in proof. The suggestion made by one archaeologist that "the Lamoka people probably lived just south of a glacial sea" has been refuted by the most recent geological evidence (page 14).

The geographic setting of the Lamoka culture falls within two physiographic provinces, viz., the Great Lakes Section of the Central Lowland Province and the Glaciated Allegheny Plateau of the Appalachian Plateaus Province (Fenneman, 1938) (see endpaper map). In the former section the Erie-Ontario lowland bordering these lakes rises from 246 feet along Lake Ontario to nearly 1000 feet where it joins the Allegheny Plateau. The surface soils of the Lake Plain, of glacial-lakes deposition for the most part, consist primarily of gravelly and sandy loam, intermixed with residues of weathered native rocks—soft Ordovician and Silurian shales, sandstones and limestones—to produce deep alkaline soils of high fertility (Howe, 1935). This well-watered lowland is crossed by numerous streams, large and small, mainly north-flowing, and dotted by swamps and marshes (including the large Montezuma Marsh) lying among the kames, eskers and drumlins which give relief to this relatively flat country. All these features, swamps included, are relics of recent (probably Port Huron) glaciation (page 12).

The Allegheny Plateau Section, adjacent on the south to the Erie-Ontario lowland, has a maximum elevation of approximately two thousand feet in the Finger Lakes region, in the heartland of the Lamoka culture. On this glaciated plateau the soil cover, largely derived from the disintegration of Devonian shales and sandstones, intermixed with glacial till, is generally thin, acid, poorly drained and of low fertility.

Only one major site of the Lamoka phase, the type station itself at Lamoka Lake, lies within this highland province in a unique setting combining, apparently, all the physiographic features essential to the food-gathering economy of these people who, lacking horticulture, depended simply and directly upon wild animals and plants for food, clothing and shelter. The close harmony involving habitat, economy and technology is evident within the limited ecosystem of the Lamoka people in the locations and contents of the major sites, which yield such inferences more readily than the camp components where only a small fraction of the material culture survives.

The preference for waterside locations, both for temporary and more permanent abode, is obvious, and moreover these locations invariably comprise the shallower and weedier sections of the larger lakes (the north ends of Seneca and Cayuga lakes, the west end of Oneida Lake); small lakes of no great depth, well adapted even now for fish life (Lamoka, Waneta, Conesus, Honeoye and Cross lakes); the margins of large marshes having considerable open water (Montezuma Marsh); or the larger, quiet-water streams, having weedy pools and bars (Genesee, Seneca, Oneida, Oswego, Chemung, Cohocton, Susquehanna rivers). It is worth mentioning here that riverine rifts, so attractive to the fishermen of the Laurentian, Point Peninsula, Owasco and other early and late cultures, did not strongly entice the Lamoka fisherman, judging from his site locations, doubtless because he, unlike the others, had no barbed bone points or harpoons for spearing, unless possibly the leister, which is more likely to have been employed in capturing waterfowl. It is also worth emphasis that no sites of this culture are known from along the shores of the deeper parts of the Finger Lakes or of Lake Ontario, a generalization broadly valid for all prehistoric New York cultures.

While Lamoka sites seem to have been

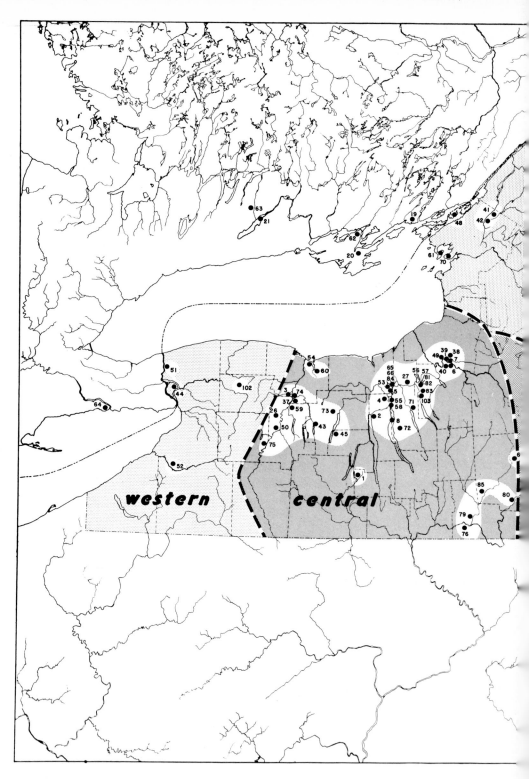

Figure 4 Locations of some important sites referred to in the text of the Archaic, Transitional and Woodland stages. 1 Lamoka Lake, 2 Geneva, 3 Woodchuck Hill, 4 Lawson, 5 Ross and Di Santo, 6 Robinson, 7 Oberlander No. 1, 8 Frontenac Island, 9 Wapanucket No. 6, Mass., 10 Donovan (Vergennes), Vt., 11 KI, Vt., 12 Bannerman, 13 Lotus Point, 14 Wading River, 15 River, 16 Bent, 17 Hoffman's Ferry, 18 Isle La Motte, Vt., 19 Collins Bay, Ont., 20 Picton, Ont., 21 East Sugar Island, Ont., 22 Snook Hill, 23 Weir, 24 Vedder, 25 Old Place, 26 Piffard, 27 O'Neil, 28 Orient No. 1, 29 Orient No. 2, 30 Jamesport, 31 Sugar Loaf Hill, 32 Stony Brook, 33 Baxter, 34 Solecki, 35 Muskeeta Cove, 36 Lake Montauk, 37 Wray, 38 Oberlander No. 2, 39 Vinette, 40 Pickins, 41 Muskalonge Lake, 42 Hunter (Red Lake), 43 Morrow, 44 Riverhaven No. 2, 45 Vine Valley, 46 Long Sault Island, 47 Rosencrans, N.J., 48 Canoe Point, 49 Wickham, 50 Squawkie Hill, 51 Lewiston, 52 Cain 53 Rector,

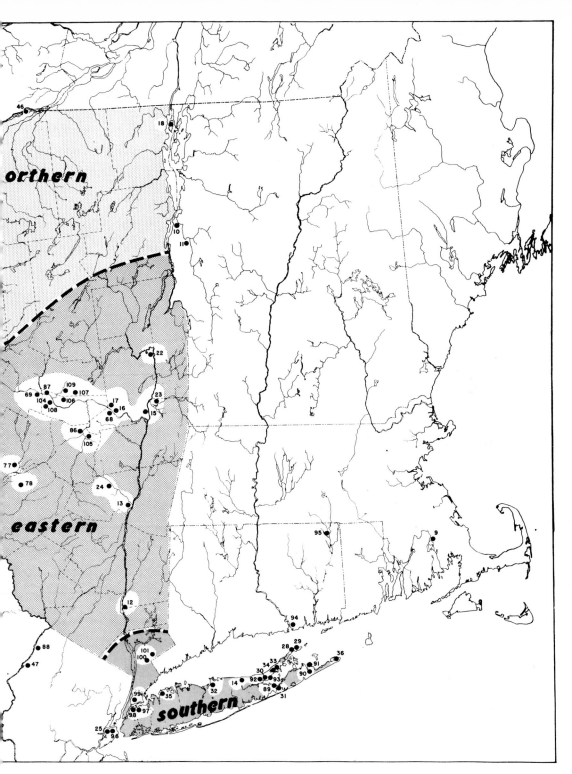

54, Sea Breeze, 55 Kipp Island, 56 Jack's Reef, 57 Felix, 58 Menard Bridge No. 1, 59 Durkee, 60 Plum Orchard, 61 Point Peninsula, 62 Bay of Quinté, Ont., 63 Brock Street, Ont., 64 Port Maitland, Ont., 65 Hunter's Home No. 1, 66 Bluff Point, 67 White, 68 Turnbull, 69 Willow Tree, 70 Pillar Point, 71 Lakeside Park, 72 Levanna, 73 Sackett, 74 Golah, 75 St. Helena, 76 Willow Point (Clark and Palmer), 77 Wilber Lake, 78 Hilltop, 79 Castle Creek, 80 Bainbridge, 81 Carpenter Brook, 82 Jack's Reef No. 2, 83 Maxon-Derby, 84 Hunter's Home No. 2, 85 Bates, 86 Enders, 87 Snell, 88 Bell-Philhower, N.J., 89 Sebonac, 90 Soak Hides, 91 Squaw Cove, 92 Conklin, 93 Wells, 94 Old Lyme, Conn., 95 South Woodstock, Conn., 96 Bowman's Brook, 97 Wilkins, 98 Grantville B, 99 Clasons Point, 100 Finch Rock House, 101 Helicker's Cave, 102 Oakfield, 103 Kelso, 104 Oak Hill, 105 Chance, 106 Getman, 107 Cayadutta, 108 Otstungo, 109 Garoga.

selected with consideration to the fishing potentials, hunting and the collecting of vegetable foods were of major importance in this forest-adapted economy. The chief food animals were the deer, turkey and passenger pigeon, as attested by the predominance of their bones found in refuse middens and utilized for implement manufacture. All three species obtain most of their food in hardwood forests, the former browsing on foliage, buds and twigs and eating such mast foods as acorns, chestnuts and beechnuts. The vegetable food of the turkey and passenger pigeon consists largely of these same nuts, plus wild cherries, grapes, and berries of the flowering dogwood and sourgum (Bent, 1932, p. 335). The acorn was also a most important food resource of the Lamoka people, as shown by the large quantities of carbonized shells, and occasional cotyledons, scattered throughout the ash beds and refuse deposits at the Lamoka Lake site. The numerous food-grinding implements of several forms testify to the same conclusion. The coexistence of the Lamoka habitat and the hardwood forest is, therefore, a predictable ecological relationship.

Prominent constituents of the primeval forest as it was first known by white settlers of the Erie-Ontario plain were the beech, sugar maple and basswood, with some white ash, cucumber, tulip poplar and black birch (Bray, 1930). Oak-chestnut and oak-hickory stands were found along the valleys of the streams and lakes where Lamoka sites had existed in far earlier days (Smith, 1954, p. 25 and map), when it seems likely that these climax forests had also flourished here (Braun, 1950, p. 408). Oak-chestnut groves likewise occurred in the northern hardwood forest of the Allegheny Plateau, along with beech, sugar maple, black cherry, black

birch, white ash, hickory, hemlock and white pine (Bray, 1930; Smith, 1954, p. 26 and map).

When the Lamoka folk lived in this territory, almost five thousand years prior to white settlement, according to radiocarbon determinations, the climate may have been warmer than at present, and perhaps somewhat drier. Radiocarbon-dated fossil pollen profiles from the northeastern United States indicate a forest dominance at this time of oak, birch, hickory, chestnut and hemlock (Deevey and Flint, 1957; Beetham and Niering, 1961; Sears, 1948, 1963). These and other palynological findings confirm the archaeological evidence from the Lamoka sites. Attempts in 1958 to obtain pollen samples at various points and depths in the Lamoka Lake site, and to correlate these with core samples from deep borings in adjacent marshes and shallow waters of Lamoka and Waneta lakes, were only partially successful, due largely to the poor preservation of pollen from the site. The results of the lake and marsh borings have not yet become available.

Chronology

The early position of the Lamoka phase in the Archaic sequence in New York State rests principally on radiocarbon dating. The Lamoka complex at the key station occurred in refuse ranging from about one to five feet in depth. Thinly and sporadically overlying the site, especially in the northern portion, were artifacts and features of later occupations. A small part of this subsequent material, notably a few atlatl weights, a stone gouge and a small number of broad-bladed points, has a probable Laurentian provenience; most of it, however, is referable to a short occupation in early Middle Woodland times, with pottery, pits, and burials of a brachycranial people, accompanied by distinctive grave goods, patently intrusive into the older deposits (Ritchie, 1932).

The radiocarbon basis of comparison comprises a series of eight dates for the Lamoka Lake site, all obtained on charcoal from hearth samples taken from various depths and places at the site (Figure 1). These have been processed at three laboratories and the provenience details are recorded with the published results (cf. Ritchie, 1951b, p. 31). The first two dates, obtained through the courtesy of Dr. W. F. Libby, discoverer of the method of radiocarbon analysis, at the Institute for Nuclear Studies of the University of Chicago, were 3433 B.C.±250 years (C-367) and 2419 B.C.±200 years (C-288, Arnold and Libby, 1951, p. 114). The older date was preferred by the laboratory, since the sample yielding the second date was heavily contaminated with rootlets. However, some of this latter sample was requested from Chicago by the University of Michigan Memorial-Phoenix Project Radiocarbon Laboratory, and rerun. The resulting date of 2485 B.C.±400 years (M-26) closely approximated the Chicago figure (Crane, 1956, p. 667). Another specimen run by Michigan in the same year gave an age of 2575 B.C.±400 years (M-195, Crane, 1956, p. 668).

Two additional samples were collected by the writer in his excavations of 1958 in a portion of the north field where the refuse mantle was thinnest and where much of the intrusive goods occurred. They came, however, from apparently undisturbed hearths of the Lamoka culture and yielded dates of 2521 B.C.±300 years (M-911, Crane and Griffin, 1961, p. 117) and 2451 B.C.±250 years (M-912, Crane and Griffin, 1960, p. 38).

In the last work done on the site by the writer in 1962, numerous hearth samples were collected from the subsoil level, two of which have been dated by the Radiocarbon Laboratory of Yale University with the following results: 2550 B.C.±80 years (Y-1279) and 2540 B.C.±80 years (Y-1280).

It seems probable therefore that a median date for the Lamoka occupation would approximate 2500 B.C. and that the first appearance of this culture in the Northeast may be at least several centuries earlier. It is also now established that phases of the Laurentian culture were already in existence in certain parts of the Northeast, particularly in northern and eastern New York and western Vermont, before 2500 B.C. (page 84).

The Lamoka People

Of the people responsible for the Lamoka culture few skeletal remains have survived on which to base a reconstruction of their physical appearance, pathologies and injuries affecting the bony structure, and various other facts. Two sites yielded all the useful material of this kind available, Lamoka Lake and Frontenac Island. At the Geneva site a group of presumably Lamoka graves were long ago destroyed by railroad construction, and two burials found in the refuse were judged to be later intrusions; while at Scottsville, the bones of five individuals found were too badly decomposed to be of value (Ritchie, 1936).

Despite diligent search, no cemetery could be located on or near the Lamoka Lake site. Thirteen skeletons, however, complete or in fair condition, and portions of thirty-four other burials (not to mention random isolated human bones found at various depths in the refuse) were discovered on this site (Ritchie, 1932, pp.

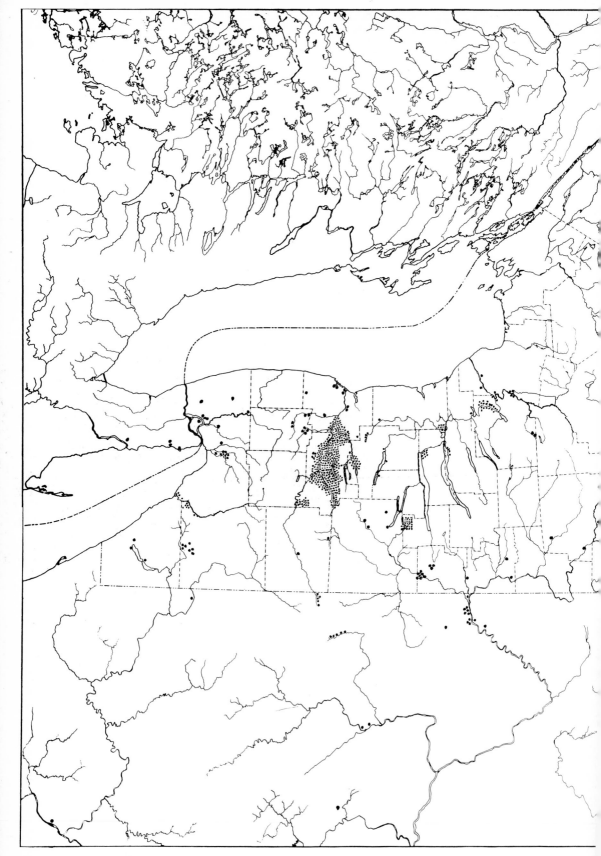

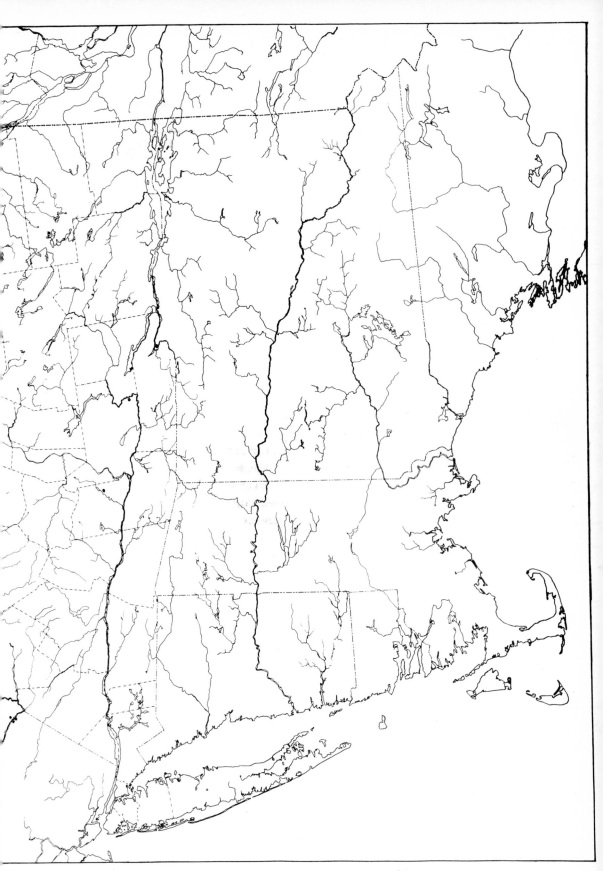

Figure 5 Distribution of the beveled adz of the Lamoka phase. Each dot represents one specimen.

45

115–30. A fourteenth, incomplete skeleton was added to the total by the writer's later excavations there in 1958 and does not enter into the following discussion). Two distinctly different physical types were represented in this material, a slender, gracile, dolichocranial or long-headed type, and a rugged, heavy-boned, brachycranial or broad-headed group. The latter consisted of three adult males whose flexed skeletons reposed in intrusive graves traceable from a near surface level into the older Lamoka middens. They were accompanied by grave goods comprising artifacts unknown from the Lamoka culture.

The dolichocranial skeletons, three male and two female, had no burial offerings and seemed to have been casual flexed burials covered with the refuse of the Lamoka community. These and other facts led to the assumption that the latter type probably belonged with the older culture, a postulation subsequently verified at Frontenac Island, as will later be shown. On the basis of our total evidence we may describe the typical Lamoka adult male as of medium height (about five feet five or six inches), slender and gracile build; with a long, narrow, oval, and high-vaulted head; a high and narrow face, with little malar (cheekbone) or alveolar (lower face) projection; a well-formed palate with a regular arrangement of teeth; a relatively narrow nose, and eyes in medium-high sockets, under weak to moderately developed brow ridges. The closest comparison with this morphological type seems to lie with the Archaic Shell Mound people of the southeastern United States, and to a lesser degree with the Basket Makers of the Southwest, with both of whom they may have had some remote genetic, as well as cultural, ties.

The scanty skeletal remains provide also the following information: the dental health of these people was good; caries was virtually absent, impactions and malocclusions were rare, and few teeth were lost in life. Most of the trouble seems to have resulted from the eating of gritty foods, largely stone dust from the grinding tools. Attrition of tooth enamel varies from slight to advanced and deposition of secondary dentine did not always keep pace with the wear, resulting in the exposure of the root canal to infection, which led to apical abscesses, and sometimes loss of teeth. Mild periodontitis and alveoloclasia seem also related to this factor.

Diseases affecting the bony tissue were uncommon and their lesions were observed on only a few adult skeletons. They can be diagnosed as mild osteoarthritis of the spine (one or two cases); mild arthritic changes following a severe compression fracture of the head of the right femur in a male, who had also suffered a bad fracture of the shaft of the same bone; moderate osteoperiostitis sequent to a fracture of the lower arm in an old male; and mild osteoporosis on a male cranium.

Traumatisms of bone were limited to the fractures enumerated, plus an apparently fatal skull fracture and several lethal dart wounds, described below in connection with probable warfare.

From this evidence one may infer, as in the case of the dentition, a relatively healthy populace, unafflicted with severe physical disabilities which register their ravages on the bones. The single case of osteoporosis suggests a nutritional deficiency of some sort in this individual. The several long-bone fractures, confined to males, are a probable index to the rigorous life of the hunter, who also met with hostile contacts with other men, as shown by projectile-point wounds.

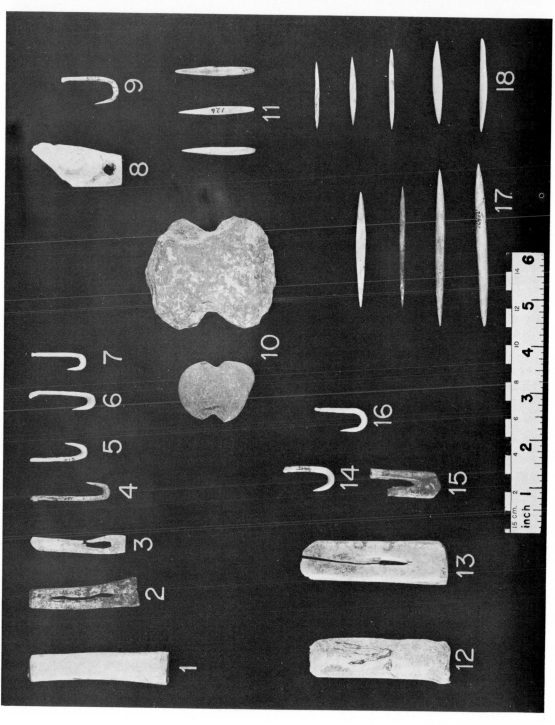

PLATE 12 Fishing tackle of the Lamoka phase. 1–3 fishhooks in process from curved bone sections; 4–7 fishhooks made by this process; 8 bone blank for fishhook made by drilling and cutting; 9 fishhook made from similar blank; 10 notched pebble netsinkers; 11 bone points perhaps for compound fishhooks; 12, 13, 15 fishhooks in process from flat bone sections; 14, 16 hooks made by this process; 17 probable bone leister points; 18 bone gorges.

Subsistence Fishing

The Lamoka people depended for subsistence upon hunting, fishing and collecting, probably in that order of importance. A considerable reliance on fishing is indicated by the abundance of equipment for that purpose, especially at the Lamoka Lake site, where the Rochester Museum's excavations alone disclosed approximately eight thousand notched pebble netsinkers (some seven hundred were also found at the Geneva site),[1] showing the predominance of net fishing over line angling (Plate 12, Figure 10). For the latter, two, and perhaps four, bone devices were employed, the gorge and the barbless hook. The former consists of a round or flat splinter of bone, from about one and a quarter to two and a half inches in length, ground to a sharp point at both ends (Plate 12, Figure 18). Gorges were found singly or in groups of from three to five at the Lamoka type station (Ritchie, 1932, Plate IX, Figure 10), while at Frontenac Island, thirty-seven specimens occurred in a heap with Burial 94, strongly suggesting their use on trot-lines. The line itself was probably composed of twisted vegetable fibers, such as Indian hemp (*Apocynum cannabinum*), and was secured about the center of the gorge. When the impaled bait was taken by a fish, the gorge turned transversely in its gullet or stomach. The smaller examples could likewise have served in the capture of waterfowl. Some short, single-pointed bone splinters may have constituted part of a compound hook with wooden shank (Plate 12, Figure 11).

[1] Quantification data for the Lamoka Lake, Geneva and Scottsville sites will be found in the trait tables for this culture in Ritchie, 1944, pp. 387–94.

Unbarbed bone fishhooks with plain, knobbed or grooved shanks occur (Plate 12, Figures 4–7, 9, 14, 16). Many rejects of manufacture in all stages from long bone to finished hook disclose the details of three major methods, utilizing respectively either a curved section of naturally hollow bird bone, or a flat piece of mammal long bone. In the first method, suitable length sections of the humerus, or sometimes the leg bones, of turkey, swan or other large birds were longitudinally bisected by grooving with a sharp flint, after which the medial area was cut or scraped away. Sometimes two hooks could be cut from opposite ends of the same blank. These hooks, finished off by grinding, retained the original curvature of the bone (Plate 12, Figures 1–3). This widely employed method continued in use in our area into Iroquois times. In the second, and less popular, method, a mammal long-bone blank was whittled or ground to the desired size before scraping out the interior. The resultant hook was flat, round in cross section, and apparently stronger than the type cut from bird bone (Plate 12, Figures 12, 13, 15). A specimen from the Scottsville site illustrates a third technique of hook making by perforating a curved mammal-bone blank. This method created a potential barb which was ignored (Plate 12, Figure 8). Millenniums later this possibility may have been observed in central New York (page 246).

The barbed bone point or harpoon was unknown in the Lamoka culture. The unique specimen with barb-like notch, pictured in the Lamoka Lake site report (Ritchie, 1932, Plate X, Figure 1) is probably a net-making tool. Fish spearing, however, may have been done with a contrivance termed a leister, as suggested by the occurrence on the major Lamoka sites of what the writer has called the double-

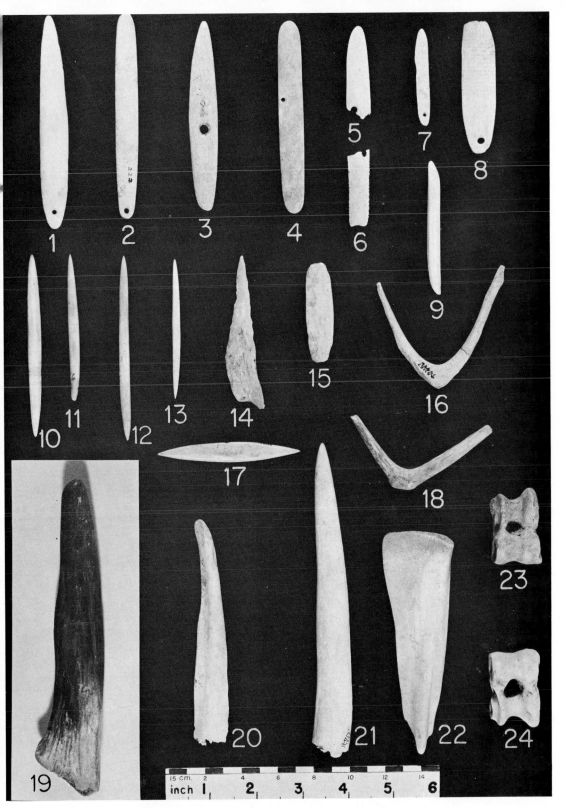

PLATE 13   Bone and antler implements of the Lamoka phase. 1–8 probable net-weaving tools; 9 polishing tool (?), 10–13, 17 sewing or weaving tools (?) (12, 13 may be leister points), 14, 15 chipped-bone point and blank; 16, 18 hook-like objects from antler and turtle bone, respectively; 19 antler flaking tool; 20 bone flaking tool; 21 antler punch; 22 deer-scapula scraper; 23, 24 socketed deer astragali.

49

pointed bone implement, a flat or rounded, bipointed, polished section of mammal long bone, three to five or more inches in length (Plate 12, Figure 17; Plate 13, Figures 12, 13). The leister consisted of a wooden shaft, twelve or more feet long, tipped with a similar bone point set firmly in the end. A hardwood grip on either side of the point spread open when the fish was struck, then held it firmly impaled upon the bone point. The leister, if known, may also have been used in capturing waterfowl. Several bone points from the Lamoka Lake site are finely scored or grooved and appear more like bodkins of some sort than leister points (Plate 13, Figures 10, 11). Adjunctive to the fishing activity are the probable net-weaving tools shown on Plate 13, Figures 1–8. They are thin, flat, elliptical sections of well-polished long bone, with rounded or bluntly pointed ends. All have a single, usually small, drilled perforation, variously situated near end, edge or center. Faint marginal nicking occurs on some specimens.

The stone plummet, a probable item of fishing paraphernalia, is totally missing from the Lamoka culture.

Very little can be recorded concerning the species of fish taken by these sundry means, since scanty evidences were preserved only at the Lamoka Lake site, where scales and jaws attributed to the pickerel, and spines of the common bullhead occurred. These fish are still present in Lamoka and connecting Waneta lakes, along with largemouth and smallmouth black bass, several kinds of sunfish, rock bass, yellow perch, suckers, and other common fish, widely dispersed in New York State waters, and doubtless among the species eaten by the Lamoka people (Roecker, 1953–54).

Subsistence Hunting

All sites of the Lamoka culture attest to the importance of hunting in the economy of their occupants. In the main, this is shown by the prevalence of projectile points, but on the large refuse-bearing stations, there is also an abundance of food-animal debris. The principal weapon was probably the javelin, propelled with the aid of a throwing board or atlatl. The stone atlatl weight (bannerstone) is not, however, an intrinsic part of Lamoka culture.

Lamoka projectile points are typically small, rude and percussion-chipped, with narrow blade, and stemmed or side-notched base which is usually left thick and unfinished (Plate 14, Figures 3–30, 34). (See typological description in Ritchie, 1961, pp. 29–30). This diagnostic point form, because of its small size (the majority fall between one and a quarter and one and three-quarters inches in length) was initially described as an arrow point (Ritchie, 1932, p. 91), but it is doubtful that the bow and arrow was known in the New World at this early date (c. 3000 B.C.). Demonstrable dart points of comparable size, but much greater age, have been discovered in Gypsum Cave, Nevada, by Harrington (Harrington, 1933, pp. 105–9).

Sites of the Lamoka culture yield a small number of long stone points of the same form, apparently for arming spears which were held in the hand (Plate 14, Figures 31–33).

Other artifacts probably connected with the hunting activity include bone daggers of several styles—trianguloid, biconvex, or round and stiletto-like in cross section, a few decorated with stripes or spirals of red ocher. They may also have been weapons of war (Plate 15, Figures 4–6).

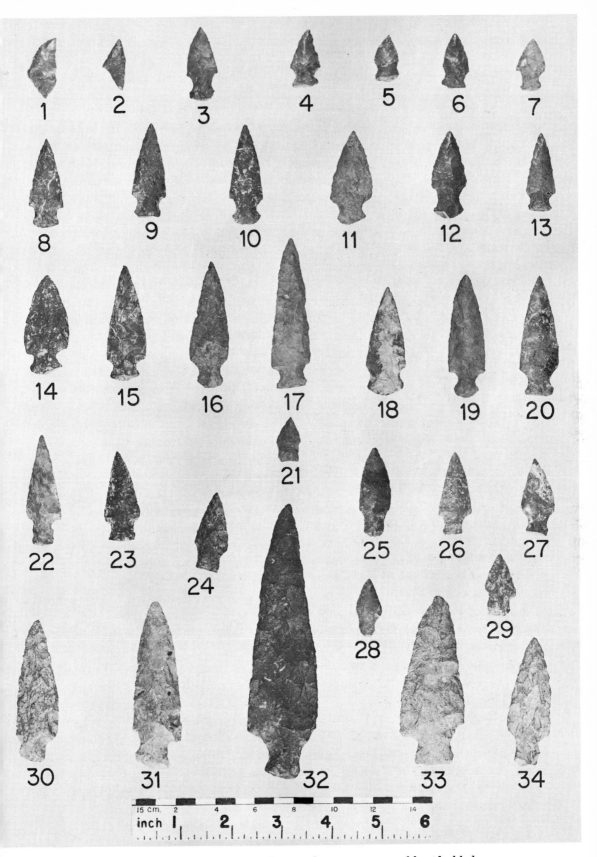

PLATE 14 Projectile points of the Lamoka phase and type. 1, 2 possible side blades;
31–33 probable spear points; all others probable javelin points.

51

Little use was made by the Lamoka people of bone projectile points and only one variety, a roughly ground, elongate, side-notched form, occurs on the larger sites (Plate 15, Figures 2, 3).

At the Scottsville site only were found two small, triangular, chipped-flint objects that suggest side blades for wooden or bone shafts (Plate 14, Figures 1, 2).

Probable projectile shaft straighteners of antler, either perforated or broadly and deeply grooved on one side, are pictured on Plate 15, Figures 1, 7–10. Several have crudely carved animal effigies or series of decorative notches at the brow end. They occurred only at the Lamoka Lake site, where twenty specimens were found.

Traps, snares and deadfalls were probably used but would leave no trace.

At the Geneva site, seven flexed burials of a small, terrier-sized dog were unearthed at various places in the refuse. Obviously this animal was held in considerable esteem to warrant an interment of the same order as accorded human members of the community. As the hunter's companion, the dog not only tracked his game, but might sometimes save him from the rushes of wounded animals, such as the bear. The dog would have been especially helpful in following and finding an animal struck, but not killed, by a dart, probably an extremely common occurrence with primitive weapons. Even with modern guns, and the revived bow-and-arrow hunting of large game animals, on-the-spot kills are not usually achieved.

The Geneva dog skeletons resemble those subsequently found on the Oberlander No. 1 and Frontenac Island Archaic sites, also in central New York (pages 96, 112) and appear to represent a similar breed. A possibly related historic, small Indian dog has been described as "fox-like,"

with erect ears, short body fur and a drooping tail (Allen, 1920, pp. 440, 461, 464).

While no dog burials were discovered at the Lamoka Lake site, dog remains occurred in the refuse, and canine and incisor teeth, variously modified, probably for necklace elements, were found (Ritchie, 1932, Plate X, Figure 10). The limb bones exhibited the same treatment as those of other animals among which they occurred, leading to the inference that at this site the dog may have provided an element of food.

Also frequently uncovered at this site were coprolites, attributed to the dog, but just possibly of human origin. Found likewise in the preserving alkaline environment of the Oberlander No. 1 and Frontenac Island sites, these objects consisted of characteristically formed, compressed masses of coarsely comminuted bone fragments, some definitely identifiable as fish vertebrae (see Ritchie, 1940, pp. 86–88).

In his examination of the refuse animal bone from the Lamoka Lake site, found in our excavations of 1958 and 1962, John E. Guilday identified the dog from limb-bone fragments and a maxilla with teeth. These remains, he says, "indicate an animal with thin, long limbs, sort of fox-terrier build. They are not as heavy and stocky as either springer spaniel or beagle" (letter of January 31, 1963). Tooth measurements indicate a more robust dentition than is found in modern dogs of comparable size.

More than 50 per cent of all animal bones from sites of the Lamoka phase were derived from the white-tailed deer (*Odocoileus virginianus*). Individuals of both sexes and of all ages were present, indicating that this animal was killed throughout the year. Nearly all the long bones were broken and split, presumably to extract the succulent marrow. The skulls were invariably broken open, probably because the

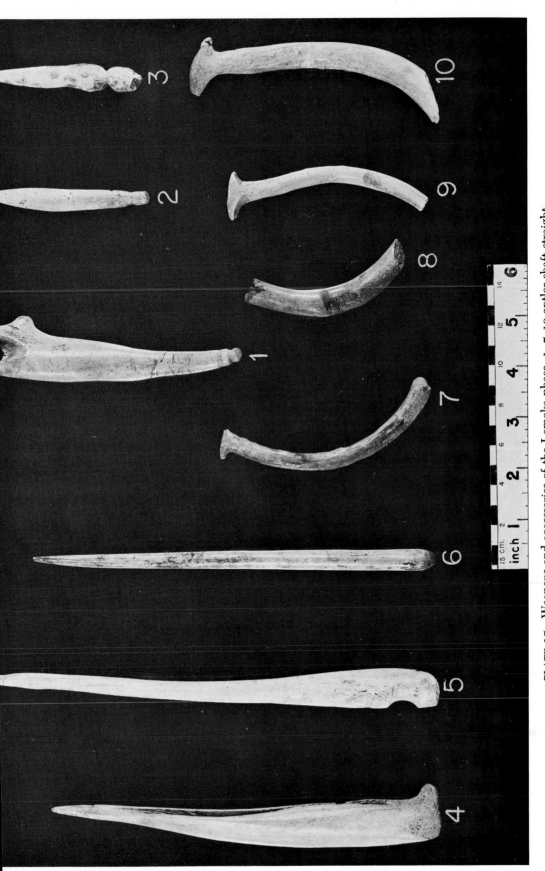

PLATE 15 Weapons and accessories of the Lamoka phase. 1, 7–10 antler shaft straighteners; 2, 3 bone projectile points; 4–6 daggers of bone and antler (6). Figure 5 has faint red spiral stripes.

brain tissue had value in tanning hides and skins.

Animal foods collected, and represented in the middens, were various turtles and frogs, and sparingly, the fresh-water mussel, although the latter was common in pits referable to the later, upper-level occupation at Lamoka Lake. If the Lamoka culture was, as has been suggested, an off-shoot of the southeastern Archaic Shell Mound culture, the relative neglect of the local shellfish is difficult to understand, unless such food became prohibited by taboo, or was unnecessary because of the sufficiency of other and superior foods. It seems more reasonable to suppose that, in common with certain other early eastern Archaic folk, they had not yet learned the esculency of such food.

At the two principal stations, Lamoka Lake and Geneva, randomly scattered human bones occurred in the refuse accumulations over the sites. In some cases several bones, apparently from the same skeleton, were closely associated. Human and game-animal bones were broken in identical fashion and intermingled in the same deposits, suggesting the practice of cannibalism by the Lamoka people.

Of the large volume of animal bone collected in the initial excavations at the Lamoka Lake site, over five hundred pounds were removed for study to the Rochester Museum of Arts and Sciences, where the assistance of osteologists at Ward's Natural Science Establishment in Rochester was obtained for their identification, the results being summarily included in the site report (Ritchie, 1932, pp. 113–15). Subsequently, on its removal to a new building, the Museum saw fit to discard this material.

The writer's more recent and limited excavations of 1958 and 1962 recovered a much smaller amount of refuse bone which, because of the extensive pillage of the site by relic collectors subsequent to his first examinations, was largely derived from dug-over and backfilled portions of the site. I believe it is chiefly for this reason that the representation of fish, frog and other small bones was so scanty in these later samples, the frail, widely scattered, diminutive bones being very difficult to recover under such conditions. The occurrence of small concentrated masses of fishbone and even scales in the primary research on the site, the usual presence in the coprolites above noted of fishbones, the more than eight thousand netsinkers, and numerous bone fishing implements, all forcefully betoken the importance of fish food at this site, despite the logical inferences to the contrary expressed in the following report, which is based, as indicated, upon an incomplete sample.

The highly competent services of John E. Guilday, Associate Curator of Comparative Anatomy at the Carnegie Museum, Pittsburgh, were obtained for the identification and other analyses of the 1958 and 1962 lots, and his report follows.

Bone Refuse from the Lamoka Lake Site

by John E. Guilday

Three thousand, four hundred and fifty bones and bone fragments were recovered from the 1958 and the 1962 New York State Museum excavations, under Dr. William A. Ritchie, at Lamoka Lake. Approximately 35 per cent (1224 fragments), all of mammal bone, were unidentified. All limb bones of large mammals had been broken for marrow extraction. Mammal remains accounted for approximately 75 per cent of the identified items, 60 per cent of the minimum number of animals present, and 99 per cent of the estimated dressed weight of meat. Birds constituted 15 per cent of the identified items, 25 per cent of the minimum number of individual animals, and 1 per cent of the estimated weight of usable meat. Birds and mammals together accounted for over 90 per cent of the identified items, over 85 per cent of the animals present, and all but an estimated 3 pounds out of an estimated 8892 pounds of meat represented by the total identified collection.[2]

Meat estimates are based upon the minimum number of a given species times an estimated average dressed weight for that form. It is impossible to know which animals were or were not consumed in all instances. Weights of individuals within one species, such as deer, or bear, vary enormously. Any estimate of meat represented is therefore a crude approximation, but it is believed to be adequate for present purposes.

Twenty-two species of mammals (exclusive of man), 9 birds, 6 reptiles, one amphibian, and 4 fish are represented. Thirty-five per cent of the forms are aquatic or semi-aquatic, 75 per cent terrestrial. Terrestrial forms, however, account for 90 per cent of the estimated meat.

[2] The excavations of 1958 and 1962, on which this figure is based, involved no more than approximately 3 per cent of the whole area of the site. Our prior and much more extensive excavations indicated a generally comparable quantity of bone refuse throughout the site. This being the case, the total weight of such debris on the site would seem to have amounted to an almost incredible 296,600 pounds. (W.A.R.)

FAUNAL LIST, VERTEBRATES FROM CULTURAL REFUSE OF THE LAMOKA LAKE SITE

Scientific name	Common name	Items	Indiv.	Est. lbs. meat
Mammals				
Canis lupus	timber wolf	3	1	50
Canis familiaris*	dog	11	1	
Urocyon cinereoargenteus	gray fox	9	3	12
Ursus americanus	black bear	24	4	800
Procyon lotor	raccoon	9	3	20
Mephitis mephitis	striped skunk	1	1	1
Lutra canadensis	otter	1	1	10
Martes pennanti	fisher	1	1	10
Lynx sp.	bobcat or lynx	4	2	20
Marmota monax	woodchuck	26	6	20
Glaucomys sp.*	flying squirrel	1	1	
Tamias striatus*	chipmunk	7	4	
Sciurus carolinensis	gray squirrel	87	14	14
Sciurus niger	fox squirrel	1	1	1
Peromyscus sp.*	deer mouse	1	1	
Microtus pennsylvanicus*	meadow mouse	1	1	
Ondatra zibethicus	muskrat	9	6	10
Castor canadensis	beaver	9	2	40
Erethizon dorsatum	porcupine	1	1	10
Sylvilagus sp.	rabbit	2	1	1
Odocoileus virginianus	white-tailed deer	1498	74	7400
Cervus canadensis	elk	2	1	350
Homo sapiens*	man	14	1	

* Not considered a food item.

Scientific name	Common name	Items	Indiv.	Est. lbs. meat
Birds				
Colymbus auritus°	horned grebe	1	1	
Branta canadensis	Canada goose	2	1	5
Bucephala albeola	bufflehead duck	2	1	1
Aix sponsa	wood duck	1	1	1
Buteo lineatus°	red-shouldered hawk	1	1	
Astur atricapillus°	goshawk	1	1	
Bonasa umbellus	ruffed grouse	4	2	2
Meleagris gallopavo	turkey	73	8	68
Ectopistes migratorius	passenger pigeon	274	43	43
Reptiles				
Chelydra serpentina	snapping turtle	2	1	3
Clemmys insculpta°	wood turtle	1	1	
Terrapene carolina°	box turtle	67	6	
Chrysemys pieta	painted turtle	8	5	
Sternotherus odoratus°	musk turtle	8	3	
Colubridae sp.°	snake	2	1	
Amphibian				
Rana sp.	small frog	6	2	
Fish				
Ictalurus nebulosus	bullhead	21	7	
Perca flavescens	perch	1	1	
Centrarchidae	sunfish family	2	2	
cf. *Catostomus commersonnii*	common sucker	1	1	
Fish species		4		

° Not considered a food item.

Ritchie, 1932, p. 115, lists the following additional forms identified by Ward's Natural Science Establishment from 1932 excavations at the site:

Alces americanus	moose	scarce
Vulpes fulvus	red fox	abundant
Mephitis mephitis	skunk	frequent
Lepus americanus	snowshoe hare	abundant
Mustela vison	mink	scarce
Mustela cf. *erminea*	weasel	scarce
Ardea herodias	great blue heron	
Aquilla chrysaetos	golden eagle	
Bubo virginianus	great horned owl	
Olor columbianus	whistling swan	
various turtles		abundant
fish		occasional
Esox lucius	pike	very large jaws

The red fox identification is doubtful. Gray fox, not red, was "abundant" in the current collection from the site. Gray fox is present, to the exclusion of red fox, in all archaeofaunas south of New York State. The prehistoric distribution of these two forms is yet to be worked out for New York. Red fox is identified from Frontenac Island (Ritchie, 1945), but the identification, also made by Ward's, cannot be verified. An unmistakable gray-fox mandible is figured (Ritchie, 1944, p. 138), from the Kipp Island site, Cayuga County, New York.

Two species may record range changes associated with the Climatic Optimum. There is strong evidence for an eastward migration of some species of plants and animals during this period. (See Smith, 1957, for a recent summary of the evidence.) The weather was presumed to be warmer and dryer than at present, enabling prairie forms to extend their ranges eastward. This is believed to have been responsible for the presence of the prairie mole (*Scalopus aquaticus*) in an archaeofauna from Pennsylvania, 75 to 100 miles east of its present range (Guilday, 1961). Radiocarbon dating would seem to make this interval coincident with the primary Lamoka occupation. At the present time[3] the fox squirrel and the box turtle enter western New York along the Lake Erie plain in Chautauqua County, about 100 miles west of the site. These animals reach their northern limits in the high Allegheny Plateau of New York and Pennsylvania about 100 miles south of Lake Lamoka. The northern limits of the box turtle are not too clear as modern records may be escaped "pets" from family vacation excursions. Dr. Edgar Reilly, Jr., Curator of Zoology, New York State Museum, is of the opinion that the box turtle is rare or local in distribution, if it occurs at all in central and western New York today. Box-turtle remains are relatively common in some sites where the reptile no longer occurs. Parmalee (1959, 1960) records box turtle from two sites in Sauk County, Wisconsin, and mentions use as cups. Bleakney (1958) records this turtle from three sites in southern Ontario, stating that they were all rattle fragments. Ritchie (1940, 1945, 1946, 1954) records box turtle from three sites in Oswego County, one

[3] There is evidence that the fox squirrel is increasing its range within the State (Hamilton, 1963).

site in Cayuga County, and one site in Livingston County, New York. Box-turtle shells, used as rattles and cups, may have been traded extraterritorially as were marine shells. Or the animals may have been taken locally, implying a range reduction to their present limits. The presence of limb bones and unworked, as well as worked, carapace and plastral fragments at Lamoka Lake suggests that these animals were taken locally at least at this site. Two Lamoka carapaces were apparently cup fragments, vertebral centra scraped off but rim unmodified, while two others were wholly unmodified. Either box turtles were collected over a wide area, hence concentrated at the site before being disposed of, or, as Reilly suggests, they may have been more widespread and common during Indian times.

The presence of fox squirrel is based upon one mandible bearing only the last molar. Identification was based upon gross size and seems reliable.

The presence of unworked box-turtle remains and fox squirrel at Lamoka, coupled with the 5000 years B.P. occupancy, is strong presumptive evidence for range adjustments coincident with the Climatic Optimum. These two species may have entered the Lamoka region during this time via the plains of Lake Erie and Lake Ontario rather than north from Pennsylvania through the uplands of the Allegheny Plateau.

Additional archaeological faunas from the area and time period involved may furnish supporting evidence.

Faunal Discussion

On the basis of the bone refuse, the Lamoka people depended almost solely upon terrestrial birds and mammals for the bulk of their meat. Mammals accounted for 75 per cent of the identified bone fragments, 60 per cent of the individual animals present, and 98 per cent of the estimated pounds of meat. Deer alone accounted for 63 per cent, 33 per cent and 86 per cent of the totals, respectively.

Birds, other than turkey and passenger pigeon, were rare. No young birds were represented. Lower leg and outer wing elements of the passenger pigeon were missing, suggesting that these elements were removed prior to cooking. No pigeon bones were charred or broken, with the exception of humeri snapped during the initial dressing. Boiling or stewing seems most probable. Pigeons, being migratory, would argue for a warm-weather occupancy during at least some period of the site's history.

The presence of netsinkers, bone fishhooks and gorges, combined with easy access to lakes, would lead one to expect a fishing industry. Fishbone constituted only .01 per cent of the sample. All 11 fish were "minnow-size"; none would have exceeded 6 inches in total length. Their combined weights were negligible. Compare this with the early historic Eschelman site (36 La 12) (Guilday, Parmalee and Tanner, 1962) on the Susquehanna River. There, fish constituted 7.6 per cent of the bone, 17 per cent of the animals and 2 per cent of the estimated meat. Judging again from bone refuse, the fishing industry of the Lamoka site was practically non-existent.

Several interpretations suggest themselves: 1) There was, in fact, no fishing industry, a situation which does not agree with the fishing implements and the accessibility to water. 2) The site may have been seasonal, the main occupation during the winter months when aquatic resources were not easily harvested. Some support is offered here by the lack of fawns and by the presence of antlered bucks as well as those with recently shed antlers, indicating fall/winter killing dates, but the presence of turtles and migratory birds argues for a warm-weather occupancy as well. 3) Fish may have been preserved by smoking and consumed elsewhere. 4) Bones of fish may have been ceremonially returned to the water. Scavenging by dogs, although there is evidence for it at the site, is not sufficient to account for the lack of fishbones. The fish fauna from lakes Lamoka and Waneta as reported by the Bureau of Fish, New York State Conservation Department, is relatively poor. The total fauna exclusive of minnows and darters consists of eel, common sucker, bullhead, chain pickerel, largemouth bass, five species of sunfish and the yellow perch. Muskellunge has been introduced. It is altogether probable, then, that a fishing industry at Lamoka was negligible. [See, however, page 54.]

Turtle and amphibian remains are negligible. Thirty-five box-turtle fragments were from a single carapace that had been a cup. The vertebral centra had been removed by scraping and the inside of the carapace had been "sanded," but the carapace rim had not been trimmed. A minimum of 6 box turtles was recovered. Of these, 2 had the vertebral centra scraped away, 2 had not. Limb bones of box turtle and snapping turtle were present, as well as shell fragments.

Deer

A minimum of 74 deer were represented by astragali count. There is a marked discrepancy in various elements present. Based upon skull parts, including isolated teeth, only 15 animals were represented. (Skull and astragali were in essential numerical balance at the Eschelman site.) This disparity is hard to account for unless many of the animals were butchered elsewhere, or unless some portions were disposed of ceremonially. There is evidence of such a custom among the historic Indians of eastern Canada.

Based upon skull fragments, at least 8 bucks (4 antlered, 4 with recently shed antlers), a doe, and 3 fawns (all over 6 months of age) were present.

In contrast to the situation at the historic Eschelman site (36 La 12) (Guilday, Parmalee and Tanner, 1962) and the late prehistoric Mt. Carbon site (46 Fa 7), skinning and butchering cuts on bones at Lamoka Lake were scarce. This may reflect a basic difference in the treatment of large game carcasses between Archaic and post-Archaic cultures. More archaeofaunas must be studied from this point of view, however, before any definite conclusions can be reached. Indians at the Eschelman and Mt. Carbon sites appear to have disarticulated the entire carcass. Lamoka Lake people seem not to have done so. This may reflect differences in food-preparation techniques.

A cut running across the condyles of the humeri and suggesting disarticulation at the elbow, present in 70 per cent of the Eschelman specimens, was noted but once. Cuts running over the dorsal surface of the astragalus and suggesting disarticulation at the hock, seen in

70 per cent of the Eschelman material, were noted in less than 10 per cent of the Lamoka collection. Detailed search in those portions of limb bones, pectoral girdles, pelvic girdles, and vertebrae known to produce butchering marks in other collections, failed to produce any consistent butchering marks. Instead, there appear many random scratches, possibly associated with defleshing, which did not appear on the Eschelman material. There is evidence of fire beds measuring approximately 55′ × 10′ × 2′ at the site, which have been interpreted (Ritchie, 1932) as the remains of fire beds associated with meat-smoking racks. If meat were stripped from the carcasses rather than the carcasses disjointed, this would account for both the lack of butchering cuts and the presence of random defleshing marks. All limb bones appear to have been broken up for the extraction of marrow. Three occipital bones and 4 atlas vertebrae appear to have been smashed into left and right halves, perhaps during brain extraction. One complete atlas bore transverse cuts inflicted during removal of the head.

These deer are assumed to be the large northern race *Odocoileus virginianus borealis*. Deer increase in average size with latitude. This situation is obscured in some areas today by stocking programs but is reflected in bones recovered from prehistoric archaeological sites.

I would like to thank Dr. Paul W. Parmalee, Curator of Zoology, Illinois State Museum, for the identification of many of the bird remains; Dr. Edgar Reilly, Jr., Curator of Zoology, New York State Museum; Neil D. Richmond, Curator, Section of Amphibians and Reptiles, Carnegie Museum; and C. W. Greene, Chief, Bureau of Fish, New York State Conservation Department for their assistance.

Subsistence Gathering

A considerable variety of wild vegetable foods doubtless comprised a significant part of the fare of this Archaic group, but direct evidence for use of the hickory nut and acorn survived only at one site, Lamoka Lake. Hickory-nut shell fragments were of sparse occurrence but large numbers of acorn hulls, and rarely cotyledons or whole fruits, were present in ash beds, in pits, and in and around hearths. Species identification was not feasible, according to botanists consulted.

All of our oaks contain varying amounts of bitter and toxic tannic acid, but the white oaks have a smaller percentage than the black-oak group. Acorns of the white oak could have been largely freed of tannic acid by roasting whole in ashes (Gifford, 1936, p. 87). Use of this method is strongly suggested by the large number of fire or ash beds at Lamoka Lake, described below. Other old methods, much used by Central California tribes, and probably known to our eastern Indians as well, consisted of immersion, without pulverizing, in water or mud, or more often pulverizing and then leaching with water in a basket or sand basin. Stone-boiling of the meal in twined or coiled baskets was the customary way of cooking it among non-potters (ibid.).

The nutrient value of acorn meal has been remarked by Heizer in the following statement: "Compared to corn meal and wheat flour, acorn meal is in no way inferior as a food. As against 1.9% of fat in corn meal and 1.0% fat in wheat flour, acorn meal contains 25.31% fat. In protein, acorns with 4.5% fall below corn meal with 9.2% and wheat flour with 11.4%. In carbohydrate, wheat flour is highest with 75.4%, corn meal next with 74.4% and acorn meal with 62.0%." (Heizer, 1958, pp. 20–21.)

Large numbers of grinding implements of several kinds, presently to be described, were doubtless related to the major role played by acorn meal in the Lamoka diet.

Food Preparation

Subsistence activities appear to be involved not only in the majority of Lamoka artifacts, but in the three principal categories of features, viz., hearths or fireplaces, fire beds or ash beds, and pits. Hearths, the commonest of these, occur even on the camp components. Typically the Lamoka hearth is a bowl-shaped depression some fourteen inches in diameter and sixteen inches in depth, containing ashes, charcoal in a soggy mass, and, rarely, burned stones. Coarse bark can often be distinguished, and sometimes twigs and sticks up to one or two inches in diameter. These features, which exist by the hundreds at all levels in the major sites, from subsoil basins almost to the surface of the refuse mantle, show that for ordinary cooking purposes, small fires were used. Their placement in shallow pits resulted in a concentrated column of heat, constituting an efficient and economical use of a small quantity of readily obtainable fuel (Plate 24). The writer has found and described hearths of this general pattern in nearly every prehistoric culture investigated by him in the Northeast, and it is worth emphasizing that Indians did not cook over our kind of bonfire.

At Lamoka Lake a few hearths had partial, thin, stone-slab coverings, perhaps for roasting strips of meat, or baking acorn-meal cakes.

Absolutely no potsherds or stone vessel fragments are intrinsic to the Lamoka culture. Hot-rock cooking in perishable vessels of bark, wood, basketry or skin is amply attested by the great numbers of heat-shattered rocks on all the sites.

Fire beds, as defined at the only site of their occurrence, Lamoka Lake (Ritchie, 1932, pp. 86–87), were massive ash accumulations ranging in length from about twenty to fifty-five feet, up to ten feet in breadth, and three feet in thickness. Not infrequently they had a laminated structure involving alternating colors—white, gray, buff—in various combinations. Charcoal granules had a profuse distribution throughout the ash, and burned acorn-hull fragments were a common inclusion, but animal bones and artifacts were virtually absent. It was believed that these features had accumulated gradually as the result of long-continued fires for drying and smoking fish and game, suspended in strips from pole scaffolds. To this surmise may be added the roasting of acorns to rid them of tannic acid, as suggested by the abundance of hull particles found throughout.

The third group of features comprises pits, found on the major sites except Geneva, where the habitation area had been destroyed, leaving only a refuse-strewn slope for investigation. Pits varied greatly in size at Lamoka Lake, from approximately three to seven feet in diameter and from three to five feet in depth. Hearths occurred in some, at different levels from base to top; others contained a few burned acorns, along with refuse bone and artifacts, lost or discarded. The larger ones may have been underground granaries for acorn storage. At the Scottsville site numerous pits, around three feet in diameter, had been dug about two feet into the sandy gravel subsoil, and since hearths were present in nearly all, they were interpreted as cooking features. We need to learn a great deal more about the different kinds of pits which occur on Indian sites of various ages nearly everywhere.

The means of creating fire in the Lamoka culture are unknown since materials for this purpose have not been identified. The earliest flint-and-pyrites fire-making kits are known from the Frontenac Island site, where they appear to have been introduced by a Laurentian group. Socketed deer astragali, found at the Scottsville site

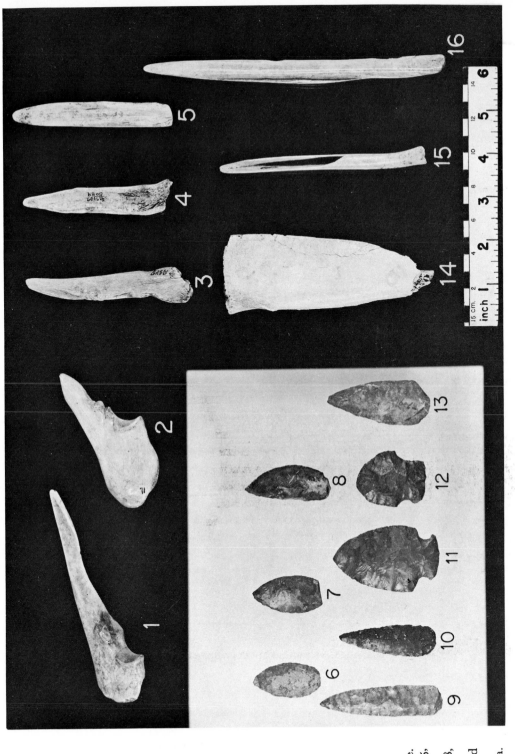

PLATE 16 Bone and stone knives of the Lamoka phase. 1–3 from the deer ulna; 4, 5, 15, 16 from mammal and bird long-bone sections; 6–8, 9, 10, 13 ovate and lanceolate forms of chipped stone; 11, 12 side-notched variety; 14 from deer scapula.

only, suggest use of the fire drill with wooden spindle (Plate 13, Figures 23, 24).

Tools concerned with the preparation of food in the Lamoka culture include the following: chipped-flint knives of ovate, lanceolate and side-notched forms (Plate 16, Figures 6–13); distinctive bone knives made from the deer ulna or scapula or from ground bone sections (Plate 16, Figures 1–5, 14–16); so-called stone choppers, perhaps actually heavy hide scrapers (Plate 17, Figures 3–6); and several varieties of milling stones or food grinders, present on all sites and in large numbers at the type station, where the full range of forms occurs. The simplest mortars consist of thick stone slabs with plane surfaces, measuring about eighteen inches across and three inches thick. Much more numerous are the well-worn specimens with a shallow or deep concave grinding surface on one or both sides (Plate 17, Figure 8). A few are unilaterally or bilaterally bowl-shaped or trough-shaped. An additional usage as whetstones for grinding and sharpening woodworking tools is exhibited by several examples. Many broken mortars seem to have served secondarily as abraders for stone and bone. Some Lamoka Lake mortars exceed fifty pounds in weight. Mortars are, for the most part, made from sandstone or graywacke boulders, locally available in the drift.

The stone muller was apparently the companion implement of the mortar (Plate 17, Figure 7). These hand stones are oval or round in outline, and some have been carefully pecked into shape from natural cobbles of sandstone, graywacke, quartzite or granite rocks. A few were used bifacially. Many are scarified or pitted from auxiliary use as hammers and/or anvils (Plate 17, Figure 2).

Cylindrical pestles, up to twenty inches in length, were also well represented at the chief Lamoka sites, apparently denoting use of the hollowed-tree-trunk mortar (Plate 17, Figure 1). While many food substances—seeds, nuts, berries, roots, dried meat—were probably reduced with these sundry implements, the evidence indicates that acorn meal formed the principal item.

Clothing and Ornaments

A discussion of the clothing of the Lamoka people is precluded by lack of any direct evidence, but probable skin-dressing implements are very numerous in the culture. These comprise a distinctive Lamoka form of thin, adz-like scraper, perhaps also employed in shaping wood (Plate 18, Figures 1–3); deer-scapula scrapers (some as sharp as knives), also diagnostic for this phase (Plate 13, Figure 22; Plate 16, Figure 14); and a large assortment of awls fashioned from various bones of the deer, bear, raccoon, lynx, beaver, fox, turkey, blue heron and other birds and mammals (forty-two varieties are listed for the Lamoka Lake site alone in Ritchie, 1944, p. 389). (Plate 19.) It is important to note the virtual lack in the Lamoka phase of any kind of chipped-flint scraper.

Personal ornaments, negligible in quantity and variety, consist of tubular bird-bone beads (Plate 20, Figures 5–7, 9, 10); a few perforated or notched mammal teeth, jaws and other bones (Plate 20, Figures 8, 15, 18–20); perforated turtle femurs (Plate 20, Figures 16, 17); drilled or notched styliform bones of the deer, which suggest the plume holders for the hair of several Plains tribes (Plate 20, Figures 11–13); and some unique antler pendants. All of these pendants carry marginal nicking and several have been embellished with triangular (in one case funnel-shaped) de-

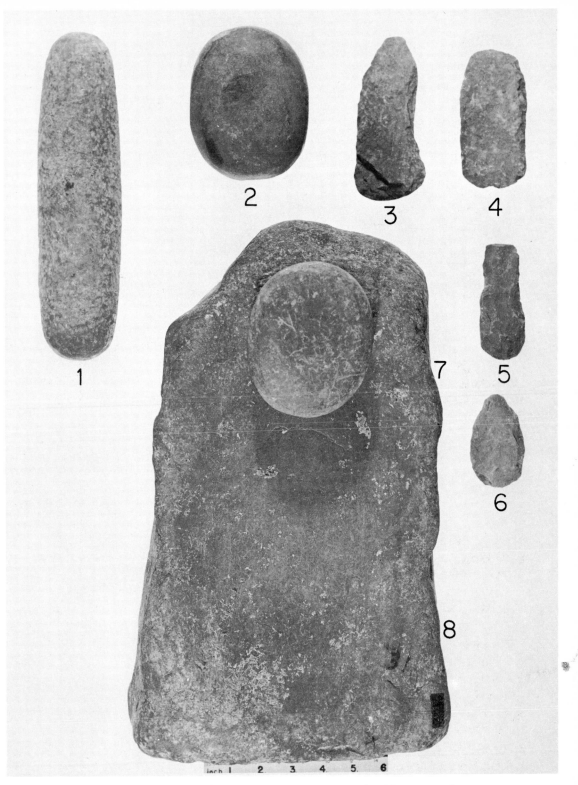

PLATE 17 Rough stone tools for food preparation in the Lamoka phase. 1 cylindrical pestle; 2 combination muller, hammer and anvilstone; 3–6 choppers; 7 muller; 8 mortar with deep concave surface.

PLATE 18 Woodworking tools of the Lamoka phase. 1–3 thin, adz-like scrapers; 4–7 variously modified beaver incisors; 8 split and ground bear canine; 9 antler chisel; 10–12 celts; 13, 16, 17 beveled adzes; 14, 15 plano-convex adzes.

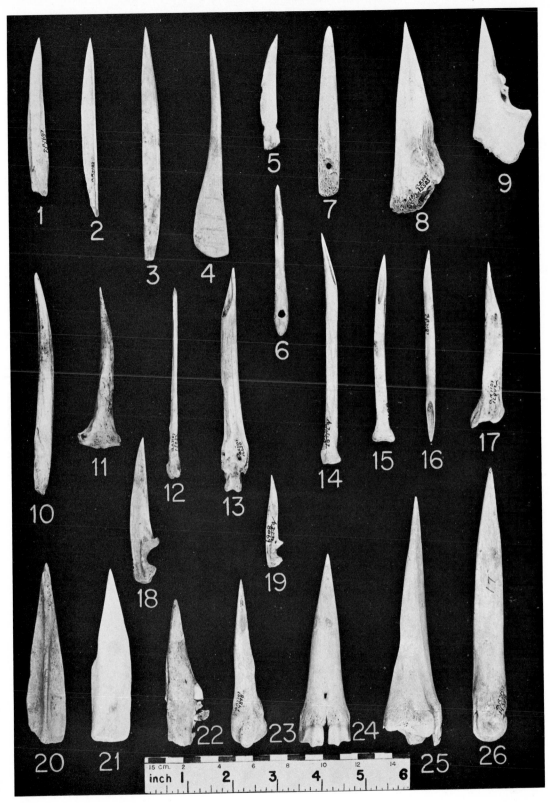

PLATE 19 Varieties of bone awls of the Lamoka phase.

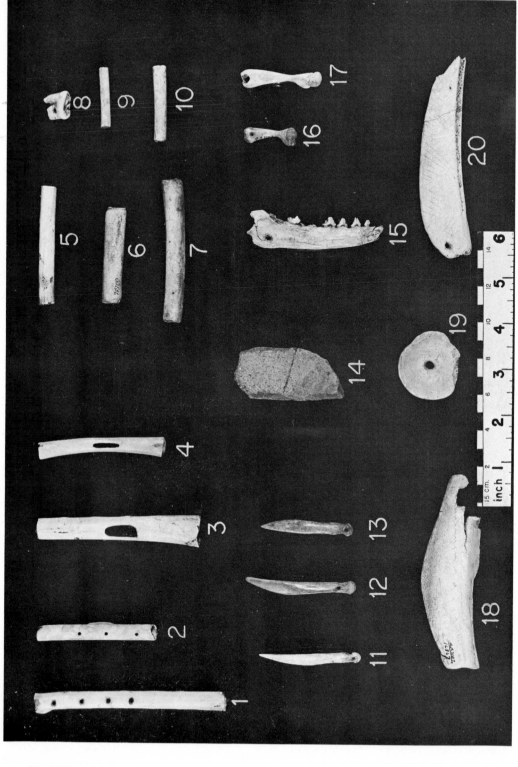

PLATE 20 Articles of amusement and personal decoration of the Lamoka phase. 1–4 flutes or whistles; 5–7, 9, 10 tubular bone beads; 8 perforated bear molar; 11–13 perforated deer styliform bones; 14 ground hematite paintstone; 15 perforated fox mandible; 16, 17 perforated turtle femurs; 18, 20 engraved and perforated deer scapulae; 19 perforated head of bear scapula.

signs in intaglio (Plate 21, Figures 1, 2, 5). These pendants, or pendant-like artifacts, seem intrinsically related morphologically to a category of problematical antler objects, and the whole group is highly specific to the Lamoka culture. The same kind of marginal nicking or "tally-marks" appears on all; some are wedge- or chisel-shaped at one end (Plate 21, Figures 7–10, 15), others bluntly pointed (Figures 11, 12, 16) or truncated (Figures 13, 14). Many are broken, as from vigorous usage (Figure 6); some are reworked; and a few are embellished with horizontal bars of red paint (Figures 6, 7, 12). As a class, they were manufactured from sections of deer-antler beam or tine, by burning or chopping away, evidently with stone axes, the undesired portions, then grinding the piece smooth on a whetstone. Many specimens were found illustrating all the production stages of this numerous and baffling group.

Red iron oxide (hematite), found on a variety of bone and antler artifacts, suggests its probable employment as a body pigment, an assumption supported by the finding of a few ground fragments of the regional fossiliferous hematite at Geneva and Scottsville (Plate 20, Figure 14) and of a small stone paint mortar (?) at Lamoka Lake (Ritchie, 1932, Plate III, Figure 4).

The Lamoka Tool Kit

Tools for felling trees and shaping wood are quite common in the Lamoka culture and include the adz, beveled adz and celt, but *not* the gouge and grooved ax. Of first importance was the plano-convex adz (Plate 18, Figures 14, 15), of which a specialized variety, called by the writer the beveled adz, is the most diagnostic single trait of the Lamoka culture, and also the most carefully made of all stone artifacts

of this phase (Plate 18, Figures 13, 16, 17; Plate 11, Figures 1, 2, 49, 50). It seems to have originated from the common adz somewhere in western New York and to have diffused throughout the Lamoka range (Figure 5). Usually of hard, fine-grained, igneous rock, it may have been especially well adapted to dugout-boat construction. Probably the facets were functionally significant, perhaps to accommodate wooden wedges for tightening the blade in its haft. Many cutting tools have been loosely described in the literature as "beveled adzes" which have no valid claim to inclusion in this very distinctive category.

The Lamoka culture also contains celts, or bilaterally symmetrical, ungrooved axes, usually rather rudely made and rectangulate in outline (Plate 18, Figures 10–12). The thin, adz-like scrapers, aforementioned (Plate 18, Figures 1–3), may also have functioned in the shaping of wood.

Bone or antler chisel-like tools (Plate 18, Figure 9), and beaver incisors, split and ground, or with modified incisal edge (Plate 18, Figures 4–7), are considered tools for the creation of wooden items, likely projectile shafts. The split and ground bear canine illustrated in the same plate, Figure 8, seems a cognate artifact. The antler punch shown on Plate 13, Figure 21, looks admirably suited to perforating tough sheets of bark, possibly lodge coverings.

More general purpose implements of the Lamoka culture include the following: unpitted and bipitted hammerstones (Plate 22, Figure 9); anvilstones (Plate 22, Figure 10); pitted stones (Plate 22, Figure 11); various combination tools showing marks of use as mullers, hammers and anvils (Plate 17, Figure 2); flint drills (Plate 22, Figures 1–8); and bone and antler flak-

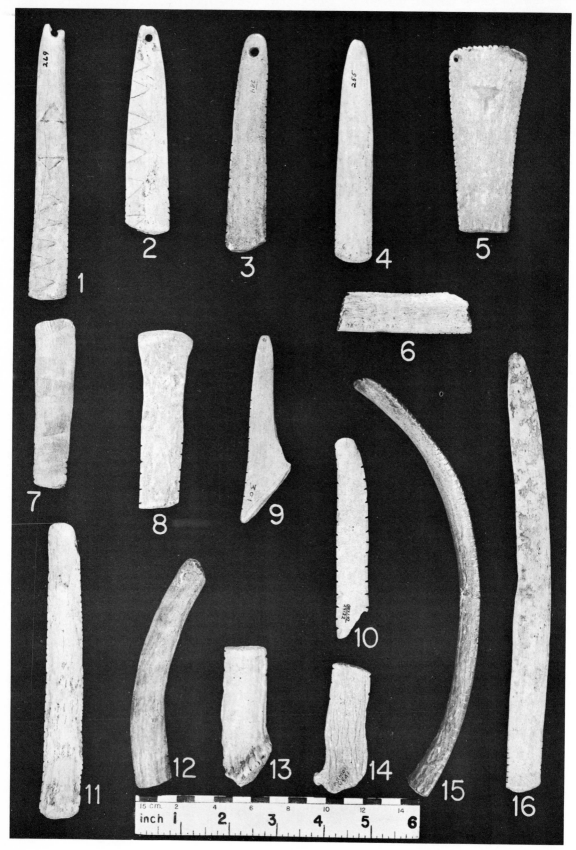

PLATE 21 Antler pendants and pendant-like artifacts of the Lamoka phase. Figures 6, 7, 12 retain traces of horizontal bands of red paint.

68

ing tools, suggesting that some of the flint chipping was accomplished with pressure techniques (Plate 13, Figures 19, 20).

No insight is afforded by the surviving relics into the recreational phase of Lamoka life. Nothing that can be interpreted as a "gaming" device was found, and the few fragments of perforated box-turtle-shell rattles (?) from Lamoka Lake may well have belonged to the later comers to this site. Flutes or whistles, found here and at Scottsville, may be musical instruments or hunting calls. They consist of the wing bones of large birds, chiefly the turkey, with single oval or multiple round perforations (Plate 20, Figures 1–4), or of plain, long tubes which can be blown upon as whistles.

Use of any form of the smoking pipe is definitely a negative trait of the Lamoka phase.

This succinct survey of Lamoka culture has disclosed little of artistic merit. It seems to have had a utilitarian orientation and a low aesthetic development, unless the art forms were expressed in impermanent media, such as bark, wood, basketry, leather, feathers, etc. A small quantity of bone carving, painting and engraving (Plate 21, Figures 1, 2, 5, 6, 7, 12; Plate 15, Figures 5, 7, 9, 10; Plate 20, Figures 18, 20) constitute about the limit of the known art accomplishments. No articles of shell, copper, mica, or polished slate have been discovered; indeed, the Lamoka appears to have been a relatively isolated, self-contained culture, with few if any trade relations outside the area of its occurrence.

Settlement Pattern

Most of the sites of the Lamoka phase represent temporary small camps from which all organic refuse has disappeared.

The Scottsville site was evidently a longer occupied camp of this sort, during which a thin refuse mantle (up to six inches deep) was accumulated, some fifty hearth pits were dug, a slight hillside midden was produced, and several burials were made. This instructive small site, never under cultivation, measured, in its habitable portion, only about 175 feet in length by 75 feet in breadth on the summit of a gravel knoll, elevated 65 feet above the flood plain of the Genesee River. Its steep slopes would have afforded some protection against surprise attack, as well as good drainage (Figure 4, site number 3) (Ritchie, 1936).

The more favorable location of the Geneva site on superior fishing waters doubtless accounted for its greater size, originally nearly two acres of the Seneca Lake bluff, close to the point of origin of the Seneca River. Despite its partial destruction in 1895 by a railroad right-of-way, it was the second-largest known site of the Lamoka phase and had probably constituted a much frequented base camp of the regional Lamoka people (Figure 4, site number 2) (Ritchie, 1936).

Data on the highly important aspects of the housing and settlement pattern of the Lamoka culture are quite limited and, with respect to the former, of recent discovery with the writer's 1962 excavations at the Lamoka Lake site. This work, restricted by time and resources, exposed the subsoil area over approximately fifteen hundred square feet in the intensively occupied northern part of this type station of the Lamoka phase, which is also the largest recorded Archaic site in New York State and probably in the whole Northeast. It lies at the head of Lamoka Lake and covers most of a level field bordering, and elevated only a few feet above, the small stream draining Waneta Lake into Lamoka Lake, near Ty-

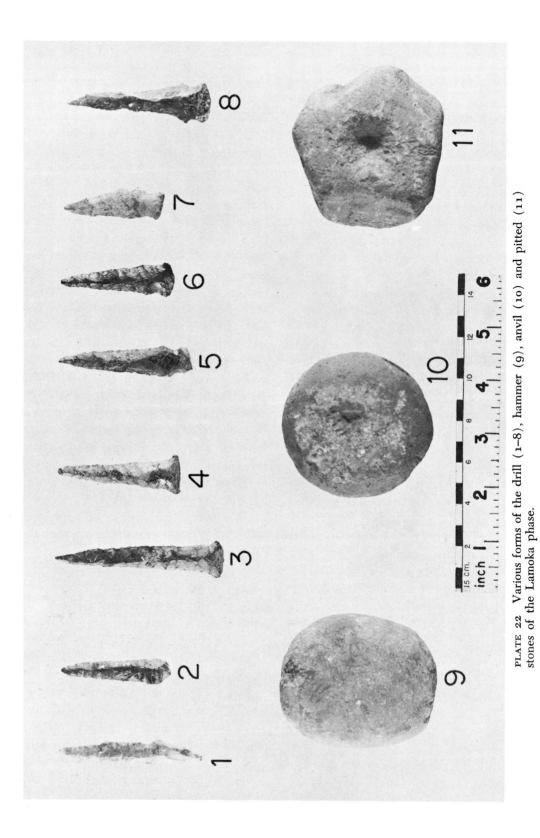

PLATE 22 Various forms of the drill (1–8), hammer (9), anvil (10) and pitted (11) stones of the Lamoka phase.

rone, Schuyler County (Figure 4, site number 1, and Plate 23). Black "Indian dirt" with much occupation detritus is strewed over an area approximately seven hundred feet long bordering the stream and from one hundred to two hundred feet eastward thereof to near the base of a long sand-and-gravel ridge, forty feet in height. While the entire area of two and a half acres has a refuse mantle nowhere less than a foot in thickness, the most intensively inhabited portion of about one acre, lying slightly north of the site's center, is refuse-covered to a maximum depth of four to five feet.

The writer's most recent excavations at the site (August 1962) were made in the northerly part of this nuclear area, where the refuse layer varied from twenty-four to thirty inches thick. As nearly everywhere on the site, the inroads of collectors, since my original excavations, had thoroughly disturbed the deposits to, or within a few

inches of, the subsoil. Their disinterest in the hearths, which had occurred throughout the midden, as providing too meager returns of artifacts, had fortunately resulted in the unmolested condition of such of these hearth features as were abundantly present in the subsoil. Also spared were the associated post molds and even the basal part of some of the lower and older pits.

The subsoil in the new excavation, as elsewhere on the site, consisted of a light-tan-colored mixture of sand and fine gravel —mostly flat, water-worn, shale pebbles— more yellow and indurated in the first few inches to a foot, probably from pressure and the heat of many fires. This soil member, like all the soil materials from sundry loci and levels throughout the site, repeatedly tested during the course of our several investigations there, showed consistently a pH of 8.0, well up in the zone where free calcium carbonate should be present, the

PLATE 23 View of part of the Lamoka Lake site (mowed meadow) looking northwestward from top of knoll to east of site. Stream connecting Waneta Lake (to right) with Lamoka Lake (to left) flows between tree rows in middle ground.

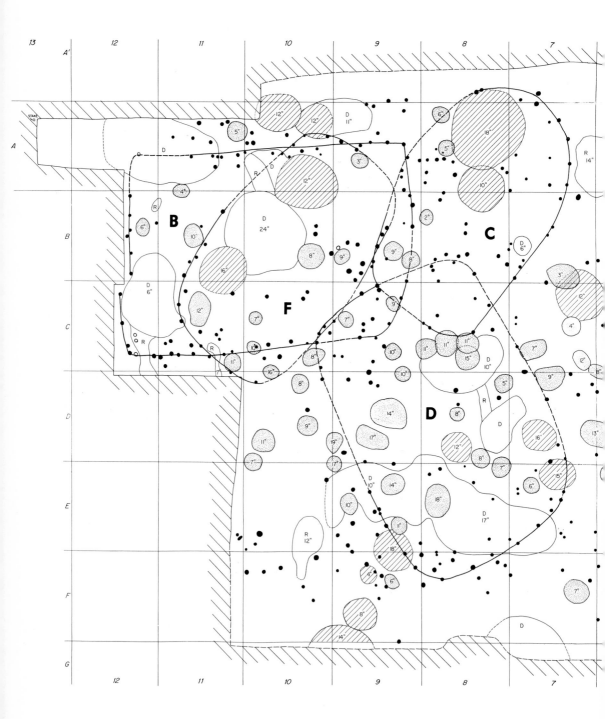

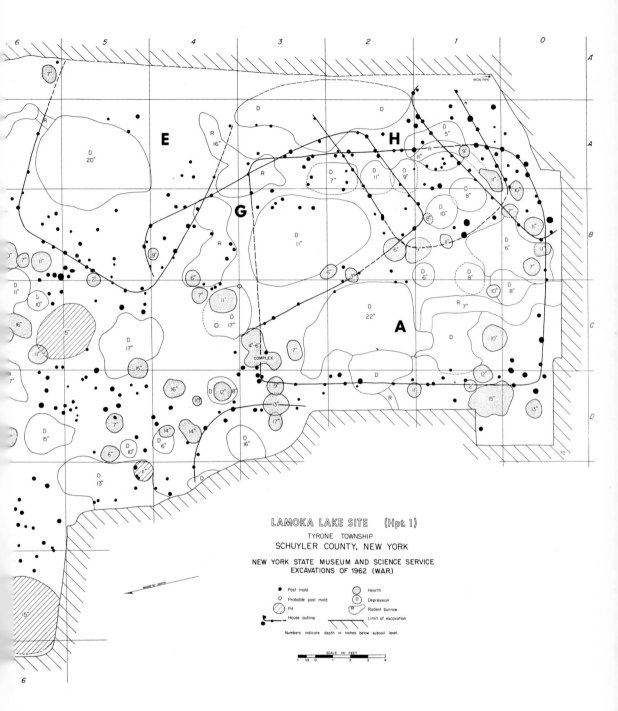

Figure 6 Area of 1962 excavations at the Lamoka Lake site, showing house floor patterns, post molds, hearths and other features.

probable primary factor responsible for the excellent preservation of the bone implements and refuse.

This light-colored basal soil also made readily possible the tracing of the numerous features—hearths, post molds, pits, and the probable natural depressions made by tree falls and animal burrows and dens—all shown on the map, Figure 6, and illustrated in part on Plate 24.

Hearths appeared as black masses of charcoal and ashes, in bowl-shaped hollows dug a few inches to a foot or more into the subsoil, sometimes clustered in a clear succession shown through overlapping (Plate 24).

Post molds, numerous and frankly confusing by their multiplicity, indicated a lengthy occupation, with much house shifting and probably repairing, like that seen on certain later sites (pages 247, 287). Some of the molds may pertain to racks for meat drying, storage, etc., and to other constructions within or outside of the abodes, but such identifications do not seem possible from the evidence uncovered.

The post molds, all validated by excavation to eliminate animal burrows and root channels, were vertical, or very slightly oblique in a few instances; tapered to long conical or blunt points; and varied from two and a quarter to three and three-quarters inches in diameter and from three to fifteen inches in depth in the subsoil. Measurements of several score indicated a mean of about two and three-quarters inches across and ten and a half inches deep in subsoil. Filled with dark soil and ashes, they occasionally yielded artifacts, more commonly pieces of refuse bone.

The map of the excavated area, Figure 6, clearly discloses the partial superposition of a number of lodges, of slightly different ages, but all refer to the Lamoka occupa-tion of the site. Laminated and compacted house-floor deposits of ash, black dirt and sand (see Ritchie, 1932, p. 87) were several times seen in direct association with linear arrangements of molds obviously representing house walls. It would, however, seem possible to trace out, more or less completely, two house floors, the larger (House A) rectangular and measuring about sixteen by thirteen feet, the smaller (House B) rectangular with dimensions of sixteen by eleven feet (Figure 6). Both are oriented parallel to the stream connecting the lakes and lie about one hundred feet east thereof near the widest part of the site. Portions of six other similar lodges (C-H) may perhaps be delineated, having measurements of approximately fourteen by nine, sixteen by eleven, ? by ten, fourteen by eight and a half, fourteen and a half by eight, and ? by seven feet, respectively.

Partitions, benches or bed platforms, and other interior arrangements appear to be lacking. No definite patterning of hearths can be ascertained, although there is some suggestion of an irregular lineal positioning of fires along the central major axis.

This form of domicile, suggested by the earlier work at the site (Ritchie, 1932, p. 87; 1956, p. 74), was doubtless framed of poles or saplings thrust into the ground, with probable arched or domed roofs and bark covers. It resembles our house-type discoveries of the much later Indians (pages 247, 282), and even the longhouse of the Iroquois, of which the Lamoka dwelling may be the earliest known prototype. The Lamoka lodge, like these later dwellings, also probably housed a communal, extended family group.

If the identification of pattern molds here suggested has intrinsic validity, it is difficult to see how more than any two of

PLATE 24   Portions of the excavated area of 1962 at the Lamoka Lake site, Schuyler Co., N.Y., showing irregularity of subsoil level with post molds, hearths and woodchuck disturbances. (See Figure 6.)

the lodges could have coexisted. Thus A and B, A and C, D or E, and B and E, G or H might have been contemporaneous, but hardly any other combination is likely. To determine the total number of such houses on the site for just the earliest period of occupation, when the posts would have invaded and imprinted themselves on the yellow subsoil, would require an excavation project far beyond ordinary resources, even if authorized by the landholder. If, however, we assume an equivalent density of post molds over the approximately one acre of the more heavily occupied portion of the site, around twenty-seven dwellings may have constituted the Lamoka community at any one time. If we risk the further assumption of six to eight occupants to a single domicile, a not implausible total population of 150 to 200 persons is indicated.

From the random distribution and frequent intrusions, one upon another, of the features throughout the site (see Ritchie, 1932, pp. 85–89), a shifting small population over several generations better fits the archaeological picture than a larger fixed group of a few years' duration.

The small foraging group that first discovered this long-uninhabited and out-of-the-way section of central New York stumbled upon an ideal environment for food gatherers. The interlinked little lakes (area of Waneta 812.8 acres, of Lamoka 588.8 acres [Roecker, 1953–54, p. 25]) immediately at hand, and the river system which drained them into the Susquehanna, supplied an abundance of fish and other aquatic life; the forested hills surrounding the site to elevations of fifteen hundred to sixteen hundred feet held a multitude of unmolested game, and contained ample groves of oak, hickory and chestnut trees. The great quantity and extraordinarily large size of the deer bones and antlers from the lower levels of the site is a noteworthy fact in support of this assumption, as is the magnitude and concentration of the site itself. With such a prolific food supply directly at hand, there was no need for further wandering, and it would appear that the group established an all-year-round settlement upon this hill-sheltered spot, directly on a connecting watercourse between the two lakes, where they and their descendants continued to reside for generations. As local game became scarcer (the supply of fish was doubtless inexhaustible to a group of this size), the range of the hunter could easily be extended by boat journeys from his door through a crux of rivers to the south, to include, without the inconvenience of a single portage, hundreds of square miles of additional forests.

Under such perfect conditions, the size of the population probably increased somewhat, but the lack of permanently storable food, except acorns, would likely tend to check unlimited growth.

This inference of a sedentary manner of life for the residents of Lamoka Lake, based upon the discovery there of the artifacts and food remains pertaining to the full range of seasonal food gathering, cannot be applied elsewhere. The normal community pattern for the Lamoka culture seems rather to have been restricted wandering, probably within a specific territory, by small bands of approximately twenty-five individuals, following a seasonal cycle, as judged from the scores of little camp sites. Except for the addition of acorn food, which required processing and grinding, and which enabled a somewhat larger and more stable population, this way of life resembled that of the Paleo-Indian, who had roamed this same region long before. At such a site as Geneva, however, we seem to see a transitional stage into a central-based wandering community pattern, for here the same band seems periodically to have returned many times to fish the lake and river.

The social organization of a Lamoka community was probably uncomplicated. By analogy with living peoples on the same level of culture, it comprised a group of nuclear or extended families, more or less loosely united by common needs, and lacking central authority beyond, perhaps, a nominal chief with advisory capacity. Social status differences were absent or negligible among the band members, who hunted and worked together and shared the food supply.

Warfare

The Lamoka Lake villagers were not entirely isolated and there is some evidence that, late in the occupational history of the site, they were defending themselves against trespass, apparently at least in part from people of their own kind, to judge from scanty skeletal testimony. This statement is based upon the following discoveries: In the upper fill of a refuse pit, only one foot below ground surface, lay, side by side, the mutilated skeletons of two young males, about nineteen and twenty-five years old, respectively. Both were headless and without hands· or feet, save for the right foot of the older man. The right arm of the first individual lay in a hearth and was partially charred. A Lamoka type projectile point was deeply imbedded, from the rear, in his eleventh dorsal vertebra. His older companion had been shot four times with similar points, three of which lay among the ribs, the fourth being firmly fixed into the anterior body of the twelfth dorsal vertebra. (For

more detail and illustrations, see Ritchie, 1932, pp. 124–27 and Plates XIV and XVIII.)

Also from a superificial position in the site, eighteen inches deep in a refuse pit, came the skeleton of a young male of the Lamoka physical type, in whose thoracic cavity was found a Lamoka point, the probable agent of death (ibid., pp. 116–18).

Mortuary Customs

The burial customs of the Lamoka people are little known. Despite an intensive search of the site and surrounding areas, no cemetery was found at Lamoka Lake. The small number of burials attributed to the Lamoka occupation there occurred at various depths and places in the refuse and comprised simple flexed interment without grave goods or any other index of social stratification. At Scottsville, the much decayed remains of five individuals were found close together in shallow graves dug into the gravel subsoil. One held the flexed skeleton of an adult male, a celt lying where the skull should have been. The others comprised two double-bundle burials, one containing a child, whose bones had been lightly sprinkled with powdered red ocher. Burials attributed to Lamoka people at Frontenac Island were all flexed, and simple grave goods were present in some cases.

Hints of the ceremonial life of the Lamoka folk are trivial and obscure. A belief in an afterlife is suggested by scanty grave goods at Frontenac Island, but it is possible that this was inspired by early Laurentian contacts, in veiw of the above-mentioned burial evidence. Rude animal-effigy heads carved on probable shaft straighteners at Lamoka Lake point toward hunting magic, present also on theoretical grounds, while red ocher, whether on implements or in graves, probably had a thaumaturgical connotation. The ax that was substituted for a skull at Scottsville likewise points in this direction. Shamanism for healing and success in hunting was doubtless a part of this culture.

Speculations on the Lamoka Culture

Although considerable time has elapsed since its discovery and initial description by the writer, the Lamoka culture is still a rather mysterious, discrete and isolated entity in central and western New York State. Cognate cultures have not as yet been found for it, although the northeastern area has since been pretty thoroughly explored. It has been compared in some detail with Archaic cultures of the Southeast (Webb and Haag, 1940; Fairbanks, 1942), which it most closely resembles in the bone constituent and differs from in many important respects, including the small use made of shellfish, the lack of the grooved ax, atlatl weight, large stemmed point, and other traits, which, by and large, have more in common with Laurentian complexes in the Northeast. One highly specific similarity consists in the sharing of the problematical antler objects (Plate 21) with the Ward site (Webb and Haag, 1940, Figure 24) and Annis Mound (Webb, 1950, Figure 14D), Kentucky. There seem to be, however, no sound reasons for postulating the derivation of the Lamoka culture from any southeastern Archaic complex (or vice versa) and radiocarbon dates denote approximate coevality for the pertinent Archaic complexes of the two areas.

Lamoka-like projectile points have a much broader geographical range than the Lamoka culture. A similar form, called the "Dustin point," occurs in the Lower Penin-

sula of Michigan. Small narrow-bladed, stemmed points are present in eastern and southern New York, especially in the Hudson Valley, where they are part of the recently defined Sylvan Lake complex (page xix). The range of "small stemmed" points of Wading River and other varieties extends across all of southern New England (page xx; Ritchie, 1965a).

The narrow, side-notched Normanskill point of the River phase of eastern New York has also been confused with the side-notched variety of the Lamoka point, prior to the identification of the River phase (page 125, compare Plates 14 and 46).

It is extremely important to keep in mind, however, that the distribution of the Lamoka *culture* does *not* include any of these areas, and the firmly established radiocarbon date for the Lamoka phase of about 2500 B.C. is several centuries earlier than that determined for the other narrow point complexes, the Sylvan Lake and Squibnocket, both about 2200 B.C., and the River phase at approximately 1900 B.C. I believe that the several varieties of small, narrow-bladed, stemmed points were related to an early "narrow point tradition," and were widely distributed among a number of discrete complexes during a fairly considerable time period, which clearly overlapped that of other cultures characterized by quite different point styles (page 143).

At the moment, the writer's best guess is that the Lamoka culture, as outlined above, had its essential development in the area where its remains are found (Figure 5), from a simpler, more generalized, and more widely disseminated and mobile hunting and fishing manifestation, which probably antedated 3000 B.C. This basic complex was in no way related to or descended from any recognized Paleo-Indian expression, in or out of the area. It may have formed part of a general eastern Appalachian Archaic cultural platform. Probably at this stage there was relatively little utilization of wild vegetable foods, for milling stones seem not to be present in the deeper site layers referred to. Rough stone tools—hammers, anvils, pitted stones, netsinkers, etc.—have been found on some sites, but no bone objects have survived.

The Lamoka culture per se seems to have developed and concentrated in central New York, probably a few centuries prior to 2500 B.C., in response to an ecosphere extremely well suited to the needs of a hunting and fishing culture. A more semi-sedentary way of life likely resulted from increasing emphasis on acorn food and the heavy grinding tools required to process it, while certain artifact forms, notably the beveled adz, appeared as improving inventions. As indicated by the close correspondence in radiocarbon dates, the first inroads of Laurentian groups into this area may have come soon after, and their pressure seems initially to have been exerted from eastern and northern New York, beyond the range of the Lamoka territory, where in all probability occurred cultures of the Laurentian tradition of pre-Lamoka age. The partial coexistence in New York State of the two very distinctive peoples and cultures seems amply attested by the evidence from Frontenac Island, later to be discussed, where, following a primary period of conflict, an amalgamation apparently resulted in the gradual assimilation and disappearance as a culture of the less dominant old Lamoka complex.

THE LAURENTIAN TRADITION

As first formulated by the writer, the Laurentian was an aspect, in the sense of the Midwestern Taxonomic System; that is, a group of related foci sharing a majority of common traits (McKern, 1939, p. 308; Ritchie, 1938, pp. 106–7; 1940, pp. 1–2, 93–98; 1944, pp. 235, 264 ff.). Subsequently it was considered in the broader light of a tradition (Ritchie, 1955a, p. 7; 1958), essentially as defined by Phillips and Willey (1953, pp. 626–28) and on page xxviii herein. Still more specifically its present use conforms to the notion of an elaborating tradition (Haury, et al., 1956, p. 44), in which an increasing complexity in the cultural pattern resulted from the addition, from time to time and place to place, of traits or attributes to the simpler, more uniform basic culture which, in the light of the evidence from New York State, was probably brought into the Northeast by people of a new brachycranial physical type (page 92).

The Laurentian may perhaps best be regarded as an extensive Archaic cultural continuum, widely spread throughout northeastern North America, with its major area of development and diffusion within southeastern Ontario, southern Quebec, northern New England, and northern New York. Its most diagnostic traits, occurring in considerable morphological variety, comprise the gouge; adz; plummet; ground slate points and knives, including the semilunar form or ulu, which occurs also in chipped stone; simple forms of the bannerstone; a variety of chipped-stone projectile points, mainly broad-bladed and side-notched forms; and the barbed bone point (Ritchie, 1940, p. 96).

Certain of these distinctive elements—the woodworking tools, ground slate implements, and barbed bone points—may derive from an old, circumpolar, boreal level of culture (Spaulding, 1946; 1955, pp. 17–18; Strong, 1930). The possibility of bone prototypes for the ground or rubbed slate points and knives was, I believe, first suggested by Ralph Linton, although the reference has escaped me, and perhaps it was by conversation only. The gouge, too, may first have appeared in bone. Both possibilities are enhanced by the discovery, albeit in contexts too late to have a direct bearing on our problem, of associated tools of these kinds in ground slate and bone (Ritchie, 1949, p. 18 and Figure 4, w and aa; 1962a, p. 99 and Plate 2, d; and Plate 38, Figure 14, herein).

It is certain, however, that in the northeastern area itself, the basic Laurentian traits, geared to the livelihood of hunters and fishermen, underwent regional specialization to various degrees, probably in response to better ecological adjustment. It is equally clear that new traits were assimilated into the gradually developing local manifestations of the Laurentian, and that these traits came chiefly from other Archaic cultures situated to the south and west of the Laurentian heartland. There is no longer any reason to believe that such Laurentian traits as the ground slate points and knives were diffused into the Northeast from Dorset or other Eskimo sources to the north, since radiocarbon dating has revealed the priority of these traits in the Laurentian over any known possible Eskimo donors (Ritchie, 1951a, 1962a).

It has so far proved impossible to trace the distribution of the primary traits of the Laurentian over the immense span of northern forests to the hypothesized Alaskan bridgehead. Recent extensive surveys by the National Museum of Canada along the shore of Lake Superior, in the Rainy River region, and in the interior of western Canada have failed to disclose significant evidences of the Laurentian over this large territory, which is characterized by the absence or extreme scarcity of ground stone tools of any kind. In Ontario, the various typological forms of the gouge, adz, slate points and knives, and stone plummets have a very sparse distribution north of the 46th Parallel, occurring rather south of the Boreal forest, and concentrated in the region between Georgian Bay and Lake Huron on the west and the vicinity of Three Rivers, Quebec, to the east (Wright, 1962; and by conversation of January 1962).

West, north and east of this region, or from the north shore of Lake Huron to the interior of the province of Quebec, Laurentian elements are weakly represented, chiefly by crudely fashioned adzes and gouges with very short and shallow troughs, chipped, for the most part, rather than pecked into shape, with partial grinding, often confined to the bit section. Associated with such tools, especially in Quebec, is a group of bifacially chipped core artifacts, comprising ovate and lanceolate blades, end and side scrapers, semilunar knives, and possibly choppers, usually made of quartzite or chalcedony (Plate 25). Side-notched points and retouched flake knives and scrapers occur on some of these sites (Burger, 1953, pp. 32–45; Rogers and Rogers, 1948, 1950), which appear more recent than sites in the Georgian Bay district that produce similar core tools (Greenman and Stanley, 1943; Lee, 1954, 1955, 1957). It would seem that on the northern periphery of its range the Laurentian tradition had merged with the surviving remnant of a much older core-tool tradition, termed by Wright the "Shield Archaic" (Wright, n.d).

South of the Great Lakes and the St. Lawrence River, cultures of the Laurentian tradition extend from the Maritime Provinces of Canada westward at least into northern Ohio, and probably into Michigan, where sporadic finds of gouges, ground

PLATE 25 Stone tools of the Shield Archaic. Found en cache on Kempt Lake, Quebec. 1, 3 end scrapers; 2, 4–7, 9, 10, 13, 16, 17 ovate knives; 8, 11 chipped ulus; 12 rude chopper or scraper; 14 gouge; 15 celt-like tool, chipped all over, slight grinding on one side of bit. Material: 14 traprock, 15 siltstone, all others smoky chalcedony or quartzite. Collection of Mrs. Otto R. Burger, New York City.

slate points, etc., are reported. These may, however, be a reflex of the trade in copper tools with Laurentian communities to the east (page 101).

In the rather amorphous Old Copper culture of the Lake Superior area, native copper counterparts exist for such diagnostic Laurentian stone traits as the gouge, adz, ground slate spear points and double-edged points or knives of several varieties —barbed, straight stemmed and with serrated stem—and even for the bannerstone, plummet, and barbed bone point. A near parallel for the semilunar knife or ulu of chipped or ground stone is also to be found in the crescentic copper knife or chopping tool having extended tang-like terminals for hafting. (For illustrations of these artifacts see West, 1929, 1932; Griffin, ed., 1961; cf. Miles, 1951.)

While it was apparent to the writer from the first that Old Copper and Laurentian crossties had existed (Ritchie, 1940, pp. 44, 98), radiocarbon dates of 5600±400 B.P. (C-836) and 7400±340 B.P. (C-837, 839) for the Oconto site in Wisconsin raised the possibility of native copper prototypes for major Laurentian tool forms (Ritzenthaler and Wittry, 1952; Ritzenthaler, 1946; Baerreis, et al., 1954; Ostberg, 1957). Currently, however, the Old Copper culture is undergoing critical scrutiny, the accuracy of the Oconto dates is being questioned, and the Old Copper seems less a specific cultural manifestation than an industry shared by a number of more or less discrete phases. Carbon-14 dates of 3450±250 B.P. for the Osceola site and 3660±250 B.P. for the Reigh site, both in Wisconsin, together with a distributional study of copper artifacts in relation to areas submerged during the Algonkian and Nipissing stages of postglacial lake history in the Michigan basin, suggest an antiquity of around 2000 B.C. for the

probable climactic stage of the Old Copper Industry (Ritzenthaler, 1958; Mason and Mason, 1961; Griffin, ed., 1961). This is about the time that the Brewerton and Frontenac phases were flourishing in central New York (pages 91, 108), and the Early Boreal Archaic, the immediate predecessor of the so-called Moorehead complex, existed in eastern Maine (Byers, 1959a, pp. 244, 249).

It is possible, as I have earlier hypothesized, that the route of entry of the formative Laurentian was "through the deciduous forest belt bordering the Great Lakes in Altithermal times" (Ritchie, 1955a, p. 8), an idea shared by Dragoo (1959, p. 223), and by Byers for his Boreal Archaic on the Atlantic seaboard, concerning which he says, "We are therefore forced to conclude that the route by which it entered the Northeast lay south of the Great Lakes or else along the Arctic littoral, a route which seems improbable if only because of lack of the characteristic implements at early times" (Byers, 1959a, p. 253).

If this is indeed the case, and since the Laurentian and Boreal Archaic are approximate cultural equivalents (Ritchie, 1940, pp. 96–98; Byers, 1959a, pp. 254–55), the adjective "Boreal" seems somewhat inappropriate, inasmuch as the forest milieu associated with the assumed nascent culture was more likely of the Lake Forest than of the Boreal Forest type. The latter, consisting chiefly of white and black spruce, balsam fir, larch and paper birch, lies north of the Great Lakes (Weaver and Clements, 1938, pp. 487–92; Braun, 1950, map), while the more hospitable Lake Forest, of conifers—white, red and jack pine, and hemlock—and stands of northern hardwoods—beech, sugar and red maple, yellow birch, white and red oak, white ash, and basswood, as the principal climax association—

probably covered then, as more recently, the larger portions of the area concerned in this discussion (Weaver and Clements, 1938, pp. 496–500; Braun, 1950, pp. 337–440). Within the Lake Forest zone the life of man on an Archaic cultural level must largely have been restricted to the hardwood forests, since there, rather than in the conifers, were to be found the mast foods and browse, and therefore the heaviest concentration of the principal game animals on which the hunter subsisted.

Irrespective of the problems of origin, the development of the Laurentian in its recognized guises was a feature of the northeastern area, doubtless in conformity with local ecological situations and cultural connections. This is especially well shown in the Ellsworth Falls, Maine, sequence in the relationship between Occupation 2 (Early Boreal Archaic), radiocarbon-dated around 2009 B.C., and its obviously derived, directly overlying Occupation 3 complex (Late Boreal Archaic), with a carbon-14 age of c. 1400 B.C., which Byers (1959a, pp. 244–47) relates to the Moorehead complex (Red Paint culture, Moorehead, 1922; Maine Cemetery complex, Smith, 1948).

Thus, over several millenniums, arose a still undetermined number of regionally elaborated phases, some, as the Brewerton, Vergennes, Frontenac and Moorehead complexes, relatively well known, others, like the Vosburg, Tadoussac and Old Stone cultures of Labrador, poorly defined or still unrecognized. The generic similarity among the various manifestations was subsumed by the writer under the term "Laurentian" (Ritchie, 1938, pp. 106–8; 1940, pp. 96–98; 1944, pp. 264, 268) and more recently by Byers in his tentative dual division of "Maritime Boreal Archaic" and "Laurentian Boreal Archaic" (Byers, 1959a, p. 255).

Of this recognized unity within diversity he remarks as follows: "On a larger scale the same principle applies to the entire Boreal Archaic. This would include Frontenac, Brewerton, Vosburg, Vergennes, Tadoussac, the Moorehead complex, Newfoundland Aberrant, and the Old Stone culture of Labrador. All show points in common. They are as familiar as a contemporary class picture from another school—the clothes and poses are familiar, but the faces are different" (Byers, 1959a, p. 254).

THE VOSBURG PHASE

The hypothetical Vosburg phase was first tentatively postulated by the writer to account for a rather variable series of stone artifacts from surface sites in the Hudson-Mohawk region of eastern New York (Ritchie, 1944, pp. 257–59). The trait list for these sites closely paralleled those for the Brewerton and Vergennes phases. With the latter the agreement is now seen to be even closer, since the discovery of the KI site and the redefinition of the Vergennes phase (page 84). The chief distinctions between the Brewerton and Vosburg phases are the absence from assemblages attributed to the latter of native copper tools and ground slate double-edged knives or points, and the presence in much greater numbers of the slate semilunar knife or ulu.

Very characteristic of Vosburg sites is a distinctive form of projectile point, well made, with corner-notches and basal grinding, appropriately called the Vosburg type (Ritchie, 1961, p. 55). This point has not, however, been found to the exclusion of all other forms on any site, nor does it even predominate in most.

Components assigned to the Vosburg

phase have been excavated, since 1951, on sites in the Hudson Valley (Ritchie, 1958, pp. 8–34), and one station, the Bannerman site in Dutchess County (Figure 4, site number 12), has been radiocarbon-dated at 2524 B.C.±300 years (ibid., p. 67). More recently, Robert E. Funk's excavation of the Sylvan Lake Rockshelter has disclosed an apparent Vosburg horizon (Sylvan Lake 2) at this stratified site. A hearth feature which he interprets to mark the lower range of the Vosburg component has been dated at 2780 B.C.±80 years (Y-1535) (Funk, 1965, pp. 145–46; 1966).

Long and diligent efforts to isolate a clear-cut, recurring composite, sufficiently discrete and well enough differentiated from the Vergennes and Brewerton phases, have as yet not adequately succeeded, and the Vosburg remains, as in 1944, a tentatively recognized entity of the Laurentian tradition. My present feeling is that it represents the culture in eastern New York of various groups of hunting-fishing-gathering peoples, sharing contemporaneously with the Brewerton groups of central and western New York, and with the Vergennes groups, especially the later ones, inhabiting upper eastern New York, western Vermont and adjacent parts of Quebec, in the Laurentian cultural tradition. I regard it as the base culture of much of this whole area, upon which the subsequent historical developments were reared through internal changes and outside influences and contacts.

THE VERGENNES PHASE

Of the cycle of related local variants of the Laurentian cultural tradition the Brewerton phase, discussed in the next section, is the best known, mainly through the ex-cavation of two large sites at Brewerton on the Oneida River. The Vergennes phase, centered along Otter Creek and Lake Champlain in western Vermont, but extending into Quebec and northern and eastern New York, has recently been given sharper delineation through the discovery of the KI site, as described below and the Bridge site, referred to on page xviii. Only the elusive Vosburg phase remains, as of this writing, without adequate verification for want of sufficient site data.

As first conceived by Bailey on the basis of his excavations at the Donovan site on Dead Creek, a tributary of Otter Creek, near Vergennes, Vermont (Figure 4, site number 10), the "Vergennes focus" included a considerable range of projectile-point forms, together with a variety of pottery styles which in the light of present knowledge can be referred to Middle and Late Woodland horizons in this region (Bailey, 1939; Ritchie, 1944, pp. 257–59). The Donovan site must now be recognized as a multicomponent camp site, lived on by different cultural groups from time to time over several millenniums. In some manner, not wholly clear, the diversified relics of these sundry sojournings became considerably intermixed, and despite Bailey's careful techniques of excavation, observed by the writer on several visits to the site, specific cultural assemblages could not be differentiated. It seems probable that this condition can best be accounted for by the combination of a shallow occupational zone (eight to fourteen inches), aboriginal disturbance through pits and other features, soil creep from an adjacent sand slope, and cultivation in historic times.

Bailey's tentatively postulated Vergennes focus is therefore much too inclusive, for it pools materials which have since been found separately on local camp sites and even, to some degree, in stratigraphic relationship on one or two of these. It does, however, contain a core complex, doubtless the oldest at the Donovan site, comprising the ground slate semilunar knife and double-edged knife or point of at least two kinds, gouge, adz, Otter Creek point, and probably the winged atlatl weight, as the most important elements. This primary complex, with a few additional traits, stands revealed as an apparently "pure" assemblage at the KI site in the same area.

Following its discovery in 1955 on a rocky, wooded island in the swampy valley of Otter Creek, Rutland County, Vermont, the KI site was sporadically excavated by Thomas E. Daniels of Orwell, Vermont, and Mrs. Kathleen Rowlands of Poultney, Vermont, until Mr. Daniels' death in 1962 (Figure 4, site number 11). In 1959 and 1960, through the courtesy of the excavators, the site was visited by the writer, who participated briefly in the excavations and received the loan of the collection for study and reporting. For a period of one week in June 1966 the site was intensively excavated by the writer and several assistants, including Robert E. Funk. Two previously undisturbed areas were explored, totalling 525 square feet. The following data are drawn from the sum total of my experience on this site.

Two soil zones were distinguished, an A zone, called stratum 1, consisting of a dark-brown humus, topped by sod or duff, measuring about three and a half inches in thickness, and underlaid by a gray podzol up to an inch thick; and a B soil, composed of two intergrading horizons, referred to for convenience as strata 2 and 3. The B soil was a fine-textured, sandy-clay, alluvium-like material, containing many water-worn pebbles and an occasional small cobble. It seems to have been water-laid at some period when Otter Creek flowed at a much higher level than at present, which I suspect was in Late Pleistocene times.

Stratum 2 was prevailingly yellowish or reddish brown, varied from approximately two to eight inches, with a usual thickness range of four to six inches. Stratum 3, resting upon the uneven, glacially worn, deeply weathered and fissured, white or light-gray marble bedrock, was tan to cocoa brown to light olive brown in its deepest parts, seemed to contain more clay than stratum 2, and ranged from one inch to one foot in thickness, with three to seven inches as the usual depth.

Artifacts; chipping debris, mostly quartzite; burned rock fragments, scattered charcoal particles and an occasional piece of calcined bone (part of the claw core of a bear and a fragmentary deer phalanx were recognizable), occurred in all three strata, from the lower part of stratum 1 to the bedrock. They were, however, four times as numerous in stratum 2, the yellow-brown or red-brown layer, as in the two other strata. The few items from the base of the humus layer, stratum 1, may be intrusive from rodent or root disturbances of the top of stratum 2. Mr. Daniels had reported no discoveries from the humus zone in the areas explored by him, and I am inclined to consider this a sterile horizon laid down after the occupation of the site.

In the main, artifacts and debitage had an apparent random horizontal distribution. No habitation zones or floors could be distinguished, but some clustering in areas a few feet in diameter was noted, possibly indicative of lodge floors.

A possible lodge floor was verbally described by Mr. Daniels as having been located on the highest (some twenty feet above swamp level) and smoothest ground.

85

Approximately fifteen feet in diameter, it was traceable by a rough circle of three-inch post molds. A low earth mound seemed to surmount the spot, hinting at the possibility of an earth-covered structure. In the floor of this feature Mr. Daniels found, under a covering of quartzite cobbles, a much decayed human skeleton, lightly sprinkled with red ocher.

The earlier excavators had reported no hearth discoveries. Our recent work disclosed four small features, interpreted as hearths. They consisted of shallow, basin-shaped areas containing burned earth, burned stones and scanty charcoal which was carefully collected for C-14 assay. The combined small sample from adjacent features 1 and 2 yielded the disappointing date of A.D. 120±80 years (Y-1815). As some concrete evidence of forest fires was uncovered at the base of the duff, I am inclined to suspect contamination of the sample by some of this later charcoal through the mechanics of root channels or small rodent burrows. Another small sample, from Feature 3, was then submitted to the Yale Radiocarbon Laboratory which obtained the unacceptable figure of 370 B.C.±100 years (Y-1855).

Present indications suggest that this site was occupied by a single small band, perhaps seasonally as a winter hunting camp. Their surviving cultural traces ally them with other Archaic-period hunters in the Northeast, but the cultural complex at the KI site seems to be uniquely free from admixture with that of any earlier or subsequent residents, probably due to the peculiar isolation of the site. This site may, therefore, at least tentatively, be regarded as a key station, and its data used to redefine the Vergennes phase. To the core complex of this culture, as enumerated for the Vergennes site, can now be added the

plummet, chopper and copper gorge. All the artifacts relate directly to hunting, fishing, the preparation of animal foods and skins, and tree-felling and wood-shaping activities, and they reflect very well the forest-adapted life of a hunter-fisher folk of the postulated Laurentian tradition. Nearly all of the artifacts from the site are fashioned from regionally available stone materials—mainly quartzite, slate and flint. No bone tools survived, although soil tests by the writer gave a pH of 6.5, or very slightly acid.

The primacy of the hunting activity in the economy of this culture is inferred from the preponderance of projectile points, apparently for the arming of darts or javelins, as judged from their size and weight. The Otter Creek type (Ritchie, 1961, pp. 40–41) greatly predominates (Plate 26), the small remainder including side-notched, eared, and triangular forms.

Plate 27, Figures 1–3, 6–8, portray six of the ten double-edged, rubbed slate knives, of stemmed, barbed and serrated-stemmed varieties; and the ulus (Figures 9–11), of which the first is the only fragment of a finished, sharp-edged tool. On Plate 28 are illustrated the adzes, gouges, celts, choppers, and other rough stone tools. Unillustrated artifact forms from the KI site include the following: ovate and lanceolate knives, all of quartzite; a few simple end scrapers; a winged drill with stemmed base; two fragmentary plummets; a copper gorge; a probable bannerstone wing fragment; various forms of abrading stones; and a considerable number of rude, rod-shaped objects, all broken, apparently unique.

The diagnostic point form of the Vergennes phase, as herein redefined, has been termed by the writer the Otter Creek point, and it can be affirmed that this type

PLATE 26 Projectile points of Otter Creek type from the KI site, Rutland Co., Vt. Collection of Thomas E. Daniels, Orwell, Vt.

PLATE 27 Ground slate implements from the KI site, Rutland Co., Vt. 1–3, 6–8 double-edged knives or points; 4, 5 slate blanks for similar points; 9–11 ulu fragments. Collection of Thomas E. Daniels, Orwell, Vt.

occupies a low-level position in its rare occurrence in Brewerton-phase sites of central New York (Plate 29, Figures 14, 20) and a similar placement in eastern New York sites where some stratigraphy is evident. These facts suggest a relatively high age for the Vergennes phase. Moreover, the Otter Creek point presents some marked morphological resemblances to the Raddatz, Osceola and other Archaic points of the central and northern Mississippi Valley, and to the Big Sandy point of Tennessee, to which a fair order of antiquity attaches. For these and other reasons, I would estimate that the Vergennes phase of culture flourished some time between 2500 and 3500 B.C., and that it was probably the earliest manifestation of the Laurentian to appear in the New York area.

THE BREWERTON PHASE

The discovery of the sites through which this culture is defined was made in 1937 at Brewerton, Onondaga County, where two large stations were found on opposite sides of the Oneida River at the foot of Oneida Lake. The locating of these sites rewarded the writer's long search to establish the context of a significant body of surface-found material, chiefly a variety of broad-bladed projectile points, the gouge, bannerstone, plummet, and ground slate point and ulu, which were variously distributed over most of New York and some surrounding areas.

The essentially Archaic character of these sites, the Robinson and Oberlander No. 1 (Figure 4, sites number 6, 7), which were excavated by the Rochester Museum of Arts and Sciences, under the writer's direction, in 1937 and 1938, was recognized at that time (Ritchie, 1940, pp. 97–98). The upper level of both sites, however, produced a small quantity of scattered potsherds which seemed to indicate the continuity of the preceramic complex into the ceramic period. Mainly for this reason the newly discovered culture assemblage at these sites was, after much thought and discussion, tentatively and with misgivings assigned to the then vaguely defined Woodland Pattern in the Midwestern Taxonomic Method. The suggestion that the nonceramic portion of the complex be classified as Archaic and the minor ceramic part as Woodland was rejected as leading to confusion. The whole assemblage at these two similar sites was therefore designated the Brewerton Focus. In this focus were also appropriately placed other surface and subsurface sites in central and western New York yielding stone materials of the same kind (Ritchie, 1940, pp. 92–93). The Brewerton Focus was, in turn, compared with site assemblages in eastern New York and Vermont, and two probably related foci, the Vosburg and Vergennes, were postulated. These several foci, linked by a small core of significant common traits, were considered to be broadly and basically related within an old culture platform having northern affinities, and accordingly, in terms of the classificatory system employed, all were assigned to a Laurentian Aspect of culture (Ritchie, 1940, pp. 92–98). Soon afterward, however, the writer's reconsideration of the total evidence led him to consign the Laurentian Aspect and, of course, its component foci, to the Archaic Pattern, thus recognizing its fundamental non-ceramic, prehorticultural, hunting, fishing, gathering base. Since some artifacts of now recognized Laurentian provenience were present in the upper level at Lamoka Lake, the Laurentian Aspect was placed above the Lamoka Focus in the Archaic segment of the cultural sequence for New

PLATE 28 Stone tools from the KI site, Rutland Co., Vt. 1, 8, 10 chipped celts; 2, 6 hammerstones; 3 bipitted stone; 4 celt or adz; 5 gouge; 7 coarse scraper or chopper; 9 chopper. Collection of Thomas E. Daniels, Orwell, Vt.

York State (Ritchie, 1944, pp. 5, 7). The probable partial persistence of the Laurentian into the earlier part of the succeeding "Intermediate" period, was also recognized (ibid., p. 10).

Distribution and Ecology

The nuclear area of the Brewerton phase is central New York, wherein occur the principal stations and a large number of surface sites. Sites of the latter character, evidently temporary camps, are recognized, however, throughout western New York, and in northern New York along the St. Lawrence and its principal tributaries. A clear-cut differentiation of the Brewerton phase from other postulated phases of the Laurentian is, however, difficult on the basis of current data.

Sites of the Brewerton phase are found both in the lowland and highland provinces of its range, chiefly in the former, where they are clearly related to present topographical features, mainly waterways and swamps. The ecological relationship of this culture closely approximates that of the preceding Lamoka. The principal difference would seem to be in the greater emphasis on hunting in the Brewerton, on fishing and acorn collecting in the Lamoka. Sites of the two cultures occur both separately and, more often, intermixed along the same rivers and lakes, and at exactly the same 380-foot elevation along an old beach line rimming the large Montezuma Marsh in central New York. As will later be adduced, the two quite distinctive and historically unrelated complexes, Lamoka and Brewerton, seem in part to have coexisted within the same range. The prevailing climatic conditions, relatively warm and dry, in the closing stages of the thermal maximum, and the related floral and faunal ecosystem were doubtless substantially the same for both cultures. Bone refuse, entirely lacking from all surface sites, was preserved in instructive quantities only at the Oberlander No. 1 site. No vegetable food remains were, however, found anywhere.

Age

Very little charcoal occurred at the Brewerton sites and none was available a decade later for radiocarbon dating. At Frontenac Island, where the Brewerton and Lamoka cultures interacted, a series of three carbon-14 dates was obtained, ranging between 2980 B.C. and 1723 B.C. At the stratified, multicomponent O'Neil site, near Weedsport, Cayuga County (Figure 4, site number 27), the writer's excavations of 1961–62 uncovered hearths in the top of the basal level which produced Brewerton-type projectile points, a tanged copper point, and other material attributable to the Brewerton culture, the first phase of occupation at the site (page 156) (Ritchie, MS. report to be published elsewhere). Charcoal samples from two of the hearths yielded, respectively, carbon-14 dates equivalent to 2050 B.C. ±220 years (I-424) (Trautman, 1963, p. 68) and 2010 B.C. ±100 years (Y-1273). A considerably older carbon-14 date of 2750 B.C. ±150 years (GSC-162) may pertain to a Brewerton related Laurentian site in Canada, the Morrison's Island No. 6 site in the Ottawa Valley of Quebec. The date was derived from scattered charcoal in the fill of a grave pit and is not certainly related to the culture, found in a habitation and burial component, which has the principal traits of the Brewerton phase but is far richer in copper tools (Kennedy, 1966). An earlier date for the Laurentian in Canada is predictable on the assumption of its having diffused southward into New York and New England (page 79).

The Brewerton People

The skeletal remains of the Brewerton people were scantily represented at the major Robinson and Oberlander No. 1 sites. Much better evidence came from Frontenac Island, and there can be very little doubt that the people associated with the Brewerton culture were morphologically, and probably genetically, of the same stock as the intrusive, upper-level, broad-headed folk at the Lamoka Lake site (page 46).

This group, in sharp contrast with the Lamoka people, can be generally described as of stocky build and medium stature (about five feet five to six inches). Their heavy-boned skeletons, with strong muscular attachments, bespeak a rugged and powerful body development. Their heads, of good cranial capacity, were broad, round, and of only medium height in the vault, with medium to heavy eyebrow and temporal ridges. The relatively short and wide face was characterized by a prominent lateral and anterior projection of the malars (cheekbones), medium to low orbits, and a short and broad nose.

There is unequivocal evidence for the persistence of this subracial type in central New York into Middle Woodland times (page 241).

The bone pathology of this group includes minor osteomas, arthritis of the spine and femoral head, and mild osteoperiostitis following injury to various long bones. Dental lesions and anomalies embrace apical abscesses, apparently largely induced by excessive attrition; periodontitis; a minute incidence of caries; and a tendency to supernumerary teeth.

A small number of fractures of long bones and vertebra, all in males, as in the Lamoka series, seems related to the more hazardous role as hunters performed by this sex.

Subsistence Activities

Hunting seems clearly to have constituted the primary subsistence activity in the Brewerton culture, as shown by the relative proportions of artifacts designed for various food-getting and preparing functions. On most of the surface sites projectile points comprise approximately 90 per cent of the surviving remains, and even at the large, subsurface stations at Brewerton, where much of the total material culture still lay *in situ*, hunting points constituted over 60 per cent of all objects, and more than 80 per cent of chipped-stone artifacts at the Robinson site, about 39 per cent and 71 per cent, respectively, at Oberlander No. 1.[1] Indeed, high projectile-point frequencies characterize all sites and phases of the Laurentian tradition.

A rather large variety of point forms occurs in the Brewerton phase, as determined by careful excavation. Broad side-notched points (Brewerton Side-Notched) predominate, however (59 per cent at Robinson, 64 per cent at Oberlander), and probably constitute the oldest point style of this phase (Plate 29, Figures 7–12, 13, 15–17, 21). Other important point types, all with relatively broad blades, include the following: Brewerton Corner-Notched, Brewerton Eared-Notched, Brewerton Eared-Triangle and various stemmed forms (Plate 29, Figures 1–6, 19, 22). (For

[1] For a complete listing, with numerical frequencies, of the traits from these key Brewerton sites, see Ritchie, 1940, pp. 98–104; 1944, pp. 374–79. Detailed descriptions and other data, including percentiles, are given in the text of the first reference.

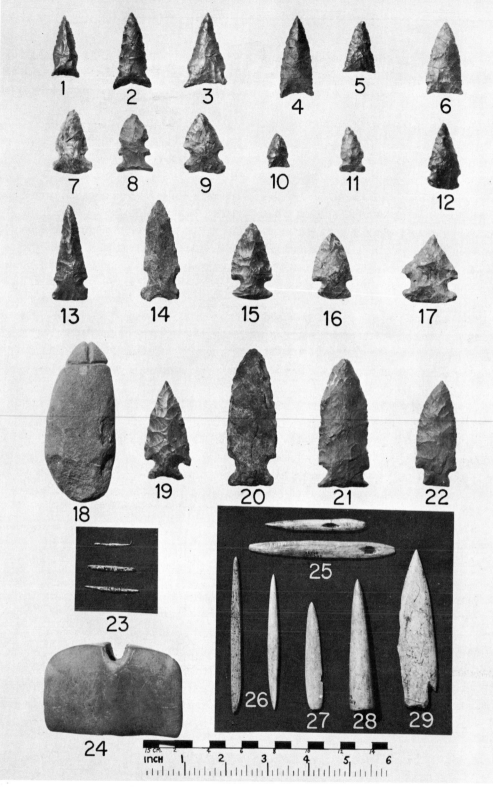

PLATE 29 Hunting and fishing equipment of the Brewerton phase. 1–3 projectile points of Brewerton Eared-Notched type; 4–6 projectile points of Brewerton Eared-Triangle type; 7–13, 15–17, 21 projectile points of Brewerton Side-Notched type; 14, 20 projectile points of Otter Creek type; 19 projectile point of Brewerton Corner-Notched type; 22 projectile point of Genesee type; 18 plummet; 23 copper gorges; 24 bannerstone or atlatl weight; 25 probable snowshoe needles; 26 probable leister points; 27 flat bone projectile point; 28 conical antler projectile point; 29 ground barbed projectile point (left side broken away).

93

typological descriptions of the Brewerton point series see Ritchie, 1961, pp. 16–20; for general descriptions see Ritchie, 1940, pp. 27–32, 64–67.)

Some quantitative differences in point styles were found at the two sites and, while present at all levels throughout the refuse deposits, some significant variations were noted in the depth frequency of the several groups. Thus at the Robinson component 79 per cent of triangular forms occurred in the upper half of the general midden, while at Oberlander No. 1, where triangular points were few in number and of nearly uniform distribution, 72 per cent of corner-notched, 78 per cent of stemmed and 75 per cent of eared points pertained to the superior horizon. At both stations, small points (under one and three-quarters inches in length) of all forms predominated in the upper half of the general midden (Robinson 57 per cent, Oberlander 70 per cent) (Plate 29, Figures 10, 11).

These facts suggest, among other things, the relative recency in the complex of the triangular, eared, stemmed and corner-notched point varieties, and a growing emphasis on the use of lighter weapons. It may be possible, although unlikely, that the bow and arrow was introduced into the culture during the latter part of the life span of the Brewerton stations.

Spear points of side-notched form, five to six inches in length, occur infrequently in this phase, and one corner-notched bone spearhead was found at the Oberlander site (Plate 29, Figure 29). Conical antler and flat bone projectile points are also present (Plate 29, Figures 27, 28).

While the majority of the heavier, non-triangular stone points appear to have been percussion chipped, for the most part from local Onondaga flint, antler and bone tools, presumably flakers for pressure chipping,

were found in small numbers (Plate 30, Figures 1, 2). The delicate fashioning of the eared and triangular points would seem to have required carefully controlled pressure reduction. Use of the javelin in the Brewerton phase is implied not only by the large, heavy projectile points, but by the discovery of stone atlatl weights of several simple forms, viz., rectangulate, oval and trapezoidal (Plate 29, Figure 24).

The lesser role of fishing in the economy of this culture is suggested by the proportionally much smaller number of fishing appliances found at the Brewerton sites, which beyond doubt were primarily summer fishing stations. The commonest items, notched netsinkers, totaled only 148 (versus over 8000 at Lamoka Lake); there were eighteen copper gorges (none of bone) (Plate 29, Figure 23); seven barbed bone points or harpoons, with single or multiple barbs and line hole, all fragmentary; and four long, double-pointed bone implements, probably leister points (Plate 29, Figure 26).

It is important to note that no bone fishhook has, to my knowledge, ever been found on a pure Brewerton or Laurentian site, and it seems probable that this important contrivance, found in the earlier Lamoka, and in all subsequent cultures, including the Lamoka-Brewerton hybrid Frontenac complex, was not originally a Laurentian trait. Stone plummets, present at the Brewerton sites and generally throughout the Laurentian, may have served as sinkers for lines equipped with gorges rather than hooks (Plate 29, Figure 18).

Stone grinding tools, consisting of cylindrical and conical pestles, mullers, and mortars with a single shallow grinding surface, were found in small numbers on both Brewerton sites (Plate 31, Figures 4–6).

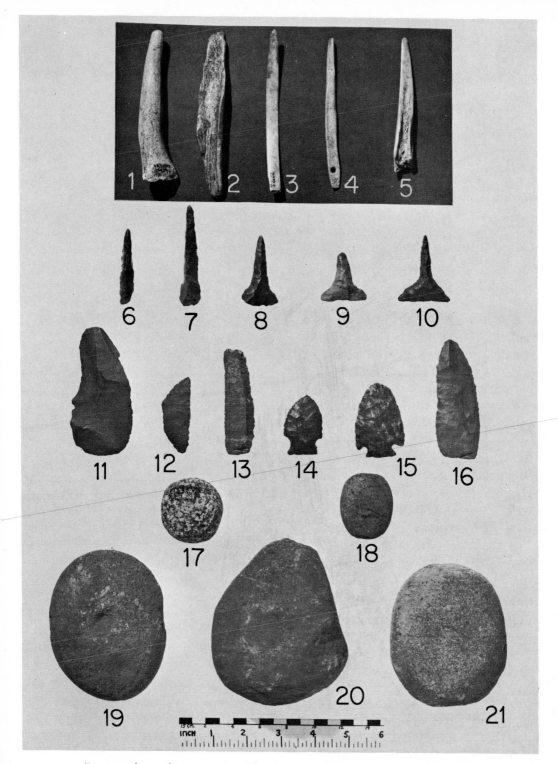

PLATE 30 Bone, antler and stone tools of the Brewerton phase. 1 antler flaker; 2 bone flaker; 3, 4 curved bone needles, probably for sewing mats; 5 bone knife; 6–10 varieties of the chipped-stone drill; 11–13 knives from retouched flakes; 14–16 corner-notched and trianguloid flint knives; 17, 18 pebble hammerstones; 19 pitted hammerstone; 20 anvilstone; 21 combination hammerstone and muller.

They alone indicate use of wild plant foods, since no direct evidence has persisted.

Food storage in subterranean pits is improbable, considering the size and character of such features, probably earth ovens, found at Brewerton (Ritchie, 1940, pp. 11–15, 56–57). Hearths, not numerous on either site, consisted of ash and charcoal lenses or of small basin-shaped depressions with burned rock and scanty ash contents (ibid., pp. 15, 54, 55). One burned stone feature, found at Oberlander No. 1 (ibid., p. 54), was probably a roasting platform, analogous to those described elsewhere in this report from Archaic and later sites. Thousands of fire-shattered rocks found throughout both stations testify to the practice of stone-boiling in this potteryless culture. As no flint strikers were recovered, fire may have been created by friction techniques.

The Brewerton hunters had for companionship and aid in tracking and cornering game a small, terrier-sized dog, apparently of the same breed as that found at the Geneva site (page 52). The flexed burials of two such dogs in the middens at the Oberlander No. 1 site attest to the regard felt for this useful animal.

Besides the grinding tools already enumerated, implements involved in the preparation of foods in this culture include several forms of the flint knife, viz., the retouched prismatic flake, large retouched flake, ovate or triangular biface blade, and side-notched form with convex edges, listed in descending order of frequency (Plate 30, Figures 11–16). One example of the semilunar knife or ulu, an unfinished chipped sandstone specimen nearly ten inches long, was found prior to our coming by the owner of the Oberlander No. 1 site,

eroding from the refuse of the site along the riverbank. (See illustration in Ritchie, 1944, p. 249.)

The so-called chopper is a prominent artifact of the Brewerton culture, and five or six forms were present on the sites under discussion (Plate 31, Figures 1–3). Choppers also turn up on nearly all camp sites of this complex, and have a wide distribution in the Laurentian and related manifestations in the Northeast. As the service edge is blunted or rounded on these rude objects, their primary purpose has been assumed to be the chopping up of game and fish, but perhaps a likelier function might have been the scraping of heavy hides, for which small flint end scrapers seem inadequate. A large hoe-shaped form, well represented at Brewerton (Plate 31, Figures 1, 2), has elsewhere, in a comparable context, been identified as a hoe, an improbable purpose in the almost certain absence of any horticultural expression in these particular cultures.

Settlement Pattern

We have no data on housing for the Brewerton culture. Despite the most diligent search, only a few evident post molds were uncovered at the Robinson and Oberlander sites. Probable lodge-floor areas were identified by spreads of sand and gravel, about six to ten feet across, thought to represent floors sanded for dryness and sanitation, interspersed with black soil and ash layers (Ritchie, 1940, pp. 8–9, 51, 54). The two large sites at Brewerton were ideally situated on a major shallows or rift in the Oneida River, directly below its

PLATE 31 Tools used in food preparation in the Brewerton phase. 1–3 choppers; 4 cylindrical pestle; 5 conical pestle; 6 muller.

source in Oneida Lake,[1] an eighty-square-mile body of relatively shallow water (maximum depth sixty feet) with many

bars, shoals and weed beds and several islands, perfectly suited to aboriginal methods of fishing. During seasonal fish runs,

[1] Oneida Lake is a remnant of postglacial Lake Iroquois at its maximum extent and it lies in the valley of the old Rome outlet of this lake, which drained through the Mohawk Valley into Lake Albany. This lake filled the Mohawk Valley below Schenectady and the wider Hudson Valley from about Glens Falls to Kingston. (See Figure 2 and page 13).

multitudes of eels, walleyed pike, northern pike, suckers, and other fish, passed through the rifts, where they could be trapped and speared. Doubtless mainly on this account the Brewerton area attracted Indian groups of nearly every culture in New York (Ritchie, 1940, 1944, 1946).

The Robinson site covered some three acres of a well-drained, nearly level terrace, fifteen to eighteen feet above the south shore of the river (Figure 4, site number 6). This occupied area was marked by a refuse mantle of black soil ten to thirty-two inches deep (Ritchie, 1940, pp. 4–50). Directly opposite, about a quarter mile away on the north bank of the river, lay the Oberlander No. 1 site, also on a level terrace, composed of sand and gravel, elevated approximately nine feet above the present surface of the river, and covering nearly two acres with refuse midden deposits up to fifty-four inches thick (ibid., pp. 50–89) (Figure 4, site number 7). The soil here was prevailingly alkaline and, in consequence, bone was generally well preserved, contrary to the conditions found at the Robinson site (ibid., pp. 9–11). Each of these sites unquestionably recorded in its deposits many centuries of seasonal use as a major fishing camp by groups of the same cultural tradition. During this long period some stylistic changes in projectile points took place, mostly of a quantitative nature; the use of copper tools declined; but some traits of the culture—for example, the stone gouge—persisted apparently unchanged throughout. Later, small parties of Meadowood and Point Peninsula people, whose main camps are known close by on both shores of the river (pages 190, 234) seem to have tarried here briefly and been responsible for the intrusion of the limited pottery, and a small amount of other material, including some pit features, into the

upper levels of both the Robinson and Oberlander No. 1 sites. This conclusion is at variance with the opinion formed at the close of the excavations on these sites, when it was suggested that minor use of pottery characterized the final stage of the Brewerton culture (Ritchie, 1940, pp. 50, 88–89). Both Vinette 1 and 2 ware types were represented in the small, scattered and generally superficially distributed sherds, which in some instances were found in intrusive pits (Ritchie, 1940, pp. 11, 14). Subsequently, at the Vinette site (Figure 4, site number 39) just west of Oberlander No. 1, these wares were found in a stratigraphic sequence denoting a chronologic differentiation (page 206) which has since been amply sustained by data from many sites throughout the Northeast. It seems probable, therefore, that slight intrusions occurred on these sites during the succeeding Early and Middle Woodland occupations of the Brewerton area. The virtual impossibility of distinguishing much of this intrusive evidence in the ground under conditions prevailing at the Brewerton sites is well worth emphasizing for its applicability to other, and doubtless frequently encountered, situations of this kind elsewhere (ibid., pp. 48, 88).

A seasonal cycle of travel is indicated for the Brewerton people, some of whose inland hunting camps, marked by an abundance of their characteristic projectile points and much lesser numbers of other stone tools—hammers, anvils, gouges, etc. —have been identified in the vicinity, both north and south of Oneida Lake, and in many other places in central and western New York. They often lie adjacent to large swamps, especially near streams which enter or emerge from them; and near big springs, well back in the hills of the Allegheny Plateau. Here, it would seem, small groups, perhaps families, passed some part of the winter, hunting and doubtless trapping.[2] Central-based camps, like those at Brewerton, and a few other lesser spots along the Oneida and confluent Seneca rivers, were gathering places for spring fishing, and the industrial vestiges in the deep middens at the Brewerton sites strongly suggest that the occupation continued on through summer and autumn into the early winter. It is even possible that some members of the band never left the sites even then. The general picture engendered by the archaeological evidence for the Brewerton culture would seem to be analogous to the way of life recorded for the Algonkian Mistassini Indians of south-central Quebec by the Rogerses (Rogers, E. S., and Rogers, J. H., 1959), and for the Penobscot, another forest tribe of the same linguistic stock in Maine (Speck, 1940, pp. 26, 35–36).

Tools and Ornaments

Several forms of chipped flint end and side scrapers are very characteristic of the Brewerton culture. Commonest is the simple ovate or "thumbnail" end scraper made from a thick flake chipped only on one face and with a steep scraping edge (Plate 32, Figure 11). Others include stemmed, and corner- and side-notched, "crescentic edge" varieties, the latter two bifacially chipped, sometimes, apparently, from reused projectile points (Plate 32, Figures 10, 12, 15–17, 19), and a possibly late triangular type chipped on both sides, which persisted into the Meadowood culture (Plate 32, Figure 18). The majority of side scrapers consist of retouched flakes (Plate 32, Figure 13), but a few specialized varieties occur (Plate 32, Figure 14). There are also a few bone scrapers made from deer scapulae (Plate 32, Figure 4).

These scrapers, and a small assortment of bone and copper awls (Plate 32, Figures 5, 6), probably had numerous functions related to needs in several categories, one of which was the preparation and working of leather and peltry into body covering. No bone needles suitable for sewing skins were found. Curved needles cut from strips of deer rib (Plate 30, Figures 3, 4), generally considered mat needles, were probably employed in sewing together rush mats, while the specimens illustrated on Plate 29, Figure 25, resemble snowshoe needles of wood and bone used by later northeastern hunting Indians.

Personal adornments are nearly non-existent; there is one short, tubular, bone bead (Plate 32, Figure 2); six bird-bone tubes, several inches in length, possibly for the same use; a grooved bear canine, perhaps a pendant (Plate 32, Figure 1); and several ground hematite paintstones from which red pigment was obtained (Plate 32, Figure 3).

A great deal of woodworking is indicated by the cutting and shaping tools of several media found at Brewerton. These did not include the grooved ax, which had no place in cultures of the Laurentian tradition. The gouge and plano-convex adz (Plate 33, Figure 13) were the principal instruments, the former occurring in two varieties, mainly a short, broad form (Plate 33, Figures 9, 10) but also a long, slender type (Plate 33, Figure 11), both widely distributed in the Laurentian. There is additionally a copper gouge or "spud" from the Robinson site (Plate 33, Figure 12), of Old Copper culture type and probable ori-

[2] Employment of the snowshoe is suggested by the discovery at the Oberlander No. 1 site of probable bone snowshoe needles (Plate 29, Figure 25; cf. Figure 20 in Speck, 1940).

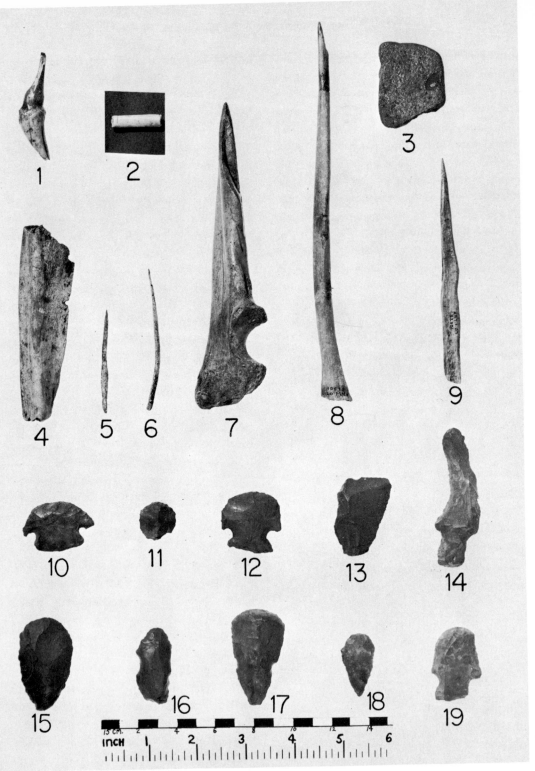

PLATE 32 Personal ornaments and general tools of the Brewerton phase. 1 grooved bear canine; 2 tubular bone bead; 3 ground hematite paintstone; 4 deer scapula scraper; 5, 6 copper awls; 7–9 bone awls; 10–19 varieties of end and side scrapers.

gin. The gouge seems to imply, especially, use of the dugout canoe. Short, rectangulate stone celts are likewise a feature of the culture, and there is one flat copper celt, also with Old Copper culture parallels, from the Robinson site (Plate 33, Figures 5, 7, 8). Many copper celts, adzes, gouges and other implements have been found in working the land in the general Brewerton area (Beauchamp, 1902).

Other contrivances concerned with the manipulation of wood and bark, both of which beyond cavil figured prominently in the Brewerton culture, comprise the following, all from the Brewerton sites: a copper chisel (?) fragment; antler punches; unique sickle-shaped flint blades (present also on numerous Brewerton camp sites and apparently diagnostic in this culture) (Plate 33, Figure 6); split and ground beaver-incisor tools of several kinds (Plate 33, Figures 1–4); some of the flint end scrapers already described; and simple whetstones doubtless used in grinding and sharpening stone and bone cutting tools; and bone awls (Plate 32, Figures 7–9).

Various multipurpose implements of the Brewerton culture comprise flint drills of six principal shapes, viz., expanded base, straight, based on rough spall, expanded notched base, T-shaped base and expanded eared base, in order of frequency (Plate 30, Figures 6–10); unpitted and pitted hammerstones (Plate 30, Figures 17–19); anvilstones (Plate 30, Figure 20); pebbles, cobbles and boulders with single or multiple conical pits, use unknown; and various combination tools employed as hammers, anvils and mullers (Plate 30, Figure 21).

Trade Connections

Native copper implements (no ornaments occur) in the Brewerton culture be-

token trade connections with the Old Copper center of the Upper Great Lakes, where typological parallels are to be found. These crossties involve other phases of the Laurentian as well, and cover a variety of tool and weapon types not actually excavated on the Brewerton sites, but found on the surface in the same area and almost certainly elements of this complex (Beauchamp, 1902). The mechanics of exchange are problematical, but the metal objects in finished form may have passed through the hands of several intermediaries between their place of origin and central New York. A route westward is perhaps identified by a light diffusion of stone gouges and a backwash of Laurentian traits south of the Great Lakes into Michigan.

A major route of diffusion through the Ottawa Valley into the St. Lawrence Valley is indicated by the recent discoveries by Clyde C. Kennedy of large numbers of copper artifacts on Laurentian habitation and burial sites on Allumette Island and Morrison's Island. The Morrison's Island No. 6 site seems closely related to sites of the Brewerton phase in New York (Kennedy, 1966), the Allumette Island complex most closely resembles that of the Vergennes phase. The collections from these sites were studied by the writer in Ottawa through the courtesy of Mr. Kennedy.

The Brewerton phase of central New York and the Vergennes phase of western Vermont are specifically interlinked, not alone by copper traits, but by the presence in the lower levels of the Brewerton sites, where nearly all the copper was found, of a few examples of the distinctive Otter Creek type projectile point of the Vergennes phase, made from the usual Vermont materials, quartzite and slate (Plate 29, Figures 14, 20) (page 86).

PLATE 33 Woodworking tools of the Brewerton phase. 1–4 beaver incisors modified for scraping and cutting; 5 copper celt; 6 sickle-shaped flint knife; 7, 8 stone celts; 9–11 stone gouges; 12 copper gouge or "spud"; 13 stone adz.

Southeastern Pennsylvania jasper artifacts, and some of argillite apparently derived from northeastern Pennsylvania and northern New Jersey, suggest limited relationships with groups to the south of New York. Water routes in each of these directions, west, east and south, are readily feasible from the Brewerton area, situated at a veritable crux of waterways in the geographical center of New York State. Yet it seems most unlikely that trading groups from the Brewerton area actually journeyed to these distant sources to the west and south. I suspect we are seeing here the very beginning of trade-route connections which were to reach their climax in Middle Woodland times. (See a further discussion of this subject on pages 119, 196, 253.)

Burial Traits

Robinson and Oberlander No. 1 were doubtless unshielded settlements fully exposed to hostile man or beast. Presence of a palisade would certainly have been recorded by some evidence, such as post molds or possibly a ditch, as at the Sackett site (page 287). That an occasional raid on the inhabitants may have taken place is suggested by the multiple and apparently hasty burial of four individuals in a common grave at the Oberlander site. In this feature occurred the peculiarly arranged and incomplete skeletons of two children and an adult female and male, the latter with a side-notched projectile point within the thorax (Ritchie, 1940, pp. 58–60).

The mortuary customs of the Brewerton people appear to have been somewhat more complex and varied than those of the Lamoka folk, although like the latter they seem not to have had regular cemetery areas, but to have disposed of their dead in haphazard fashion within the community confines, possibly even beneath the floors of the dwellings, since the latter have not definitely been identified. A shallow grave fossa, dug in or through a refuse midden, was the rule, and the corpse was covered with midden soil containing refuse bone and other discards. The extended supine position was favored, but flexed, bundled and cremated bones were found on the Brewerton sites. It is possible that the last two modes were reserved for people who died at some distant place and whose remains were subsequently brought "home" for interment. There was here, however, no grouping of the graves as though in family plots, such as will be described at Frontenac Island. Grave goods were absent or very scanty, and confined to utilitarian objects. The extended body of an old man with a diseased hip had been lightly sprinkled with red ocher at the Oberlander No. 1 site.

There was nothing about any grave or its contents to indicate a superior social status, greater personal esteem, regard, or wealth for its occupant. Nor was there any real hint of mortuary ceremonialism, such as was manifest in cemeteries of the Early Woodland period, one of which (Oberlander No. 2) (page 181) was subsequently found and excavated by the writer within a few hundred feet of the Oberlander No. 1 site.[1]

Clues, such as amulets or fetishes of a distinguishable character, to any form of magico-religious behavior were not uncovered, nor were there any objects of supposed ceremonial or even recreational character. In this connection it may be well to emphasize the absence of any kind of smoking pipe from the Brewerton, or any

[1] Details of the Robinson and Oberlander No. 1 burials are given in Ritchie, 1940, pp. 15–18, 57–64.

other Archaic manifestation in the Northeast.

The Brewerton culture, as seen archaeologically, conveys an impression of utilitarian functionalism as its dominant motif. By analogy with historic northeastern Algonkian tribes, on a generally comparable cultural level, the Brewerton people, with a simple band organization composed of consanguineous families, probably spent most of their energy in fulfilling subsistence requirements, principally through hunting activities.

THE FRONTENAC PHASE

The Frontenac phase of the Archaic cultural stage in New York was formulated on the basis of the remarkable discoveries made on Frontenac Island in Cayuga Lake through the excavations in 1939 and 1940 of the Rochester Museum of Arts and Sciences, under the writer's direction (Ritchie, 1944, pp. 268–92; 1945). In 1953 an additional excavation covering three hundred square feet was made in the southwestern quadrant of the site by the New York State Museum and Science Service, under the supervision of the writer, and the results are incorporated in this summary. Since the data from the first two excavations are fully recorded, although only summarily discussed in the publications referred to, because of wartime restrictions in printing costs, the present treatment will avoid a detailed repetition of the cultural criteria and will focus instead upon the interpretation of certain of the findings which deepen our comprehension of some of the non-material aspects of the culture, as revealed particularly in the mortuary customs.

The Frontenac Island site stands in the forefront, among the small group of key stations which have contributed vital segments of information to knowledge of the cultural sequence, chronology and interrelations in New York State prehistory. It has provided most of the human skeletal material on which our understanding of the physical types associated with the Lamoka and Brewerton phases is based; and also the best preserved, most varied and ample bone, antler and shell artifacts of the latter phase. Moreover, although hints of this nature came to light elsewhere, for example at the Brewerton sites (Ritchie, 1940, p. 91), it yielded physical and cultural data of perhaps as full and clear a character as can be hoped for from solely ancient archaeological remains, of the contact metamorphosis of these two groups. The culture-contact situation here revealed by the total evidence is one best described as site unit intrusion of the Type A3 category (i.e. fusion with dominance of the intruding culture). This has been defined as follows, and illustrated specifically, among other examples, for the Frontenac Island site:

"In an area of more or less homogeneous culture, Culture A, a different culture, Culture B, appears as one or more site-units. Subsequently only one culture is identifiable in the area, representing a fusion of elements found in both of the earlier cultures but with elements of Culture B predominating." (Willey, et al., 1956, p. 15.)

This statement of an apparent situation disclosed archaeologically at Frontenac Island (and supported by the evidence of minor sites in the same and other areas) furnishes a clue to the fate of the Lamoka people and their particular cultural assemblage. In a word, their identity both as a people and a culture seems gradually to have disappeared through progressive miscegenation and assimilation, beginning around 2000 B.C. in central New York, perhaps somewhat earlier or later elsewhere within the range of contact. Although elements of the Lamoka culture, such as its characteristic small Lamoka type projectile point, the bone fishhook, stone chopper, and probably other traits, persisted for varying periods in succeeding cultures (the bone fishhook down to historic times), and other trait items became involved in sundry recombinations (see Ritchie, 1945, p. 21), the Lamoka culture as a specific entity passed into limbo. The peculiar physical type of its carriers (page 46) likewise seems to have disappeared as a genetic complex, but in hybrid form it would seem to have persisted within the area from the period of Frontenac Island contact until, at least, Middle Woodland times, as suggested by the scanty data for the local Point Peninsula manifestations (Ritchie, 1944, p. 186).

But if the ancient Lamoka culture and its people were thus assimilated, in the manner of long-subsequent tribal groups such as the Huron, Neutral and Erie by the Confederated Iroquois Nations, is it any more likely that their unknown language survived than the dialects of the three mentioned recent Iroquoian groups? The hypothesis which ascribes the introduction of the Iroquoian language into the Northeast by migrating Lamokans from the Southeast (Byers, 1961, p. 49) seems to the writer dubious in the extreme.

The Frontenac Island Site

Frontenac Island, the only island in the Finger Lakes, lies one half mile off the village of Union Springs on the east shore of Cayuga Lake, seven miles south of its foot, in Cayuga County (Figure 4, site number 8). A small island, slightly under an acre in extent, it consists of a resistant mass of fissured fossiliferous Cobleskill limestone of Upper Silurian age, actually a local coral reef in the Paleozoic sea, elevated about eight feet above the present lake level (380 feet above mean sea level). There is not the slightest reason to believe that the relationship of land to water was essentially different over four thousand years ago when the island was first occupied. A thin, sterile clay subsoil containing water-worn pebbles overlies the nearly level bedrock and varies in depth from zero to about six inches. It was probably deposited by a stream flowing from the mainland, of which a vestige still remains, when the island was submerged by an arm of Lake Iroquois (Figure 2). An old duff or humus zone, one to three inches thick, containing a few artifacts, rests upon the subsoil where present. The entire island is covered with a mantle of dark Indian refuse, ranging from ten inches deep at the northern end where it directly invests the rock, to more than twenty-nine inches at the southern end. Artifacts were found, with notable quantitative and qualitative variations, throughout the refuse cover; while most of the burials and other features occurred within its lower level or were intrusive therefrom into the subsoil or bedrock crevices. No physical stratigraphy was present, the refuse appearing in general homogeneous from top to bottom.

An upper-level occupational zone averaging approximately seven inches in depth was differentiated by its cultural content, which pertained to several complexes and time periods. This part of the site, Frontenac Island 2, will not figure in the following discussion, but will again be referred to in appropriate sections of this work.

The Indians' selection of Frontenac Island as a semipermanent camp site, abandoned probably only in midwinter, depended primarily on its ideal situation with respect to excellent fishing grounds, comprising adjacent and nearby shoals, and shallow water with soft weedy bottom extending northward to the foot of the lake, which is drained by the Seneca River, and surrounded by an extension of the great Montezuma Marsh. The exuberance in this area of fish, wildfowl and deer in 1670 astonished the Jesuit, Peter Raffeix (quoted in Ritchie, 1945, p. 2), and there is every reason to suppose that, in Archaic times when the population was only a fraction of that in the historic Cayuga Iroquois period, animal-food resources were even greater.

Our excavations on the island unearthed many food-animal bones, broken in the usual way, including those of mammals, birds, reptiles and fish (Ritchie, 1945, p. 8).

Food of the Frontenac Islanders

During the State Museum excavations of 1953, involving three hundred square feet of Trench 9 in the thinner refuse mantle of the southwest quadrant of the site, a relatively small sample of animal bone was obtained. Most of this pertained to mammals, lesser amounts to birds, reptiles, fish and mollusks. In the latter categories were about two quarts each of small fishbones and mussel shells, most of the fish pertaining to the bullhead group (*Ictalurus* sp.), of the mollusks to the genus *Elliptio*, ac-

cording to Dr. Edgar M. Reilly, Curator of Zoology, New York State Museum.

Subsequently, in March 1963, the larger part of the bone sample—minus the fish remains, which could not be located in the Museum storage—was submitted for identification and other analysis to John E. Guilday, Associate Curator of Comparative Anatomy at the Carnegie Museum, whose report follows:

"Six hundred and eight bone fragments were available for study. Four hundred and eighty-three or 80 per cent were identifiable. All of the unidentified bone fragments were from large mammal limb bones that had been shattered for marrow extraction. The high per cent of identified material is unusual.

"The sample is a small one in terms of bones, but inasmuch as at least 30 deer are represented, and if other species are present in their true *in situ* proportions [true for all except fish, as already remarked], it appears to be a significant one.

"The faunal remains from the Frontenac Island site agree with the Lamoka material in several important points: the emphasis on big game, the lack of aquatic resources other than mammals, the lack of butchering marks on the bones. Deer, bear and elk accounted for 93 per cent of the estimated weight of meat, raccoons 2.6 per cent, aquatic mammals 1.25 per cent, other aquatic resources only .12 per cent, and birds of all types a mere .28 per cent.

"At least three of the deer represented by the 30 individuals accounted for were bucks with antlers firmly attached, fall or early winter kills. Eleven mandibles representing eight deer were, based upon degree of tooth wear, all adult, the youngest over one year, the oldest in excess of eight years of age.

"Butchering marks on deer were virtually

non-existent although detailed search was made for them.

"Three elk astragali were examined. Two of them, representing two animals, bore butchering marks indicative of disarticulation of the hock joint. There was not enough elk material present to attempt any further observations on butchering."

FAUNAL LIST—FRONTENAC ISLAND

Species		Items	%	Indiv.	%	Est. lbs. meat	%
Total		483		68		4606 lb.	
Mammals		468	97%	58	87%	4553 lb.	98.8%
Canis familiaris	dog	1	0.2%	1	1.4%	–	–
Canis lupus	gray wolf	5	1.0%	1	1.4%	30 lbs.	.6%
Ursus americanus	black bear	30	6.2%	3	4.2%	600 lbs.	13.0%
Procyon lotor	raccoon	15	3.1%	8	11.7%	120 lbs.	2.6%
Lutra canadensis	otter	2	0.4%	1	1.4%	10 lbs.	0.2%
Lynx sp.	bobcat or lynx	1	0.2%	1	1.4%	15 lbs.	.3%
Marmota monax	woodchuck	1	0.2%	1	1.4%	5 lbs.	.1%
Sciurus carolinensis	gray squirrel	9	1.8%	4	5.6%	4 lbs.	.08%
Ondatra zibethicus	muskrat	5	1.0%	2	2.8%	4 lbs.	.08%
Castor canadensis	beaver	11	2.3%	3	4.2%	45 lbs.	.97%
Erethizon dorsatum	porcupine	5	1.0%	2	2.8%	20 lbs.	.4%
Odocoileus virginianus	Virginia deer	352	72.8%	30	44.0%	3000 lbs.	65.0%
Cervus canadensis	elk	24	4.9%	2	2.8%	700 lbs.	15.2%
Birds		9	1.8%	4	5.6%	13 lbs.	.27%
Meleagris gallopavo	turkey	3	.6%	1	1.4%	9 lbs.	.19%
Bonasa umbellus	ruffed grouse	1	.2%	1	1.4%	1 lb.	.02%
Ectopistes migratorius	pass. pigeon	1	.2%	1	1.4%	1 lb.	.02%
duck species		1	.2%	1	1.4%	2 lbs.	.04%
unidentified bird		3	.6%	–	–	–	–
Reptiles		5	1.0%	3	4.2%	3 lbs.	.06%
Terrapene carolina	box turtle	1	.2%	1	1.4%	–	–
Clemmys insculpta	wood turtle	1	.2%	1	1.4%	–	–
Chelydra serpentina	snapping turtle	1	.2%	1	1.4%	3 lbs.	.06%
Fish		2	.4%	2	1.4%	3 lbs.	.06%
Esox lucius	northern pike	1	.2%	1	1.4%	3 lbs.	.06%
Ictalurus sp.	bullhead	1	.2%	1	1.4%	–	–

Radiocarbon Dates

Three radiocarbon dates, obtained by as many laboratories, on charcoal samples taken from hearths at various loci and depths in the refuse mantle suggest that the first inhabitants arrived around 2500 B.C. and the most recent occupants of the Frontenac phase (Frontenac Island 1) departed for the last time some five hundred years later.[1] This estimate places the total period of the island's habitation within the Xerothermic interval of maximum warmth and dryness, which has been correlated with an oak-hickory forest maximum in the northeastern United States.

Hunting, Fishing, Food Processing and Other Equipment

The subsistence pattern of the Frontenac Islanders appears to have been typical of the Archaic cultural stage, as already de-

[1] The earliest date, 2980 B.C. ±260 years, obtained by the solid-carbon method (C-191, Arnold and Libby, 1951, p. 114), was based on a hearth sample from near the bottom of the deposits in Trench 4, Section 4, where this intrusive feature had destroyed the lower portion of extended Burial 47, which lay upon bedrock, twenty-three and a half inches below the surface (Ritchie, 1945, pp. 6, 57, 115). It was surmised that this feature dated from the initial period of Lamoka-Laurentian contact on the site (Ritchie, 1951b, p. 31).

Two younger dates resulted from assays, by the gas method, of samples collected during the 1953 excavations in Trench 9, Section 2. The first, 2013 B.C. ±80 years (Y-459, Deevey, Gralenski and Hoffren, 1959, p. 161) from feature 8, at a depth of twenty-two inches; the second, 1723 B.C. ±250 years (W-545, Rubin and Alexander, 1960, p. 180) from feature 9 only a foot north of feature 8 and twenty and a half inches below the surface. These hearths, each about a foot in diameter and four inches thick, lay at opposite ends of a mass of boiling-stones (page 113) and there were no immediate artifact associations. Their overlapping dates seem too young and suggest the possibility of contamination by the thick root mass from the vegetation cover on this part of the island.

scribed for the Lamoka and Brewerton phases. The complete, quantified, comparative trait list for all three groups has been published elsewhere (Ritchie, 1945, pp. 30–46). The typologies of the hunting and fishing equipment were, however, enriched by a few new contrivances, chiefly the forms of the projectile point and the barbed bone point, and there were quantitative differences of some apparent significance within the total category of artifacts for food securing and processing. Thus, ground slate points of two varieties were found here: one broad, plain-stemmed example (Plate 34, Figure 29) among the grave goods of Burial 78 (Plate 43), and a narrow point with faceted blade and serrated stem (Plate 34, Figure 28) in the deep refuse. There was also a fragment of a probable ground slate ulu (Ritchie, 1945, Plate 8, Figure 21). The crescentic atlatl weight, with seven examples, was the only variety of the "bannerstone" found here (Plate 34, Figure 33) and this form was not present at the Brewerton stations (see Plate 29, Figure 24), although it is known from other components of the Brewerton phase (Ritchie, 1940, Plate XXXII, Figure 16, from the Smoky Hollow site). A novel form of probable shaft straightener is shown on Plate 34, Figure 31, while several additions to the barbed-bone-point inventory for the Brewerton phase appear on Plate 35, Figures 10, 11. Unique objects concerned with the food complex at Frontenac Island comprise antler spoons (Plate 36, Figures 15, 16), a cup made from an excavated basal section of shed elk antler (Plate 36, Figure 14) and probable dishes, found in very poor condition, from the carapace of the box and wood turtles.

Stone food-grinding implements for processing wild vegetable substances were represented by a total of only twenty-two

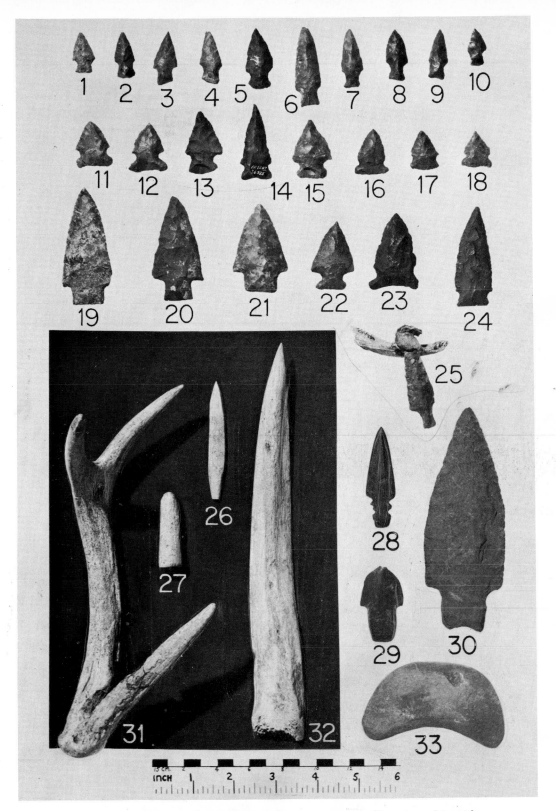

PLATE 34 Hunting weapons of the Frontenac phase. 1–10 projectile points of Lamoka type; 11–18 projectile points of Brewerton Side-Notched type; 19–21, 30, projectile points (30 is a spearhead) of Genesee type; 22 projectile point of Brewerton Corner-Notched type; 23 projectile point of Brewerton Eared-Notched type; 24 untyped projectile point; 25 Lamoka point imbedded in bony excrescence on human rib; 26 flat bone projectile point; 27 blunt, conical, antler projectile point; 28, 29 ground slate points or knives; 31 antler shaft straightener; 32 bone dagger (faintly striped with red paint); 33 atlatl weight or bannerstone.

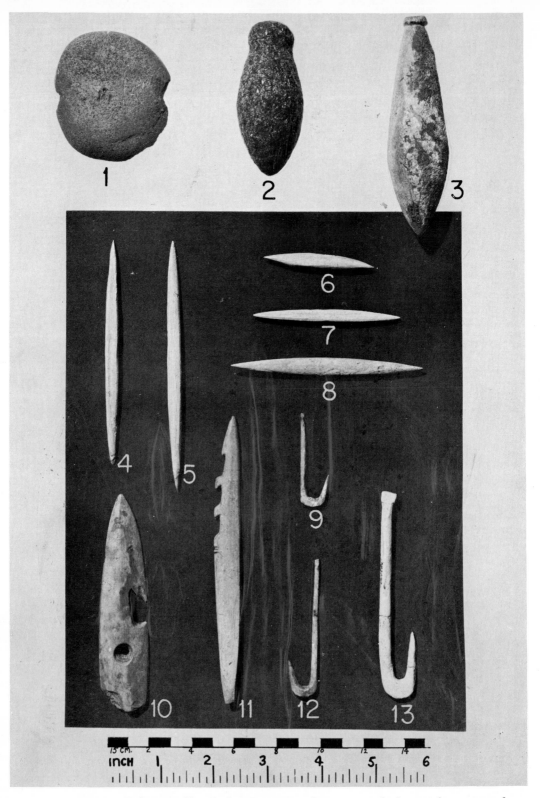

PLATE 35 Fishing tackle of the Frontenac phase. 1 notched netsinker; 2, 3 plummets; 4, 5 probable leister points; 6–8 bone gorges; 9, 12, 13 bone fishhooks; 10, 11 barbed bone points.

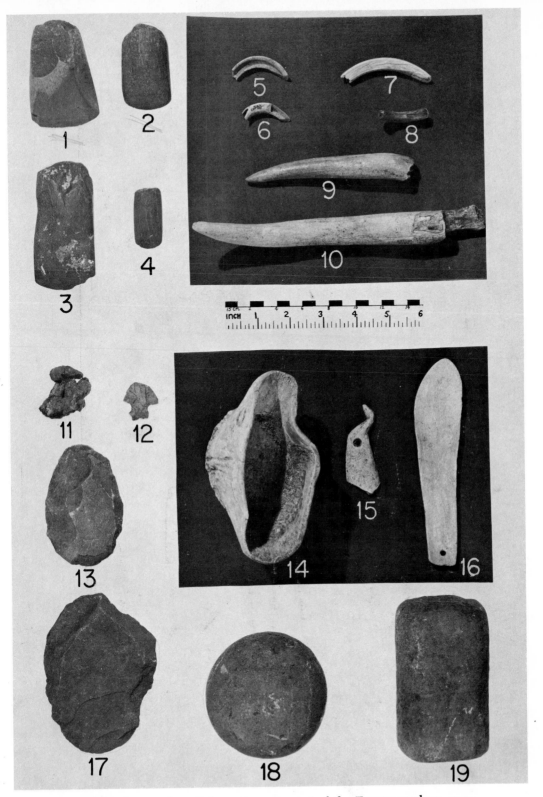

PLATE 36 Woodworking tools and domestic equipment of the Frontenac phase. 1, 2, 4 plano-convex adzes; 3 celt; 5–8 beaver-incisor cutting tools; 9 antler punch; 10 antler chisel; 11, 12 fire-making set composed of iron pyrites and flint striker made from projectile point; 13, 17 choppers; 14 cup from shed elk antler; 15, 16 antler spoons; 18 muller; 19 short pestle.

artifacts, comprising shallow mortars, mullers, and cylindrical pestles (Plate 36, Figures 18, 19), and were thus relatively and absolutely scarce at Frontenac Island, as were the carbonized remains of acorns, hickory nuts and butternuts, facts suggesting a small use of vegetal products. This is logical enough at a primarily summer camp where activities pivoted about fishing, as attested by the abundance of fishing gear, comprising notched stone netsinkers (Plate 35, Figure 1), bone fishhooks (manufactured by two methods already described, page 48) (Plate 35, Figures 9, 12, 13); bone gorges (Plate 35, Figures 6–8); barbed bone points of several forms (Plate 35, Figures 10, 11); probable leister points (Plate 35, Figures 4, 5) and stone plummets (Plate 35, Figures 2, 3). I believe the latter were employed as sinkers in hook-and-line or trot-line fishing, and in the first capacity they might have performed the additional service of sounding or feeling the bottom, as modern fishermen (the writer included) employ a lead plummet-like sinker. Accurate knowledge of the character of the bottom and depth of the water is indispensable for angling success. Strangely, no bone tools of the kind thought to be for net weaving in the Lamoka culture (Plate 13, Figures 1–8) were recovered at Frontenac Island.

While fishing appears to have predominated at this site, hunting must have been actively pursued, utilizing a wide variety of stone, bone and antler projectile points (Plate 34, Figures 1–30); the atlatl weight (Plate 34, Figure 33); the bone dagger, sometimes ornamented with red paint (Plate 34, Figure 32); the shaft straightener (Plate 34, Figure 31); and, for pursuing game and bringing it to bay, dogs of two breeds, one of terrier size (nine examples), the other as big as a collie (three

examples) (see Ritchie, 1945, p. 7). The first variety was known to the Lamoka and Brewerton peoples (pages 52, 96), but the big dog appears here for the first time. Incidentally, it or a similar breed continued in use in the New York area until historic times, as attested by subsequently mentioned discoveries.

An affectionate regard for the dog is indicated by separate burials in six cases; while recognition of his invaluable services to the hunter seems a logical inference from the fact that in all other instances save one, an infant (Burial 23), dog burials were the accompaniment of males, usually provided with hunting and other equipment.

For want of a more suitable place of mention, I interject here a brief word concerning the intentional burial of an adult bald eagle at the Frontenac Island site (Ritchie, 1945, p. 8 and Plate 4, Figure 3). One might conjecture whether it was kept as a pet, or for its valuable feathers, or in connection with some ritualistic practice.

Among the woodworking and general-purpose tools of the Frontenac phase the following should be mentioned as of obvious significance in the culture: flake knives, some made from prismatic flakes with retouched edge (Plate 37, Figure 8); ovate and triangulate knives (Plate 37, Figures 6, 7, 14); side- or corner-notched knives with convex edges (Plate 37, Figure 15); drills of a variety of styles, chiefly straight, with expanded base, or with T-shaped base (Plate 37, Figures 1–5); celts (Plate 36, Figure 3); plano-convex and beveled adzes (Plate 36, Figures 1, 2, 4); gouges, one of stone, two of bone (Plate 38, Figure 14); unpitted and oval bipitted hammerstones (Plate 37, Figures 13, 16); anvilstones (Plate 37, Figure 17); pitted stones of unknown function; whetstones (Plate 37, Figures 12, 18); choppers of several shapes (Plate 36, Figures 13, 17); bone and antler flakers (Plate 37, Figures 9, 10); knives, chisels and gravers made from beaver incisors (Plate 36, Figures 5–8); and antler punches and chisels (Plate 36, Figures 9, 10).

For the first time in the cultural sequence in New York, a method of fire making was disclosed by the discovery with several burials, two males and a female, of iron pyrites masses, altered through decay to limonite, in one instance (Burial 94) with a striker made from a flint point (Plate 36, Figures 11, 12). Hearths or fireplaces of the same kind as described for the Lamoka Lake site (page 60) were numerous and present throughout the refuse mantle at Frontenac Island. There was also a burned stone platform, about fifty inches in diameter and seven inches in thickness, thought to be a cooking feature, and very similar to those uncovered on the Bent site and elsewhere (pages 126, 159).

Of unusual interest, and unique occurrence, were hoards of water-worn pebbles, two to three inches in diameter, chiefly of limestone from the mainland beaches, which were obviously assembled for use as stone-boilers. There ten of these features (four found in 1953), the number of individual stones in each ranging from 70 to 438. Many of them were closely associated with hearths, and the shattered fragments resulting from their use were present everywhere on the site (Plate 42). (See Ritchie, 1945, pp. 6–7 for fuller descriptions of the hearths and other features mentioned here.)

No insight was obtained through the excavations to the character of housing at Frontenac Island. Probably flimsy, bark- or rush-covered shelters were sufficient during the periods of the year when the island was inhabited. Beyond question the lodges

were shifted about from time to time to utilize the entire small available surface, and the hearth pits were dug in any convenient place. Over the centuries there came to be overlapping, as well as superposition, of hearths, and especially of graves, as will be noted below.

Dress and Ornament

A unique, eyed bone needle (Plate 38, Figure 10), found, curiously enough, within the skull of an adult woman (Burial 28), offers a clue to the dress of these Archaic people, since it suggests the possibility of tailored skin garments. Beyond this, it is only possible to add that bone and stone scrapers of several varieties (Plate 38, Figures 8, 9, 11, 12, 15), the latter not numerous for a site of this size, would seem to indicate the preparation of skins and hides on the site, while a multitude of awls, mostly of bone (Plate 38, Figures 1–7) but also of copper (Plate 38, Figure 13), hints at their manufacture into garments and other articles.

More light is shed on personal decoration by the grave goods at Frontenac Island than by discoveries at any other Archaic station in the Northeast. In many instances these were probably carried to the grave as adornments to the body (necklaces, bracelets, pendants) or as embellishments to the clothing, showing that the corpse was dressed, presumably in his best raiment, not simply wrapped in a robe or shroud. Some of the items may have been intended primarily or entirely as charms or amulets, the animal teeth and claws particularly.

The list includes devices in several media —bone, antler, animal teeth, shell and stone —and in several categories. The most extraordinary specimen is a unique, six-tooth

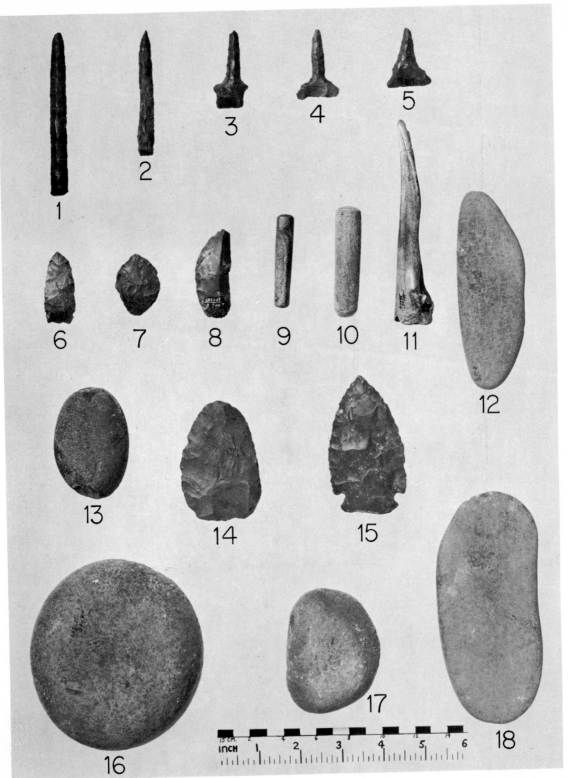

PLATE 37 Tools of the Frontenac phase. 1–5 flint drills; 6, 7, 14 trianguloid and ovate knives; 8 knife from retouched flake; 9, 10 antler chipping tools; 11 deer-ulna knife; 12, 18 tabular whetstones; 13 pebble hammerstone; 15 corner-notched knife; 16 bipitted hammerstone; 17 anvilstone.

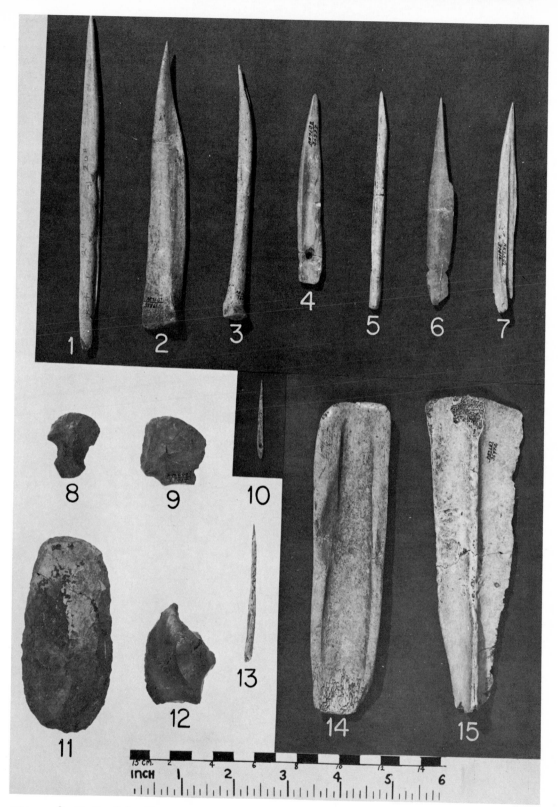

PLATE 38 Tools of the Frontenac phase. 1–7 bone awls; 8 stemmed end scraper; 9 simple end scraper; 10 eyed bone needle; 11 large double-ended scraper; 12 side scraper from retouched flake; 13 copper awl; 14 bone gorge; 15 deer-scapula scraper.

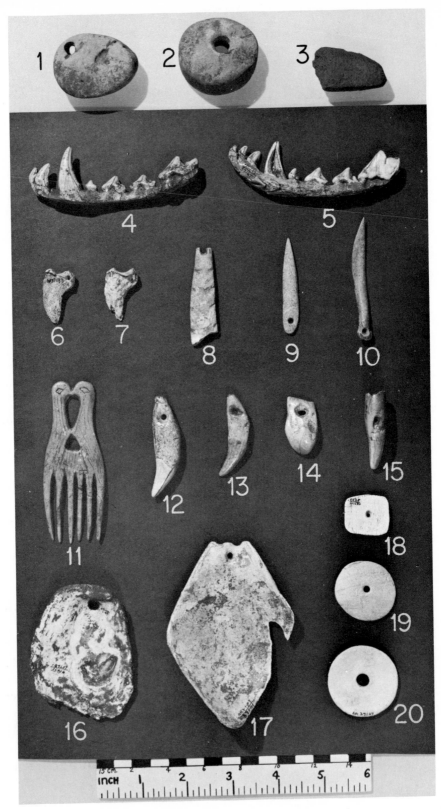

PLATE 39 Personal ornaments of the Frontenac phase. 1, 2 naturally perforated, water-worn pebbles; 3 hematite paintstone; 4, 5 pair of wolf mandibles with ground-off bases; 6, 7 claw cores of the black bear; 8 fragmentary antler pendant; 9 imitation and 10 actual styliform bone of deer, perforated for plume holders (?); 11 effigy antler comb; 12 perforated black-bear canine; 13 perforated wolf canine; 14 perforated elk canine; 15 canine of immature black bear drilled through anterior root wall; 16 oyster-shell pendant; 17–20 varieties of marine-shell pendants.

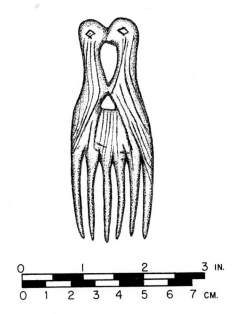

0   1   2   3 IN.

0   1   2   3   4   5   6   7 CM.

PLATE 40 Drawing of effigy antler comb shown on Plate 39, Figure 11. Frontenac phase.

antler comb, with effigy top depicting two inward-facing birds' heads with united beaks, the eyes outlined as incised rhomboids, and other incising present over the entire front side (Plate 39, Figure 11, and Plate 40). Probably the oldest known bone comb from North America, this ornament formed part of the rich mortuary offerings of a young adult man, about nineteen years of age, shown in his grave (Burial 78) in Plate 43. Besides this comb, the articles lying over or near the lower left arm include the long-bone flute shown in Plate 41, Figure 8, the ground slate point and a whetstone, doubtless used to keep it sharp (Plate 34, Figure 29; Plate 37, Figure 12), a chopper, drills, antler flaker, beaver-incisor engraver, bone awl, antler punch, and iron pyrites for fire making.

The perforated canines of the bear, wolf and elk figured as necklace elements or jacket (?) ornaments in several graves. Those of the bear were of two styles, the adult tooth with apex perforated (Plate 39, Figure 12) and the immature tooth with incomplete root formation, perforated through one lateral wall (Plate 39, Figure 15). Twenty such teeth, representing at least five young bears, were found distributed from the neck to the pelvis of a child (Burial 19), as though sewed upon a shirt or jacket front; along with bone awls, a worked beaver incisor, a shell pendant and an effigy antler spoon fragment (Plate 36, Figure 15). Perforated elk canines, found in two graves, a cluster of three under the chin of Burial 4, are illustrated on Plate 39, Figure 14; wolf canines in Figure 13 of the same plate.

Ground wolf mandibles, which seem to have been hair ornaments, occurred in pairs, one set with a male burial (number 105), lying on either side of the skull (Plate 39, Figures 4, 5). Molar teeth of the wolf with ground base, evidently from similar ornaments, occurred singly in other graves.

Claw cores of a small species of hawk and of the black bear were present in a number of graves. The chitinous cover, which may have been basally perforated for suspension or attachment, had of course decayed away. While some were found singly among the little mound of assorted grave goods, most of them came from Burial 111, that of an adult man, and were scattered over the chest, arms and around the right wrist, as though sewed upon a shirt or jacket and made into a bracelet (Plate 39, Figures 6, 7). This was an especially well accoutered grave, with offerings too numerous to repeat here (for list, burial photographs and other data on this grave, see Ritchie, 1945, pp. 71–72, 148–51. Most of the grave goods are also illustrated on Plates 10–12).

Notched, engraved and painted antler pendants, as well as the pendant-like arti-

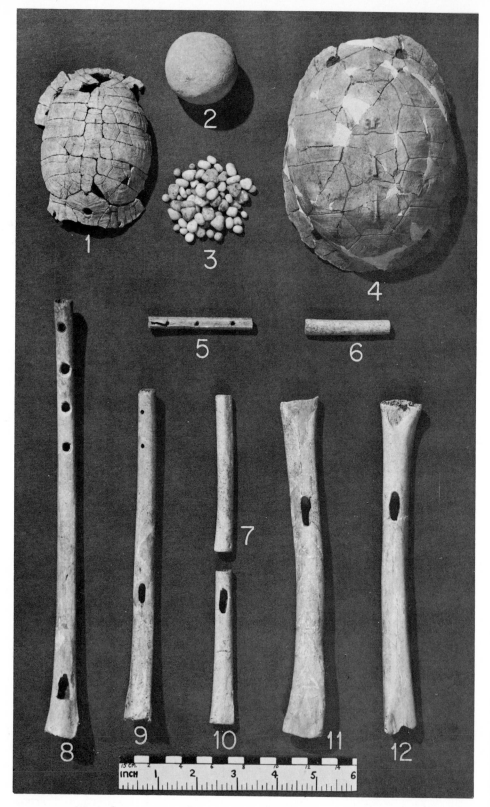

PLATE 41 Musical or ceremonial instruments of the Frontenac phase. 1 rattle made from wood-turtle shell; 2 spherical pebble, probably a toy; 3, 4 rattle made from box-turtle shell and quartz pebbles found inside it; 5, 8–12 varieties of bone flutes or whistles; 6, 7 bone tubes, probably whistles.

facts described for the Lamoka phase (page 62), were found both as grave goods and in the refuse at Frontenac Island and constitute one of the many close links with the Lamoka culture (Plate 39, Figure 8).

Shell ornaments, on the other hand, are a new increment, not recovered previously from New York Archaic sites. Nearly all were found as grave goods in positions suggesting their use as pendants or necklace elements. The drilled, but otherwise unmodified, oyster valve, shown on Plate 39, Figure 16, is from Burial 23 previously referred to (page 112). More elaborate are the pyriform pendants and discoidal (one rectangular) objects of conch shell shown on Plate 39, Figures 17–20. Nearly all such objects came from the graves of children and a young woman (Burials 82 and 94, in particular). Also found were two small shell receptacles, one cut from the larger end of a conch (Burial 81), the other a local mussel valve filled with red paint (Burial 57).

Among the problematical articles, perhaps ornaments, were imperforate or perforated styliform bones of the deer (Plate 39, Figure 10) and bone imitations thereof (Figure 9, same plate), found in a number of cases near the skull, which may have been the pin-like fasteners to the hair of plumes, or other ornaments attached to cords, analogous to those of several Plains tribes, made of wood or bone.

In the problematical category also are the naturally perforated and water-worn limestone pebbles, of oval or irregular shape (Plate 39, Figures 1, 2), found as definite mortuary associations with three burials, eleven of the thirteen specimens with an adult male (Burial 135).

Three ground and faceted paintstones (Plate 39, Figure 3), all of Clinton fossil-iferous hematite found in this region, permit conclusion of the inventory of personal ornaments with the statement that red ocher pigment was doubtless employed, not only for the embellishment of bone weapons (daggers) and ornaments (antler pendants), but also for the face and body. A light sprinkling of this paint over the corpse was recorded in ten graves.

The marine-shell artifacts, fashioned from various sections of the common whelk or conch shell of the Atlantic coast, and the native copper awls (nine in number), most likely derived from the copper mining and working Lake Superior area, comprise the only indications of trade relationships with outside regions found at Frontenac Island. The Brewerton complex involved at Frontenac Island was the undoubted source of the copper objects (page 101). One is tempted to raise the question whether the presence here in central New York of exotic material derived from several distant sources points to the distinct possibility that in this relatively late phase of the Archaic cultural stage in the Northeast, definite trading channels were becoming established, perhaps through structured friendships with groups favorably situated either for direct exchange of the desired commodities, or as middlemen. It seems extremely doubtful that journeys to distant parts were made by our local Archaic groups, whose whole way of life, as revealed archaeologically, conveys the impression of provincialism. This is not to deny the universality of human contact and influence suggested by the wider distributions of many Archaic culture traits, but it is clear that, at the Brewerton and Frontenac level, the well-marked trade connections of Middle Woodland times, especially in the Hopewellian manifestation, were in an incipient stage of development.

Combat

Trade and contact outside the area sometimes led to warfare and raiding, but such evidences of hostilities as came to light at Frontenac Island indicate friction only between the two groups involved in the Frontenac contact situation, viz., the Lamoka and Brewerton. It is probable that this enmity gradually subsided with the progressive assimilation of the former, as suggested by the archaeological criteria for physical and cultural interaction.

While traumatic lesions, mainly long-bone fractures, apparently suffered accidentally, were observed on the skeletons of both sexes (along with arthritic and dental pathologies like those already described on pages 46, 92, for similar groups), a second group of injuries, obviously resulting from wounds, was confined to adult males. They seem referable to combat, since they comprise skull fractures, both healed and fatal, and projectile damage involving bone. One case of particular note (Burial 67) exhibits surgery to the skull, in an unsuccessful effort to remove a deeply imbedded flint point tip. (For details and illustrations, see Ritchie, 1945, pp. 10–13; Plate 7, Figure 2; Plates 51, 52.) In several male burials, projectile points were found in positions, as within the thoracic cavity, suggesting that they constituted the instruments of death (Plate 34, Figure 25).

Aesthetic and Recreational Activities

Whether for recreational or ceremonial purposes (or for both), the Frontenac Islanders had such contrivances as bone flutes and whistles of several styles, and rattles made from the multiply perforated (for handle attachment) box-turtle shell, with small white quartz pebbles as shakers (Plate 41, Figures 1, 3, 4). It is surely not without significance that all these instruments were found as burial furniture of adult males, ranging in age from approximately nineteen to forty-four, where such determination was feasible (Plate 43). In some cases (Burials 77, 111), more than one flute accompanied the body, which was usually provided with an assortment of other, and utilitarian, equipment.

The simple forms of the Lamoka flute or whistle have been described and illustrated (page 69). Those from Frontenac Island combine the single features of the Lamoka types, and greatly elaborate them (Plate 41, Figures 5, 8–12). The variously perforated flute, and perhaps the turtle-shell rattle, are Lamoka-culture derivatives in the Frontenac phase, only the simple bone tube, possibly a whistle, occurs also in the Brewerton phase (Plate 41, Figures 6, 7).

Whatever aesthetic expression of the Frontenac people went into the creation of highly perishable objects can never be determined. Existing evidence from bone and antler devices, already referred to for the most part, comprises simple and rather rude carving of animal heads (Plate 36, Figure 15; Plate 39, Figure 11), engraving or incising on a bone flute (Plate 41, Figure 11), and on the bone comb illustrated on Plate 40; and striping with red ocher (Plate 34, Figure 32).

Mortuary Customs and Some Social and Religious Inferences

During the long Archaic stage of occupation at Frontenac Island, many burials were made in shallow graves dug into the refuse or through some part of it and the shallow subsoil to reach bedrock. Where wide crevices occurred in the latter, burials were put therein at the deepest level possible. While no explored portion of the island was without graves, there was a notable tendency to concentrate them where the refuse was thickest, or over the eastern and southern sections (see map of excavations in Ritchie, 1945). Remains of 159 individuals were uncovered in the major investigations, of four others during the limited excavations of 1953. This constitutes by far the largest skeletal series from an Archaic station in the eastern United States north of Kentucky, and it has provided data of great significance to various problems concerning early human populations in this area.

Although fairly well preserved because of the high soil alkalinity (pH over 8 in most places), with free calcium carbonate present, nearly every skeleton was extensively pressure-fractured (Plates 42, 43). Complete restoration was possible, however, of forty-five adult skulls (twenty-nine males, sixteen females), and a number of others were partially reassembled. Metrical and morphological studies of the series showed that two fundamentally different groups were present, the dolichocranial type already described as the Lamoka people (page 46) and the brachycranial type of the Brewerton phase, found also intrusively at Lamoka Lake (pages 46, 92). Probable hybridization involving these two groups was indicated by a mesocranial subtype showing various other intermediate characteristics of the skull and face (Ritchie, 1945, pp. 18–20, 83–89). Correlations of these physical groups with segments of the cultural assemblage, as shown in burial mode and typology of grave goods, revealed that grave goods of Lamoka type were associated principally with flexed burials and the dolichocranial form of skull; grave goods of Brewerton Lau-

rentian type occurred almost exclusively with extended burials and the brachycranial skull form; while grave goods combining traits distinctive of both the Lamoka and Brewerton phases were found only with extended burials and with skulls of both morphological types, leading to the conclusions already stated on page 104. (See full data in Ritchie, 1945, pp. 17–22.)

Some further inferences may now be attempted from these data, directed toward a fuller comprehension of the socio-religious and related aspects of the culture. To begin with there were definite suggestions concerning the relative social significance of the sexes, and some hints on the sexual division of labor. There were also unmistakable indications of social stratification, involving the dominance and importance of males of the invading brachycranial group. Age, as well as sex, was a factor of worth in this society, if we are to base our assumptions on burial offerings, and there were slender, but striking, tokens of parental sentiment.

These statements rest upon the following observations, which can be checked from the published data, and are adduced here in the same order as the postulations.

Over 60 per cent of the adult (but not senile) males were provided with mortuary accompaniments, while only 34 per cent of the adult females were so supplied. With a single exception, an infant (Burial 23), all dog associations were with males, who had also been given all the musical instruments, most of the fishing tackle and hunting gear, including daggers as well as projectile points, and the tools, such as drills, flakers, beaver-incisor gravers, etc.

Burial gifts to women were scanty, with one exception (Burial 94), consisting of a few ornaments (perforated elk incisors, shell and antler pendants, plume holders

PLATE 42 Loosely flexed burial of child with accompanying skull of young woman at Frontenac Island site. Part of a mass of boiling-stones at anterior edge of grave. Photograph courtesy of the Rochester Museum of Arts and Sciences.

PLATE 43 Extended burial of young man with rich offerings over left arm at Frontenac Island site. Photograph courtesy of the Rochester Museum of Arts and Sciences.

(?), hawk claws, and a mussel shell full of red paint) and such implements as a bone needle, harpoon, plummet, gorges, celt, awls, bone knives and scrapers, worked beaver incisors, a chopper, spoon, fire-making kit, and a few flint points, perhaps really knives.

Where present among the males, there was a striking differential in the quantity, and to some extent quality, of the grave goods. A small number of individuals, all referable by skull form or burial mode to the brachycranial group, and all interred in the extended position, were extraordinarily well accoutered (for example, Burials 66, 78, 79 and especially 111) (Plate

43). These men, some of them as young as around nineteen, were clearly very important personages, or much beloved.

There is a strong suggestion that we have here the roots of a social hierarchy, in this instance evidently founded upon conquest, which were to expand more fully in the succeeding period in our area, and parallel at that or a slightly later time, such a classic example of social order, as seen in the Adena culture.

In scrutinizing the burials of other age groups at Frontenac Island, we observe that of twenty infant graves, only fifteen per cent had even a minimum of offerings, such as a projectile point or awl, a perforated tooth, or simply a sprinkle of red ocher. Outstanding in the small series was Burial 23, with more eloquent testimony of parental grief. This body had been buried in the probably still warm ashes of a hearth, an oyster-shell pendant lay on its chest, and a puppy of about the same size as the baby had been immolated and flexed directly upon it in intimate companionship (Ritchie, 1945, Plates 29, 30).

Young children appear to have been held in higher regard, since 50 per cent of the fourteen graves had been furnished with some provision for, we presume, a contemplated personal permanence. Certain of these burials are worth a few remarks; number 19, for example, had the twenty bear teeth sewed on shirt or jacket (page 117), along with bone awls, a beaver-incisor tool, a shell pendant, and about half of an antler spoon with effigy handle. The old fracture line showed that the spoon had been defective when placed in the grave. This consignment of old, broken or worn-out articles for the use of the dead will be met with later on as a matter of regular practice in the Early and Middle Woodland cultures.

A child of around five (Burial 82) with no fewer than six conch-shell neck ornaments, and two plume holders (?), was well endowed for this culture. A nine-year-old (Burial 112) had at his right hand a spheroidal water-shaped pebble nearly two inches in diameter, apparently a toy (Plate 41, Figure 2).

The most provocative interment (number 64A) was of a child approximately three years old, who had placed against his right side the skull of a young woman, obviously decapitated since the articulated cervical vertebrae were still in place (Plate 42). Was this a favored child of the upper social stratum for whom some lesser surrogate mother, perhaps a captive woman, had been immolated?

Among the adolescents, of which only six were found, the percentage of mortuary bestowals rises to 66 per cent, highest of any group at the site, but the amounts were trivial.

At the bottom of the group were the old people (estimated at over sixty years of age from cranial and pubic-bone criteria) with only three men, wholly unprovided for, and one woman who was equipped with a bone awl and a whetstone to keep it sharp for the old-age task of sewing.

Among other general observations should be mentioned what appeared to be family burial plots, suggested by concentrations of graves, contributed to over a long period, since later burials disturbed to varying extent prior ones (Ritchie, 1945, p. 10 and Plates 20, 47–50). Cremations and bone bundles found therein may mean that persons dying far from home and transportable only in one of these conditions were interred among their kinsmen. This sentiment has been recorded for many primitive folk, including the Penobscot hunters of Maine (Speck, 1940, p. 259), whose way of life, it seems to me, provides some illuminating parallels and analogies for our Laurentian groups.

THE RIVER PHASE

In the past few years, because of fortunate site discoveries in eastern New York, particularly in the Hudson and Mohawk valleys, it has been possible to recognize three heretofore unknown Late Archaic cultures, termed respectively the River phase, the Snook Kill phase, and the Sylvan Lake complex, the latter only recently defined (page xix). The characteristic projectile-point types of these phases were previously recorded from surface and some excavated sites with mixed cultural components within the area, but no unequivocal association of traits could be established prior to the finding of closed or relatively "pure" unicultural sites. A similar condition still exists in the same region with respect to other probable Archaic complexes, including the putative Vosburg phase.

What the writer has called the River phase takes its name from the River site (Coh. 8-3), situated on the west bank of the Hudson, about two and a half miles north of Waterford, Saratoga County (Figure 4, site number 15), which was named and excavated by William J. Kirby of Cohoes and Thomas F. Finn, Jr., of De-Freestville between 1941 and 1949. In the latter year, when most of the site had been dug away, it was reported to the writer, whose investigation is elsewhere discussed in detail (Ritchie, 1958, pp. 34, 43–53, 55–58).

At least two components were present at the River site, an upper one of Late Point Peninsula provenience separated from the lower component of the River phase by a sterile six-inch alluvial layer. Geological interpretations of the site suggest a somewhat higher water plane for the Hudson at the period of first occupation.

Essentially modern conditions seem to have prevailed at the much larger Bent site of the River phase, located in the Mohawk Valley and presently to be described. At the latter site, radiocarbon dates of 1350 and 1930 B.C. would make the culture coeval with some part of the presumptive Younger Peron High sea level, dated between c. 2000–1000 B.C., when mean sea level is said to have attained a maximum elevation of ten feet above its modern level. This transgression of the sea is believed by Fairbridge to have been correlated with a climatic interval of hotter and drier summers (Fairbridge, 1958, pp. 477–78). Such a rise of sea level might have affected the upper Hudson River where the River site is located, but could not have influenced the Mohawk River, above the falls at Cohoes.

The Bent site (Ams. 73) is situated on the Mohawk some thirteen miles above these falls, but, like the River site, on the flood plain, one mile west of Scotia, Schenectady County (Figure 4, site number 16). It lies approximately one thousand feet north of the present river shore on gently rising ground, some eight feet above the normal level of the river. The site is flanked by two postglacial river terraces and still farther north by the steeper and higher glacially veneered slopes of the original valley. The terraces, at elevations of twenty and forty feet, respectively, above the stream, are delta remnants of sand and gravel laid down by the swollen Iroquois stage of the Mohawk River, near the close of the Port Huron stadial, when the icy waters of Lake Iroquois were discharging through the Rome outlet into the standing waters of Lake Albany. With subsidence of the Lake Albany waters, following the drainage of Lake Iroquois through Covey Pass into the St. Lawrence Valley (page 14) and the subsequent lowering of the Mohawk level, the Mohawk River began its erosion of the delta deposits west of Scotia, creating in its meanderings the two terraces referred to. Since reaching its present level, the river has been depositing clays and silts along its channel in a narrow flood plain, covering the older coarser deposits, and lapping against the lower terrace. The site, a concise description of which follows, is intrinsically related to this later stage of the river's history.

The Bent site was reported to the writer in the fall of 1959 by Arthur C. Glamm, Jr., of Schenectady, who had found artifacts exposed by bulldozer operations in the commercial removal of topsoil. Investigation showed that the material was coming from a buried silt stratum, and that it represented on a much more generous scale the little-known complex from the lower level of the River site. Excavations by the New York State Museum and Science Service, conducted by Robert E. Funk and the writer, assisted by several members of the Van Epps-Hartley Chapter, New York State Archeological Association, were carried out in 1960–61.

The site was found to be of extraordinary size for the Archaic stage, test pits showing material distributed over approximately five acres. Seven major zones of deposition were recognized, all representing floodplain deposits of silt resulting from successive inundations by the river over a long period. These zones were distinguished principally by differences in color and texture, and in amounts and kinds of cultural remains. Two zones only, C and E, need

concern us here. (Ritchie and Funk have prepared a full site report.)

Zone C, the principal occupation stratum, was dark brown to black in color, depending on the amount of charcoal and other organic contents, averaged eleven inches in thickness, and lay between twenty and thirty-one inches below the surface. Most of the features and artifacts of the River phase came from this layer. The features consisted of hearths with burned stones; irregular beds of burned stones, probably for roasting meat and leaching acorns (Plate 44); and shallow pits, possibly for acorn storage. No postmold patterns or other satisfactory evidences of housing were discovered.

Zone E, separated from C by a nearly sterile silt band averaging twenty-one inches in thickness, produced scanty evidence, in the form of hearths, calcined animal bone, and projectile points, of the Sylvan Lake occupation characterized by small stemmed points of Wading River type.

The artifact assemblage from Zone C at the Bent site provides the fullest insight yet available into the life of the River-phase people. The approximately one thousand artifacts, all of stone, appear to have been solely concerned with the subsistence activities of an Archaic community.

Before describing them, some additional data on distribution and other aspects of the culture are in order. Surface occurrence of the diagnostic Normanskill point type seems fairly well confined to eastern New York, with the nuclear area in the lower Mohawk Valley and the Hudson Valley from about Glens Falls to Kingston, including the valleys of the principal tributaries, especially the Normanskill at Albany, from which the point type was named (Ritchie, 1961, pp. 37–38).

PLATE 44   Burned rock feature on the Bent site, Schenectady Co., N.Y. River phase.

Although the River and Bent sites lie along major watercourses, surface finds indicative of small components of this culture also occur on sandy terraces well above these rivers and their tributaries, some of them at distances of several miles inland from the rivers. There is one example of a small component of this culture, discovered, excavated and reported to the writer by John A. Swart of Amsterdam, New York, on a narrow terrace about sixty feet above the north bank of Chaughtanoonda Creek, near its confluence with the Mohawk, just south of Hoffman's Ferry, Schenectady County (Figure 4, site number 17).

Charcoal, in sufficient quantities for radiocarbon dating the River phase, was recovered from several hearths and a burned stone feature at the Bent site. Two of these samples have now been dated at 1350 B.C. ±200 years (M-1187) (Crane and Griffin, 1963, p. 243) and 1930 B.C.±100 years (Y-1169). The older date of 1930 B.C. is believed to be the more accurate one. By about 1470 B.C. the Snook Kill phase was established in the same area (page 134), but no indication of the overlap or contact of River and Snook Kill cultures has been observed. On the other hand, both at the River and Bent sites (as well as on most of the surface components), the broad-bladed points of the Laurentian tradition (radiocarbon-dated in the lower Hudson River at about 2524 B.C., page 84) have been found in small numbers.

Nothing whatever is known about the people themselves, as no human skeletal

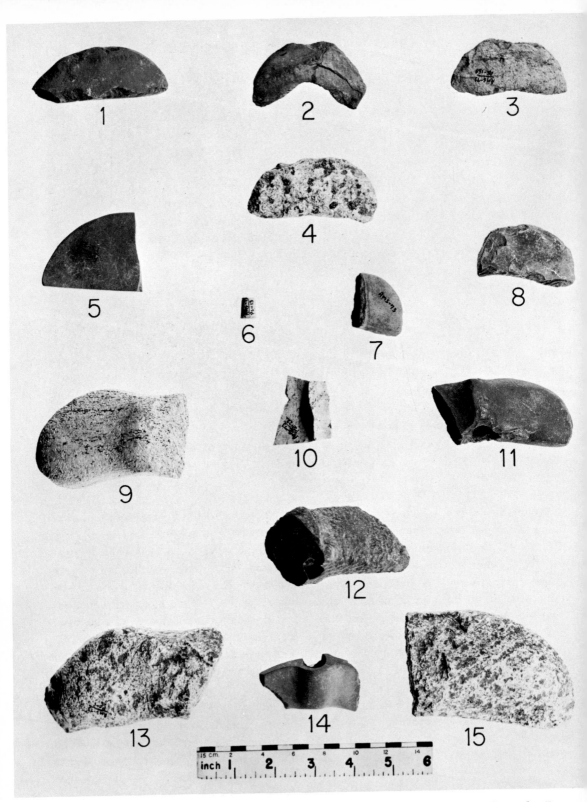

PLATE 45 Notched and perforated varieties of winged bannerstones from the Bent site, Schenectady Co., N.Y. River phase. 6 is a core section.

remains of this phase are available for study. Soil conditions on the River and Bent sites were sufficiently acid (*p*H 6.0) to destroy, over so long a period, all unburned osseous material, food animal as well as human, if the latter had existed there. No cremations have been found either, hence the mortuary customs of the River people remain enigmatic.

The subsistence pattern can in part be reconstructed from the surviving stone artifacts and from some carbonized vegetable remains, which did not include any horticultural products. From this assemblage one may infer the importance of the hunting activity, since about 40 per cent of the total artifact content at the Bent site, and an even higher proportion of the River site remains, consists of projectile points and atlatl weights or bannerstones of notched crescentic or perforated winged forms (Plate 45). The javelin or short spear, propelled with the atlatl or dart-thrower, and tipped with the small, narrow-bladed, side-notched Normanskill point, was obviously the principal hunting weapon (Plate 46). A few longer points of the same form suggest spearheads for more heavily shafted weapons to be held in the hand. Some bits of carbonized deer bone were found at the Bent site, and this animal was probably of foremost importance among the hunters of this group, as of virtually all known earlier and later groups in the Northeast area.

Notched pebble netsinkers were plentiful at the Bent site, testifying to the significant role of fishing. It is probable that bone gorges, fishhooks and harpoons were also used here, and especially at the River site, which was situated along an extensive rift in the Hudson, and where only one sinker-like object was found.

Wild plant foods, recovered from the Bent site only, consist of carbonized acorn cotyledons, of an unidentifiable species of oak. These were found in connection with burned stone features (Plate 44), which seem to have been in part used for roasting the acorns to drive off the toxic tannic acid, after which they were ground into meal, either on shallow mealing stones with mullers, or in tree-trunk mortars with cylindrical stone pestles. Beyond doubt other wild plant foods were extensively employed.

Several of these long stone pestles, found on the Bent and Hoffman's Ferry sites, were of especial interest in having the top carved into an animal-head effigy, apparently a bear in all cases (Plate 47). These are culturally unique in New York State and have their closest known parallels in eastern New England from Maine to Rhode Island (Willoughby, 1935, pp. 150–51).

No pottery or stone vessels were known to the River people, who doubtless boiled part of their food in perishable bark or wooden vessels, using the stone-boiling method of dropping heated stones into the liquid contents; broiled over small fireplaces; and roasted or baked both meat and vegetable foods on the large stone platforms. Their method of making fire was undisclosed. No flint strike-a-lights were present on any site of this culture, suggesting that friction rather than percussion methods may have prevailed. If the domestic dog existed, his bones, too, have disappeared.

Chipped-stone artifacts dominate the surviving cultural remnants and include, besides projectile points, simple ovate and trianguloid knife blades. Scrapers have not been found, and there is only one drill point, from the Bent site. Many of the projectile points seem, however, sufficiently slender to have served for drilling, yet none

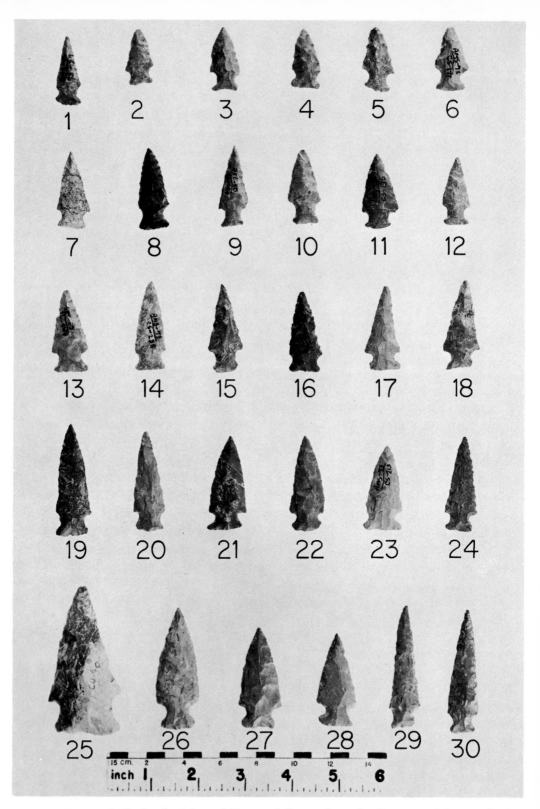

PLATE 46 Projectile points of Normanskill type from the Bent site, Schenectady Co., N.Y. River phase.

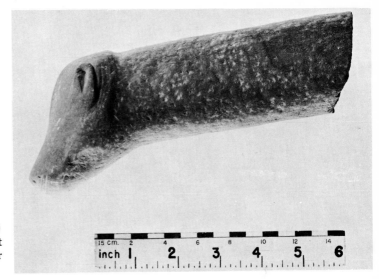

PLATE 47 Fragment of bear (?) effigy elongate pestle from the Bent site, Schenectady Co., N.Y. River phase.

shows indicative use marks. The only drilling process depicted on artifacts of the River phase was the hollow-core technique, used on the perforated category of atlatl weights (Plate 45, Figures 6, 7, 9–15).

Hammerstones, mainly of the unpitted, battered-pebble type, and anvilstones, some of specialized character, studied in connection with the flint artifacts and debitage, suggest chipped-stone tool manufacture by rest percussion techniques (Ritchie, 1958, p. 49).

Tools for felling trees and working wood, scarce on sites of the River phase, comprise the plano-convex adz, the shallow-lipped gouge, and a single probable reworked celt. These tools may have functioned chiefly in the making of dugout canoes, since there are no indications of substantial housing or stockaded settlements. They, like the atlatl weights and certain of the pestles, were manufactured mainly by pecking and grinding, employing a variety of hammerstones and abraders.

Of evident importance in the River culture, at least on the Bent site, is a relatively large group of single or multiple, conically pitted stones, of undetermined function. Some specimens perhaps served to scour off the hard charred surface of wooden fire spindles, a postulated part of the apparatus of fire making in this culture (Ritchie, 1929, pp. 11–12).

The lack of any satisfactory evidence of house type has been remarked. Only a few isolated post molds were discovered and there were no traces of trampled or sanded floors. The dwellings were probably small, simple, flimsy shelters of poles and bark. Some of the hearths found at the Bent site may have been inside such structures, as suggested by the relative abundance of industrial remains generally immediately peripheral to these features. As already observed, the Bent site, covering an area of some five acres, seems too large to have been totally occupied at one time by a group in the Archaic stage of culture in the Northeast area, yet its industrial contents, relating to the food quest, betoken habitation throughout the year. Perhaps

131

the most logical assumption, in our present state of knowledge, is to regard the Bent site as a central-base settlement, more or less continuously occupied by some portion of the population, even during the seasonal hunting and foraging expeditions usually required to sustain a non-agricultural community. Shifting lodge sites of small nuclear family groups, over an area unconfined by fortifications of any kind, would most satisfactorily account for the relatively large size of the site. The River site was certainly very much smaller, while the other known components of this culture appear to have been mere camp sites covering about a quarter of an acre, producing for the most part only a thin surface-scatter of artifacts, chiefly Normanskill points, and no trace of refuse.

Because the artifact inventory of the River phase is limited, to date, to objects of apparently utilitarian purpose, contrived of demonstrably regional, indeed, very local, raw stone materials, without trace of an exotic form or substance, the inference seems warranted that the River folk were essentially a provincial group, with a central-based wandering community pattern, like that of the Lamoka and certain other Archaic peoples in the Northeast, already described.

THE GLACIAL KAME CULTURE

Although not yet reported for New York, the probability that the Glacial Kame culture will be found in this state is greatly enhanced by a recent discovery on its northeastern border, at Isle La Motte, Grand Isle County, Vermont, near the northern end of Lake Champlain (Figure 4, site number 18). The locus of this find, taken in connection with the distribution of known Glacial Kame sites, leads to the

further prediction that the new discoveries will be made in the northern area of the state, most likely in the St. Lawrence and Lake Champlain valleys.

In July of 1962, workmen digging gravel in the town pit of Isle La Motte unearthed a number of human bones and accompanying artifacts enveloped in red ocher. Late in August the writer received word of this accidental disclosure from Mrs. Lois M. Callan of St. Lambert, Province of Quebec, a summer resident on the island, and Miss Mabel C. Holcomb, a local occupant and vice-president of the Isle La Motte Historical Society, with a request for advice and assistance. An investigation made soon afterward, with the help of R. Arthur Johnson, member of the New York State Archeological Association, led to the cultural identification of the site and to the acquisition through excavation, of additional information which establishes an outpost of Glacial Kame culture in upper New England, some two hundred miles in an air line east of its previously known limit in southern Ontario.

The site lay near the western edge of a high level terrace, approximately one hundred feet above the present surface of Lake Champlain. The steeply cut face of the gravel pit revealed an exposure of about thirty-five feet of Champlain Sea sediments, consisting at the base of well-sorted sands with several contrasting horizons of fossil molluscan fauna, overlaid by extremely coarse gravels and associated finer materials. These may represent a till-derived deposit developed in this region and perhaps subjected to reworking by a later marine inundation responsible for the three- to four-foot capping of reddish clay with some gravel and fine, indurated, tan-colored sand forming the upper layer, directly beneath the humus zone.

Undercutting of a portion of this bank by power machinery had caused the human bones enveloped in red ocher in the upper sand layer to slump into the pit, where they were seen by the operator. Work at this point was halted while the site was visited and test pitted by various people prior to our investigations. The bones, not seen by the writer, were taken to Burlington, while most of the artifacts recovered from the talus remained in the custody of Miss Holcomb, acting for the local historical society, through whose courtesy they were loaned to the New York State Museum and Science Service for study, photography and publication.

In his inspection of the site the writer collected cremated fragments of human bone, stained red with ocher, in the dugover talus deposit, suggesting that such burials had probably been shoveled out unnoticed in the past.

The area for about fifty feet adjacent to the place where the grave or graves (two areas of red ocher were observed by the workmen) had appeared was test trenched and pitted, insofar as conditions created by surface bulldozing and prior disturbance permitted, resulting in the discovery of two additional graves. The first one, near the edge of the pit, lay only four inches beneath the stripped surface, resting upon the tough clay-gravel mixture, in a saucer-shaped depression hardly more than a foot below the previous surface. Red ocher stained a patch of sand measuring thirty-four by thirty by four inches, within which were found about three quarts of burned adult human bone fragments, cremated elsewhere, sections of an unburned long bone and skull of a child, and a calcined portion of a bone-splinter awl and a fire-shattered flint scrap.

The second burial, located some thirty-five feet to the northwest, was also very shallow, in contrast to the usually greater depth for graves of this culture. Beneath an unbroken humus layer eight inches thick and three inches of firm tan sand, the top of a concentrated ocher mass, about fifteen inches in diameter and ten inches deep, was uncovered. Mixed throughout the red paint were cremated bones of an adolescent, minus many anatomical parts, and two copper adzes with characteristic gouge-shaped lips, apparently a cultural diagnostic, illustrated on Plate 48, Figures 6, 7. Almost certainly the grave contents had been interred in a bag or basket. The bone fragments, carelessly and only partially gathered up from the crematory, situated somewhere else, had been mingled with the blood-red ocher, perhaps a symbolic life-restorer, and the copper tools, untouched by fire, added to the bundle.

Incidentally, it is of interest to add that copper adzes of this type almost always occur in pairs in graves of this culture, as though provision had been made to supply a sharp replacement. There were two and probably three instances of this at Isle La Motte, one at Picton (Ritchie, 1949, pp. 30–31, Figures 8, 11 x, y), and another at the Muskalonge Lake site in northern New York, assigned to the Early Meadowood phase (page 181) and believed to show Glacial Kame influence (Ritchie, 1955, pp. 18, 36, Plate 11, Figures 10, 11).

Most of the artifacts recovered as grave goods at the Isle La Motte site and available at the time are pictured on Plate 48. The site inventory, typical of the Glacial Kame culture, is as follows: five copper adzes with gouge-shaped bit (two from Burial 2, as noted above, three found in the talus of two graves) (Figures 6, 7); fifteen thick rolled copper beads, one half to five eighths of an inch in length, several still on a bast fiber thong; 140+ discoidal shell beads (Figure 2); a discoidal, three-hole shell gorget (Figure 1); a narrow rectanguloid shell gorget (Figure 5); portions of three sandal-sole shell gorgets, one exhibiting repair by edge grinding and lacing holes (Figures 3, 4); 125+ lumps of unworked galena, of hazelnut to walnut size (Figure 8); and a projectile-point fragment, thin and finely chipped, suggesting the Meadowood type. Unfortunately the base was not recovered.

The shell is all of marine provenience. The galena (lead sulphide) crystals are incrusted with cerussite (lead carbonate), a product of decay since burial, according to an analysis made by Professor Alfred J. Frueh, Jr., Department of Geological Sciences, McGill University. Identification of fragments of burned leather, probably from a shroud, found like most of the other articles in the talus, was confirmed by Professor Eric O. Callen, Macdonald College, McGill University.

The major contribution of this small cemetery of five or six graves, some multiple, and probably as many more unobserved cremations lost in the gravel digging, accrues not from its burial traits and artifact typology, which are indeed classic for the Glacial Kame culture, but from its location far to the east of the previously recorded easternmost component at Collins Bay, Ontario, investigated by the writer in 1952 (Ritchie, 1955, pp. 72–73) (Figure 4, site number 19). The recognized distribution has heretofore included southern Michigan, northwestern Ohio, northeastern Indiana, and southern Ontario from near the Detroit River eastward to Picton (Cunningham, 1948). A probable new discovery pertaining to this culture has recently been brought to my attention by Neil Coppieters of Chatham, Ontario. It consists of a single

grave, again with the multiple interment of cremated and unburned human remains in red ocher with mortuary furniture, from a sand dune near Sarnia, Ontario (letter of November 3, 1963).

At Picton, Prince Edward County, Ontario (Figure 4, site number 20), the only professionally excavated burial site of this culture was explored in 1948 by a Rochester Museum expedition led by the writer, and eleven graves in red ocher were found, several containing more than one individual, disposed of by cremation, flexed inhumation, bone bundle and extended burial. With but a single exception, grave goods of characteristic kinds occurred with these burials (Ritchie, 1949, pp. 24–45).

So far we have no carbon-14 dates for a site certainly of the Glacial Kame culture. It appears to belong to the Late Archaic stage of hunting-fishing-gathering, close perhaps to the transition into Early Woodland, or between approximately 1600 and 1000 B.C. (See, however, page 200.) Elements of the Glacial Kame culture have been remarked for the Meadowood phase, with which it may slightly overlap in the latter's northern range (Ritchie, 1955, pp. 71–72).

THE SNOOK KILL PHASE

In a publication of 1958 the writer included a preliminary account of a newly recognized cultural complex in eastern New York, which he named from the first identified site located on the Snook Kill in Saratoga County (Ritchie, 1958, pp. 91–98) (Figure 4, site number 22). Two additional large sites have since been found in eastern New York, and two lesser components seem identifiable in southern New York. Moreover, the diagnostic Snook

PLATE 48 Grave goods of marine shell, copper and galena, from the Isle La Motte site, Grand Isle Co., Vt., of the Glacial Kame culture. 1 circular shell pendant; 2 discoidal shell beads; 3, 4 portions of sandal-sole shell gorgets; 5 elongate shell gorget; 6, 7 copper adzes; 8 galena nodules. Collection of the Isle La Motte Historical Society.

Kill point type (Ritchie, 1961, pp. 47–48) appears to have a wider range in the Northeast, occurring in Connecticut, Massachusetts and Vermont. In eastern Massachusetts, where it has been found in stratified sites, it clearly occupies the same Late Archaic position in the sequence as in New York, where it has been radiocarbon-dated from the type site. The Snook Kill phase would therefore seem to be part of a wide cultural horizon of Late Archaic times, linked with eastern Pennsylvania and probably farther south. Currently I view it as the earliest aspect of the Susquehanna tradition in the Northeast, probably related to the broad-point cultures of the Transitional stage into which it merges. Further discussion and speculation will be given following a brief description of the Snook Kill culture.

The physiographic setting of the eastern New York sites is distinctive, in each case involving a high, level, well-drained, sandy or gravelly river or stream terrace. The southern New York sites, too, are adjacent to waterways, as are some of the seemingly related New England sites. Because there is no evidence that fishing was of consequence in the culture, the site locations seem rather to have been orientated toward mobility by water transportation.

The eastern New York sites are large; thus at the Snook Kill component the relics and features, while more concentrated close to the stream, are scattered thinly over some four acres of a twenty-five-foot terrace. The only dark soil, however, is found in the fire pits. The Vedder site in Greene County covers approximately one and a half acres atop a sand-terrace remnant of glacial Lake Albany, some fifty feet above the flood plain of the Catskill (Figure 4, site number 24). Pits with burned stone, but no organic refuse, are reported found

on this site. The most productive site of all, on the W. H. Weir farm, brought to the writer's notice by James H. Zell of Albany, occupies at least two acres of a glacial terrace some 110 feet above the Hoosic River, and along a small spring-fed tributary, in Rensselaer County (Figure 4, site number 23). Abundant flint debitage and several hundred artifacts have been found, including a cache of twenty-four projectile points, but no trace of dark soil, pits or other features.

The sole radiocarbon date for the Snook Kill culture was obtained on charcoal found in a cooking pit on the type site by the discoverers and excavators of the site, Mr. and Mrs. William H. Rice of Gansevoort, New York. This date of 1470 B.C.±100 years (Y-1170) (Stuiver, Deevey and Rouse, 1963, p. 331) places the Snook Kill phase in very Late Archaic times for New York. A single stone potsherd from the Weir site suggests that the dawn of the Transitional stage, as defined by the writer (see above), was not far distant. The phase, therefore, has been placed on the sequence chart (Figure 1) at the threshold of the Transitional. Radiocarbon-dated pollen spectra for eastern North America suggest that this was a time when the warm, dry climatic episode of the earlier Archaic period was trending toward the cooler and moister conditions which have persisted, with minor oscillations, into the present. The floral cover seems to have consisted principally of oak, chestnut, birch and hemlock. Lacking animal remains from the Snook Kill sites, we can only speculate that the fauna probably differed little from that described for the earlier Archaic cultures in New York.

Human skeletal remains, from which it might be possible to make certain inferences regarding the physical characteristics, pathology and related facts about the people of the Snook Kill culture, are virtually absent. No graves have been reported on the eastern New York sites or on Staten Island. Two cremation burials that seem by their related projectile points to belong to this culture were found on eastern Long Island and do not help us in this regard (page 138).

From the surviving stone artifacts of the Snook Kill culture it can be inferred that hunting was the primary activity, and that it was conducted with thrusting spears having long points, and shorter throwing spears or javelins with lighter points, used, however, without the weighted atlatl, since "bannerstones" do not occur in this culture. Snook Kill points, thick, and coarsely chipped for the most part, probably by a percussion technique, are predominantly broad-bladed and stemmed (Plate 49, Figures 1–18, 22, 23), but more slender forms occur, some stemmed, others with wide, shallow side-notches (Plate 49, Figures 19–21, 24). Since both broad- and narrow-bladed examples were present in the cache of twenty-four points found by Mr. Zell, the differences may have been functional, not chronological.

While the loss through decay of the bone constituent would account for the absence of part of the fishing tackle, the total want of the common notched pebble, or other form of netsinker, suggests the small use of fish in the diet of these people. This fact contrasts with the report of heavy netsinkers from some sites of the related Lehigh complex in Pennsylvania (page 154).

Nor are the usual food-grinding devices —pestles, mullers, mortars, etc.—known in the Snook Kill complex. Unless the wooden mortar and pestle were employed, it seems unlikely that wild vegetal foods constituted a major portion of the subsistence. What

seemed to the finders to be charred wild cherrystones are described from a pit on the Snook Kill site, but no trace of any other wild or cultivated plant was observed, nor is it probable that the Snook Kill pits were dug for storage of food. Rather, the high content of burned stones, charcoal, ash, etc., makes probable their use as roasting or baking ovens, primarily for meat, as further suggested by the burned bone fragments, present in some.

If the dog was present as an aid to the hunter, which seems likely from its earlier and later ocurrence in the same area, the proof still awaits discovery.

House forms and settlement patterns are also matters of mystery. Since the artifacts and chipping debris occur scattered thinly over fairly large areas on the chief sites, a number of small components is indicated, or alternatively, a wide spacing of the dwelling units, as in the Adena culture, together with a lack of fortification. The camp refuse seems simply to have been scattered at random, rather than dumped into middens or empty pits, hence it has completely disappeared. Finally, the data at our command do not attest to long inhabitancy at any component; rather, a camp-type community is indicated. The usual corollaries of this restricted wandering way of life are a low areal population density and small-sized communities composed of nuclear-family or joint-household groups which live and travel together, within a limited territory, in loosely knit bands of fewer than one hundred people (Beardsley, et al., 1956, pp. 136–38).

There are few clues to the dress and ornamentation of the Snook Kill people. The characteristic thick stemmed scrapers, usually with well-worn edge (Plate 49, Figures 25, 26), may have been skin scrapers, wood scrapers, or both. Small discoidal shell beads and red ocher were present as grave goods with the Long Island cremations attributed to this culture, and the bone flutes from the same graves comprise the sole evidence for possible aesthetic or recreational activities (see below). There are no smoking pipes.

Fire making by percussion with the flint striker and iron-pyrites anvil seems demonstrated by the finding of well-battered flints made from broken projectile points (Plate 49, Figure 27).

The stone artifacts seem large and coarsely made, strictly utilitarian and tradition-bound, and very limited in variety. Aside from the hunting points already discussed, there are a considerable number of chipped flint knives, large, broad-bladed, nearly stemless and frequently asymmetrical (Plate 49, Figures 29–33); hoe-shaped choppers (heavy hide scrapers?) (Plate 49, Figure 28); a few expanded base drills; pebble hammerstones; anvilstones; and a small number of crude tree-felling and woodworking tools—celts, adzes and a single gouge—pecked and poorly ground into shape. The wood-shaping tools presumably served the transportation need in the manufacture of dugout canoes, for it seems, from the site locations, that water travel was the principal mode of locomotion.

Yet there is very little to indicate trade or contact relations with other groups—a few argillite, rhyolite and jasper points, and a single stone potsherd—and much to reflect the relative isolation of a simple, self-reliant, hunting group, mobile within its limited territory.

Mention has been made of cremation burials thought to belong to the Snook Kill phase on eastern Long Island. These were found in 1954 by Melville L. King of Easthampton, on the Great Pond site on Lake Montauk (formerly called Great Pond),

Easthampton Township, Long Island (Figure 4, site number 36). Here the flank of a knoll was covered by a shell midden three feet deep, consisting mainly of hard clams and whelk.

Two burials were found, eleven feet apart, each in a shallow, two-foot-wide depression in the sand subsoil, opening from the base of the midden. Each grave held a small heap of burned adult human bones imbedded in red ocher, much less than an entire human skeleton, not cremated *in situ*. Offerings of the same kind lay among the two heaps, viz., a long-bone whistle or flute of bird bone with a single oval perforation near one end; 600 and 150, respectively, small, thin, white, discoidal shell beads; and five and three, respectively, projectile points of quartzite, slate and rhyolite, showing close typological affinities with both the broad and narrow variants of the Snook Kill point.

According to the finder, ten or twelve similar points occurred in the immediate vicinity of the graves, together with the unmodified maxillary fragments and teeth of a wolf. It is also plausibly claimed that steatite potsherds came from and near the base of the midden, at about the same depth as the Snook Kill points, while Vinette 1 potsherds occurred, without such points, at a higher level. Sebonac pottery and bonework occurred in the upper horizon of shells.

In July 1956 the writer, after studying and in part photographing Mr. King's uncatalogued collection, visited the site with him and made some exploratory trenches in the heavily molested midden. He was able to verify by his own discoveries the relative position in the midden of Vinette 1, Sebonac, and even a little Niantic pottery, which came from near the surface.

While unconvincing in itself because of

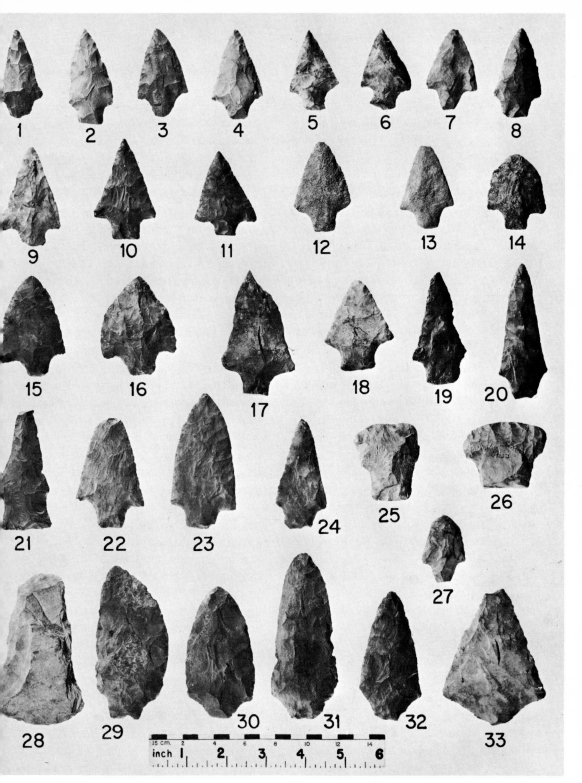

PLATE 49 Projectile points (1–24); stemmed end scrapers (25, 26); strike-a-light (27); chopper (28); and knives (29–33) of the Snook Kill phase from the Weir site, Rensselaer Co., N.Y. Collection of James H. Zell, Albany, N.Y.

poor collecting methods, the suggested cultural sequence at Great Pond finds some support at the second southern New York site referred with greater certainty to the Snook Kill phase. This is the Old Place site on the east bank of the Arthur Kill, in northwestern Staten Island (Figure 4, site number 25). Its situation on land too swampy, it would seem, to have invited Indian habitation, suggests a relatively recent elevation of sea level, as noted at Grannis Island on the Connecticut coast (Sargent, 1952) and elsewhere in the Northeast.

The site was excavated by Albert J. Anderson and Donald L. Sainz, local amateurs, and the collection from this and other Staten Island sites was studied by the writer in February 1962 through the courtesy of Mr. Anderson (page 147). This analysis pointed to a vertical distribution of the materials at Old Place in which a small but typical Snook Kill assemblage of points and scrapers—of quartzite, rhyolite, argillite, jasper and flint—occurred in the lowest few inches of a homogeneous tan-colored sand, forty-two inches deep. From a slightly higher level came Poplar Island points with a small intermixture of Bare Island points, and an unfinished bipennate atlatl weight. Above this rather vague zone were found mostly Bare Island points of argillite, apparently with a few narrow stemmed and weakly corner-notched points, of the same material, like those found in a similar association in the Kent-Hally site on Bare Island in the lower Susquehanna River (Kinsey, 1959, Plate 5, Figures 7–11).

More secure data on the relative position in the developmental sequences of the Northeast of complexes dominated by points which, upon actual inspection by the writer, bear unmistakable typological affinities with the Snook Kill type, come from eastern Massachusetts. For example, at the Foster's Cove site on the Shawsheen River in the northeastern part of the state, Bullen discovered such points (called "corner-removed"), made of felsite and slate, in the lower zone of the site, in association with the semilunar knife and stone gouge. From slightly higher in the same, yellow-brown sand stratum came small stemmed and small triangular points of quartz. The superincumbent loam stratum produced throughout a predominance of large triangular points, together with potsherds, of coarsely tempered grit at the lower levels, vegetable-tempered and fine-grit-tempered above (Bullen, 1949, pp. 23–34).

A congruent story was told by the Norton site on Lagoon Pond, Vineyard Haven, Martha's Vineyard, Massachusetts, where the stratigraphic succession consisted of layers of crushed shell, brown earth, and yellow earth grading into the sterile subsoil. Excavations by a local student, E. Gale Huntington, who kindly showed me both the site and his collection, produced a generally similar ordering of materials as found by Bullen on the mainland.

The earliest occupants of the yellow-earth zone had used large Snook Kill, or Snook Kill-like, points of slate and slaty rocks, and apparently small stemmed points of quartz. A carbon-14 date of about A.D. 500 (Y-583) for this level is adjudged much too late by the excavator, who estimates 1000 B.C. as closer to fact, in which the writer concurs.

From the overlying brown earth came narrow stemmed and side-notched points, some of the former closely resembling the Bare Island type, steatite potsherds and grit-tempered pottery. In the uppermost stratum, the crushed shell, broad triangular points prevailed, along with shell-tempered potsherds. A radiocarbon date of around

A.D. 900 (Y-582), obtained near the bottom of the shell, is thought to be fairly accurate (Huntington, 1959).

A stratified cultural sequence pertinent to the Snook Kill problem was found by the writer and a small party of graduate-student assistants during the summer of 1964, on the north shore of Squibnocket Pond, Town of Gay Head, Martha's Vineyard, in a major site excavation, through the courtesy of Henry Hornblower II, of Boston, the landowner. The following concise summation is taken from the writer's complete report (Ritchie, 1969).

A fivefold physical stratigraphy was apparent, with crushed bay scallop shell and black soil constituting the uppermost layer (stratum 1A) just beneath the sterile sod line. Little refuse bone was present in this stratum, radiocarbon-dated at A.D. $1380 \pm$ 80 years (Y-1528). This layer and pits originating therefrom produced, along with artifacts of lesser diagnostic nature, triangular points of Levanna type and shell-tempered pottery decorated with scallop shell or cord impressions, attributable to the Late Woodland stage of occupation.

The irregularly intergrading 1B stratum differed chiefly in containing much coarsely broken and whole shell of most of the local shellfish species, much refuse bone of mammals, birds, fish and amphibians, and quite different artifacts which included among the principal forms, Wading River points of quartz and grooved and side-notched pebble sinkers.

The Snook Kill, or very similar, points and scrapers—nearly all of gray-green argillite—occurred with choppers and an adz, in the next lower layer, a cocoa-brown sandy soil of variable thickness, evidently an old humus or A soil (stratum 2), along with mammal bones, especially of the deer, and relatively fewer shells, for the most part

whole valves of the quahog, oyster and long clam. A small number of Susquehanna Broad and Orient Fishtail points of various materials also came from this stratum.

Below the brown sand, the heavy shell midden reappeared as stratum 3. Crushed and whole shells, chiefly of the quahog, were present, with much mammal, fish and bird bone, and a resumption of the quartz industry of the lower portion of stratum 1. With the Wading River points occurred small lobate stemmed points (Squibnocket Stemmed) and small triangles (Squibnocket Triangle), also of quartz, with concave bases and convex edges, plummets and choppers. This Squibnocket complex has been C-14 dated on hearth charcoal to 2190 B.C. $\pm$ 100 years (Y-1529).

Stratum 3 rested upon the tan-colored subsoil, the first few inches of which were heavily mottled with brown humus stains, perhaps through leaching from above. In this basal horizon, termed stratum 4, were found a small number of classic Laurentian point types—Otter Creek, Brewerton Eared-Notched and Brewerton Eared-Triangle— and a few other artifacts. A radiocarbon date of 2270 B.C. $\pm$ 160 years (Y-1530) has been obtained from a hearth in this stratum.

Further Snook Kill data were obtained by the writer's excavations in 1967 on the Lester Peterson site in Chilmark, Martha's Vineyard, where Snook Kill and Susquehanna Broad points of green argillite occurred with quartz points of Wading River type in stratum 3, dated at 2070 B.C. $\pm$ 115 (I-3103), beneath an Early Woodland horizon with Vinette 1 pottery, dated at 590 B.C. $\pm$ 105 (I-3101) (Ritchie, 1969).

The writer would place in his category of Snook Kill points what is termed the "Corner-Removed No. 7 type" in Massachusetts, one of several point types attributed there to the "Stone Bowl culture period," with an estimated antiquity of approximately 3000 B.C. (Fowler, 1961, pp. 6, 8; compare his Figure 7 illustrating this type with the Snook Kill points pictured on Plate 49, herein). This chronological estimate is almost certainly some seventeen hundred years too great, since the steatite-using horizon in southern New England was doubtless coeval with its approximate equivalent Transitional stage in New York (page 150). In the latter state, however, the Snook Kill phase and point type just precede this stage, pertaining rather to the terminal Archaic, and as already stated, a radiocarbon date of 1470 B.C.±100 years, which is highly compatible with our established dated sequence for New York (Figure 1), has been obtained at a Snook Kill culture site.

The Snook Kill point belongs to the family of broad points which largely characterize the Transitional stage. I suspect as its immediate prototype and likely ancestor the Lehigh Broad point of a little-known complex centering on the Lehigh and upper Delaware rivers of eastern Pennsylvania (page 154). The roots of the Snook Kill phase are probably to be sought in this complex. Eastern Pennsylvania was also the potential source of the foreign stone materials found at the geographically intermediate Old Place site on Staten Island and in trace quantities at the Weir site. Still more remotely, the Savannah River point of the Southeast, and the broad-bladed, stemmed point and stemmed scraper types of the Long site in Lebanon County, Pennsylvania, appeal to me as reasonable antecedents to Snook Kill forms.

THE ARCHAIC IN COASTAL NEW YORK

Several attempts have been made to define a broad cultural manifestation to which the term Coastal Archaic could be applied in contradistinction to other regional Archaic manifestations, but the problem is still with us (Skinner, 1909a; Ritchie, 1938, pp. 103–6; 1944, pp. 102–12; Sears, 1954, pp. 28–36; Byers, 1959a, pp. 236–43). The current perspective indicates that, rather than a particular cultural assemblage of this kind, a number of inland phases of the Archaic stage reached the coastal region at different times and from different directions, there to become adapted to a marine littoral environment, essentially, to a principal dietary reliance on shellfish. The slender available evidence does not suggest that fishing, especially pelagic fishing, or the hunting of sea mammals, such as whales, seals and porpoises, was practiced in the New York area during this early period. Evidence of these activities has, however, been found by the writer on Martha's Vineyard, Massachusetts (Ritchie, 1969).

The coastal-dwelling Archaic groups did not lose contact with their inland congeners, with whom cultural interchanges took place, and it is indeed difficult to separate them on the basis of surviving artifact differences. A prominent criterion of this nature is found, however, in the grooved ax, which in the New York and adjacent tidewater area of our present concern seems to have been a characteristic tool of the coastal inhabitants from later Archaic times onward, although by no means confined thereto. Both fully grooved and three-quarter-grooved axes occur, the former variety appearing to be the earlier. Archaic cultures of the Southeast seem to have been the source of diffusion of this element. The continued acculturation and the specialized development of the coastal-dwelling groups, beginning it would seem with the Orient, resulted in some subsequent differentiations, chiefly ceramic, which distinguish such Late Woodland groups as the Sebonac, Bowmans Brook, Clasons Point (pages 266–72) and probably others from their inland contemporaries.

In the coastal and tidewater area of New York the Archaic stage is represented by numerous, small, nearly always multicomponent sites, variously situated on tidal inlets, coves and bays, particularly at the heads of the latter, and on fresh-water ponds on Long Island, Shelter Island, Fishers Island, Manhattan Island and Staten Island, and along the lower Hudson River on terraces and knolls, at various elevations having no consistent relationship to the particular cultural complex. Efforts at the correlation of some of these sites with the postulated sea-level fluctuations of Fairbridge (1958, 1960, 1960a) (pages 124, 168) have not, I think, yielded conclusive results (Salwen, 1962; Brennan, 1962). Most of the sites spared by construction or other modern activities have been heavily molested by relic collectors over a very long period and relatively few have received attention from competent amateur or professional archaeologists.

The Archaic occupation of the southern and lower eastern subareas of New York involved elements of several traditions, namely, the Laurentian, "narrow point" and Susquehanna. The unfortunate lack of any excavated well-stratified site makes it difficult or impossible clearly to define the order of appearance here of the first two of these traditions and the evidence, such as it is, suggests that the situation in the coastal district of the state may have been somewhat at variance with that for upstate New York.

In the first place, the Laurentian tradition, as it is represented in the rather poorly defined Vosburg phase of eastern New York, is not demonstrably present on Long Island or on Staten Island. Certain characteristic Laurentian traits, notably the ground slate ulu, stone gouge and plummet, do, however, occur sporadically, usually as surface finds and rarely in context, as at Garvie Point, Glen Cove, Long Island (Patterson, 1955).

Strongly represented in the coastal area are broad, rather heavy projectile points, side-notched or stemmed, which as a class suggest some similar point forms in the various manifestations of the Laurentian tradition. Such points were found by the writer in stratigraphic relationship below a large component of the Orient phase, Susquehanna tradition, at Stony Brook, Long Island (Ritchie, 1959, pp. 18, 32–33, 47). Points of this kind have been interpreted as indicating Laurentian extensions into the coastal area and there is still no categorical reason to deny this possibility (Smith, 1950, pp. 142–143; Ritchie, 1959, pp. 47, 84, 87). It must, however, clearly be stated that no indubitable Laurentian complex or phase of culture can as yet be identified in this area.

Nor is it possible unequivocally to demonstrate the stratigraphic horizon in which such broad points occur in relation to the narrow points of another tradition which is even better represented in the coastal region. To this tradition, as yet without an acceptable designation, belong the Sylvan Lake complex (page xix) and the probably related Squibnocket complex in New England (page xxi). The Sylvan Lake complex is now recognized as pertaining both to eastern and southern New York.

The largest recognized and most completely explored site of this character in the coastal district is the Wading River station on eastern Long Island (Figure 4, site number 14) (Ritchie, 1959, pp. 78–88). The rude, notched, winged atlatl weight, the rough, side-notched chopper and the polished rectangular celt were present on this site of a hunting and shellfish-using people. Deer bone was very plentiful, and slight to moderate amounts of shell detritus, chiefly of the soft-shelled clam and oyster, with lesser amounts of hard-shelled clam, scallop and periwinkle, occurred in the midden.

Radiocarbon dates for Archaic cultures on Long Island and Staten Island have not yet been obtained. In the middle Hudson Valley, the stratified Sylvan Lake Rockshelter has provided a very important dated sequence, already discussed (page xx). Pertinent here are the dates for the Sylvan Lake complex, with its narrow point tradition, and the deeper Vosburg level of the Laurentian tradition. The dates are, respectively, 2210 B.C.±140 years (Y-1536) and 2780 B.C.±80 years (Y-1535). Another date for the Vosburg level in the lower Hudson Valley is 2524 B.C.±300 years (M-287) (page 84).

These dates and the dated, parallel Martha's Vineyard sequence (page 141) support the assumption that in eastern New York and eastern Massachusetts, culture manifestations referable to the Laurentian tradition underlie those of the narrow point tradition, with which they overlap. For the New York coastal area, however, some recent and significant new information on this problem has been acquired through the work of Louis A. Brennan and his associates, Sigfus Olafson and Mauck Brammer, in several sites on the lower Hudson in Westchester County, and particularly on the Twombly Landing site, on the Hudson, in Palisades Park, New Jersey (Brennan, 1962, pp. 140, 147, 154; 1963, p. 11; 1967). At this site a narrow-bladed, stemmed, small point, conforming to my Wading River type, was found within two feet of a hearth which produced the dated charcoal, on the same stratigraphic level,

beneath an intact heap of shell. Two conformable radiocarbon measurements indicate that the fire was kindled between about 2775 B.C.±60 (GX-0762) and 2800 B.C.±160 (Y-1761) (Brennan, 1967, p. 10). Such an antiquity, if confirmed by subsequent discoveries, would show the coexistence in different parts of the Northeast of two completely discrete traditions, the Laurentian, centered in the north, and the narrow point tradition, presumably centered well south in the Middle Atlantic region.

Further support for this possibility exists in the Laurentian dates of 2010 B.C.±100 (Y-1273) and 2050 B.C.±220 (I-424) for a site in central New York (page 91) and of 2750 B.C.±150 (GSC-162) for a site in the Ottawa Valley (page 91), and the cluster of dates for the Lamoka Lake site of around 2500 B.C. (page 43), the latter site pertaining to the narrow point tradition, which Brennan has termed the "Taconic tradition" (Brennan, 1967, p. 5). The writer, while in some substantial agreement with Brennan (ibid., pp. 10–12), regards this term with disfavor, as connoting an essential relationship with the narrow Taconic mountainous region, whereas in reality it seems to me that the point form is widely spread throughout the coastal plain, piedmont and much of the Appalachian highland province. For this reason, the alternate term "Appalachian tradition" has been proposed by Robert E. Funk, but is also not entirely satisfactory.

Irrespective of the name which will ultimately be agreed upon for this narrow point tradition, which includes points of the Lamoka, Bare Island, Popular Island, Wading River and other types, an antiquity comparable with that for the Laurentian now seems probable. In the coastal area of New York and New Jersey this may represent the basic Archaic tradition. Farther north, in eastern New York and southern New England, it obviously appears later on some sites. On other sites an overlapping of the two traditions seems to be indicated by the evidence. In central New York the picture is not yet sufficiently clear, beyond the fact of cultural interaction involving the two traditions, as seen particularly at Frontenac Island (page 104).

The Culture Sequence on Staten Island

Throughout the area we are considering, other even less well-known Archaic complexes were present. They are chiefly represented by surface and subsurface finds of projectile points of such recognized types as Poplar Island, Bare Island and Rossville. (Ritchie, 1961). Unlike the Laurentian, which affected the coastal area from the north, the cultural influences responsible for this group of points lay to the south, probably largely in the lower Susquehanna Valley and Middle Atlantic area. They entered the New York coastal region through New Jersey, and most of the located sites are on Staten Island, which is much more closely related archaeologically to the latter state than to any other part of New York. Several of these point types have been found on Staten Island in apparent stratigraphic relationship, as will in part be noted in the following sections (pages 145–49).

Most of the material pertains, however, to the Poplar Island and Bare Island complexes, and the writer is indebted to Albert J. Anderson and Donald L. Sainz of Staten Island for permission to study and utilize their excavated collections.

The largely postulated and virtually unknown Poplar Island complex, which may contain the rectangular bannerstone or atlatl weight and rough chopper, has as its diagnostic trait a slender-bladed projectile point with rounded shoulders and a fairly long, constricted stem, tapering to a narrow, rounded base (Witthoft, 1959, p. 83; Kinsey, 1959, p. 115; Ritchie, 1961, pp. 44–45). In New Jersey it is commonly referred to as a "fish-spear" (Cross, 1941, pp. 33, 57). Most such points are of siltstone or argillite, but rhyolite, quartz, quartzite and other materials, including rarely flint, were employed.

From the evidence at the Kent-Hally site in the lower Susquehanna Valley of Pennsylvania, Kinsey suggests a Late Archaic age for this point type. Witthoft, on the evidence from Duncan's Island in the same area, would place the type somewhat earlier in the Archaic (Witthoft, 1959, p. 82). Both archaeologists agree, however, that the Poplar Island and the Bare Island point types are nearly contemporaneous; or that their temporal ranges overlap, and with this opinion our Staten Island data are in general agreement.

The Bare Island point, sometimes confused with the Lamoka type, is also a slender-bladed projectile, but the stem is straight with parallel sides and the base is also straight (Kinsey, 1959, p. 115; Ritchie, 1961, pp. 14–15). Quartz and quartzite predominate as preferred materials in the southern part of its geographic range, which is much broader, including, with the far more common cognate Wading River type, southern New England, than that of the Poplar Island point, with flint as the commonest stone in the Hudson Valley north of Greene County, where the Poplar Island point is absent or very rare.

The Bare Island complex has been defined, chiefly on the basis of the Kent-Hally

145

site, as a Late Archaic hunting culture characterized by Bare Island points as the major type, Poplar Island points and large corner-notched points as minority forms, T-shaped drills, slate crescents, bipinnate atlatl weights, various rough stone tools including choppers of several shapes, mullers, milling stones and cylindrical pestles, and steatite bowls (Kinsey, 1959, pp. 129–31). The presence of the latter would assign the complex to the Transitional stage, as I regard it (page 150). The proximity of the Kent-Hally site to steatite outcrops in Pennsylvania and Maryland probably resulted in the earlier use of this material in that area than in New York State.

Three Staten Island sites in particular record the presence in coastal New York of the Bare Island complex, and possibly of a discrete and slightly earlier Poplar Island complex, in a rough sequence, according to the excavators, Messrs. Anderson and Sainz. They have designated these sites Bowman's Brook A, Old Place and Arlington Place A-1.

The Bowman's Brook A site is a multicomponent station forming part of the large site complex which formerly existed at Mariners' Harbor, on the northwestern shore of Staten Island (Skinner, 1909, pp. 5–9). Here was located the type component of the Bowmans Brook Focus, East River Aspect, on which Skinner excavated in 1906, during the course of construction over a large tract, of the Milliken Brothers' steel plant (Smith, 1950, pp. 122–23, 176–77). This foundry no longer exists, and the partially cleared area was undergoing extensive leveling by bulldozer for a new industrial enterprise when the finds, now to be described, were made, evidently in a portion of the area close to Skinner's Bowman's Brook, Site 2 (Skinner, 1909, Figure 1, p. 6).

Anderson and Sainz, digging in a small, partially bulldozed, partially trash-covered section formerly under foundry buildings, discovered a series of components of different cultures and apparently of different ages, enclosed in a homogeneous, tan-colored sand which covers the whole northern shore area. The series was not directly superimposed, the components being horizontally separated by unascertained distances, hence the validity of the sequence is subject to some degree of doubt. Five levels or occupational horizons were recognized on the basis of projectile-point typology and relative depth, but only one of these levels was distinguishable by soil differences, consisting of the addition of charcoal granules to the sand. This horizon, number 4, also produced the only feature found, a hearth with accompanying burned stone fragments. The following sequence is said to have occurred here.

Level 1. A probable original surface level relating to the Bowmans Brook phase, now almost entirely destroyed. A single Levanna type point, characteristic of this phase, was found on the bulldozed surface.

Level 2. At the northern edge of the excavated area occurred what appeared to be the original humus level, some five inches thick, overlaid by a modern accumulation of cinders and trash. In a four- to five-inch zone of unstained sand immediately beneath the humus were found six broad-bladed, side-notched and corner-notched points of flint and quartzite, resembling Middle Woodland forms, Brewerton types, and an end scraper chipped on both sides.

Level 3. In a narrow zone of clean sand, only a few inches thick, reached at about one foot below the stripped surface, from which sand of indeterminate depth had been removed, was found a small Bare Island-point association. This relic-bearing horizon seemed to lie about half a foot deeper than Level 2, which produced the notched points. Eight stemmed points were found, one of quartz, the others of argillite, together with a lanceolate and an ovate knife of argillite and flint respectively, and a probable notched bannerstone, thick, and crudely chipped from a cherty stone.

Level 4. At approximately seventeen inches below the bulldozed surface the level containing the hearth and scattered charcoal granules was reached. Although the modern scraped surface was slightly irregular, and no datum point for the excavation was established, it would seem that horizon 4 lay a few inches deeper in the sand than number 3.

The hearth itself consisted of a mass of charcoal (saved for possible carbon-14 dating) and ashes, about ten inches in diameter, in a shallow, bowl-shaped depression of heat-reddened sand, surrounded by fire-shattered pieces of rock, among which lay the basal portion of a Poplar Island point. In the vicinity of this feature, and within the five- to six-inch charcoal-flecked zone which enclosed it, the investigators found six more Poplar Island points, all of heavily weathered argillite in a variety of colors—purple, red, brown, gray and black. No other artifacts were present.

Level 5. The deepest occurrence of artifacts at the site was reported at approximately twenty-eight to thirty-two inches from the scraped surface, in clean sand. The nine projectile points found here were of narrow stemmed form, rudely chipped of flint, except for two of quartzite. The smallest specimens resemble most closely the Wading River and the Squibnocket Stemmed types, the two largest have sim-

ilarities to the Bare Island type. Three other point fragments with broader blades, one with a long, narrow, lobate stem, are said to have come from the same level of the site. There are also five rude, simple end scrapers, one very thick, of flint and jasper.

The Old Place site lies on the east bank of the Arthur Kill, immediately north of the Goethals Bridge abutment, in the northwestern section of Staten Island. It is presently situated on land too swampy, it would seem, to have invited Indian habitation, suggesting the probability that a recent elevation of sea level has here, as at Grannis Island on the Connecticut coast (Sargent, 1952), Grassy Island in the Taunton River, Massachusetts (Johnson and Raup, 1947), and elsewhere in the Northeast, created the prevailing wet conditions.

There is dubious evidence that the Snook Kill points found at this site came from the lower level. A concentration of Poplar Island points, along with a small percentage of Bare Island points, also made of argillite, and an unfinished short-winged bannerstone, is said to have occurred below a concentration of Bare Island points of argillite, apparently associated with a flint end scraper, a flint strike-a-light, and a few narrow stemmed and weakly corner-notched argillite points, similar to some found in the Kent-Hally site on Bare Island in the lower Susquehanna River (Kinsey, 1959, Plate 5, Figures 7–11).

About half a mile inland (south) of the Bowman's Brook cluster of sites, occurs another group centering along South Avenue, Arlington. One of these, designated Arlington Place A-1 by Anderson, has been bulldozed, with the removal of an undetermined amount of topsoil. In remnants of the humus, triangular points have been found. Some ten to fourteen inches below the present truncated surface, in red sand, an occupational zone six to eight inches thick yielded over fifty projectile points of Poplar Island and Bare Island types, in a proportion of about one to three. Argillite, badly weathered, was the principal material, but a few Bare Island specimens were of slate, quartzite and flint. Two Orient Fishtail points, of slate and jasper, respectively, were also present in the intermixture, according to Anderson.

The Archaic sequence on Staten Island, as indicated by the summarized data, evidently falls in the narrow point tradition of the Late Archaic segment in the Northeast. The closest connections for the Staten Island manifestations, as might be anticipated from its geographical relations, are with adjacent eastern New Jersey, where the same artifact types, many made from identical stone materials, are well known (Cross, 1941). Probably a similar sequence could be established there also, but as yet no clear cultural order has been worked out.

A very close parallel for most of the sequence is to be found in the lower Susquehanna Valley of Pennsylvania, especially at the Kent-Hally site on Bare Island, where both the typology and lithology closely match the Staten Island assemblages. It would seem that Staten Island lies near the northern extremity of a Middle Atlantic cultural province of Late Archaic and Transitional age which extended southward an indefinite distance into coastal Virginia.

The Staten Island succession, as tentatively elucidated, suggests that a pure Poplar Island complex may be represented in Level 4 at the Bowman's Brook A site. Unfortunately, this small site and sample may be misleading, and only the projectile points of this still poorly defined complex

at Poplar Island and Duncan Island in the lower Susquehanna Valley (Witthoft, 1959, pp. 82–83) were present. On the other Staten Island sites where Poplar Island points were found underground—Old Place, Travis, Wort and Arlington Place A-1—they occurred intermixed with the Bare Island type, in varying proportions not readily determinable from the data, but at the last-mentioned site Bare Island points were about three times as frequent as those of Poplar Island style, a relative frequency close to that reported at the Bare Island type site (Kinsey, 1959, p. 115).

It would appear possible that on Staten Island an earlier Poplar Island complex of short duration was assimilated by a Bare Island complex, to produce the assemblage seen on most of the Staten Island sites. This looks like a culture-contact situation generally congruent with that described elsewhere (page 104) for the Frontenac phase in central New York, but the Staten Island data are much too thin to carry the same conviction.

Found with the intermixed Poplar Island and Bare Island points on various of the Staten Island sites, and presumably forming part of the composite complex, were the following artifact varieties: bipinnate bannerstones (Old Place, Travis, Arlington Place); notched bannerstones (Bowman's Brook, Old Place); fully grooved axes (Travis, Arlington Place); chipped knives of lanceolate, ovate and trianguloid forms (Bowman's Brook, Arlington Place); end scrapers (Old Place, Arlington Place): flint strike-a-light (Old Place); cylindrical pestles (Travis, Arlington Place); grooved sinker, pitted and unpitted hammerstones, and steatite potsherds (Arlington Place).

The finding of steatite postsherds on only one of these sites indicates, along with the typological evidence, that most of the sites belong to the Late Archaic, rather than to the Transitional horizon, on Staten Island.

It is of interest to compare this limited inventory with the hypothesized Poplar Island complex of Witthoft (1959, p. 83) and with the Bare Island trait list as tentatively given by Kinsey (1959, pp. 129, 131). The chief correspondences with the former are the winged bannerstones, fully grooved axes (Witthoft also includes the three-quarter-grooved form which occurs on Staten Island but without known context) and cylindrical pestles. Knives and end scrapers, found on some of the Staten Island sites, are negative Poplar Island traits, while the choppers of the latter complex are not reported from Staten Island in this connection, although they occur on undesignated sites there.

With Bare Island certain of the Staten Island sites under discussion share bipinnate bannerstones, steatite bowls, the grooved ax (? for Bare Island), cylindrical pestles and hammerstones. Bare Island drills, slate crescents, choppers, mullers, whetstones and chipped disks are unreported from the Staten Island complex, while the notched bannerstones, grooved sinker, knives, scrapers and a few other Staten Island traits are unlisted for the Bare Island complex.

At the Kent-Hally site the scanty pottery, all of Vinette 1 type, or its derivative, Modified Interior Vinette 1, was confined to the upper level, while nearly all of the "semilozenge" points (which comprised only 8.7 per cent of the total site sample) came from the top two levels (Kinsey, 1959, pp. 114, 115, 124–25, 128). This point category includes the Orient Fishtail and Susquehanna Broad types, the first associated with steatite vessels and Vinette 1 and related pottery on Long Island (Ritchie, 1959), the second with similar associations in central New York (pages 159, 173). The association of various forms of this group of "semilozenge" points with Early Woodland pottery on Staten Island sites, at Rossville, Page Avenue and Old Place, is therefore no surprise.

On Staten Island (and throughout New Jersey) the minor role of the Laurentian tradition is attested by the scarcity of such characteristic objects, mostly surface-found, as stone gouges, plummets, rubbed slate ulus and broad, side-notched projectile points.

III   The Transitional Stage—
from Stone Pots to Early Ceramics
(c. 1300–1000 B.C.)

A Transitional stage of culture connecting the Late Archaic and Early Woodland stages in the northeastern United States has long been recognized (Witthoft, 1949, pp. 171–72; 1953; 1954, pp. 43–44; Ritchie, 1951, p. 131), but even now most of the constitutent complexes of this stage, which spanned the interval between approximately 1300 and 1000 B.C., are little known. The Transitional stage, as I am regarding it, was essentially preceramic, but during this relatively short period of about three hundred years, carved soapstone vessels, together with new varieties of projectile points, including both broad "semilozenge" and narrow "fishtail" forms, came into common use within much of the area from the Potomac and Chesapeake Bay region to central New York and northern Massachusetts. The ancestry of these traits is yet to be determined, but it apparently lies to the south of our area, in Archaic cultures of the Middle Atlantic region.

In the Northeast, the recognized cultures of the Transitional stage include the Orient phase, described on page 164, and the newly defined and still earlier Frost Island phase. The Frost Island phase, as adumbrated on page 156, is based primarily on our recent discoveries at the O'Neil site in central New York, discussed on page 156, where a middle-level stratum was found to represent an apparently unmixed complex of the people who used the soapstone pots and the Susquehanna Broad points and who spread into New York from eastern Pennsylvania, as one of a related group of participants in what Witthoft has called the Susquehanna Soapstone culture, and what I refer to as the Susquehanna tradition.

This culture, with an apparent hearth in southeastern Pennsylvania, has its principal industries in soapstone (steatite) and rhyolite (or more properly, aporhyolite, metamorphosed lavas from the South Mountain district of Franklin and Adams counties, near Gettysburg, Pennsylvania; Witthoft, 1953, pp. 8–9). Witthoft recognizes at least three, and probably five, complexes within this culture, chiefly differentiated by a distinguishing form of broad point. Since each of these complexes, or at least their point styles, figures in our discussion of New York prehistory and is unequivocally derived from eastern Pennsylvania, a concise digest of Witthoft's material is appropriate.

According to Witthoft (1953, pp. 7–16), the basic and oldest complex contains the Susquehanna Broad spear point. This complex, however, overlaps in time and in geographical range with the other complexes associated with its derived projectile forms, viz., the Perkiomen, Lehigh, "serpent-head" and "fishtail" points. It has, moreover, the broadest distribution of all. From a presumed center in the lower Susquehanna Valley of Pennsylvania, its small sites are scattered southward into the Chesapeake Bay region of Maryland, westward in Pennsylvania to include the watershed of the West Branch of the Susquehanna and the upper Conemaugh River, and eastward along the Susquehanna watershed. We have now traced it northward throughout central New York, where two components of special significance will later be described (page 156). Susquehanna Broad points and probably related steatite vessel sherds occur scattered also in southern and eastern New York, especially along the Hudson and Mohawk valleys.

This distinctive point type, nearly always made of rhyolite in Pennsylvania, and often of this material in New York, where it was also translated into the local flints (Ritchie, 1961, pp. 53–54) (Plate 51, Figures 5–18), is part of a complex which contains the following traits: drills, scrapers and graving points all having the same basal shape as the point type, and probably in many cases created from damaged projectile points by rechipping. The scrapers are notable in their lack of beveling, and the battered, rounded edges of some specimens suggest (to me) use as strike-a-lights. No other chipped types are known, nor are there any utilized flakes. Netsinkers from long, oval pebbles, end-notched, and sometimes side-notched also, are abundant on the Pennsylvania sites, testifying to the important role of fishing in this culture. The numerous soapstone pots, quarried from the extensively worked steatite outcrops at Christiana, Lancaster County, and else-

where in the lower Susquehanna Valley of Pennsylvania and Maryland, are oval to rectangular in outline, with flat bottoms, straight or sloping sides, and usually a lug at either end. These handles, as well as the pot lip, are often notched, apparently for ornamentation (Plate 52, Figure 7). Cracked vessels were often drilled and laced together. Broken ones were cut up to make thick, doughnut-shaped beads, usually with notched edges; heavy rectangular gorgets, having slightly rounded corners and two to six perforations drilled from both sides; and ladles or spoons. The complex also contains unpitted and pitted pebble hammerstones, anvils, adzes, cupstones and rectangular notched shale gorgets.

While found only on some sites of the Susquehanna Soapstone culture, Witthoft believes "Selden Island Steatite Tempered Pottery" (Marcey Creek Plain pottery, Manson, 1948, p. 225; Evans, 1955, pp. 54–55) to be an intrinsic part of this complex (Witthoft, 1953, p. 12). Manson illustrates only one specimen of what I would identify as a Susquehanna Broad point from the upper level of the Marcey Creek site on the Potomac River opposite Washington. Associated points, all of quartzite, rhyolite and quartz, seem to me to resemble Savannah River styles, although several are relatively narrow and suggest a relationship with the fishtail forms of Pennsylvania and New York (Manson, 1948, Plate XXIII, A). Associated stone artifacts were a perforated winged bannerstone fragment, a fully grooved ax, and a doughnut-shaped object of steatite, strongly suggesting the so-called "perforated netsinkers" of the same material, characteristic of the Savannah River Focus (Claflin, 1931, pp. 31–32). Sixty-two per cent of the pottery from this level was of the steatite-tempered plain ware, pertaining to flat-bottomed, nearly straight-sided, lugged vessels of oval outline, identified by the finder as direct copies of the steatite vessels from the preceramic lower level of the site, where they were accompanied by larger spear points of the same Savannah River-like kinds found in the superimposed stratum.

This plain, thick, friable ware, coarsely tempered with steatite fragments from crushed soapstone potsherds, is apparently the earliest pottery of the Middle Atlantic region. A variant with finer and less abundant tempering is reported to have been present in the lower level which produced the Susquehanna Soapstone complex at the Wilson site in East Towanda, Pennsylvania (McCann, 1962, pp. 53–55), tending to support Witthoft's contention. Vinette 1 sherds are said to have occurred at a higher level in the same site (ibid., p. 55).

While Marcey Creek Plain pottery has a rare and sporadic occurrence as far north as central New York, its associations in this state are uncertain, and such pottery as can now be related to the Susquehanna Broad point complex is of Vinette 1 type (page 159).

The people of the Susquehanna Soapstone culture, as described by Witthoft, had a riverine orientation, their small but numerous sites being scattered along the banks of the major streams within the territory of their range, chiefly the great watershed of the Susquehanna River. They occupy the many islands in the river, and are found on the high parts of the flood plain along the stream edge. Apparently these folk were canoe wanderers, who visited the back country only to replenish their supplies of steatite and rhyolite. They were hunters of large and small game; fishermen, at least with nets; but they did not ordinarily eat the river shellfish. Nor

are they known to have stored food in pits. A very large surface site of this culture at Milan Station, near Athens, Pennsylvania, tested by the writer in 1959, failed to produce a single pit. Cooking pits were, however, present on the O'Neil site component of this culture in central New York (page 159).

Witthoft (1953, p. 14) believes that "The Susquehanna Soapstone Culture represents a very distinct and marked change in every detail of material culture and way of life from earlier times in the Susquehanna Valley." In New York State, this change in material culture seems not to have involved any distinctively different manner of living. Thus, in New York, the camp sites of this culture occur in precisely the same locations along the large streams and lakes as do those of Archaic and Woodland peoples, indeed, very often on the same loci—as, for example, Frontenac Island in Cayuga Lake, the Piffard site, and the O'Neil site on the Seneca River, all with earlier and later components. There is little to suggest on these and other sites any marked difference in the way of life of any of the various occupants.

Witthoft surmises that the broad spear points (javelin or dart points in the main, by my definition; 1961, pp. 5–6) of the several aforementioned related types derive from "certain heavy, rough, crudely corner-notched rhyolite points found among other Archaic types in the area included between the Lower Susquehanna and the Juniata Rivers" (Witthoft, 1953, p. 15, and by conversation of February 20, 1962). I suspect, however, that he has found an even better potential prototype in the broad stemmed points of the Long site, a surface component situated on a high rounded hilltop overlooking Swatara Creek, a tributary of the lower Susquehanna in

Lebanon County, Pennsylvania (Witthoft, 1959, p. 82 and Figure 1, g-i). These points, of Hardiston quartzite from nearby outcrops, show strong similarities to the Savannah River point of the Southeast and to the Snook Kill point of eastern New York. The stemmed-scraper type of the Long site is identical with that of the Snook Kill complex. Witthoft considers the Long site complex Early Archaic, around seven thousand years old, but this estimate seems to me excessive.

Having seen his material at Harrisburg, through Witthoft's courtesy, it is difficult to escape the strong impression that the Long site points may represent the local ancestral form for the Lehigh Broad point of Pennsylvania and the indubitably related Late Archaic Snook Kill type of New York, both of which have very close resemblances to the broad stemmed points of the Savannah River Focus (Claflin, 1931; Caldwell, 1952, pp. 312–14). On a slightly later level, I suspect, the Perkiomen and Susquehanna forms emerged from a Lehigh background in the same area of Pennsylvania. In addition to those mentioned, the category of "corner-removed" points of New England appears to have been genetically related to the Long and Savannah River styles.

The Perkiomen and Lehigh complexes have their respective centers east of the Susquehanna watershed, the former in the Schuylkill Valley and the drainage systems entering from the north; the latter in the area drained by the Lehigh and the upper Delaware (Witthoft, 1953, pp. 16–22). The jasper quarries of Berks, Lehigh and Bucks counties, Pennsylvania, furnished the bulk of the stone for the Perkiomen points, but rhyolite was extensively used. Lehigh points were mainly fashioned from jasper or black flint. Jasper, rhyolite and argillite,

all Pennsylvania materials are included in the lithology of the Snook Kill points of eastern New York, which typologically overlap, and were almost certainly derived from, the Lehigh type (Ritchie, 1961, pp. 47–48).

Perkiomen points have a thin surface scatter in central New York, especially along the Seneca River (Ritchie, 1961, p. 99); in eastern New York, particularly the Hudson Valley, where they are rarely present in the upper levels of some sites (Ritchie, 1958, Plate 5, Figure 3); in southern New York, where also two specimens seen by the writer in the Anderson collection were said to have been excavated, along with the greater portion of a Vinette 1 pot, suggesting the persistence of this point form into Early Woodland times, at the Rossville No. 1 site on the Arthur Kill, in southwestern Staten Island; and in the Genesee Valley on the margin of western New York.

In this latter locality a discovery of great interest was made on the Piffard site (Figure 4, site number 26), near the hamlet of the same name, in Livingston County. This unusual, important and multicomponent site of the Archaic and Transitional periods covers about half an acre of a level, sandy-loam terrace along a tiny brook, one and a quarter miles west of the meandering Genesee, at an elevation of eighty feet above the flood plain of the river. Revealed during topsoil stripping, it was extensively excavated in 1946–47 by Robert R. Hill of Rochester and John P. Jones of Cuylerville, through whose courtesy the site and collections were later studied by the writer, who also conducted excavations in the small remaining portion.

While most of the material pertained to the Lamoka phase (page 38), and lesser amounts to the Brewerton or Frontenac

phases, surface finds of steatite pot fragments, and refuse recoveries of a few Vinette 1 sherds were made by the first excavators, who also opened some thirteen
graves, whose wall outlines were intrusive
into the Archaic refuse. Two were cremations, the others flexed; red ocher was present in all but three, and the scanty grave
goods matched our finds at Frontenac Island.

A unique find among this group of graves
and of exceptional interest was Burial 13,
the cremated remains of, apparently, a
young adult, which lay in a pit eighteen
inches across and twenty-two inches deep.
No traces of burning *in situ* were present.
The mortuary furnishings comprised between fifty and sixty broad points of the
Perkiomen type, all made from native
Onondaga flint, intentionally broken or
"killed," for the most part, but not by fire,
and elsewhere, since many of the fragments
are missing (Plate 50). Red ocher covered
the intermixed mass of bones and points.
To my knowledge, this is the only burial
anywhere which can be attributed to the
makers of the Perkiomen points.

The Perkiomen complex in Pennsylvania
is very imperfectly known. Soapstone vessel sherds are rare, but beads of this material, and end-notched netsinkers, both resembling traits of the Susquehanna Broad
point complex, are present. Drills and
scrapers, and "drill-tipped" tools, all based
on typical broken spear points, occur, as
do hammerstones and adzes, to form a
close parallel with the Susquehanna Broad
point complex.

Sites of the Perkiomen complex in Pennsylvania are small, rarely pure, have no
pits or graves, but occasional caches. They
are said to be less closely related to major
streams than the Susquehanna Broad point
sites, and often to lie within large tracts of

swamp on small streams, suggesting more
emphasis on hunting than on fishing and
less mobility through water travel.

The picture of the Lehigh complex is
even more obscure. Soapstone pot fragments occur on some of the always small
sites, together with cruciform drills (like
those of the Savannah River Focus),
chipped from the characteristic points, and
heavy netsinkers. The slender indications
point to a way of life as wandering hunters and fishers with canoe transport, like
that associated with the Susquehanna
Broad point complex.

Actually, of all the Susquehanna Soapstone cultures which originated in Pennsylvania and penetrated northward through
the Susquehanna and Delaware river systems into New York State, the Lehigh-de-
rived Snook Kill complex, apparently the
earliest of all these cultures, is the most
developed and best-known; in fact, the
trait assemblage and site characteristics of
the Snook Kill in eastern New York, while
leaving much to be determined, are better
elucidated than the parent Lehigh complex
of Pennsylvania (page 153).

Two variant point types, regarded by
Witthoft as later developments from the
Susquehanna Broad form, remain for brief
consideration. They are his "serpent-head"
and narrow "fishtail" points, both of which
seem to have had Vinette 1 pottery associations in Pennsylvania (Witthoft, 1953,
pp. 22–23). The first is concentrated in the
Lehigh and middle Delaware valleys, the
second along the middle and upper Delaware River. In New York State the "serpent-head" variant is dubiously represented, but the narrow "fishtail" style
achieves a high development in the Orient
Fishtail type (Ritchie, 1961, p. 39), found
chiefly in eastern and southern New York,
and the diagnostic point form of the Ori-

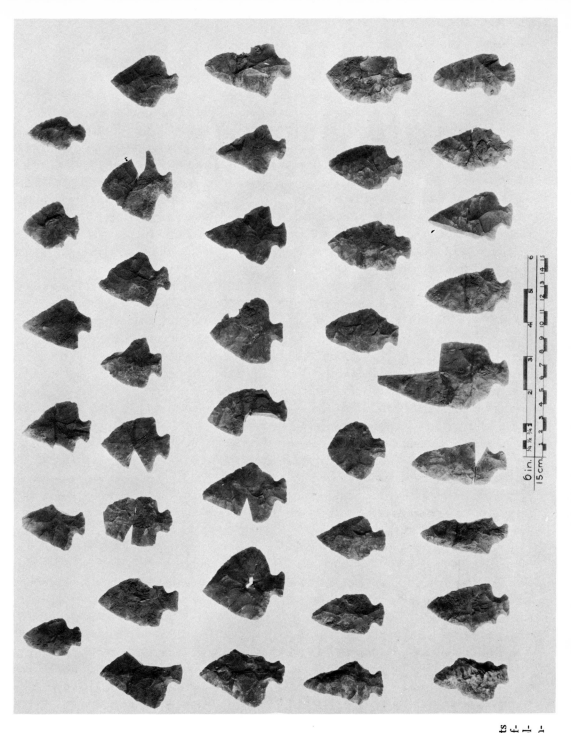

PLATE 50 Perkiomen-type points from cremated burial on the Piffard site, Livingston Co., N.Y. Collection of Robert R. Hill, Rochester, N.Y.

ent phase of Long Island, radiocarbon-dated between 1043 B.C.±300 years and 763 B.C.±220 years. This Transitional to Early Woodland culture is described on page 164. While there are as yet no carbon-14 dates for any Pennsylvania sites or cultures, it is quite probable that the Orient phase in New York and the unknown Pennsylvania complex to which the comparable fishtail point belongs were contemporaneous, and some of the materials of Orient points on Long Island, jasper and argillite in particular, may have been quarried in southeastern Pennsylvania, possibly along with some of the steatite of the accompanying stone cooking vessels. Thus the Orient phase, like the other Transitional-period complexes discussed, doubtless had some of its roots in eastern Pennsylvania, although its major development and climax seem to have taken place, with stimuli from southern New England, on eastern Long Island, several centuries subsequent to the radiocarbon-dated Frost Island phase, next to be considered, to which the Susquehanna Broad point in New York pertains. Hence, as Witthoft states, "During the Transitional Period, we can see a number of cultural subareas which make up one big culture area, included within the drainage basins of the Potomac, the Susquehanna, and the Hudson-Mohawk" (Witthoft, 1953, p. 16). He could have extended this range to have included Long Island and the Finger Lakes -Seneca River region of central New York.

THE FROST ISLAND PHASE

As has been remarked (page 150), the exegesis of the Frost Island phase rests for the most part on discoveries made in 1961–62 by the New York State Museum and Science Service, under the writer's direction, on the E. J. O'Neil farm, Township of Cato, Cayuga County (Wpt. 11-4) (Figure 4, site number 27). Finds made here in a radiocarbon-dated horizon apparently constitute a true assemblage of related traits. The site, the subject of a full report to be published elsewhere, is situated at the southern end of a drumlin, on the first or twenty-foot terrace above the flood plain of the Seneca River, which evidently flowed at the base of the terrace in Indian times. The old meander channel encloses a piece of swampy land called Frost Island, now lying between the site and the river.

Three distinct soil strata were traced. The deepest, stratum 3, a brown sand, produced artifacts of the Brewerton phase and hearths, radiocarbon-dated around 2000 B.C. (page 91). The middle stratum, number 2, an old humus layer, consisted of black, compact soil, abounding in fire-broken stones, either scattered or in concentrations. This layer constituted an archaeological find of cardinal importance, for it yielded an apparently uncontaminated, *in situ* complex of artifacts and features, which form the basis of my definition of the Frost Island phase. Moreover, this complex has been radiocarbon-dated from one of the hearth samples. The uppermost layer, stratum 1, of brown sandy loam, resulted in most of the pit and other features found on the site, and in artifacts relating to Middle and Late Woodland cultures of Point Peninsula and Owasco proveniences. Later references will be made to these finds, which were also carbon-14 assayed.

In only one other New York site known to the writer, viz., the upper level at Frontenac Island (page 105), have Susquehanna Broad points been found in any number underground. There they occurred with drills having similar semilozenge-shaped bases, steatite vessel fragments and

Vinette 1 sherds, as at O'Neil's, but inter-mixed with later Middle Woodland, Point Peninsula materials (Ritchie, 1945, Plate 6).

An evidently single-component, subsur-face site, with Frost Island affinities, has been reported at East Towanda, Bradford County, Pennsylvania, although here a sub-stantial part of the material was recovered, not *in situ,* but from the eroding Susque-hanna River bank (Witthoft, 1953, p. 13; McCann, 1962).

At this site, however, a variety of Marcey Creek Plain ware was present with the soapstone sherds at the lowest level, while a little Vinette 1 pottery was recovered at a higher horizon (McCann, 1962, pp. 53–55). The Marcey Creek sherds pertained to steatite-tempered pots, modeled after the stone bowls, being oval with slightly everted walls, having flat bases which pro-ject slightly beyond the walls to form a "heel," and often bearing lugs at either end. This early pottery seems clearly to reflect the introduction into the Middle Atlantic area, probably from farther south and by stimulus diffusion, of the initial knowledge of ceramics.

Surface sites where occur the same dis-tinctive Susquehanna Broad points, soap-stone potsherds, and occasionally other ar-tifacts of the now recognized Frost Island complex have a wide distribution along the Susquehanna River and its tributaries in New York, especially the Unadilla, Che-nango, Tioughnioga, Chemung and Cohoc-ton. Through the latter the culture proba-bly reached the Genesee Valley, where it is sporadically found. It is well represented in the Finger Lakes district of central New York, and the contiguous Seneca, Oneida and Oswego river valleys. It is present with lesser intensity in the Delaware, Hudson and Mohawk valleys. In New York, there-

fore, it is primarily a central New York manifestation.

Everywhere throughout its range the sites occupy a riverine setting, never far from the main stream, in fact usually upon the bank of the first terrace or the higher por-tions of the flood plain. Sites are small, indicative of mere camps, but they may overlap extensively or, as apparently at O'Neil's, occur as superimposed compo-nents marking a succession of temporary sojourning places by the same group.

We have only the one radiocarbon de-termination from the O'Neil site to fix the time of the Frost Island culture, viz., 1250 B.C.$\pm$100 years (Y-1274). This would seem to mark its approximate arrival at the O'Neil site, since the hearth yielding the charcoal came from near the base of stra-tum 2, and therefore probably in central New York as well. Witthoft has suggested 1500 B.C. for the beginning of the Susque-hanna Soapstone culture in Pennsylvania (McCann, 1962, p. 55), and this is likely; while a date of about the same magnitude, 1470 B.C.$\pm$100 years, for the Late Archaic Snook Kill phase, bordering on the Transi-tional stage, has already been noted for eastern New York (page 136), and pro-vides substantial support.

There are no data on the somatology of the Frost Island people; the few possibly pertinent burials (page 163) being crema-tions.

Hunting doubtless constituted the pri-mary subsistence activity, the dart or jave-lin and probably the hand-held spear being the major weapons, tipped with Susque-hanana Broad-type points (Plate 51, Fig-ures 5–14, 17, 18) (Ritchie, 1961, pp. 53–54) chipped from rhyolite or flint, the latter most common in New York where rhyolite sources are lacking.

Fishing with nets is indicated by the

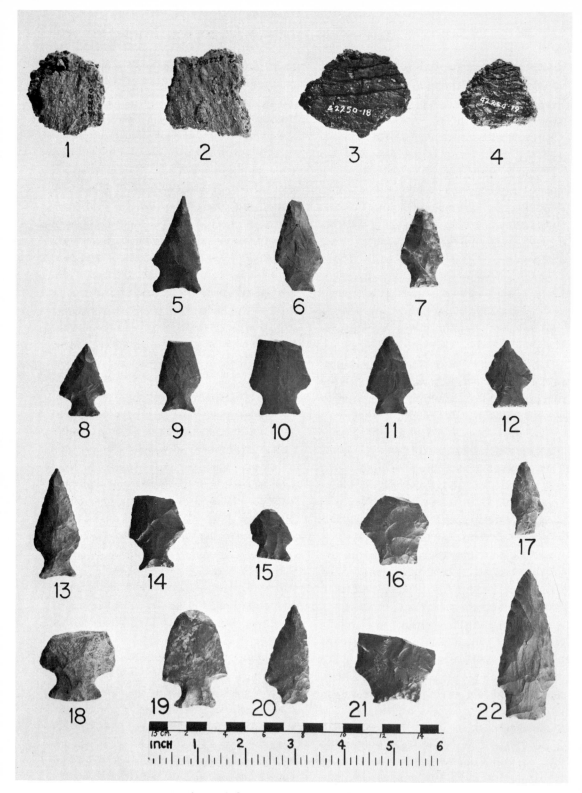

PLATE 51 Artifacts of the Frost Island phase from the O'Neil site, Cayuga Co., N.Y. 1–4 Vinette 1 type potsherds (1, 2 exterior, 3, 4 interior surfaces); 5–14, 18 Susquehanna Broad points; 15 Susquehanna Broad point showing use as strike-a-light; 16, 21 basal sections of semilozenge-shaped knives; 17 narrow variant of Susquehanna Broad point; 19 Susquehanna Broad point modified for end scraper; 20 asymmetric knife; 22 Genesee-type point.

presence on some of the sites of notched pebble netsinkers (Plate 53, Figure 7).

While the use of wild vegetable foods is highly likely, any knowledge of agriculture at this early time is very doubtful. Storage pits have not been identified, nor do we have any of the usual implements for food grinding. Cooking was done in stone pots or by baking on beds of heated stones, placed, apparently, in shallow pits (Plate 54). Late in the phase was added the limited use of Vinette 1 pottery vessels.

Data on house form are lacking. The settlements were certainly small and temporary, involving components covering a third of an acre or less, and comprising probably not more than twenty-five to forty people. Reiterated occupancy of a propitious locale is suggested, the O'Neil-site ground midden, for example, indicating periodic usage by the same or similar cultural groups.

Nothing is known concerning the dress and ornaments of these people. Rude crescentic gorgets with two perforations, made from broken steatite pots, have been found by the writer on two sites of this phase in New York. Witthoft (1953, p. 12) also reports "heavy gorgets cut from soapstone sherds, rectangular with slightly rounded corners, with two, four or six holes drilled from both sides."

The list of artifacts attributable to the Frost Island phase is very limited; few bone or antler forms have survived; most of the articles are of chipped or rough stone, with very little ground or polished stonework in evidence. All objects, except as noted, may be classified as tools. There are no smoking pipes. Knives, end scrapers, drills and strike-a-lights occur with the typical bases of the Susquehanna Broad points, and many if not all of these implements may be secondary modifications of such points (Plate 51, Figures 15, 19). In addition,

there are probable knives of semilozenge or pentagonal shape, having the general outline of the characteristic point type (Plate 51, Figures 16, 21); and an asymmetric, side-notched style (Plate 51, Figure 20), reported also from the Wilson site (McCann, 1962, p. 52).

Adzes, chipped and partially ground into shape, are a part of this complex. Although Witthoft (1953, p. 12) speaks of "heavy adze blades, long, of oval cross section," as occurring on Pennsylvania sites of the Susquehanna Soapstone culture, all New York specimens known to the writer from surface sites and the O'Neil station are small tools, ranging from about three and a half to five inches in length, some oval, others plano-convex in cross section (Plate 53, Figures 1–3). The similarity of these artifacts to certain of the tools used in quarrying and shaping the steatite pots is noticeable. (Compare Plate 53, Figures 1, 3, with Holmes, 1897, Plate XCIV.)

A remarkable peculiarity of the New York specimens is their light, porous, leached condition. Examples submitted for analysis to geologists of the New York State Museum and Science Service show that they were made (by chipping and grinding) from an impure calcareous chert, from which the carbonates have leached away leaving only the silica. As the rock in this condition does not possess conchoidal fracture, the tools were certainly worked out prior to the leaching, the cause of which is problematical.

Rough stone implements (Plate 53) include unpitted pebble and bipitted pebble hammerstones (Figures 4, 8), anvilstones (Figure 5), multiple pitted stones of unknown purpose (Figure 10), apparently a simple form of the so-called sinewstone (Figure 9), and the chopper (Figure 6).

The stone bowls or vessels, several times

PLATE 52 Soapstone pot fragments of the Frost Island phase from the O'Neil site, Cayuga Co., N.Y. 1, 6, 7 rim sections (7 has a notched lug); 2, 5 vertical wall fragments showing flat bottom; 3, 4 wall sherds.

PLATE 53   Stone tools of the Frost Island phase from the O'Neil site, Cayuga Co., N.Y. 1–3 chipped and ground plano-convex adzes (2 is deeply eroded); 4 plain pebble hammerstone; 5 multiple-pitted anvilstone; 6 chopper; 7 notched netsinker; 8 bipitted hammerstone; 9 simple sinewstone, reverse shows use as whetstone; 10 multiple pitted stone.

referred to, and known only from fragments, seem to have been oval or rectangular in shape, with flat or nearly flat bottoms and straight or slightly outsloping sides. Lobate or squarish lugs appear on either end of many of the pots. Lips and lugs, nicked or notched transversely, presumably a decorative feature, are not uncommon. Holes bored for lacing together cracked sections are very prevalent, indicating that the vessels were used as long as possible (Plate 52).

Broken utensils were sometimes cut up for gorgets, as already mentioned, and according to Witthoft (1953, p. 12) for thick, doughnut-like beads, and spoons or ladles, none of which has so far been noted on a New York site.

Nearly all the stone vessels of the Susquehanna Soapstone culture show the marks of the quarry pick, a chisel- or narrow celt-like cutting tool employed in carving them out of blocks of stones, quarried presumably around Christiana, Lancaster County, Pennsylvania (Witthoft, 1953, p. 13; Crozier, 1939). These vertical or oblique tool marks are present on the exterior surface of nearly every vessel fragment pertaining to this culture, while the interior surface is always rubbed smooth, probably with sand and water or a sandstone hone (Plate 52). It is important to note again the difference in this respect between the stone pots of the Susquehanna Soapstone culture and the Orient phase. The latter, like those of New England to which they are most closely related, are in nearly every instance smoothed both inside and out, and as a further difference, have chiefly rounded rather than flat bottoms (page 171). These distinctions have led me to suppose that, although the common hearth of the stone-pot industry of the eastern United States may have been situated in

the steatite-rich Virginia-North Carolina Piedmont region, with diffusions in all directions, two secondary sources of dissemination in steatite-producing regions can be distinguished, one in the Potomac and upper Chesapeake Bay area, including southeastern Pennsylvania and the vicinity of Washington (Holmes, 1897, pp. 113–33), giving rise to the materials of the Susquehanna Soapstone culture; another perhaps of slightly lesser antiquity, in southern New England, to which the Orient stone vessels relate (Ritchie, 1959, p. 62).

Steatite, or more properly amphibole-talc (Ritchie, 1959, pp. 63–64), while furnishing an extraordinary material for cooking pots because of its property of long retention of latent heat, is also very heavy, and stone vessels are cumbersome to transport. Both for this reason and because of the site locations, canoe transportation is strongly indicated, and the writer shares Witthoft's conception of an essentially riverine way of life, the back country being frequented only for fresh supplies of the stone materials, steatite and rhyolite.

When once the little bands of travelers, in their probable dugout boats, had penetrated and established themselves in New York, it is questionable whether journeys were made back to the nearest quarry centers in southern Pennsylvania for the traditional stone materials. Perhaps some trade was conducted from group to group along the rivers linking the far-separated areas. Locally available flint was substituted for the rhyolite, as is patent from our finds on all New York sites (Plate 51). In the main the traditional form was copied faithfully, but some variations on the basic style are manifest (Plate 51, Figure 17).

The want of any suitable stone substitute for the steatite pot may have hastened the adoption of the Vinette 1 ware which was

PLATE 54 Burned stone feature of the Frost Island phase on O'Neil site, Cayuga Co., N.Y.

being introduced into the New York area not later than 1000 B.C. (Ritchie, 1962).

The mortuary customs of the Frost Island people, as of all the groups encompassed in the Susquehanna Soapstone culture, are as yet unelucidated. I suspect the practice of cremation, without, however, the elaborate cult aspects seen in the slightly overlapping Orient phase. Burial 142 at Frontenac Island was a cremation with associated "killed" rhyolite blades of semilozenge shape, probably related to the Frost Island component in the upper level of the site (Ritchie, 1945, p. 79); Burial 13

at Piffard, with an offering of similarly treated Perkiomen points, although not of the Frost Island phase, was also a cremation with red ocher (page 154).

We are equally in the dark regarding the religio-ceremonial aspects of the Frost Island culture. Inferences from the surviving stone relics, chiefly tools, weapons, and utensils, point to a prosaic, utilitarian bias, and suggest that the general manner of life of the Archaic cultural stage was still in vogue.

The Frost Island complex may have followed a still unrecognized complex in New

York, and a very poorly defined one in Pennsylvania, containing the Perkiomen Broad point (page 153), or the two complexes may have been partly coeval. Thus far, the Perkiomen point (Ritchie, 1961, pp. 42–43) is represented mainly by scattered specimens, probably related to the steatite potsherds found on some of the same surface sites, and by an offering of such points with a cremation on the Piffard site (pages 153–54).

The Frost Island phase seems to have expired without clear survivals. Some still unclassified projectile points from central New York suggest vestigial remnants of the broad-bladed Susquehanna varieties. Vinette 1 pottery, the first areal introduction of which seems to have been into the Frost Island assemblage (Plate 51, Figures 1–4), increased in frequency in the succeeding Early Woodland stage, represented in the same area by the Meadowood culture (page 179). Since the oldest carbon-14 date for the Meadowood phase is 998 B.C. ±170 years (C-192), derived from the Oberlander No. 2 site on which, and the related Vinette site, several steatite potsherds and Susquehanna Broad points were found (Ritchie, 1944, pp. 156, 162, 164), there may have occurred a slight overlapping of these two cultures, with the final submergence of the Frost Island phase in central New York taking place at about this time.

THE ORIENT PHASE

The first discovered site of this culture, Orient No. 1, was a cemetery situated on a sand hill close to Orient, near the northeastern end of Long Island. In the same year (1935), and only an eighth of a mile away, a second hilltop burial ground, Orient

No. 2, was found by the same excavators, Roy Latham of Orient, and fellow members of the Long Island Chapter, New York State Archeological Association. Two years later, this group located and dug a still larger burial site of the same extraordinary type, on the summit of Sugar Loaf Hill, in the Shinnecock Hills, on the southern fork of eastern Long Island, and in 1940 they began work at the fourth site of this kind, similarly located on a hilltop at Jamesport, about twenty miles west of the original discovery. A fifth cemetery of unknown size, but apparently much the smallest of all, was destroyed in bulldozing operations on a hill near Cutchogue (Figure 4, sites number 28–31, 34) in 1959, and in part perhaps earlier, and investigations made there in the summer of 1961 by the New York State Museum and Science Service are described below.

The data for an Orient Focus were summarized by the writer following his examination of the Long Island Chapter's finds, through the courtesy of Roy Latham and Charles F. Goddard (Ritchie, 1944, pp. 227–35), and the possibility was suggested, due to the absence of recognized habitation sites and because of trait linkages in southern New England, that the Indians responsible for the Orient cemeteries might have resided in Connecticut, and only visited eastern Long Island by canoe passage across Long Island Sound "for the purpose of disposing of their dead in a complicated funeral ritual" (ibid., p. 232, footnote 3). In his analysis of coastal New York, Smith (1950, p. 150) follows somewhat the same idea, concluding that the Orient Focus was "the burial complex of the people responsible for the North Beach focus" on Long Island.

Clarification came with the excavation in 1955 and 1956 by the writer for the New

York State Museum and Science Service of a major habitation site of the Orient culture at Stony Brook (Skt. 1-1), near the north-central shore of Long Island (Figure 4, site number 32) (Ritchie, 1959). In the summer of 1961 additional data of this kind were secured by the State Museum group on the Baxter site (Sag. 3) near New Suffolk, Long Island (Figure 4, site number 33), described later on, and it is now unequivocal that the Orient culture was native to Long Island. Its characteristic fishtail projectile points and soapstone pot fragments have a nearly island-wide surface distribution, and they have been found in upper New York City (Skinner, 1919, pp. 64, 70), on Staten Island, in the Hudson Valley north at least to Catskill, where they occur stratigraphically between Archaic and Middle Woodland levels in the Lotus Point site (Ritchie, 1958, pp. 25–34, 100), and sporadically in eastern New Jersey, Connecticut and Rhode Island (Ritchie, 1959, pp. 10, 49, 90). In addition to the Stony Brook and Baxter sites, a habitation site of undetermined extent, but apparently small, is known from Muskeeta Cove,[1] near the village of Glen Cove at the western end of Long Island (Figure 4, site number 35). A visit by the writer in 1955, through the courtesy of Edward Patterson of Sea Cliff, confirmed the occurrence of Orient Fishtail points and steatite potsherds in red sand directly beneath a virtually sterile shell spread. The known burial sites of the culture, however, are confined to the eastern third of Long Island, despite intensive search by the writer and others over a much broader area.

[1] According to the Nassau Archeological Society, which reported the site, this is the older and correct spelling, although the Sea Cliff, New York, 7.5-minute quadrangle (1954) gives it as "Mosquito Cove."

Time Span

A compact and consistent series of five radiocarbon dates for Stony Brook and three of the four major burial sites, ranging between 1043 B.C. and 763 B.C., indicates a minimum time span of around three hundred years for the Orient culture (Figure 1). This period seems to correlate with a progressively cooling climatic phase and a consequent drop in sea level, believed by Fairbridge to amount to approximately ten feet during its maximum or "Pelham Bay Emergence," radiocarbon-dated c. 876 B.C. ±220 years (C-943, Libby, 1954a, p. 735) on wood from a "drowned forest" at Pelham Bay, New York (Fairbridge, 1958, pp. 477–78; 1960, p. 51).

While this change in sea level could hardly affect the burial locations, all on the highest available hills where they occur, it might have a definite bearing on the selection of living sites, since we now know that the Orient people were heavy users of shellfish foods. It also raises the possibility that the scarcity of Orient settlement sites may in part be owing to their having had near-shore situations, which are now submerged. Other factors, however, such as shelter from cold winds, were clearly involved in site selection, a matter further explored below.

Food and Its Preparation

Clues to the subsistence basis of the Orient culture afford the only direct surviving evidence of the floristic and faunal associations of the period, and they do not suggest any substantial differences from the present biotic or climatic environments. The fossil pollen record for the Northeast points to an oak-hickory forest dominance at this time (Deevey and Flint, 1957), and carbonized hickory nuts were the only vegetable remains (except wood charcoal of unidentifiable species) found in the pit features at Stony Brook.

Shellfish appear to have provided the primary source of food, and they were doubtless abundant and easily gathered from mud flats, shallow bays and stream estuaries all around Long Island. The Orient midden at Stony Brook (Midden A) and its appertaining pits were rich in shellfish detritus, which comprised an estimated 65 per cent of the total volume, the remainder being stained sand, burned stones, charcoal particles, animal bones, etc. Many of the shells were crushed from trampling on the surface of the living area; others, especially in the cooking pits, were massed and whole. The following species were present in order of frequency: oyster (*Ostrea virginica*), some individuals as much as ten inches in length; bay scallop (*Pecten irradians*); hard-shelled clam or quahog (*Venus mercenaria*); long clam or soft-shelled clam (*Mya arenaria*); a gastropod of the genus *Littorina* (commonly called a periwinkle); channeled whelk (*Busycon canaliculatum*); and ark (*Arca* sp. ?).

Most of the shell remains from the much smaller Baxter site were saved for study and they are discussed below under the description of the site (page 169).

Although soil conditions were excellent for the preservation of osseous matter at Stony Brook, where a *p*H of 8.0 was general throughout Midden A, the quantity of animal bones (and of bone artifacts) was low, denoting a limited use for this class of food. Since this was a reversal of the conditions found in the deeper and older midden on the site (Midden B), pertaining to an Archaic occupation (page 143), it is

possible that already by *c.* 974 B.C. the supply of large game on Long Island was running low, and the inexhaustible reserves of shellfish were largely depended upon for maintaining a population of no great size. As usual, the bone refuse was well broken, presumably to obtain marrow, brains and bone grease. The white-tailed deer (*Odocoileus virginianus*), also as usual, was the chief game animal, and the turkey (*Meleagris gallopavo*) the most used bird. Other species taken for some purpose were the common box turtle (*Terrapene carolina*), woodchuck (*Marmota monax*), raccoon (*Procyon lotor*), gray fox (*Urocyon cinereoargenteus*), mink (*Mustela vison*), and various small rodents and ducks.

Bones and antlers of the deer, and bones of medium-sized birds, were found by us in calcined condition as probable food offerings in a grave (Feature 1) in the Orient cemetery at Jamesport, and at Stony Brook the bones of a dog occurred under conditions suggesting its use for food. Very likely, however, the chief value of this animal was as aid and companion to the hunter. Finally, a small number of deer bones (twenty) were present at the Baxter site.

No fishbones were found at Stony Brook or the Baxter site. If fish were included in the diet, some evidence should have been present, as such remains are preserved in the shell middens of later sites on Long Island. Moreover, no articles of fishing gear came to light in middens or graves, not even a netsinker.

The pre-Orient Archaic people of Long Island, one of whose middens, as already mentioned, lay directly beneath the Orient occupation at Stony Brook, seem also to have neglected fishing but, in contrast to their successors, they made relatively little use of shellfish, their main dependence being on hunting, with the deer as the favorite game animal. Similar conditions were found by us at the Wading River site (Mrh. 1-2) (Figure 4, site number 14) of another Archaic group on Long Island (Ritchie, 1959, pp. 46–47, 81–82) (page 143). The progressive shift to a main reliance on shellfish food seen at both these sites suggests, in addition to a possible correlation with a growing scarcity of large game, a changing cultural orientation from an inland pattern of forest hunting, ages old in the Archaic traditions of the eastern United States, toward the sea; at first a littoral preoccupation with shellfish gathering, finally, the development (or adoption from neighboring areas) of an offshore fishing activity, employing barbed bone points and bone fishhooks, some of composite form, as well as nets, as inferred from stone sinkers. This stage in the evolution of the subsistence economy on Long Island appears to have been reached in Middle Woodland time. A generally congruent development in Maine is noted by Byers (1959a, p. 234). Some supporting data were found by the writer on Martha's Vineyard, Massachusetts, during his excavations of 1964 (page 141).

Doubtless wild vegetable foods comprised a significant part of the Orient people's diet, but the preserved evidence consists only of a few carbonized hickory nuts from Stony Brook. Rude elongate stone pestles found as grave goods in some of the cemeteries further suggests the employment of short wooden mortars as grinding devices (Ritchie, 1944, Plate 107, Figures 23, 24).

In the cooking of foods there is ample evidence of the following methods: stone-boiling; baking in pits or earth ovens, with or without use of heated stones; roasting on stone platforms; and boiling in stone pots and, to a limited extent, later in the period

of Orient occupation, in pottery vessels. Fire was made by percussion, with nodules of iron pyrites and quartz or flint strikers, and fire-making kits form part of the furniture of nearly every burial (Plate 55, Figures 1, 2).

Settlement Sites

Very little is known concerning the Orient dwellings and settlement patterns, since no house floors or post-mold arrangements could be discovered at the Stony Brook or Baxter sites. Shelters were probably flimsy, temporary, and small affairs of poles and bark or mats. Such lodges were set up in camp spots selected for convenience to food resources, a potable water supply, and shelter from cold westerly and northerly winds. The present location of the Stony Brook site is the gentle south-facing sand slope, on the low bank of a tidal stream flowing through a wide expanse of salt marsh and tidal flats into Smithtown Bay of Long Island Sound. Behind it, to the north, rises a high morainal ridge, from the base of which springs formerly flowed.

The site today seems ideally located with respect to existing land and hydrographic features, but if mean sea level were some ten feet lower than at present, as has been postulated by Fairbridge (page 169), it would, as stated by Salwen, probably lie on a small fresh-water stream flowing through low meadowland, and thus have an inland rather than a coastal character, while probably still maintaining direct canoe access to the Sound. The predominance of oyster shells over other shellfish remains in the refuse may indicate the then greater accessibility of this species in the deeper waters of Smithtown Bay, while quahogs or hard-shelled clams, of lesser

PLATE 55 Artifacts of the Orient phase from the Baxter site, Long Island. 1, 2 quartz strike-a-lights; 3, 4 projectile points of Bare Island type; 5–7, 9–11, 13–15 projectile points of Orient Fishtail type; 8 drill; 12 steatite potsherd; 16 hematite paintstone.

abundance in the middens, were gathered from the then much shrunken tidal flats nearby (Salwen, 1962, pp. 48–51).

The Baxter site lies on nearly level sand on the west side of Downs Creek, a tidal inlet emptying into Peconic Bay about a quarter mile to the south. It faces southeast across the open salt marsh and meadow, and probably had a dense forest barrier to the wind from the west. Incidentally, this pattern of location on the west bank of a short tidal stream was found by our Long Island survey to be the general rule for sites of all periods and cultures. Currently eight to ten feet above present mean sea level, and only a few hundred yards distant from tidal flats which even today produce hard-shelled clams in abundance, it had, theoretically, a much different setting during the "Pelham Bay Low" when sea level reached some ten feet below the present level. In his reconstruction of the Orient environment at the site, Salwen envisions a setting on "a small freshwater stream, or a very narrow tidal estuary, which flows a little over a mile to the south before reaching Peconic Bay. The bay itself is shallower than at present, with extensive tidal flats bordering the mainland and surrounding Robins Island" (Salwen, 1962, pp. 51–53).

The heavy predominance of the hard-shelled clam in the Baxter-site refuse is thus explained and contrasted with the situation at the Stony Brook site, where oyster valves prevailed over all other shellfish remains, presumably because of their then ready availability in Smithtown Bay.

Recently, serious doubt has been raised concerning the fluctuation of the sea level as postulated by Fairbridge. Radiocarbon age determinations of peat and wood samples from the Connecticut coast indicate rather a continuous submergence over the last seven thousand years, apparently as the result of a world-wide, or eustatic, rise of sea level. According to Bloom and Stuiver (1963, p. 334), "The radiocarbon dates and general stratigraphic relationships demonstrate that submergence has been continuous on the Connecticut coast for at least 7000 years and probably for over 11,000 years, with no evidence of pauses or reversals in the submergent trend. From 7000 to 3000 years ago submergence was at the rate of 0.6 foot per century; during the last 3000 years the rate has been only half as great. It is significant that not one of several hundred borings in Connecticut tidal marshes showed more than 10 feet of salt-marsh peat overlying bay mud. Apparently, sediment accumulation and salt-marsh growth have been able to keep pace with submergence only during the last 3000 years; prior to that time the more rapid submergence maintained open, although shallow, estuaries and lagoons on the sites of the present salt marshes." (Cf. Sears, 1963; Shepard, 1964.)

The Baxter site is very small, covering only some six hundred square feet, of which 131 square feet had been explored by Ralph Solecki, its discoverer, in 1938, and by Solecki and Bert Salwen, both of Columbia University, in 1960. In July 1961 most of the remainder was excavated by the writer and a party of four student assistants, through the courtesy of the owner, William J. Baxter, and our Columbia colleagues.

Although small and shallow, the site was well stratified, with two artifact-bearing layers, the uppermost, in the A1 soil of the humus zone, grading downward into a dark-brown, organic-stained sand. In this six- to seven-inch occupation level, and in two shallow pits originating from it, were found a small quantity of Late Woodland potsherds and broad triangular projectile points.

The underlying Orient culture horizon, a

seven- to eight-inch zone of orange or reddish-brown sand (B2 soil), produced burned stones, scattered or in thin lenses suggesting hearths, quartz rejectage, and a sparse representation of typical Orient artifacts—Orient Fishtail points, a drill, a strike-a-light, a steatite potsherd and a paintstone—as the most important items, all represented on Plate 55. Two Late Archaic, Wading River type points were also found at the very base of the Orient stratum (Plate 55, Figures 3, 4).

No charcoal was present and only a small quantity, mostly calcined, of mammal bones, identifiable as deer. Nearly twenty-four pounds of shellfish remains were recovered, however, 99 per cent pertaining to the hard clam, 0.8 per cent to the oyster, and 0.2 per cent to the channeled or knobbed whelk. Stratigraphic analysis clearly revealed the virtually identical percentile distribution of these remains between the Woodland and the Orient levels. Our finding, based upon the total shellfish debris, is at variance with the earlier results of the column-sampling method at the site (Salwen, 1962, pp. 51–53), and since it indicates no significant changes in the dietary of the Orient people and their Woodland-period successors of much later date, when in all probability essentially modern conditions prevailed on Long Island, it casts further doubt upon the validity of the correlation of Orient sites with major differences in sea levels.

The skeletal remains of the Orient people are much too scanty to afford an adequate conception of their physical appearance. An infant burial occurred at Stony Brook, and the much decayed bones of an adult were found in a grave pit at Orient No. 2. All other human physical traces have disintegrated in the highly acid sand (pH 5.0–5.5) of the burial hills, or are represented by cremated bone fragments.

Ornaments, Weapons, Tools

Their apparel has entirely disappeared, but, because of its more durable nature, there remain a few vestiges of personal ornamentation, viz., a crude discoidal shell bead (diameter about one half inch); several rather rough, circular, centrally perforated claystone pendants (about two and a half inches in diameter); ellipsoidal and rectanguloid stone gorgets, some rudely incised (Plate 56); and a considerable number of paintstones of graphite and hematite (Plate 55, Figure 16). Quantities of the latter, ground into powder, were used in the mortuary ritualism.

PLATE 56 Engraved slate gorget of the Orient phase from burial on the Jamesport site, Long Island. Length 4¾ inches. Photograph courtesy of Carl Schuster, Woodstock, N.Y.

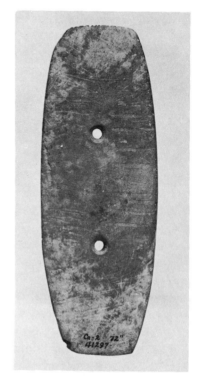

Most of the surviving artifacts belong in the category of hunting equipment, the principal item being a highly distinctive form of projectile point, designated the Orient Fishtail type (Plate 55, Figures 5–7, 9–11, 13–15). This slender, gracefully formed point is found in all habitation and burial sites, in nearly every grave, and constitutes over 88 per cent of the points used in this culture (Ritchie, 1959, pp. 31–32; 1961, p. 39). The small remainder comprises side-notched points, narrow to medium-wide; and narrow, stemmed forms. The materials of these javelin and spear heads are local glacial pebbles of quartz, quartzite, slate, siltstone and felsite, in approximately that order of frequency. Points made of argillite, jasper and flint also occur, and some of these appear to be importations from eastern Pennsylvania and eastern New York. All chipped stone seems to have been worked by percussion methods. Unpitted hammerstones are present, made from quartz or flint pebbles, some faceted or beveled in an unusual manner.

Use of the dart thrower in propelling the javelin is supported by the rare discovery in the burial sites of weights (bannerstones) of two types, a simple winged form with slightly grooved face (Ritchie, 1959, Plate 30, Figure 20), and a short tubular variety, oval in cross section, with one grooved side for accommodation of the dart shaft (Ritchie, 1944, Plate 107, Figure 22).

Tree-felling and wood-shaping tools embrace rare fully grooved axes, rude rectanguloid celts and plano-convex adzes, grooved back adzes, and a single small gouge (Ritchie, 1944, Plate 107, Figures 19–22, 25–27). Other tools comprise ovate and trianguloid knives of quartz; straight, stemmed, or fishtail base drills of quartz or flint (Plate 55, Figure 8); and a few anvilstones. There are no scrapers of any kind, no utilized chips, no articles of copper, and no pipes.

Utensils of Stone and Clay

Stone utensils are numerous; those of clay are rare. A considerable diversity in size and shape characterizes the stone pots, which may be oval, rectangular, nearly circular, or trough-shaped in outline, with rounded corners, generally rounded bases, and slightly outsloping to vertical walls. Most have squarish or lobate lugs at either end, just below the rounded lip, which is sometimes decorated with a series of shallow nicks (Plate 57, Figures 1–3; Plate 58; cf. Ritchie, 1944, Plate 108; 1959, Plates 29, 44). Size range is from around five and a half to eighteen inches in length and two to six inches in height. Some exhibit cracks and lacing holes; many are smoke-stained and grease-incrusted, indicating their utilitarian function; all are broken—intentionally for the most part, in the case of grave goods—if only by knocking out a hole in the bottom.

The material of those found and submitted by us for expert analysis is amphibole-talc, which was probably quarried and worked into shape at some of the southern New England aboriginal quarries in Rhode Island, Connecticut and Massachusetts. (See discussion in Ritchie, 1959, pp. 62–64.) Not only is the material as a whole characteristic of New England rather than southeastern Pennsylvania, but the technique of smoothing the outside as well as the interior of the vessel, and the tendency toward rounder bases, are also indicative of the same source. Thus, I have postulated (ibid., p. 62) that, although the original center of the whole stone-pot industry of the eastern United States in the Transitional period may have been situated in the Virginia-North Carolina Piedmont re-

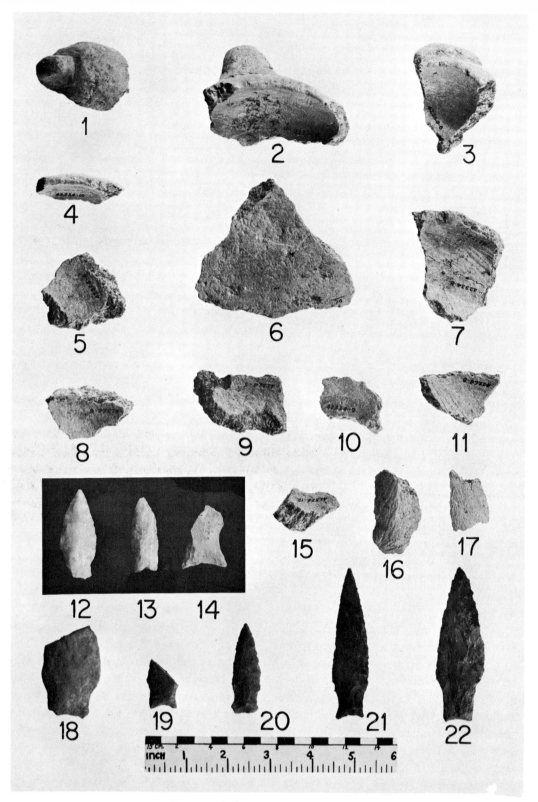

PLATE 57   Grave offerings of the Orient phase from the Solecki site, Long Island.
1–11, 15–17 steatite potsherds; 12–14, 18–22 Orient Fishtail points.

gion, there were probably two secondary centers of development and diffusion for the stone vessels of the Northeast, those of the Orient complex and southern New England stemming from the latter area; those of inland New York, Pennsylvania and New Jersey, all associated with the broad-point cultures, spreading out from southeastern Pennsylvania (page 162).

Pottery seems not to have been part of the earliest Orient complex, although sherds of two pots occurred at the oldest radiocarbon-dated cemetery on Sugar Loaf Hill. No ceramic potsherds were found at the Orient No. 1 and No. 2 cemeteries, in the lower levels of Midden A at Stony Brook, or in the Orient horizon at the Baxter site. Parts of a single, rather trough-shaped clay vessel with lugs and nearly vertical walls, cord-marked on the exterior and part way down the inside, and a direct copy of a stone vessel with Vinette 1 surface treatment and paste characteristics, came from the Jamesport cemetery, and a second similar pot, together with a cylindrical vessel, came from the Sugar Loaf Hill burial pit. This pottery is grit-tempered with crystalline aplastic and resembles the Stony Brook Corded variety from the Stony Brook site (Latham, 1953; Ritchie, 1959, pp. 37–38, 51–52, 66–67, 74).

The Orient phase thus illustrates the stone-pot-using Transitional stage of cultural development on Long Island, linking the preceramic Late Archaic with the Early Woodland ceramic stage, which was becoming established in this area toward the end of Orient times (Ritchie, 1959, p. 89).

Both the lithology and typology of the stone pots point to southern New England connections. The better-known quarry and workshop sites of the steatite industry closest to Long Island are at or near Providence, Rhode Island, and Portland and Bristol, Connecticut (Putnam, 1878; Willoughby, 1935, pp. 157–61; Dunn, 1945, pp. 49–52).

Cultural Connections

Moreover, a burial site with strong Orient-phase traits has been reported from Lakeville, Plymouth County, Massachusetts, only some thirty miles east of the Providence quarries (Lord, 1962; Robbins, 1963). The Hawes site was largely destroyed by gravel digging half a century ago, and a recent examination proved inadequate to determine whether the probably cremated burials with "killed" stone pots and projectile points had been placed in single-grave pits, a communal burial pit, or a combination of both, as in the Orient cemeteries of New York. Clearly most of the burial goods from this site match the Long Island materials. The stone pots conform in shapes and finishing techniques (compare Lord, 1962, Figure 1, with Ritchie, 1944, Plate 108; 1959, Plates 29, 44); Orient Fishtail points are present (Lord, 1962, Figures 2, 12, 13, 15–17; compare with Ritchie, 1944, Plate 107, Figures 4–9; 1959, Plate 20, Figures 2–19, et al.); and side-notched forms occur like some found in the Orient burial sites of New York (compare Lord, 1962, Figures 2, 2–5, 8, 11, 14, with Ritchie, 1959, Plate 32, Figure 4; Plate 33, Figures 18–20). Distinctive differences comprise the long, slender, stemless or stemmed points (Lord, 1962, Figure 2, 1, 2, 4, 6–11), not so far known for the Orient phase in New York.

It therefore seems probable that in Orient times, contact and trade relations existed across Long Island Sound. Parties of workmen from Long Island may have visited the New England quarries for soapstone vessels, or such vessels in the finished

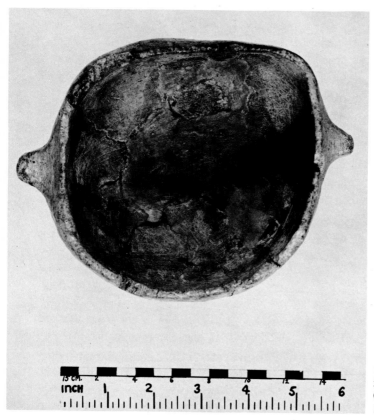

PLATE 58 Restored steatite pot from the Van Orden site, Greene Co., N.Y. Collection of Carl S. Sundler, West Albany, N.Y.

state may have been imported into New York from the New England Indians. The Hawes site, and other less well defined evidence, leads me to believe that the Orient phase, in all its essential characteristics, will yet be found in southeastern New England. In a recent intensive study of cremation cemeteries in eastern Massachusetts, Dincauze has postulated an ancestral connection between what she terms the Coburn group of the Susquehanna tradition, best represented at the Coburn site on Cape Cod (Kremp, 1961), and the Orient phase (Dincauze, 1968).

Slight indications of Orient cultural contacts with eastern Pennsylvania and eastern New York have been alluded to as the probable sources of the small number of chipped-stone implements made of argillite, jasper and Deepkill flint found in the Orient cemeteries. The distribution of Orient Fishtail points and soapstone pots (Plate 58) encompasses this region, but, on the whole, the Orient phase conveys the distinct impression of having achieved its climax on Long Island.

Except for its mortuary aspects, it would seem to have been quite prosaic and utilitarian, the product of a small population of semisedentary food gatherers firmly rooted in regional Archaic traditions. There is no evidence for aesthetic or recreational activities beyond a little rude incised embellishment on some of the stone gorgets and the possible use of turtle-shell rattles, inferred from the finding at Orient No. 2

174

of heaps of small quartz pebbles, such as are known to have been used in articles of this kind in the Archaic Frontenac phase in central New York (Plate 41, Figures 1, 3, 4).

Burial Ritualism

From what we can reconstruct of their burial customs, ceremonial ritualism of considerable complexity was involved in this supermundane aspect of Orient culture. As discussed in more detail elsewhere (Ritchie, 1959, pp. 54, 77, 88–92), the Orient people surely shared with certain of their inland contemporaries a religious ritualism concerned with the well-being of the dead, which was at this time, around 1000 B.C., well established in the Northeast and elsewhere in the eastern United States (Ritchie, 1955). The Orient culture not only shared the great majority of basic traits of this mortuary cult (ibid., pp. 61–65), but it added two of it own, viz., use of large communal burial pits, associated, it would appear, with periodic and elaborate magical observances, probably under shamanistic direction, and the addition of utensils of stone and clay to the grave offerings.

Unfortunately, the finders and excavators of the four Orient cemeteries have left us no description or account of their work beyond a few notes (Latham, 1953), nor is it likely, barring the discovery and professional excavation of another site of this kind, that satisfactory data on this intricate and intriguing subject will ever become available. The writer's search for such a site, involving the deep trenching and test pitting of more than a dozen promising hills on central and eastern Long Island, has to date been fruitless.

The hope raised by the most recent discovery of Orient cultural remains obviously from a burial site (Rih. 4-2) (Figure 4, site number 34) near Cutchogue, Long Island, suffered the same disappointment as the earlier reconnaissances when the site was thoroughly tested in 1961 by the State Museum field party led by the writer.

Apparently this site, unlike the others, had contained only a small number of individual graves, but it occupied a similar situation on the summit of a sand knoll, on the property of Julian Solecki. In 1959, in grading, a bulldozer cut away the upper few feet, revealing faint red stains in the white sand and a number of Orient Fishtail points and stone pot fragments, most of which are pictured on Plate 57. Through Mr. Solecki's brother, Professor Ralph Solecki of Columbia University, word reached the writer in the winter of 1960. The site was explored in the following summer by a system of trenches and test pits, but the only additional finds consisted of twenty steatite pot fragments, pertaining to one or more vessels, and another Orient point, shown in part on Plate 57.

It seems a logical inference from the Solecki site that small cemeteries were also a trait of the Orient culture, but that they conformed to the customary pattern in the selecting of locale and in providing the usual grave goods. This small burial ground may have been related to the Baxter site, distant only one fourth of a mile in an air line to the southeast (page 169).

In 1953 and 1956, respectively, the State Museum's investigations, conducted by the writer at the two still-available burial sites at Jamesport and Sugar Loaf Hill, yielded significant new information helping to clarify the earlier published summary (Ritchie, 1944, pp. 227–35) and affording two additional carbon-14 dates. These researches have been reported in detail elsewhere (Ritchie, 1959, pp. 49–74). The burial customs of the Orient people, as currently understood, need therefore only be outlined, as follows:

1) Burial was made in a definite cemetery, invariably at the summit of the highest hill in the selected district of eastern Long Island, not, as in earlier Archaic times, more or less at random in the refuse of the settlement. In fact, these cemeteries appear to lie at some considerable distance from the habitation site or sites they were designed to serve, and to have constituted a sacred precinct of the dead, a distinctive aspect of the religious ideology which was emerging at this period in various parts of the eastern United States. It may also be that specific cemeteries belonged to particular groups having their own territoral ranges on Long Island. Since radiocarbon dates for the Orient No. 2 cemetery and the Stony Brook site are exactly the same (944 B.C.±250 years, M-494, M-587, Crane and Griffin, 1958, pp. 1100–1101), it is tempting to speculate whether the occupants of the latter site made a canoe voyage (or voyages) more than half the length of Long Island to inter their dead at this chosen spot.

2) Burial features were of two kinds, individual graves and large communal burial pits. At the first discovered site, Orient No. 1, and at the Solecki site only the former occurred, elsewhere the two were combined in the same cemetery.

Individual graves, circular or oval in shape, ranged from about thirty-three to ninety-six inches in depth, although most are said to have varied from thirty-five to fifty-three inches. Deposits of grave goods, including red ocher in some cases, occurred at the base of all, while in the deepest example, found at Orient No. 2, decayed remnants of a human skeleton suggested a bundle burial.

A grave of this kind found in our excavations at Sugar Loaf Hill in 1956, measured six feet in length on a northwest-southeast axis, four and a half feet in maximum breadth, and thirty-three inches deep. Two separate clusters of grave goods lay at opposite ends, between which, presumably, a flexed or bundle burial had decayed away in the acid sand (pH 5.5). Nearly everything had been enveloped in and covered with a dark-stained sand, layered in part, filled with charcoal particles and containing a few unidentifiable bits of burned bone. A radiocarbon date for this charcoal was the oldest obtained for the Orient culture, viz., 1043 B.C.±300 years (M-586, Crane and Griffin, 1958, p. 1101) (Ritchie, 1959, pp. 67–74). The dark sand found here, and in our re-exploration of the Jamesport site, was clearly the scrapings from a funeral fire made elsewhere, in which animal food was consumed, and it provided the key to the comprehension of reported discoveries by the prior investigators.

More spectacular, and best developed in the Orient culture, were the large mortuary pits which occurred on three of the four sites, in each case with the major axis aligned east and west. At Orient No. 2, this structure is said to have measured about thirty by twenty feet with a depth exceeding five feet; at Sugar Loaf Hill thirty by twenty-seven by seven feet; and at Jamesport thirty by eighteen by eight feet. A smaller variant of this type apparently also occurred at Orient No. 2 and Sugar Loaf Hill; one example at the latter site was said to have measured eleven by six by seven feet.

3) Various features are reported found on the floor of these mortuary pits, including deposits of red ocher up to two bushels in volume; a circle of large stones, five feet in diameter; and many "fireplaces" containing charcoal and cremated human

bones; all features having one or more directly associated "caches" of burial offerings. The latter in nearly every case included a fire-making kit, a number of projectile points, one or more "killed" stone vessels, a hammerstone and a paintstone, and they frequently included an adz or celt. Of more sporadic distribution among the offerings were knives, drills, pendants, gorgets, pestles, grooved axes and bannerstones. The typical basic grave lot therefore provided for hunting game, kindling fire, and cooking food, with a cosmetic kit thrown in. Some of the richer lots, with more of the common goods and extras, may reflect differences in social status or personal regard for the individual. Because so few body traces remain, it is impossible to determine whether sex and age were factors here, or indeed, whether a whole or a selected population is represented in the great mortuary pits. The smaller multiple-burial structures and the individual graves may also have been connected with a social hierarchy, although it seems more probable that they were consigned to later burials within the sacred precincts.

Many of our problems would surely be less acute if the excavation methods employed by the finders of these cemeteries had been more adequate, and if offers of professional advice and assistance had been accepted. The work was done by digging a series of deep shafts into the productive areas and enlarging them at the bottom until nothing more could be found, the holes being completely filled in at the close of each day's work. It was thus impossible to observe most of the details which could have led to a true comprehension of these remarkable structures.

A small section of the large pit at Jamesport, missed by the previous diggers, was found in our 1953 examination of the site and has been discussed in detail in the site report (Ritchie, 1959, pp. 52–67). Here two unmolested features of the kind referred to as "fireplaces," with associated "caches" of burial offerings, proved, like our burial just described from Sugar Loaf Hill, to be secondary deposits of burned material, including identifiable bird and deer bones, which had served as grave coverings (Plate 59). It appears most probable that, as part of the ritualism attached, here as elsewhere, to the mortuary cult, the contents of a funeral fire kindled outside the pit were scattered over the remains of the deceased and his other offering of tools, utensils, weapons, ornaments, etc. Not improbably perishable articles were consumed in the flames, along with food offerings, including animal foods, a feast in which perhaps the living participated with the dead. Red ocher had been poured over the fire residue in one of the new Jamesport features mentioned. A charcoal sample from the burned material assayed at 763 B.C.$\pm$220 years (W-543) (Rubin and Alexander, 1960, p. 180), the youngest of the five Orient dates.

It is certain, however, from evidence examined by the writer, that human cremations formed part of the discoveries of the Long Island Chapter at these sites, but the proportion of such burials to flesh or bone inhumations in the Orient burial complex can be determined only if another site is found and properly investigated.

Then, too, we may perhaps learn whether the big pits were enclosed in a charnel house or open to the sky; whether a single great ceremony took place (as in the periodic Huron Feast of the Dead) at which bodies of recently deceased persons, and corpses in various stages of decay down to bare-bone bundles, were committed to the ground in a lengthy and detailed ceremony; or whether, as need arose through the occasion of a death, the pit

PLATE 59 Orient-phase burial feature with grave offerings of "killed" steatite pots and other objects in great burial pit at the Jamesport site, Long Island.

was used, and the corpse covered with fire residue, sand, and often ocher, until the entire floor area had been utilized, when occurred the final ceremony of filling the common grave and scattering therein the loose and random artifacts always found in the fill, in addition to the individual commitments.

About these Orient cemeteries the writer senses a pervading aura of high religious drama, in marked contrast to the impression of prosaic everyday life conveyed by his humble findings in the settlement sites of the same people. There is also, one feels sure, a good deal of lost symbolism, some of it of more universal nature, in which high places, the east, the sun, fire and red ocher figure as elements of a vigorous religious movement, apparently focused upon the perpetuation of life after death, and the care and welfare of the deceased. (See further discussion of this in Ritchie, 1955.)

IV The Woodland Stage—
Development of Ceramics,
Agriculture and Village Life
(c. 1000 B.C.–A.D. 1600)

The term "Woodland," long in use by American archaeologists to refer variously to cultures or items of culture, prehistoric or ethnological, received some semblance of clarification at the First Woodland Conference, held at the University of Chicago in 1941, in which the writer participated (Anon., 1943). Since that event a considerable number of investigators, especially in the Woodland core area extending from Manitoba, Minnesota, Iowa and northern Missouri eastward across the United States and Canada, have further clarified and refined the concept through the elucidation of pertinent regional manifestations, better chronologies and much discussion, in professional papers and in informal sessions. The result has been a threefold subdivision into what is commonly called the Early, Middle and Late Woodland "periods," stressing the temporal aspects of the cultural developments. There is much need, however, for a fuller interpretation of the Woodland concept.

To outline these developments, with particular regard to the area of our current focus, it is to cultures of the Early Woodland stage, beginning around 1000 B.C., that the first significant use of pottery can be attributed, although Vinette 1 ware and related pottery have their initial, feeble inception in the preceding Transitional stage (pages 159, 173).

Smoking pipes of tubular varieties—the cigar-shaped and the specialized blocked-end type—are Early Woodland innovations. Gorgets (defined as having two or more perforations), which appeared first in Transitional times, now occurred in an assortment of distinctive and, like the pipe forms, culturally assignable styles. Birdstones, boatstones and bar amulets also belong here, as do the earliest known copper ornaments—tubular beads. Copper tools, of course, but not ornaments, except in the case of the probably Late Archaic Glacial Kame culture, not yet actually found in New York (page 132), are much older, with an Archaic provenience in our area (page 82).

A well-developed mortuary ceremonialism, having its roots and antecedents in Late Archaic and Transitional cultures of the Northeast (page 175), is likewise a major feature of the Early Woodland stage, during which a few burial mounds may have been constructed in New York State (page 201).

There is in our area during the Early Woodland no indisputable testimony for knowledge or use of cultigens, or for any salient or significant shift from the prior subsistence pattern or general way of life of the several groups.

The Middle Woodland stage, starting perhaps, several centuries B.C. in our area, is differentiated by such criteria as the arrival of the classic Woodland styles of stamped or impressed pottery—dentate, pseudo-scallop-shell, rocker-stamped (dentate and plain varieties), cord-ornamented, etc.—from an apparent center in the Upper Great Lakes region; and the local development or introduction from a southern or southwesterly direction of the elbow pipe, and of the platform pipe, the latter definitely part of the Hopewellian mound-building complex which, in our area as elsewhere, was associated with the apogee of mortuary ceremonialism. Agriculture may have had a minor role in New York during the latter part of this stage.

The cultural continuity into the Late Woodland stage, beginning around A.D. 1000, was so even and apparently so largely of an internal developmental character in our area as to create difficulty of demarcation from its late Middle Woodland antecedents. Pottery of traditional classic Woodland lineage underwent progressive modifications, as did pipe styles derived from the straight and elbow forms. Descriptions in some detail are given in the following pages.

A principal distinction setting off Late from Middle Woodland cultures is the now obvious fact of the importance of cultigens —corn, beans and squash demonstrably—in the economy. This change accompanied, *pari passu,* a major alteration in settlement pattern, with large villages, the later ones protected by palisades, containing a sessile or semisedentary, augmenting population, dwelling communally in longhouses.

An equally notable divergence is the absence from Late Woodland cultures of any apparent evidence of mortuary ceremonialism. This had waned progressively through the late Middle Woodland to virtual extinction by the close of the stage.

THE MEADOWOOD PHASE

This culture was formerly included in the Point Peninsula Focus of the Vine Valley Aspect, Woodland Pattern (Ritchie, 1944, pp. 112 ff.) and subsequently designated the Point Peninsula 1 Focus of the Early Woodland period.

As explained in the following section on the Point Peninsula culture (page 205), the Meadowood is now regarded as a separate historic entity from the Point Peninsula and is placed in the Early Woodland stage in New York because of its established Vinette 1 ceramic associations (Figure 1).

It has seemed to the writer appropriate to name this phase the "Meadowood," after the estate of Delos Wray at West Rush, Monroe County, New York, where the first excavated site of the complex, a small cemetery, was found in 1930 by Charles F. Wray, who invited the writer's participation (Ritchie, 1944, pp. 125–26). The same designation has previously been accorded the major point type of this culture (Ritchie, 1961, pp. 35–36).

While Meadowood points have virtually a state-wide distribution, with rare representation in the eastern and southern parts of the state and adjacent areas, the known Meadowood sites, mainly burial components, are found in northern, central and western New York, with five of the eight sites in the central section (Figure 4, sites number 37–44). Six of these sites have already been described in print, viz., Wray, Oberlander No. 2, Vinette (lower component), Pickins, Muskalonge Lake (earlier finds) (Ritchie, 1944), Muskalonge Lake (later finds) and Hunter site on Red Lake (Ritchie, 1955). (See page xxii for new sites.)

Brief references are made throughout the following account to the still largely unpublished Riverhaven No. 2 habitation site (Kochan, 1961) and the Morrow burial site. The latter, situated on nearly level land near the north end of Honeoye Lake, Ontario County, New York, was accidentally disclosed by land-development operations in the fall of 1956. Great damage was inflicted on the site by collectors prior to announcement of discovery, when the New York State Museum and the Rochester Museum of Arts and Sciences carried out salvage excavations, resulting in the recovery of some important data. It is believed that between thirty-five and forty burial pits were clustered in an area of some sixty by forty feet. All known burial modes for the Meadowood culture occurred here, with some *in situ* pit cremations. Grave goods seem to have been present with most burials, and they included a carbonized fish net and basketry, at least three birdstones, many gorgets, a tube pipe, and considerable amounts of red ocher.

Eleven burials excavated by the writer, one with an offering of forty-two mortuary blades, are described in detail in his unpublished site report.

The site distribution of the Meadowood phase indicates a preference for relatively flat terrain and propitious fishing grounds on sizable streams and small lakes, and all of the components lie within, or adjacent to, the Central Lowland Province (see endpaper map).

Period of Occupation

The period at which this culture flourished is rather accurately known, inasmuch as three of the sites have been radiocarbon-dated as follows: Oberlander No. 2, 998 B.C. $\pm$170 years (C-192, Arnold and Libby, 1951, p. 114); Hunter, 841 B.C. $\pm$68 years (Y-981, Stuiver and Deevey, 1962, p. 225; a previously published date for this site, obtained by the solid-carbon method from the same grave sample, was 2448 B.C. $\pm$260 years, C-794, Libby, 1954, p. 137; Ritchie, 1955, p. 66; 1962, pp. 583–84); and Morrow, 563 B.C. $\pm$250 years (M-640, Crane and Griffin, 1959, p. 183) and 630 B.C. $\pm$100 years (Y-1171, Stuiver, Deevey and Rouse, 1963, pp. 331–32). (See pages xxiii, xxiv for new dates).

The fossil-pollen spectrum for the Northeast during the period between *c.* 1000 and 600 B.C. reveals a predominantly hemlock-hardwoods (chiefly oak, hickory and beech) forest cover, suggesting a prevailing climatic condition moister and probably cooler than in the preceding Xerothermic interval.

In this environment the Meadowood people pursued a fishing, hunting, and presumably gathering subsistence pattern which appears from the tangible evidence to have generally conformed to that of their already described predecessors of the Late Archaic and Transitional periods. The presence of actual, although small, cemeteries, and of probable storage pits, does, however, point toward the inception of a more stable pattern of living.

Despite the fact that most of the Meadowood sites are cemeteries, no adequate description of the physical characteristics of the people is possible, since cremation was

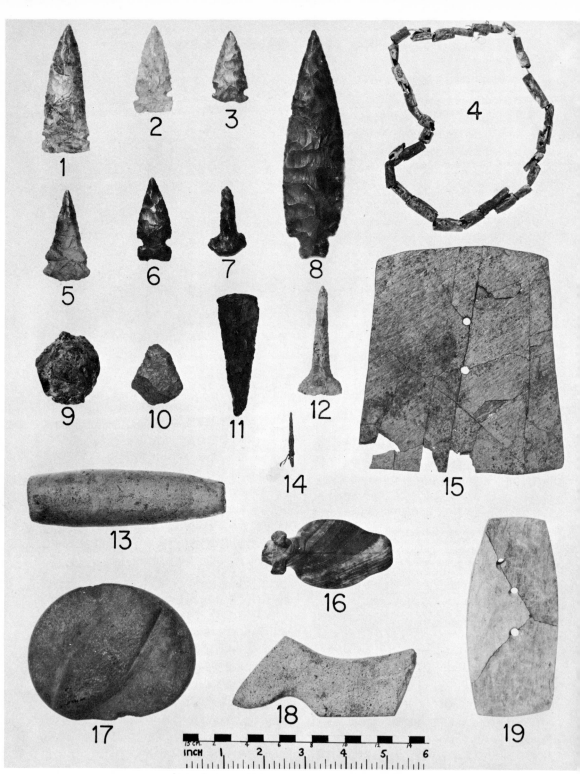

PLATE 60 Artifacts from burials of the Meadowood phase. 1–3, 5, 6 Meadowood-type points; 4 necklace of tubular copper beads; 7, 12 flint drills; 8 spear point or knife of Fulton Turkey Tail type (base is damaged); 9 nodule of iron pyrites (altered to limonite) and 10 flint strike-a-light, elements of a fire-making kit; 11 triangular end scraper; 13 tubular pottery pipe; 14 copper awl; 15 trapezoidal gorget; 16 birdstone of "pop-eyed" form with expanded, barred base; 17 abrading stone of specialized type; 18 unfinished bar-type birdstone; 19 rectanguloid gorget. Provenience: 4, 13 Wray site, all others Oberlander No. 2 site.

extensively practiced and unburned inhumations have, for the most part, completely or largely decayed. A small series of four adults, only one definitely a male, from the Wray site, indicates that, at least for this particular group, the head form was long or moderately long and narrow, and of medium height; with face of medium breadth (in one case relatively narrow), orbits of medium height, and a narrow nose.

The Food Quest and Its Attributes

The primary subsistence activities, hunting and fishing, are represented by the majority of the artifacts found in the habitation sites or as mortuary furnishings for the dead. Projectile points, suggesting by their fairly large size javelin rather than arrow armaments, although atlatl weights do not occur, unless perchance the birdstone was so used, lead numerically. These points, ranging in length from about one and five eighths to three and a half inches, are extremely thin and very skillfully made by a well-controlled pressure-flaking technique. Called by the writer Meadowood points, this side-notched form is diagnostic of the culture under consideration (Ritchie, 1961, pp. 35–36) (Plate 60, Figures 1–3, 5, 6; Plate 64, Figures 12–16). Some examples have expanded bases and beveled or serrated edges (Plate 60, Figures 2, 5).

At one site, Muskalonge Lake, seven generally similar, but slightly corner-notched points were found in one of the graves (Ritchie, 1955, Plate 11, Figures 1–6).

The great majority of Meadowood points, wherever found, have been fashioned from a western New York variety of Onondaga flint of mottled gray-and-brown color. Extensive quarry and workshop sites of this high-grade stone are known from the vicinity of Diver's Lake, Genesee County (page 8).

This is also the material employed in the masterful chipping of the extremely thin, leaf-shaped cache or mortuary blades, which occur chiefly in deposits, ranging up to about 1500, but usually numbering between approximately 100 and 250 blades (Plate 61). It is still not certain whether these artifacts were included with the burial furniture only to supply in the spirit world the ready raw material for quick and easy elaboration into projectile points, knives, drills and scrapers (as is suggested by their presence in habitation sites—page 183), or whether they had, like the red ocher with which they are often associated, some symbolic function, perhaps as a species of wealth to maintain the status or prestige of the departed in his new abode. (See detailed description and discussion of these objects in Ritchie, 1955, pp. 42–45, 59–60, 65, 68.)

A bone flaker was found at the Wray site (Ritchie, 1944, Plate 54, Figure 46) and a remarkable, unique copper flaking tool in a carved wooden handle came from a grave at Muskalonge Lake (Plates 62, 63). Large antler flaking tools, like those of the Kipp Island phase, probably hafted like chipping mallets, occurred at the Riverhaven No. 2 site (Plate 65, Figures 8–12). Identical artifacts are present in some Hopewellian mounds in Ohio and Michigan.

A spike-shaped, probable projectile point of bone from the Wray site (Ritchie, 1944, Plate 54, Figure 47); what may be an antler club spike from the Pickins site (ibid., Plate 70, Figure 49); and what seems to be a section of a flat bone dagger from the Oberlander No. 2 cemetery complete the small weapon inventory known for the Meadowood phase, unless the two

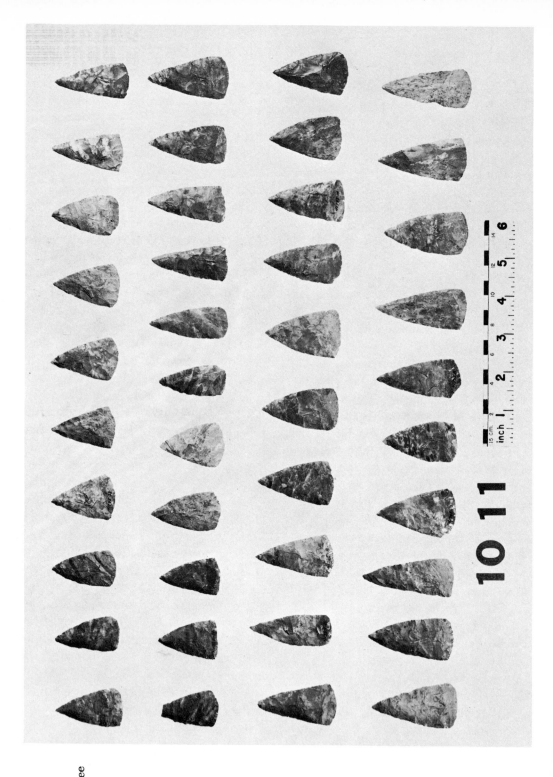

PLATE 61 Mortuary or cache blades of the Meadowood phase. From burials 10, 11, Morrow site, Ontario Co., N.Y. (See Plate 71.)

PLATE 62   Copper flaking tool in wooden handle, Meadowood phase, from the Muska-longe Lake site, Jefferson Co., N.Y.

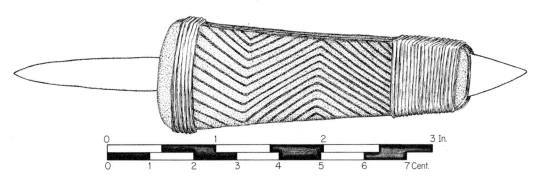

PLATE 63   Attempted restoration of copper flaking tool shown in Plate 62. Short cop-per point probably for notching flint projectiles.

grooved ovate pebbles from the Vinette site are bolas-stones, rather than netsinkers (Ritchie, 1944, Plate 75, Figures 50, 51); and the blade of Fulton Turkey Tail type from the Oberlander No. 2 site (Plate 60, Figure 8), and from surface sites of this culture, are spear points rather than knives (Ritchie, 1961, p. 23).

Use of the dog is shown by scanty re-mains of this animal found cremated with human bones at the Oberlander No. 2 site.

The considerable importance of the fish-

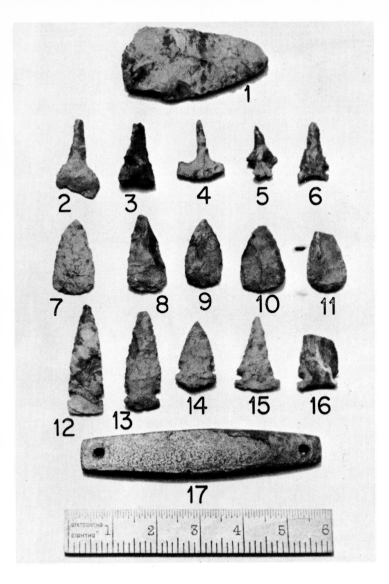

PLATE 64 Artifacts of the Meadowood phase from the Riverhaven No. 2 site, Erie Co., N.Y. 1 ovate knife; 2–6 various forms of the drill; 7–11 thin, leaf-shaped, cache blades; 12–16 Meadowood points; 17 rectanguloid or bar gorget. Collection of Edward Kochan, Niagara Falls, N.Y.

ing industry in the economy of these people is chiefly indicated by the locations of all sites, although very little actual fishing tackle has survived destruction by burning and soil acidity. Surprisingly, the small number of bone articles found at the Wray, Morrow and Riverhaven No. 2 sites did not include the fishhook or gorge, and there is only one example of a single, unilaterally barbed bone point (Plate 65, Figure 7).

These sites and the Vinette station produced flat, notched netsinkers, some of those at Riverhaven being chipped around the entire periphery. A thick, ovate-shaped, natural pebble with notched or grooved ends came from the Morrow site, and in one burial a group of such objects, obviously sinkers, was actually still attached by a double cord to a carbonized fish net (Plate 66). Tragically, this unique specimen, rolled into a compact mass along one side of the grave, and reduced to a carbonized state by the crematory fire, was dug out by a collector and only fragments were salvaged. The material was apparently Indian-hemp fiber, twisted into a

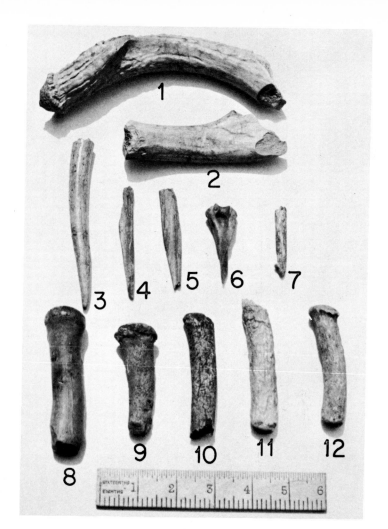

PLATE 65 Antler and bone tools of the Meadowood phase from the Riverhaven No. 2 site, Erie Co., N.Y. 1, 2 cut sections of deer antler; 3–6 antler and bone awls; 7 unibarbed bone point; 8–12 large antler flaking tools. Collection of Edward Kochan, Niagara Falls, N.Y.

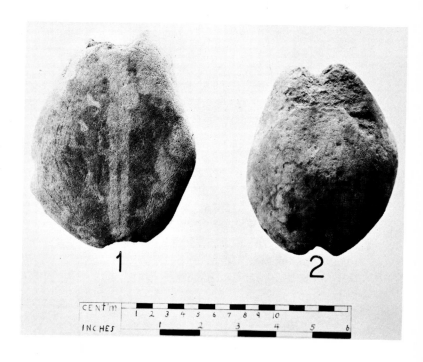

PLATE 66 Ovate pebble netsinkers with notched ends. Note imprint on left-hand specimen of double cord attachment to net shown on Plate 67. Meadowood phase, Morrow site, Ontario Co., N.Y. Photograph courtesy of the Rochester Museum of Arts and Sciences.

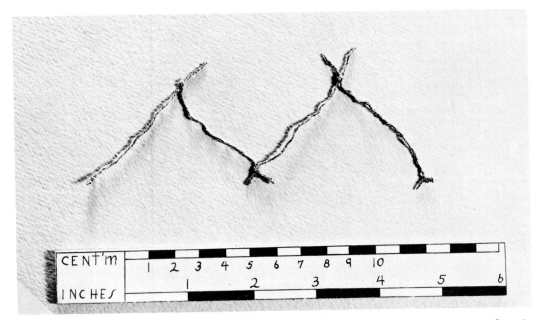

PLATE 67 Fragment of carbonized fish net, Meadowood phase, Morrow site, Ontario Co., N.Y. Photograph courtesy of the Rochester Museum of Arts and Sciences.

cord of small diameter, which was woven into a net with about a two-inch mesh (Plate 67).

Food-animal remains, mostly in a very poorly preserved state, occurred sparsely at the Vinette, Morrow and Riverhaven No. 2 sites, and comprised chiefly fish-bones, of which the common or brown bull-head (*Ictalurus nebulosus*) was identified, and bones of the deer, bear, beaver, turkey and various turtles. Burned dog, deer and fish remains were present with human cremations at the Oberlander No. 2 site, apparently food offerings, except for perhaps the dog.

Pits with U-shaped cross sections were found on the cemetery knoll at the Oberlander No. 2 site, although mostly in a separate area from the graves. At this component, at the Wray site, and probably also at Morrow's, it appeared that some of the burials had been made in abandoned storage pits, because of the black, humus-like soil covering the bottom. What resembled at the time of discovery a corncob fragment, further discussed below, came from such a feature at the Wray site. These pits ranged in size from approximately two feet in diameter and fifteen inches in depth to over twice these dimensions, and had either round or oval orals. It is now suspected, in the light of later evidence from the Indian River sites in northern New York, that some of these sterile pits may have been graves without offerings in which the uncremated human bones have completely disintegrated.

The presence of probable food-storage pits, and indeed the fact of the cemetery itself, point toward more group stability than is attested for the cultures on earlier time levels, already considered. Although we have as yet no data on housing and settlement patterns, and no preserved plant remains, there is a haunting suggestion about these sites of an incipient shift toward an economy and cultural orientation of semisedentary character. Wild plant foods, and a plentiful supply of that reliable food resource the so-called "coarse fish"— bullheads, suckers, perch, sunfish, etc.— rather than cultigens, probably provided the basis of the economy.

Mention has been made of a carbonized "corncob" from the Wray site, which seems to contradict this statement. This object, about an inch in length, was found by Charles F. Wray and the writer at the bottom of Burial 10. This grave held the flexed skeleton of an adult male (?), interred apparently in an abandoned storage pit twenty-six inches deep. Black, crumbly, organic soil, to a depth of nine inches, covered the pit bottom and the skeleton, which had minor mortuary offerings. What appeared to the finders as a split corncob fragment, denuded of kernels, lay within this black deposit (Ritchie, 1944, p. 126). Although the potential magnitude of the evidence was not fully appreciated in 1930, the untreated specimen was enclosed in cotton, boxed, labeled, and stored with the site collection at the Rochester Museum of Arts and Sciences. Some years later it was found to have disintegrated into an unidentifiable mass of tiny scale-like flakes and granules. Since the matter has by others been misstated in print, it is here correctly recorded, with the conclusion that the question is still unresolved whether the Meadowood people, perhaps in the later part of their occupation (the Wray site, anomalous in its lack of cremations and in other respects, has not been radiocarbon-dated due to lack of suitable saved material), had received and begun the culti-

vation of corn. The special tragedy in the destruction of the Morrow site (page 181) lies in the fact that many of its pits (?) and graves are known to have been rich in a black organic material, like that from Wray's, which may have preserved the evidence we so assiduously seek on this important point.

It is of interest to note, in this connection, the discovery of seeds of *Chenopodium* (goosefoot) and *Polygonum* (smartweed) in the grave fill of cremations on the Hodges and Promranky sites in Michigan (Binford, 1963, pp. 139, 183), both of the Pomranky complex or Red Ocher culture, which is closely related to the Meadowood phase (page 200). Seeds of uncultivated *Chenopodium* were prehistorically employed in making flour, while the shoots and leaves of this plant were edible as greens.

Implements and utensils concerned with the preparation of food are of very limited occurrence, probably because most of the Meadowood sites are burial components, and in this culture grave goods did not include pottery. A muller from the Vinette site is the only grinding tool recovered, a fact which harmonizes poorly with our just concluded speculation. Pottery, of Vinette 1 ware, however, was abundant at this site, and steatite pot fragments also sparingly occurred here and in the fill of one of the burials at the neighboring, related, Oberlander No. 2 site. Vinette 1 sherds were also definitely a part of the Meadowood complex at the Riverhaven No. 2 site. A considerable number of such sherds came from Feature 4, Locus 1 at the Muskalonge Lake site (Ritchie, 1955, pp. 21, 39), and from the immediate vicinity of several features at the Hunter site on Red Lake (ibid., pp. 26, 33, 50–51). There can thus be no reasonable question that the Meadowood people cooked in pottery vessels of Vinette 1 ware, and possibly to a very limited extent in the early period, in soapstone vessels as well, which device represented a continuity from the cultures of the immediately preceding Transitional period, with which the Meadowood horizon temporally overlaps (Figure 1 and page 164).

Cooking seems also to have been accomplished with hot stones, not only by boiling, but in baking pits, similar to those from the Stony Brook site (page 166), as suggested by limited evidence from the Muskalonge Lake site (Ritchie, 1955, pp. 18–19, 20–21).

Fire making by percussion with flint and pyrites is well attested by the discovery of such kits in most of the graves (Plate 60, Figures 9, 10). This fact also highlights the heavy emphasis on fire seen in the mortuary aspects of this culture (page 199).

Sites

The lack of settlement-pattern data has already been remarked. Of the eight Meadowood components known and listed on the map, Figure 4, sites number 37–44, only Vinette (Ritchie, 1944, pp. 160–66; Ritchie and MacNeish, 1949, pp. 118–19) and Riverhaven No. 2 are habitation sites. The first is the occupation site for the Oberlander No. 2 cemetery (Ritchie, 1944, pp. 152–60); no burials have as yet been found associated with the latter. Some slight refuse deposits were found on the Indian River burial sites (Ritchie, 1955, pp. 21, 25, 26), and they may have been present near the Morrow cemetery. The small size of Meadowood sites bears testimony to a diminutive population, probably no larger than the little bands of some thirty to fifty people which we have postulated for their Archaic predecessors.

The Vinette habitation site (Syr. 2-2; Figure 4, site number 39) at Brewerton, New York, on which the writer excavated in 1938, 1940, 1942, and 1949, as portions became available in garden and lawn and beneath a cottage, encompassed approximately one fifth of an acre along the north shore of the Oneida River. The Riverhaven No. 2 station (Twa. 3-3) may be slightly larger, although most of the refuse lies upon a fifty-foot-long, narrow, crescent-shaped bench or terrace, only a few feet above the level of the Niagara River, on the easternmost promontory of Grand Island, Erie County, New York.

The site was found and explored during 1960–61 by Edward Kochan of Niagara Falls, with some assistance and advice from Dr. Marian E. White of the University of Buffalo (Kochan, 1961). It was visited and studied by the writer through the courtesy of Mr. Kochan, to whom thanks are also expressed for permission to publish these data.

Test pits dug in the field six feet above the terrace level produced chipping refuse and artifacts which unequivocally connect both loci. Excavation on the terrace disclosed, beneath a sterile, root-filled surface layer of sandy humus up to eight inches thick, a sandy stratum four to six inches deep, slightly lighter in color, and heavily intermixed with chips and other rejectage of flint knapping. The 975 catalogued artifacts of stone, bone, antler and pottery, plus food-animal remains, chiefly fishbone, occurred in this stratum and in ash deposits filling large, irregular depressions just beneath it, and extending to a depth of twenty-four inches from the surface. Nothing was found in the tough dark clay subsoil.

The typology of the assemblage, which still awaits radiocarbon dating, definitely pertains to the Meadowood phase. On Plate 64, Figures 12–16 show the classic Meadowood-type projectile points, and Figures 7–11 the equally diagnostic thin, leaf-shaped blades. So many of these blades, prominent in the mortuary offerings of this culture, occurred whole, broken or in process at the site, that Mr. Kochan has hypothesized a center here for their manufacture from the regional, high-grade Onondaga flint (Kochan, n.d.).

Other artifacts from the site, including Vinette 1 potsherds, which occurred in small numbers throughout the midden layer, in direct association with the points, blades and other characteristic artifacts, and must thus be regarded as intrinsic to the complex, are illustrated on Plates 64, 65 and 68, and referred to in appropriate context below. (See pages xxii–xxiv for recent data on habitation sites of this culture.)

Dress and Ornament

Information on dress and ornament of the Meadowood folk is very scanty. Bone and copper awls suggest skin-working (Plate 65, Figures 3–6; Plate 60, Figure 14); as do flint end scrapers, unifacially or bifacially chipped (Plate 60, Figure 11); and there is one example from the Oberlander No. 2 cemetery of a distinctive form of the "sinewstone," made from an oval, thick, flat pebble, with a medial ridge formed by deep grooves crossing either side transversely, in opposite directions (Plate 60, Figure 17). The writer has seen two other specimens of this kind from surface sites yielding Meadowood points. Personal ornaments comprise rolled, tubular, fairly thick sheet-copper beads of large diameter (Plate 60, Figure 4); small, spheroidal copper beads; a short, bird-bone tube or

bead; and small discoidal beads of white and purple marine shell. (For illustration of small copper and shell beads, see Ritchie, 1955, Plate 11, Figure 8.)

Stone gorgets, presumed to be ornaments or status markers, are numerous and diversified in the Meadowood phase, and include the following forms:

1) A large, trapezoidal style, with several minor variants, which seems to be diagnostic of this culture. It was found on four of the burial sites—Oberlander No. 2, Muskalonge Lake, Hunter and Morrow (Plate 60, Figure 15; Plate 69, Figures 3, 4).

2) A narrow rectangular form with one side medially keeled or ridged. Muskalonge Lake site only (Ritchie, 1955, Plate 15, Figure 3).

3) A similar form without the keel. Riverhaven No. 2 site only (Plate 64, Figure 17).

4) Dumb-bell shaped. Hunter site only (Ritchie, 1955, Plate 23, Figure 13).

5) Rectanguloid with excurvate edges. From the Wray and Oberlander No. 2 sites (Plate 60, Figure 19).

6) Rhomboidal. Morrow site only.

Hematite, limonite and graphite paint-stones, and the extensive use of powdered red ocher in the mortuary rites, are well-documented Meadowood traits.

Tool Inventory

Birdstones, of unknown significance (their use as atlatl weights is questionable), are, like gorgets, characteristic elements of the Meadowood phase. Two forms are represented, the bar type, with or without "pop-eyes" (Plate 60, Figure 18; Plate 69, Figure 6), and the expanded body type with two transverse basal ridges

PLATE 68 Potsherds of Vinette 1 type and tubular pottery pipe fragment. Meadowood phase, Riverhaven No. 2 site, Erie Co., N.Y. Collection of Edward Kochan, Niagara Falls, N.Y.

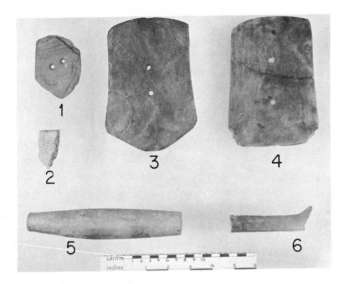

PLATE 69 Grave offerings of the Meadowood phase from the Morrow site, Ontario Co., N.Y. 1 reworked gorget fragment; 2 Vinette 1 potsherd (in grave fill); 3, 4 trapezoidal gorgets; 5 tubular pottery pipe; 6 reworked section of bar birdstone. Courtesy of the Rochester Museum of Arts and Sciences.

(Plate 60, Figure 16). The truncated or bust form of the Adena-Middlesex manifestations is not known for the Meadowood culture.

A forest environment and considerable use of wood in the culture are indicated by the occurrence in some numbers of pecked and polished stone, and copper-plano-convex adzes, some with gouge-shaped lip; chipped and pecked and polished rectanguloid celts; the already described, probably multipurpose end scrapers (Plate 60, Figure 11); and side scrapers made from a retouched flake. Beaver incisors hafted in antler, presumed wood-carving tools; also unhafted incisors of the same animal having the incisal edge ground chisel-shape, gouge-shape or to a lateral point, are shared with the several phases of the Point Peninsula culture, and with the Middlesex phase as well.

The inventory of what may be regarded as more general-utility tools includes the following:

1) Knives of several varieties—broad flake with retouched edge; prismatic blade, with or without marginal retouching; bifacially chipped triangular, broad or narrow (Plate 64, Figure 1); large, lanceolate, ceremonial (?) (Ritchie, 1955, Plate 15, Figure 1); and probably some of the side-notched points with strongly excurvate edges.

2) Drills or perforators—with expanded, rounded, rectangular or side-notched base (one variant of the latter has a very short point). Sometimes the rounded base is retouched for an end scraper (Plate 60, Figures 7, 12; Plate 64, Figures 2–6).

3) Hammerstones—both unpitted and bipitted pebble varieties. One specimen from the Vinette site is a phallic effigy, unique for this culture and the earliest known New York example, secondarily employed as a hammerstone (Ritchie, 1944, Plate 75, Figure 53).

4) Anvilstones—of common scarified pebble form.

5) Abradingstones—tabular form most common; some have deeply rubbed hollows, some incisions, as though for sharpening awls.

193

6) Rough, chopper-like tools.

7) Needles—one burned fragment of a thin, curved, perforated, mat-making (?) needle came from a cremation at the Oberlander No. 2 site.

Vinette 1 Pottery, Pipes and Basketry

The writer's first excavation at the Vinette site in Brewerton discovered the exterior-interior cord-impressed variety of pottery which characterized the lowest levels of the site (Ritchie, 1944, p. 164), and which he later (1946, pp. 13, 16) described as "Vinette 1 ware," "a moderately thick, coarse to medium grit-tempered, gray to black or buff colored ware, derived from fairly large, unornamented, straight-sided, conoidal-based vessels, cord- or fabric-roughened over the entire surface, both outside and inside." In a subsequent further elaboration it was indicated that while on the exterior surface the cord-markings run in various directions, although they tend to be vertical, they always run in a horizontal direction on the interior. The lip is rounded and sometimes almost pointed. Coil breaks are frequently observable on the sherds (Ritchie and MacNeish, 1949, p. 100) (Plate 68, herein).

The early position of Vinette 1 ware in the Northeast was also recognized and discussed by the writer (1946, pp. 16–17), and is sustained by all subsequent evidence. Sporadically represented in the cultures of the Transitional period (pages 159, 173), Vinette 1 pottery had become established in the New York area by Meadowood times. Sherds of this pottery have been found on all sites of the Meadowood complex except Wray and Pickins (little is really known about the latter—see Ritchie, 1944, pp. 150–52). Never occur-

ring as grave goods, the pottery is understandably rare at burial components; nevertheless a few sherds came from among the Morrow-site graves (Plate 69, Figure 2), and many were found on the surface or in thin refuse deposits with Meadowood artifact associations at the Indian River sites (Ritchie, 1955).

Apart from the basal component at the Vinette station, the best evidence for the intrinsic relationship of Vinette 1 ware with the Meadowood complex occurs at the recently discovered Riverhaven No. 2 site, on the Niagara River, as already noted (page 191). (See page xxiv for new data.)

It is also of interest in this connection to call attention to another ceramic trait in the Meadowood phase, viz., the plain, cigar-shaped, tubular pipe of grit-tempered paste, like that employed in the construction of the Vinette 1 pottery. One example of this earliest pipe form in the Northeast has been found in graves at each of the following sites: Wray (Plate 60, Figure 13), Oberlander No. 2, Muskalonge Lake, and Morrow (Plate 69, Figure 5), and a fragmentary specimen has been recovered in the midden at the Riverhaven No. 2 site (Plate 68, Figure 4).

At the Morrow site was found the only direct evidence for the use of cordage and basketry by the Meadowood people. The unique fish net of twisted Indian-hemp (?) fiber has already been referred to on page 185 (Plate 67). What seem to be basketry fragments were recovered by another collector from one of the graves after the earth-scraping machinery had cut most of it away. Much charred organic material is said to have been present in this feature, apparently a cremation *in situ*, with several characteristic Meadowood artifacts.

The four or five small fragments, the largest only about two and a half inches

PLATE 70 Carbonized fragments of basketry, Meadowood phase, Morrow site, Ontario Co., N.Y. Courtesy of the Rochester Museum of Arts and Sciences.

long, are difficult to identify. Three pieces seem to show a split-twig foundation and twisted basswood (?) fiber binders (Plate 70), somewhat similar to specimens from the Castle Creek site of the late Owasco culture (Plate 93). After examining a photograph of the fragment illustrated in Plate 70, top, Dr. Gene Weltfish commented as follows: "What I think I see is twined basketry with upward-leaning stitches toward the right and an overcast rim with a stick foundation." (Letter of June 18, 1958.)

Trade Connections

The Meadowood is the earliest recognized culture in the New York area to give evidence of fairly diversified trade relationships with distant regions, a process which continued here through much of the succeeding Middle Woodland period, and which has close parallels during Early and Middle Woodland times elsewhere in the eastern United States. The location of Meadowood sites on rivers and lakes, all part of an extensive system of interlinked waterways, doubtless facilitated this intercommunication, possibly through a system of trading partners, which probably took place by canoe travel, as in earlier times, rather than by overland forest trails, as among the Iroquois and other Late Woodland tribes.

These trade routes point in all directions from central New York, eastward to the Atlantic coast for the marine-shell beads; evidently to the north in Quebec for the smoky chalcedony ceremonial (?) knife; southward into eastern Pennsylvania for jasper and the steatite pots; but chiefly westward toward the Upper Great Lakes, where also the strongest cultural ties are found, for the copper tools and ornaments,

the striped slate gorgets and birdstones, and the Harrison County, Indiana, flint "Turkey Tail" knives or spears (Ritchie, 1961, p. 23).

Despite the apparently wide connections, our data preserve no hints of warfare, perhaps due in large part to the great scarcity of human skeletal remains. It would seem that the Meadowood folk enjoyed a half millennium or so of relative security in northern, central and western New York State, contemporaneously with some of the Orient people in southern and probably lower eastern New York, and, we may suppose, with remnant groups of other peoples of the Transitional, and even of Late Archaic, stages of cultural development in this area.

Mortuary Ceremonialism

The archaeological discoveries pertaining to the Meadowood phase afford more insight into the mortuary customs than into any other aspect of the culture, mainly because most of the components are burial sites, which unmistakably reveal a strong orientation toward activities concerned with the welfare of the dead, of sufficient complexity and intensity to suggest the presence of a more or less formalized body of belief and ritual, performed, presumably, to insure the safety and comfort of the deceased in the spirit world. This burial cult may also have involved elements of concern for the living, in re-establishing social cohesion in the bereaved group, and perhaps in providing for their protection against supernatural danger from the ghost.

These thaumaturgical rites, probably conducted by or under shamanistic auspices, seem to have varied in elaboration, perhaps in accordance with the status of the individual in a social hierarchy. The testimony of the graves certainly argues in this direction, for there were obvious differences in the care taken in the preparation of the burial and in the amount and quality of its furniture. Unfortunately, because of the thoroughness of the majority of cremations, which have reduced the bones to mere dust and fragments, and to the extensive or complete decay of unburned remains in the acid soils of most cemeteries, it is usually impossible to determine the relationship between these burial variables and such factors as sex and age. Where these can be ascertained with some confidence, the adult males were favored in both respects, as was the case at Frontenac Island, a community in the Late Archaic stage of culture (page 121).

The major traits of burial in the Meadowood phase, discussed more fully elsewhere (Ritchie, 1955, pp. 61–65), may be summarized as follows: cremation predominated, of green or new bones and, more rarely, of dry old bones (Plate 71). In either case the body must have been kept above ground, probably in a charnel house of some kind, for a period sufficient to allow for the decay of most of the flesh. Skeletal remains rarely occur well enough oriented anatomically to show at least ligamentous attachments of some of the parts, but scant proof has yet been adduced of the cremation of corpses in the flesh. Unburned bone bundles are rare, but they may have been more common than indicated, since most uncremated skeletal remains have perished through decay. Flexed burials occur (Plate 71), as do multiple burials of each kind, and combinations of all three modes, viz., cremated and bundle, cremated and flexed, and flexed and bundle. These facts suggest, as in the definitely related Orient burial practices (page 175), the performance of periodic burial services,

with individuals of a social unit (family? clan?) being interred together in a common grave in the Meadowood culture.

Cremation was carried out *in situ* in the grave pits on some of the sites (Oberlander No. 2 and Morrow), on surface crematories of stone on others (Indian River sites), and indeterminately elsewhere. Use of leather shrouds for the bone bundles is attested at two of the sites (Oberlander No. 2 and Hunter). Burial of the incinerated remains in bark-lined pits followed in most cases, but unburied cremations were discovered on the stone crematories at the Hunter site, Red Lake (Ritchie, 1955, pp. 24–26). The grave pits were sometimes dug in levels or with ramps to facilitate the ritualistic observances. No great care was exercised in most cases in gathering up the burned residue from the crematories for final interment. Along with the burned bones in some of the grave pits where cremation was *not* carried out *in situ*, occur fragments of the pyre charcoal, burned bits of the leather shrouds, and even fire-shattered rocks from the stone crematories, along with parts of fire-destroyed articles of grave goods. It is also of interest to note that unburned offerings were sometimes added to such graves and, more strangely, there are instances where the human remains were not burned but the artifacts in the same grave were (Ritchie, 1955, pp. 15–18, 27–29).

Burial took place either in a small cemetery of fairly closely spaced, sometimes actually intersecting or intrusively overlying graves, numbering from ten (Wray site) to approximately thirty-five (Morrow site), or in well-separated loci, each with a few (two to five or six) graves, as at the Indian River sites. A natural, mound-like knoll was chosen, and in all but two components (Wray and Morrow) it was high and prominent in the local landscape. In

PLATE 71 Multiple burial of the Meadowood phase on the Morrow site, Ontario Co., N.Y. Number 11 a cremation, 10 a flexed male skeleton, both with offerings of mortuary blades shown on Plate 61.

some cemeteries the graves were situated mainly or wholly on the east-facing portion of the upper slope or summit, hinting that the rising sun played a role in some part of the ceremony.

In all save one cemetery (Oberlander No. 2), use was made of powdered hematite or red ocher, which was sprinkled or more liberally poured over the grave contents, human and artifactual, or included in a bag or pouch in certain of the graves. Presumably, this substance had a symbolic significance, perhaps as a "quickening" agent or "restorer of life" from its blood-red color (see discussion in Ritchie, 1955, p. 64).

Mortuary offerings are present in the majority of the graves of the Meadowood culture, irrespective of the mode of burial. The quantity and quality, however, vary considerably from grave to grave, as already observed. In addition to whole and unblemished artifacts, and apparently new mortuary blades especially manufactured for this purpose, the grave goods often include intentionally broken objects, as well as reworked fragmentary items (Plate 69, Figures 1, 6), old worn-out and discarded things, and even, apparently, an occasional long-treasured heirloom (Ritchie, 1955, Plate 23, Figure 13; Plate 28, Figure 16, and p. 59).

Food, too, but never pottery vessels, was included in the provisions for the dead. Burned bones of the deer and dog accompanied the human cremations at the Oberlander No. 2 site, while at this and the Wray site, unburned mammal, bird and fishbones, probably food remains, were recovered from some of the graves.

Bone and antler, as raw materials for artifact manufacture in the other world, as inferred from its partial preparation or selected character, were also a provision for the deceased in some cases. Most impressive were the deposits of new, exquisitely chipped, extremely thin, ovate or triangulate blades, which vary considerably in size, usually by lots, present in one or more graves at all but the Wray site, and ranging in number from about 40 to about 1500, with approximately 100 to 250 as the usual quantity (Plate 61). Whether these were intended simply as "blanks" for the convenience of the departed in specializing projectile points and other chipped-stone implements, or whether they represent conspicuous wealth lavished on a particular individual to enhance his prestige in the spirit world, cannot be determined from the surviving evidence. (See, for fuller description and discussion, Ritchie, 1955, pp. 42–45, 59–60, 65 and Plates 9, 24.)

Fire surely played a significant part in the mortuary ceremonialism. Fire-making sets, comprising one or more anvils of iron pyrites, always altered to limonite through decay, and one or more flint strike-a-lights of various forms, are part of the contents of most graves (Plate 60, Figures 9, 10). These items were either rolled in bark (birch bark?), which served as tinder, and has sometimes left its imprint on the limonite mass, or the entire kit was enclosed in a bag or pouch, as indicated by the compact arrangement.

As conjectured by the writer (1955, 1959), the burial complex of the Orient and Meadowood phases reflects the presence in the Northeast during Late Transitional and Early Woodland times of a mortuary ceremonialism which was to reach its climax elsewhere in the eastern United States in the Middle Woodland period. Even with the greatly revised carbon-14 dating for the Hunter site (page 181), the ritualism of the Meadowood seems to have preceded the generally similar manifestation in the Adena by at least two hundred years.

This developing concern for the supermundane well-being of the dead was foreshadowed in the Late Archaic stage in the burial practices at a number of sites in the Northeast. Among these the Frontenac Island site, radiocarbon-dated between c. 2980 and 1723 B.C., has already been described on page 104. In eastern Massachusetts similar evidence has been found on the Titicut site, the Boats site (Rose, 1953), the Coburn site on Cape Cod (Kremp, 1961), the Mansion Inn site at Wayland (Mansfield, 1961), and on the Wapanucket No. 6 component, radiocarbon-dated c. 2292 B.C., referred to above on page 35 (Robbins, 1960), the Wapanucket No. 8 component (Robbins, by correspondence) and several other New England sites (Dincauze, 1966). The use of red ocher, cremation and the intentional destruction of grave offerings is recorded for most of these sites. With the passage of time and the extension of contacts this mortuary ceremonialism became not only more elaborate, but increasingly esoteric as well, being definitely directed in the Adena and Hopewellian cultures toward selected individuals in a social hierarchy.

Some of the more obvious parallels between the burial cult in the Northeast and in the Adena-Hopewellian are the empha-

sis on cremation and other extensive ceremonial use of fire; evident employment of
a charnel house; grave offerings on a progressively lavish scale, dependent upon increasingly wide trade connections to secure
exotic materials; heavy use of red ocher;
destruction of grave offerings by fire and
mechanical breakage; and certain similarities in the general artifact categories (e.g.,
gorgets, birdstones, tubular pipes, cache or
mortuary blades, copper tools and ornaments, discoidal beads, large ceremonial
knives, galena, etc.).

The selection of natural knolls as cemetery sites among the Meadowood and
Orient peoples may have been the basic
idea underlying the construction of artifi-
cial burial mounds by the later Adena and
Hopewellian groups, as previously hypothesized (Ritchie, 1955, pp. 7, 61), and in
both areas one sees the setting apart, as
"sacred precincts," of cemeteries, and
mounds and earthworks, from habitation
centers.

Cultural Relations

The closest relationship between the
Meadowood and cultures outside the New
York area is to be found to the west, in the
Red Ocher and intimately related Glacial
Kame cultures of the Upper Great Lakes
region (Ritzenthaler and Quimby, 1962,
pp. 253–56). With the Red Ocher culture
centered in southeastern Wisconsin, northern Illinois, northern Indiana, and southern
Michigan, and especially with the Pomranky complex thereof, found around Saginaw Bay, Michigan, the Meadowood phase
shares the following significant traits: use
of red ocher to cover the burial; flexed,
cremated and bundle burial in deep grave
pits; large "ceremonial" blades, ellipsoidal

in shape; "Turkey Tail" blades of Harrison
County, Indiana, flint; large caches of
mortuary blades, small and somewhat
crude and asymmetrical in the Red Ocher,
larger, symmetrical and beautifully made
in the Meadowood and to some extent in
the Pomranky complex; thick rolled or
thinner tubular copper beads; copper awls
and celts; bar-type birdstones; three-holed
rectanguloid gorgets; cigar-shaped tubular
pipes (of stone in the Red Ocher, of pottery in the Meadowood); unworked galena
cubes; celts and Early Woodland pottery
(in some Red Ocher sites) (Ritzenthaler
and Quimby, 1962, pp. 246–50; Binford,
1963, 1963a).

The principal Glacial Kame and Meadowood parallels comprise: the bar birdstone;
tubular pipe (as in Red Ocher); copper
celt and adz (some with gouge-shaped lip),
bead and awl; shell disk bead; rectanguloid gorget (of stone only in the Meadowood); red ocher with burials in deep pits;
and the practice of cremation (Cunningham, 1948; Ritchie, 1949, pp. 24–45; 1955,
pp. 71–75).

The Feeheley site near Saginaw, Michigan, believed to belong to the Glacial
Kame culture (Taggart, n.d.), has been
radiocarbon-dated at approximately 1900
B.C. (M-1139, Crane and Griffin, 1962, p.
186). Several age determinations exist for
the Red Ocher culture. The earliest, 1210
B.C.±300 years, based on a sample of
human bone (M-659, Crane and Griffin,
1960, p. 34), comes from the Andrews site
in Saginaw County, Michigan, which has
apparently (it is still unpublished) extremely close parallels with the Meadowood phase, and particularly with the Indian River sites thereof. (In October 1963
the writer inspected the material from the
Andrews, Hodges and Pomranky sites of
the Pomranky complex at the Museum of

Anthropology, University of Michigan, and confirmed this impression.)

As the Hunter site in New York is radio-carbon-dated on charcoal at 841 B.C.± 68 years (page 181), or approximately 370 years later than the Andrews station in Michigan, the writer's earlier hypothesis of primary Upper Great Lakes influences for the Meadowood is accordingly strengthened (Ritchie, 1955, pp. 78–79). Within the compass of the standard deviations, however, the two sites could be of identical age.

The Andrews site is said to represent an Early Red Ocher cultural manifestation on a Late Archaic or prepottery level. A Late Red Ocher complex, of the Early Woodland stage, is thought (Ritzenthaler and Quimby, 1962, p. 257) to be represented at the Sny-Magill Mound 43, Clayton County, Iowa (Beaubien, 1953, pp. 57–60), dated at 470 B.C.±250 years (M-305, Crane and Griffin, 1958, p. 1099). Its Red Ocher affiliations are, however, open to serious doubt, and the dentate rocker-stamped pottery found in this mound (Beaubien, 1953, p. 61) would seem to relate it to the Middle Woodland period. Its late date, too, is more consistent with dates of the second, or Early Point Peninsula tradition, which seems to have overlapped slightly with the Meadowood in New York and perhaps with the latest stages of the Red Ocher complex in the Midwest.

THE MIDDLESEX PHASE

The Middlesex phase is a rather amorphous cultural manifestation of the Northeast, perhaps because it is known solely from burial places, not one of which was professionally explored. The sites are rare and, in the absence of recognizable surface indications or habitation components, virtually impossible to find by normal investigative methods. Hence, with the single exception of the Long Sault Island mounds, all discoveries have been fortuitous, in most instances as the result of commercial gravel and sand digging in a knoll or terrace near a river or lake.

The designation and first description of the Middlesex complex were provided by the writer in 1937, the Vine Valley site in the town of Middlesex, Yates County, New York, being regarded as the type station (Figure 4, site number 45), and affinities with the Adena culture of Ohio were postulated on the grounds of certain shared traits, particularly a diagnostic tubular pipe form, which was termed the "blocked-end tube" (Ritchie, 1937). Then, and in subsequent discussions, it was concluded that the Middlesex "focus" in New York and New England represented infusions of elements of the Adena culture of Ohio into regional native cultures of the Northeast (Ritchie, 1938, pp. 100–3; 1944, pp. 112–15, 186–87; 1951, pp. 131–33).

More recently, however, as the result of additional Middlesex data, fuller analyses of the Adena culture (Webb and Snow, 1945; Webb and Baby, 1957), important discoveries of Adena in the Chesapeake Bay district, in Delaware and in New Jersey, and closer personal familiarity with Adena as well as Middlesex materials, a somewhat different interpretation has been arrived at independently by Dr. Don W. Dragoo and the writer. The newer concept regards Middlesex as essentially Adena in the north, the locally varying products of contact metamorphosis of actual splinter groups of Adena people and already resident groups, rather than random trait diffusions from an Ohio center (Ritchie and Dragoo, 1959, 1960).

The total body of evidence, analyzed in the last reference, has appeared to us to support the hypothesis that a strong movement or expansion of Hopewell people from the Illinois Valley into the central and upper Ohio Valley resulted in the social and political disruption of the Adena civilization, with the displacement of some of the more dissatisfied groups. An actual transfer of a sizable body of Adena people and their treasures, probably via the Monongahela and Potomac valleys to Chesapeake Bay, is virtually certain on the evidence of the Sandy Hill and West River sites in Maryland.

From this new center in the east, dispersal northward can be traced through Delaware—the Felton site and the new St. Jones River site (Dragoo, 1961)—and New Jersey—Rosencrans site—into central and eastern New York and New England, via the Delaware, Hudson and Connecticut rivers. The peculiar grouping of the burial sites in the Connecticut, Mohawk and Lake Champlain valleys (Ritchie and Dragoo, 1960, Figure 1), suggests that in these sections of the Northeast the newcomers were able to obtain tenure, either by force or more probably by consent of the local residents, with whom in time they were culturally and physically assimilated. A less well defined route along the Ohio and Allegheny rivers may also have led from the parent area into western and central New York.

The south-to-north direction of dispersal is unequivocally attested by the fact that a high percentage of the classic Adena-type artifacts in Middlesex sites are made from stone materials native to the Ohio River basin, but exotic in the north, viz., fireclay or Ohio pipestone which occurs near Portsmouth, Ohio; Flint Ridge, Ohio, chalcedony; Ohio banded slate; Indiana limestone; and Harrison County, Indiana, nodular flint. Furthermore, the ratio of specifically Adena elements to those of local origin in the Middlesex-site complexes varies inversely with the distance of the sites from the Adena centers to the south, ranging from nearly 100 per cent at Sandy Hill, Maryland, and 89 per cent at Rosencrans, New Jersey (Figure 4, site number 47), to between 64 per cent and 82 per cent in the western Vermont sites and 75 per cent at Long Sault Island in the St. Lawrence River.

Analysis of the nineteen burial components attributed to the Middlesex phase yields a total of ninety-two traits, seventy-four pertaining to artifacts, eighteen to burial practices. Slightly over half (55.4 per cent) are present in the Adena culture, some of them (35.8 per cent) being highly diagnostic thereof, the remaining 44.6 per cent consist of elements not recorded for Adena. Most of the latter, which occur on only one or two of the sites, can be accommodated within the Point Peninsula culture, apparently the already well established host culture, especially in central New York. (See Tables 1–5, pp. 70–80, Figure 2, and pp. 56–57 in Ritchie and Dragoo, 1960.)

The most widely prevalent artifacts on Middlesex sites are also those most distinctive of the Adena culture, comprising in particular the following items, some of which are illustrated on Plate 72: the blocked-end tubular pipe (Figure 16); large leaf-shaped and lanceolate knife (Figure 12); javelin and spear heads with straight or lobate stem or side-notched; ovoid and trianguloid cache blades (Figure 2); copper celt (Figure 18); copper awl, usually square in cross section; boatstone, sometimes of copper; bar amulet (Figures 17, 19); truncated or bust type of birdstone; several styles of gorget (Figure 14) and pendant (Figures 6, 7); cylindri-

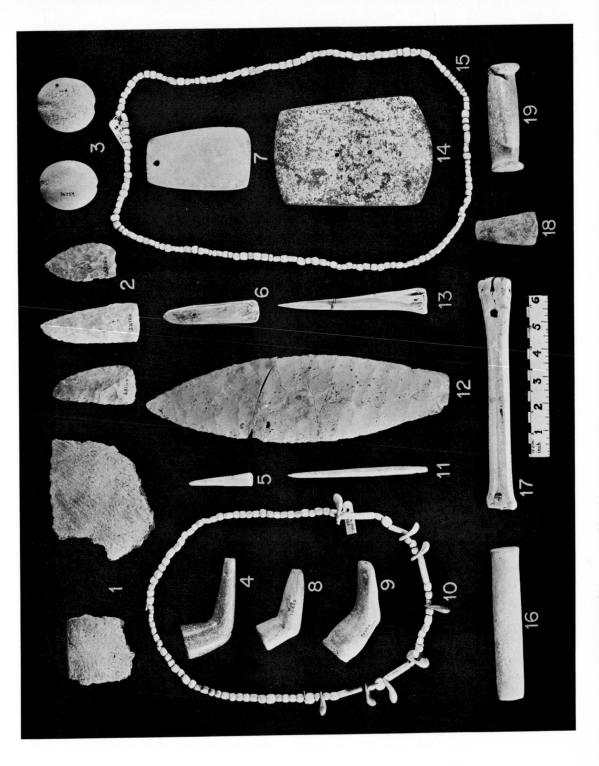

PLATE 72 Artifacts attributed to the Middlesex phase from the Vine Valley site, Yates Co., N.Y. 1 Vinette 1 potsherds; 2 cache blades; 3 grooved sinkers or bolas-stones; 4, 8, 9 plain obtuse-angle elbow pipes, of stone (4) and pottery; 5 conical antler projectile point; 6, 7 pendants of bone (6) and stone; 10 necklace of cylindrical and barrel-shaped shell beads and elk canines; 11, 13 bone awls; 12 lanceolate knife; 14 stone gorget; 15 necklace of barrel-shaped shell beads; 16 blocked-end tubular pipe; 17 probable bar amulet made from a deer metapodial bone, a unique object; 18 copper celt; 19 stone bar amulet.

cal copper beads; discoidal, barrel-shaped and cylindrical shell beads (Figures 10, 15); and *Marginella*-shell beads. Extensive use was made of powdered red ocher to cover the flexed, extended (rare), bundled or cremated human remains and their usual accompaniment of grave offerings, a number of which appear to have ritualistic rather than secular significance. Many of them are obviously treasures from the homeland, carefully conserved, since they are rarely found except in graves.

While these facts proclaim Middlesex participation in a widely prevalent mortuary ceremonialism, the use of burial mounds and certain other specialized mortuary traits of Adena seem to have been abandoned, the sole known exception being the mounds on Long Sault Island in the St. Lawrence River, curiously enough the outpost most remote of any now known from the Adena heartland (Ritchie and Dragoo, 1960, pp. 39–56) (Figure 4, site number 46). It seems likely that the dispersed small bands of Adena people, while clinging to some of their ideological and religious beliefs, as reflected in their burial practices, would have been compelled by the disintegration of the socio-political system to forego such major accomplishments, requiring sufficient common labor and authority, as the erection of large mounds and earthworks.

Because all recognized Middlesex sites are burial components, and because, as has been noted, secular objects constitute only a part of the grave goods, it seems unfeasible to attempt a reconstruction of Middlesex culture in accordance with the outline followed in this work.

Nor can a description be offered of the physical appearance of the people buried in the Middlesex graves, because of the almost total lack of skeletal remains due to destruction or loss of those found by accident, poor preservation, and the practice of cremation. Three adult male crania from the Vine Valley site belonged to fairly robust individuals having rather broad heads, wide faces and broad noses. Being undeformed, they offer scant basis for comparison with surviving Adena crania, representing in all cases a socially selected few individuals accorded the special privilege of mound burial, who had been subjected to infant head-shaping, to produce a hyperbrachycephalism.

Concerning the period during which the postulated infiltration of Adena people and their culture took place into the Northeast, we have the typological testimony of the Adena artifacts which point to later stages of Adena development, as currently known, and a few radiocarbon dates for the West River, Maryland, St. Jones River, Delaware, and Rosencrans, New Jersey, sites, derived from charcoal resulting from *in situ* cremations on all components. The West River series of eight dates is, however, more confusing than enlightening in its lack of consistency and wide variance from 360 B.C.± 200 years (M-416A) to A.D. 325±400 years (M-418). Close to the earliest date for West River is the 380 B.C.±80 years determination for the St. Jones River site (Y-933) (Stuiver, Deevey and Rouse, 1963, pp. 330–31). The single date for the Rosencrans site is unexpectedly even earlier, at 610 B.C.±120 years (Y-1384). It was derived from a grave pit measuring three by four by three feet in which classic Adena-Middlesex artifacts were found in direct association with the burned human bones by Dr. Lewis M. Haggerty of Hackensack, New Jersey, who kindly provided the writer with the sample. (Carpenter, 1950, pp. 299–303, has described this site.)

In West Virginia, radiocarbon dates of

290 B.C.±150 years (M-976), 240 B.C.± 200 years (M-975) and 70 B.C.±150 years (M-974) have been obtained from different areas of the Cresap Mound excavated by Don W. Dragoo (Dragoo, 1963), and 350 B.C.±200 years (M-903) from the Welcome Mound excavated by F. M. Setzler.

THE EARLY POINT PENINSULA CULTURE

In a previous major synthesis (Ritchie, 1944, pp. 115–21), the Point Peninsula culture, which the writer named from a burial site on Point Peninsula, at the east end of Lake Ontario, Jefferson County, New York (Nichols, 1928), was described as a single focus, but, in accord with the then existing data, a dual or even tripartite division was suggested (Ritchie, 1944, p. 116), one group being represented by the Northrop, Wray, Oberlander No. 2, Vinette, Pickins and Muskalonge Lake sites, another by the Point Peninsula, René Menard Bridge No. 1 and No. 2, Jack's Reef, Kipp Island, Fall Brook, Durkee, Bay of Quinté, and Port Maitland components, and a possible third by the Sea Breeze site.[1] This latter site, with its relatively strong showing of Hopewellian traits, was considered of potentially intermediate status between the two other groups.

The fragmentary nature of the data available at the time of writing induced the writer tentatively to combine the sundry sites into a single cultural focus while stating, however, that "he would . . . if the observed tendencies are corroborated by future research, emphasize the possibility of ultimate differentiation into at least two foci, of which sites 3 and 4 in the trait table (Oberlander No. 2 and Vinette) and site

[1] All these sites are described in Ritchie, 1944, pp. 121–81; cf. Ritchie, 1955, for later discoveries at the Muskalonge Lake site.

12 (Kipp Island) constitute respectively the type components" (ibid., p. 116). It was also pointed out that the first group of sites, with certain Middlesex (Adena) traits, was probably the older one, the second group, having Intrusive Mound culture elements (Ritchie, 1937), was the more recent, while the Hopewellian influence noted at the Sea Breeze site seemed to denote for it an intermediate stage of development in the Point Peninsula sequence (Ritchie, 1944, p. 116).

Major artifact assemblages correlated with these hypothesized groups of sites were as follows: with group 1, gorgets, birdstones, cigar-shaped tubular pottery pipes, thin side-notched points and cache blades, and rolled tubular copper beads; with group 2, pendants, bar amulets, stone tubular pipes, slightly bent elbow pipes of stone and clay, platform pipes, thick cache blades, corner-notched points, triangular points, combs, large antler flakers, and barbed bone and antler points; and with group 3, distinctive narrow rectangular gorgets, corner-notched points, prismatic flake knives and mica. It was remarked, however, that the Sea Breeze site (group 3) shared with the components of the two other groups the diagnostic Point Peninsula trait of the antler-hafted beaver-incisor cutting or engraving tool, as well as certain other elements of both the presumed earlier and later groups. Thus the whole site series presented a kind of continuity with "each site . . . likened to the segment of a circle, the sum forming considerably less than a complete orb" (ibid., p. 116).

While the picture in 1964 is still far from clear, sufficient evidence has accumulated since 1944 to bolster the hypothesized subdivision of the Point Peninsula culture, indeed, to split it into at least two historically separate cultural traditions, one of which, now called the Meadowood and already discussed, is no longer grouped with the Point Peninsula, as previously stated (page 180).

The second tradition I am now regarding as the basis for the new Point Peninsula formulation, a modification, in the light of the more recent data, of my synthesis of 1944, as revised in 1951 (Ritchie, 1951). Even more clearly than the Meadowood, it has its earlier roots and closest affinities to the west of New York, in the Upper Great Lakes area both of Canada and the United States. This connection is clearly indicated by ceramic linkages within the Vinette 2 ware series which characterizes this tradition. The appearance of this group of pseudo-scallop-shell, dentate, complex-dentate, and rocker-stamped styles is taken as the marker for the inception of the Point Peninsula culture of the Middle Woodland period in the Northeast.

The complex in which this pottery first appears in the New York area is poorly known, and the components are small and usually obscured by intermixture with earlier or later components. Thus at present we have no satisfactory type or closed site for what I am currently designating the Early Point Peninsula culture. However, what seems to be a typical component, as judged from the pottery unearthed (Plate 73), was discovered and partly excavated by the writer on Canoe Point, Grindstone Island, in the St. Lawrence River, Jefferson County, New York (Figure 4, site number 48), and on this slender basis a Canoe Point phase is tentatively postulated, the term, as will subsequently be seen, being singularly appropriate for the culture it denotes (pages 208, 211).

The middle and upper levels at the Vinette site at Brewerton in central New York show this assemblage in stratigraphic relationship to the Meadowood phase, which is represented by the lower component at this site with Vinette 1 pottery and chipped and polished stone artifacts (Ritchie, 1944, pp. 160–64; Ritchie and MacNeish, 1949, p. 118). An apparent continuity in the ceramic and stone typologies at the Vinette site was chiefly responsible for the writer's previous inclusion of what is now being termed the Meadowood phase in the Point Peninsula sequence, and on current evidence it still seems likely that the two cultures overlapped slightly in time and more extensively in space, with some concurrent use of Vinette 1 and Vinette 2 wares.

The lower level at the nearby Wickham site reveals the temporal relationship of Point Peninsula to the Owasco culture in the superimposed stratum (Ritchie, 1946), while at the recently excavated O'Neil site, also in central New York, a Point Peninsula sequence stratigraphically forms part of the upper horizon in this radiocarbon-dated, multicomponent site, involving the Archaic Brewerton phase at the base and the Frost Island phase of the Transitional period in the middle zone (page 156).

In southeastern Ontario on East Sugar Island in Rice Lake; at the Parker site on Percy Reach, Trent River; and elsewhere the writer found evidence that an Early Point Peninsula group with dentate, corded, rocker-stamped, pseudo-scallop-shell-marked, and even incised pottery types overlapped with the local culture of the Laurentian tradition, containing ground slate and ground bone points (Ritchie, 1949, pp. 17–19). Apparently this was the earliest pottery of this district, no Vinette 1 ware having been seen or reported (ibid., p. 2). Vinette 1 pottery occurs, however, in the Ottawa Valley and elsewhere in eastern Ontario (Mitchell, 1963); and at

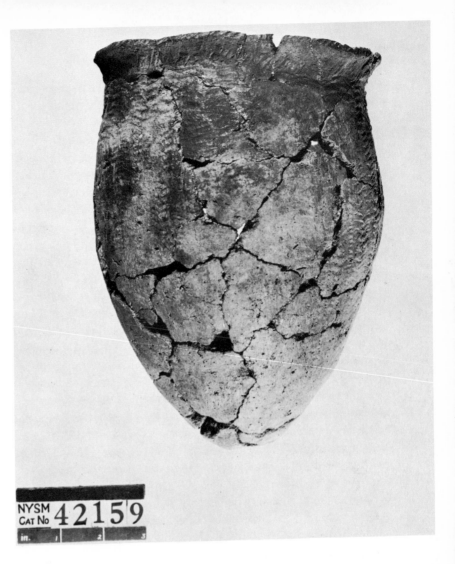

PLATE 73 Early Point Peninsula pottery vessel of Point Peninsula Rocker-Stamped type from Canoe Point, Grindstone Island, Jefferson Co., N.Y.

NYSM CAT No 42159

Frank Bay, Lake Nipissing, it was found at the bottom of the earliest Point Peninsula stratum (Ridley, 1954, p. 43).

While the relative chronological position of the Point Peninsula is thus rather clearly defined, at least in central New York and southeastern Ontario, we have as yet few actual carbon-14 determinations for any of the developmental stages of this culture. In western Ontario two sites tentatively assigned to the Early Point Peninsula have been so dated. These are the Burley site, near Port Franks on Lake Huron, at 668 B.C.±220 years (Jury and Jury, 1952, pp. 70, 73), and the Donaldson site on the Saugeen River, Bruce Peninsula, at 519 B.C. ±60 years (Wright and Anderson, 1963, p. 50). At the latter site Wright believes that the pottery exhibits a combination of the paste traits of Vinette 1 with the decorative styles and techniques of the Vinette 2 ware (Point Peninsula) series.

In New York State, only one radiocarbon date has so far been obtained which apparently applies to the Early Point Peninsula horizon, and this date, A.D. 240±80 years (Y-1277) is much later than the Canadian chronology. It was derived from hearth charcoal excavated in 1962 by the writer's party on the O'Neil site, on the Sen-

207

eca River, Cayuga County, New York (Figure 4, site number 27). The feature was evidently intrusive into the very top of stratum 2 (pertaining to the Frost Island phase, page 157) from near the base of stratum 1, from which level pottery and other Early Point Peninsula artifacts were obtained. (The writer's report on the important O'Neil site, Wpt. 11-4, is in manuscript.)

The area of distribution of the Early Point Peninsula culture is very large, comprising most or all of southern Ontario, lying below or on the southern part of the Laurentian Shield, the St. Lawrence Valley and its tributary Richelieu River, and Lake Champlain. The western limits of the range probably reach into southern Manitoba and certainly include northern Minnesota. On the east, the culture can be traced across northern Maine and New Hampshire into New Brunswick. These peripheral limits are vaguely defined, and almost entirely on the basis of ceramic remains, and the same is true on the southern marches, which include southern New York and New England, and to the north beyond the Height of Land separating the drainage of the Great Lakes and St. Lawrence River from that of Hudson Bay.

It must also be obvious that no single phase manifestation occurs over so large a territory. We are referring rather to a cultural tradition (still almost a pottery tradition at this writing), as defined above (page xxviii), characterized principally by a concatenation of pottery types, displaying throughout a remarkable consistency in paste characteristics; body, rim and lip shapes; techniques of ornamentation; and design motifs. A near identity in some sherds has been observed by the writer in finds made as far separated as Minnesota and New Hampshire.

On first becoming cognizant of this ceramic series at the Vinette and Wickham sites in central New York, the writer, to differentiate them from his Vinette 1 (which is both a ware and a type), designated them a Vinette 2 ware group (Ritchie, 1946, pp. 13–14), subsequently, with MacNeish, breaking the group down into type categories (Ritchie and Mac-Neish, 1949, pp. 100–4). Urgently needed to clarify the picture is intensive site investigation throughout the area, which, it is believed, would result in the formulation of a number of phase manifestations within the Early Point Peninsula culture.

Although very widespread, the cultural heartland appears to lie between Lake Huron and Georgian Bay on the west, the Ottawa River on the north, the Richelieu River and Lake Champlain on the east, the north shore of Lake Erie, Oneida Lake and the Seneca River of central New York on the south.

Typical Components

Within this core area are to be found a large number of camp sites, most of them small with but a thin refuse mantle, and located on the shores, particularly on promontories, coves and islands, of the myriad lakes and streams to be found in this region of low relief, encompassed mainly within the Great Lakes and St. Lawrence lowland provinces (Figure 4). Currently at least, the region is characterized by a humid continental forest climate and, as probably in Point Peninsula times, by a heavy forest cover of hemlock, white pine and northern hardwoods, principally sugar maple, beech, basswood and yellow birch (Braun, 1950, pp. 337–93). Major game animals of the Canadian fauna, represented by refuse bone in the middens, include the deer, black bear, moose, beaver and raccoon, but the general scarcity of such remains and the paucity of projectile points, as well as the situation of the sites themselves, argue that hunting was of less importance to the occupants of these sites than was fishing and collecting of fresh-water mussels, as judged from the relative abundance of fishing gear and the organic remnants of these aquatic animals. An extensive use of the wild rice beds which are known to have thrived in many of these lakes, and still do in some, may plausibly be postulated.

This inferred subsistence pattern may pertain only to warm-season occupation of fishing camps; winters may have been spent ranging the forests in small groups, as among the Algonkian bands of the Ottawa River area and their kinsmen to the west, the Chippewa; and the discovery and excavation of these winter camp sites might convey a different impression of the culture. None of the sites so far excavated has yielded post molds, hence the form of shelter employed by these Point Peninsula people is still undiscovered. Perhaps, especially in summer, it was a flimsy wigwam affair of poles with bark or mat covers, which rested almost upon the surface of the ground.

At the Donaldson site, however, which is referred to this culture, Wright has uncovered the post-mold patterns of at least two houses. They appear to have been rectanguloid structures measuring approximately seventeen by twenty-three feet and eleven by seventeen feet, respectively, and containing one or two hearths (Wright and Anderson, 1963, pp. 11–15).

What may prove to be in part an "ancestral" complex for the Early Point Peninsula in New York, or at least a definitely related one, was recently excavated by

James V. Wright on Heron Bay on the Pic River, on the north shore of Lake Superior in Ontario. Seen by the writer at the National Museum of Canada in January 1962, through the courtesy of Dr. Wright, the assemblage, found in a stained-sand stratum about one foot in thickness, under a one- to two-inch duff zone, on an eight-foot terrace above the river, comprises predominantly pseudo-scallop-shell-decorated and punctated pottery, with narrow, rounded or wedge-shaped lips and conical bases; a small quantity of dentate-stamped sherds of the same shape; thick side-notched projectile points ranging in length from about one to three and a quarter inches; simple end scrapers and notched spokeshave scrapers; flake knives with retouched edges and ovate bifacially chipped knives; simple bone awls; beaver-incisor tools with chisel-shaped edge and obliquely ground lateral edge; the conical, antler, toggle-head harpoon and probably the barbed bone harpoon; flat, bone, snowshoe (?) needles; tubular bone and discoidal shell beads; a carved bone wristlet; many copper artifacts including a conical projectile point, awls, small chisels, gorges, probable compound fishhook points, beads and bangles. The very few ground stone implements comprised a small semilunar blade and two slate spalls with edge-grinding, and in rough stone there were end- and side-notched netsinkers, flat whetstones and unpitted pebble hammerstones. Much red ocher, powdered and in the form of paintstones, occurred, but no burials were discovered.

Wright believes that this complex, which he assigns to the Early Laurel Focus, Middle Woodland period, contributed not only to the Early Point Peninsula, as now defined by the writer, but also to the later Black Duck Focus of the northern Minnesota-southwestern Ontario area (Wright, 1967).

Another undated western Ontario site, attributable to the Point Peninsula culture, is the later component at the Inverhuron site on the Bruce Peninsula (Kenyon, 1957, pp. 15–22).

With the dentate-stamped, rocker-stamped, corded-stick and other techniques of decoration appearing on small to medium-sized, conoidal-based, all-over-decorated and interior-channeled vessels, is a small assemblage of thick, side-notched projectile points, simple end and side scrapers, hammerstones, choppers, end-notched pebble netsinkers, a copper fishhook, simple bone awls, and a pointed beaver-incisor graving tool.

The Kant site in the Ottawa Valley, Wilberforce Township, Renfrew County, Ontario, is a still larger site, excavated by Professor J. Norman Emerson for the National Museum of Canada in 1947 (Emerson, 1955). Three related components apparently occur at the site, and ceramic seriations would seem to place the site as a whole within a Point Peninsula developmental continuum intermediate between the middle levels at the Vinette site and the lower levels of the Wickham site in central New York (ibid., p. 39).

Stone artifacts, surface finds for the most part, include side-notched and stemmed projectile points, of forms familiar in this context both in Canada and New York, end scrapers, an expanded base drill, and a group of generally large and rudely made plano-convex adzes. A single copper fishhook was also found. Several burials discovered here are discussed below (page 213).

On Thorah Island in Lake Simcoe, York County, Ontario, another Point Peninsula site is undergoing exploration by Paul W. Sweetman of Toronto, who has kindly made his data available to me at the University of Toronto. This typical site is stratified, with the Middle Woodland horizon at the bottom in a three- to five-inch stained sand-and-ash layer, overlaid by about a foot of dark soil and humus which has produced Iroquoian remains of several late prehistoric complexes. Fishbones, mussel shells, but no mammal bones (deer bones are present in the Iroquoian middens), occur in the Point Peninsula deposit, together with a large number of notched pebble netsinkers, and a predominance of Point Peninsula Rocker-Stamped sherds, executed with dentate stamps for the most part, with a small percentage done in corded or pseudo-scallop-shell imprints. Minor amounts of the classic St. Lawrence Pseudo Scallop Shell type, with wedge-shaped, slightly everted lip, occur, as do Vinette Dentate, corded punctate, and cord-decorated untyped varieties, some of the latter sufficiently complex to suggest a late place in the Point Peninsula sequence.

Two thin, rather narrow, side-notched projectile points and a beaver incisor with chisel edge comprise the remaining Point Peninsula finds here.

A very instructive, stratigraphically correlated, Point Peninsula sequence was excavated by the writer in 1948 on East Sugar Island in Rice Lake, Otonabee Township, Peterborough County, Ontario, and has elsewhere been described and analyzed (Ritchie, 1949, pp. 3–24) (cf. page 206 herein). The basal stratum, of black dirt, contained Laurentian material, including projectile points of flint, ground slate and ground bone, in apparent association with Vinette Complex Dentate, Point Peninsula Corded, Point Peninsula Rocker-Stamped, St. Lawrence Pseudo Scallop Shell, and Wickham Incised pottery types, and even a few sherds of Jack's Reef Corded Punctate, a type which appears late in the New York Point Peninsula succession (Ritchie, 1949, Figure 4, p. 19).

In the next higher stratum, of crushed mussel shells and black dirt, the Laurentian elements had disappeared, quantitative and minor qualitative ceramic changes were present, and the projectile points were related to Point Peninsula forms.

The third level, an ash or ashy zone, extended this continuum with diminishing amounts of the earlier ceramic types, and the addition of the stone gorget, barbed bone point, smoking pipe, and new pottery styles transitional into those of the fourth stratum.

This fourth, or loam horizon, while still definitely continuous with the underlying levels, produced a predominance of sherds belonging to what is now called the Pickering Focus, a newly defined Late Point Peninsula manifestation in Ontario, known principally from the Miller site near Toronto. This stage of Point Peninsula development leads on into the Uren stage of the Iroquois through an easy transition, as shown at the Bennett site in the same area (Wright, 1966).

The upper part of the loam and sod at East Sugar Island also produced a few late prehistoric Iroquois sherds, points and pipe stems.

This illuminating Point Peninsula developmental sequence at East Sugar Island has strong parallels at the key Frank Bay site on Lake Nipissing, about 180 miles in a direct line to the northwest (Ridley, 1954, pp. 43–47). Here, however, Vinette 1 sherds were found at the base of the remarkable stratigraphic series. The Point Peninsula sequence at these two sites affords a substantial outline of the development of this culture in eastern Ontario in

the Middle and Late Woodland periods. In central New York the Middle Woodland part of the sequence is very similar, but the Pickering and related Glen Meyer phases of the Late Woodland period in Ontario are in New York represented by the even better elucidated Owasco culture, to be described later on. In both areas the later stages of the Point Peninsula grade into the incipient stages of the regional Iroquoian cultures.

Both in Canada and in New York, as will presently be seen, other cultural influences from outside impinged, at various times, on the Point Peninsula continuum, resulting in modifications of varying kind and intensity, according to locality affected. In some parts of the total range of the Point Peninsula culture, these influences seem scarcely to have penetrated at all, while in others, closer to the points of entry of the exotic diffusions, profound changes of many kinds took place, as will appear in the following section on the Kipp Island phase.

Subsistence Pattern

As mentioned above, the subsistence pattern of the Early Point Peninsula culture seems to have been oriented around fishing, to a lesser extent hunting, with probably a considerable reliance on wild-rice gathering. Fishbones, and even occasionally fish scales, occur on all sites where osseous matter is preserved, where they are usually more abundant than the bones of mammals.

Fishing gear found on one or more of these sites comprises notched flat pebble netsinkers, common on most sites; grooved ovate pebbles, probably for netsinkers; presumable bone fishhook barbs for compound hooks; the copper fishhook and gorge; the conical antler toggle-head harpoon; and barbed bone points, with multiple bilateral angular barbs. No bone fishhooks have been reported.

The hunting activity is represented by the bones of various animals, principally the deer, bear, beaver, turkey and waterfowl, usually occurring in small quantities; and by hunting gear consisting only of projectile points, also scarce on all sites of this culture. Three styles of chipped-stone projectile points can be recognized, two of them side-notched, and a rarer stemmed variety.

The most characteristic side-notched form has broad notches with sloping shoulder and tang, and an unground convex base. It is usually medium thick, and varies in length from about one and a quarter to two and a half inches. The less frequent side-notched style is thinner, has narrower, sharp and bold notches, and usually a squarish, unsmoothed base. It apparently persisted into Late Point Peninsula times, when with certain refinements it became a popular point of the Kipp Island phase (see Plate 82, Figures 7, 8, 13, 14).

The stemmed variety of the Early Point Peninsula assemblages has rounded shoulders, and the stem is usually slightly expanded toward the convex base.

Most of the points of all kinds found in this culture are fairly well chipped from local flints. Antler and bone flaking tools have been found on some sites.

The food animals gathered by the Early Point Peninsula groups included the freshwater mussel, which was probably also dried, and various turtles, frogs, etc. Wild vegetal foods certainly included the hickory nut and beechnut, both found by the writer on the O'Neil site, and most probably wild rice where it was available.

There is no evidence for agriculture, ei-

ther as tools or carbonized plant remains. Mortars, pestles and mullers have not been reported. Pits found on the O'Neil site may have been employed for food storage, but such features have not elsewhere been recorded.

Early Point Peninsula sites yield meagerly of artifacts. Aside from those described, they include small numbers of end and side scrapers, expanded-base drills, prismatic-flake and ovate knives, pebble hammerstones, anvilstones, flat whetstones, probably the chopper or heavy hide scraper, chipped and partially ground adzes and celts, and probably small copper chisels. Evidently much use was made of wood, for the most numerous bone artifacts on nearly·every site are beaver incisors, modified, by grinding, into chisels, gravers and scrapers. Some of these teeth were set into deer-antler hafts, in a familiar form which occurs in cultures from the Meadowood through the Kipp Island.

Probable skin-working tools embrace, besides scrapers, also used in wood shaping, simple bone awls and rare copper awls. The flat bone needle was most likely employed in sewing rush mats.

Ornaments for the body or clothing comprise, according to the slender evidence, rectangular stone gorgets; short, rolled, tubular copper beads; tubular bone beads; discoidal shell beads; and powdered red ocher.

No smoking pipes of stone or clay are currently known from this culture, and it does not seem that the Early Point Peninsula people knew the use of tobacco.

The Early Point Peninsula material culture, with its exiguous inventory of stone and bone traits, conveys an impression of impoverishment in everything but ceramics. Quite likely it was rich in bark and wooden artifacts, as is the case with the northeastern Algonkian forest cultures, to some of which it may have been ancestral. The component manifestations point to small, mobile, probably bark-canoe-traveling, fishermen, hunters and wild-rice gatherers, with little baggage. Even their pottery vessels were small and readily portable.

Pottery, the best-known and most distinctive part of the material culture, is in general well made and decorated. It pertains to cooking pots of approximately two- to four-quart capacity, medium to coarse grit-tempered, with conoidal bases and nearly straight to moderately everted collarless rims (Plate 73). Prevailing characteristics are a narrow, rounded, or wedge-shaped, out-turned lip; more pinched and outflaring in the oldest examples, but becoming progressively rounder in intermediate stages, which develop into a slightly flattened form in later times (see Plates 78, 85).

Another common characteristic of this Vinette 2 pottery group is what the writer has called interior channeling, produced by a scraping tool used to finish off the interior surface of these coiled or fillet-constructed pots. The groups of parallel striae, of varying breadths and depths, sometimes cross each other obliquely (Plate 78, Figure 17).

Another usual trait is a smooth exterior body finish, over which was laid a decorative pattern covering much or all of the surface in an "over-all" design (Plate 73; Plate 78, Figures 11, 12).

Decoration was chiefly accomplished by the stamping technique, although incising or trailing, apparently in some cases executed with a rude comb, occurs on certain of the sites, especially in later components of this culture. Various stamps were employed to produce simple or complex den-

tate impressions; also what the writer has termed a pseudo-scallop-shell design, since it so closely simulates, on a smaller scale, the wavy or meandering imprint of a true scallop shell, as frequently found on coastal pottery; and cord-wound stick impressions, laid on in sundry ways.

Dentate, pseudo-scallop-shell, corded and even plain stamps were utilized to create one of the commonest decorative treatments of Vinette 2 ware, viz., rocker-stamping (Plate 73; Plate 78, Figures 5, 9, 12). Simple linear designs executed in pseudo-scallop-shell or dentate imprints seem, however, to predominate among the very earliest examples of this ware, particularly in Canada, while rocker-stamping, cord impressions, and still later trailing or broad incising, appear subsequently in the decorative sequence.

Plain exterior surfaces, which carry the bulk of the embellishment, combined with channeled interiors, gradually give way to cord-malleated exteriors and smooth interior surfaces, during the later part of the developmental sequence, as it is currently imperfectly known for the Point Peninsula (page 230).

The reader is referred to Ritchie and MacNeish, 1949, for a fuller treatment of this whole subject of Point Peninsula pottery.

Burial Traits

There are few data concerning the burial practices of Early Point Peninsula cultural groups. At the probably pertinent Donaldson site (page 209) Wright exhumed twelve flexed individuals, only four of which were adults, from six graves. Burial gifts of *Marginella*-shell beads, short tubular copper beads, ground and perforated bear canines, side-notched points, end scrapers, and a little powdered red ocher occurred in small quantities and only with some of the infants and children (Wright and Anderson, 1963, pp. 4–11).

Single and multiple flexed and bundle burials of adults were present at the Kant site in three graves. A liberal sprinkling of red ocher on one skeleton of a young adult female constituted the only surviving mortuary offering (Emerson, 1955, pp. 27–37).

Evidently, it can at least provisionally be concluded that among Early Point Peninsula groups in Ontario and New York State, mortuary customs were relatively undeveloped, by comparison with the preceding Meadowood and succeeding Late Point Peninsula cultures, being characterized by simple flexed or bundle interments, with little or no grave goods and the scanty use of red ocher.

Whether the practice of cremation should be added to the list of Early Point Peninsula burial modes is still uncertain. Many cremations were found at the extensive Ault Park site, situated on a sand terrace overlooking the Long Sault Rapids of the St. Lawrence River, opposite Long Sault Island, in the southeast corner of Ontario, but the few grave furnishings pointed rather to the earlier Meadowood phase. The site was excavated by the University of Toronto, under the direction of J. Norman Emerson, as part of the St. Lawrence Seaway salvage program, and the large amount of material found there has been studied in Toronto by the writer through the courtesy of Dr. Emerson.

Early Point Peninsula pottery types predominated in the collection, St. Lawrence Pseudo Scallop Shell numerically leading the list. However, there were also present moderate quantities of Late Point Peninsula types (e.g., Wickham Punctate, Jack's Reef Dentate Collar), also Vinette 1 sherds.

The latter probably were related to the Meadowood component, represented here by Meadowood-type points and mortuary blades, some of which were found with a cremation in red ocher.

Laurentian chipped and ground stone artifacts were in the majority, and as cremation is also a recognized trait of this tradition (page 103), the Ault Park site is not very helpful with our present problem.

Two adult male skeletons, one each from the Donaldson and Kant sites, were in sufficiently sound condition to admit of varying degrees of morphological and metrical study. They are quite similar in having rugged, broad and high skulls, and faces of medium height, with wide low orbits and broad noses (Wright and Anderson, 1963, pp. 95–103; Popham, 1955, pp. 61–65). This "Walcolid" type conforms very closely with the brachycranic type of the Laurentian and Frontenac Archaic population in New York State (pages 92, 121; cf. Neumann, 1952, pp. 21–23).

THE SQUAWKIE HILL PHASE

The presence of burial mounds in western New York was noticed soon after the area was settled in the late eighteenth century and by the early 1900s the major portion of these tumuli had already been dug into by "treasure hunters" or simply for curiosity. Squier (1851) briefly described a few mound structures and correctly related them to the "Mound Builders" of Ohio. Parker (1922, pp. 83–93) recognized a "Mound-Builder occupation" of New York and listed, along with the principal regions of mound occurrence, twenty-six traits which he believed belonged to this culture (ibid., p. 86). While most of these are good Hopewellian traits, others, although allegedly from mound sites in New York, can no longer be attributed to the "Mound Builders," especially the Hopewellian people. Among these traits are stone gouges, bannerstones, birdstones, discoidal stones, concave disks, and native copper spear heads, the cultural provenience for most of which is given elsewhere in the present volume. Some of the sites enumerated by Parker for the Mound-Builder occupation have also on later knowledge been assigned to other cultures, in particular the Vine Valley site (Parker, 1922, p. 92), which is regarded as containing an important component of the Middlesex phase (page 201).

A New York Focus, Hopewellian phase, was defined by the writer (Ritchie, 1944, pp. 202–27), based chiefly upon his excavations of several mounds in the Genesee Valley (Ritchie, 1938a). Two of these mounds were part of the small group situated on Squawkie Hill, overlooking the north bank of the Genesee River, where it emerges from its deep postglacial gorge near Mount Morris, Livingston County (ibid., pp. 4–18) (Figure 4, site number 50). This site, also mentioned by Parker (1922, p. 92), was the locus in 1899 and 1900 of mound finds which included burials in stone cist graves, accompanied by such unequivocally Hopewellian artifacts as curved-base platform pipes of Ohio fireclay, a copper ear ornament, a copper ax, pearl beads, and flake knives of Flint Ridge chalcedony (Ritchie, 1938a, pp. 4–6 and Plates 5, 7; 1944, pp. 206–8 and Plates 92, 93).

Since the several Squawkie Hill discoveries provided perhaps the first concrete evidence of a definite Hopewellian linkage for the New York burial mounds, it seems appropriate in this revision of the cultural sequence and chronology of the area to call this complex the Squawkie Hill phase of the Hopewellian cultural manifestation in the Northeast. The term "Thomas Focus,"

apparently in honor of Cyrus Thomas, the early mound explorer for the Bureau of Ethnology, Smithsonian Institution, was applied to this Hopewellian-influenced manifestation by Schmitt (1952, p. 61), but the writer feels that locality nomenclature is preferable in designating cultural complexes.

The Squawkie Hill phase is still imprecisely defined. In fact, in the absence of habitation sites and with the limited cultural and skeletal data available, it is impossible or imprudent to attempt a reconstruction of either the manner of life or the physical appearance of these people. Projectile points, chiefly of large size, probably for arming javelins and hand-held spears, and bone fishhooks proclaim the already ages-old basic hunting-fishing economy in our area, which, however, has as yet supplied no trace of cultigens, although maize horticulture is now definitely established for the Hopewell culture of Illinois and Ohio.

Distribution and Age

Some of the burial and artifact traits of the Squawkie Hill phase are traceable to the southern Ohio Hopewell center, and the obvious routes of dispersal include the Ohio, Beaver and Allegheny rivers and their tributaries in Pennsylvania, and the Allegheny, Conewango, and probably the Genesee, partly by an overland movement in the vicinity of Belmont, Allegany County, in New York. By way of the Niagara and Detroit rivers similar influences penetrated into southern Ontario.

Regional centers of expression or development are found in northwestern Pennsylvania and adjacent southwestern New York, and in the Rice Lake-Trent River district of Ontario. Central New York appears to have been peripheral to the main area of distribution in southwestern New York. A small number of low mounds are recorded for the district lying between Irondequoit Bay, Monroe County, and Onondaga Lake, Onondaga County, and in this same territory occur a few non-mound burial sites which include some Hopewellian-type grave goods. Still farther east across New York State into southern New England no burial mounds or cemeteries of this kind are known, although a scarce and random distribution of trace artifacts is present.

The prevailing picture suggests a restricted, relatively short-term manifestation, falling probably within a century or two either side of A.D. 160, the only radiocarbon date thus far obtained for a Hopewellian-related mound in New York (page 217). The archaeological record indicates the probability that in New York State the Hopewellian culture fused with local resident complexes of the latter part of the Early Point Peninsula culture, Middle Woodland stage, to produce the mixed cultural composites which I am subsuming under the term Squawkie Hill phase. In brief, to varying degrees within the affected region the existing social groups were suffused with Hopewellian religious ideas, practices and material cultural elements, some of which were doubtless cult-related. Sites of the Squawkie Hill phase may thus be said to exhibit differential amounts of Hopewellian ingredients, usually as a diluted mixture. Whether or not actual migrant Hopewell people, small budded-off or shatter groups from the major centers down the Ohio Valley, were responsible for this process, as earlier inferred by the writer (Ritchie, 1938a, pp. 39–40), is still debatable.

Burial sites, chiefly mounds, in New York, Pennsylvania and Ontario, contrast considerably in character and in the kind and amount of materials they contain for which a Hopewellian nexus can be established. Because of the prevalent notion that all mounds in the northeastern area were of Hopewellian origin, some with only dubious connections with this culture have been so described. It now seems likely that certain of these components, notably the Long Sault Island mounds in the St. Lawrence River, were constructed by people under Adena influence (Ritchie and Dragoo, 1960, pp. 39–56) (page 201). Others, of amorphous nature, show few and weak Hopewellian linkages and their attribution to the Hopewell-influenced period in our area is difficult to expound, in the absence in all instances but one of radiocarbon dates. In this single exception, the Williams Mound on Conewango Creek in northwestern Pennsylvania (Guthe, 1951), the date of 845 B.C.±300 years (M-51) (Crane, 1956, p. 667) seems much too early to relate it to the Hopewell time period, particularly in the Northeast. Typical of this anomalous group is the undated Frog Mound in the Genesee Valley (Guthe, 1959), and the Serpent Mound site on Rice Lake, Ontario (Johnston, 1958, 1958a, 1959, 1960), which, however, the radiocarbon date of A.D. 128±200 years (M-850) (Crane and Griffin, 1959, p. 183) places in the later Hopewell temporal zone, when Hopewellian influences on the Northeast appear to have been strongest.

The principal excavated and described mound sites referable to the Squawkie Hill phase because of their distinctive Hopewellian mound, burial and artifact traits are as follows: in western New York, the Squawkie Hill and Geneseo mounds (Ritchie, 1938a; 1944, pp. 202–27), and the Wheatland, Killbuck and Vandalia mounds (Carpenter, 1950, p. 307; 1950a); in western Pennsylvania, the Sugar Run mounds

(Bliss, 1942), the Irvine, Cornplanter and Corydon mounds (Thomas, 1894, pp. 499–502; Carpenter, 1956), the Nelson mound (Carpenter and Schoff, 1951), and the Danner mound (Clark, Lantz and Robinson, 1960). A good summary of the Middle Woodland sites of this upper Ohio Valley area is given by Mayer-Oakes (1955, pp. 63–67, 81–87, 96–98, 153–55).

The Lewiston Mound

A recently discovered mound at Lewiston, Niagara County, New York (Nfs. 1-2) (Figure 4, site number 51), excavated by Richard L. McCarthy, of Lockport, and associates of the Ondiara Archeological Society, is referable to the Squawkie Hill phase, for which it has supplied the first radiocarbon age determination.

The location of the feature is a plateau, 337 feet above sea level, overlooking the Niagara Gorge, at the base of a ridge called the "Second Mountain" by the French garrison of Fort Niagara. Slightly oval in outline, the structure measures approximately seventy by sixty feet, with an estimated maximum central elevation of six feet. Over 50 per cent of the mound fabric consists of fragments of the native Medina sandstone, ranging from a few ounces to several hundred pounds in size, intermixed in no apparent order with clay soil, also from the immediate vicinity. Since over a very long period the mound has been tampered with by curious diggers, it is possible that an internal rock structuring of some kind has been disrupted.

In August 1962 the writer briefly participated with McCarthy and his group in the excavations. A dark compact floor level was discerned, evidently an old duff layer which had not been removed, and a number of artifacts were then recovered from this horizon. Human bones, all in very poor condition, were also seen at various places and depths in the mound.

According to the excavators, two types of burial occur, bundle and cremation. Since these exist in all quarters of the tumulus, and from the floor to within a foot or so of the surface, they seem to have been interred over quite some period of time and the mound to have grown by accretion of soil and rock placed over the progressively added human remains. If so, this mound more closely resembles the LeVesconte mound in southern Ontario (page 218) than those in the southwestern part of New York State, adjacent Pennsylvania, and the upper Genesee Valley.

A sporadic scatter of charcoal and artifacts also was present throughout the Lewiston mound. At several loci, however, charcoal concentrations were discovered, marking the positions of extensive fires which affected the surrounding soil and rocks. One such fire-spot occupied the central floor area; another was found higher up, although well within the mound structure. A corpse or bone bundle had been cremated in this fire, charcoal of which was collected and sent to the writer. Assayed at the Yale University Radiocarbon Laboratory (Y-1276), the resulting date of A.D. 160 ±80 years provides a figure cogent and compatible with the chronological succession obtained for the prehistoric cultural sequence in New York State (Figure 1), and closely equating with new carbon-14 age determinations for late Hopewell in Ohio (by correspondence and conversation with Raymond S. Baby, Ohio State Museum).

The burial associations of this cremation consisted of two large corner-notched points, one fire-scarred, of local Onondaga flint. Similar points were found with or near other burials in the mound, or scattered in the fill. One or two of these points conform with the Snyders type of established Hopewellian provenience, and the material of one such point fragment is Flint Ridge chalcedony. For the most part, however, they are narrower variants of the classic Snyders form.

The total material, mostly from the mound fill, generously lent for study, includes the following artifact categories: corner-notched points, as already described, the prevailing form; crude side-notched and stemmed points; large triangular points; crude stemmed end scrapers; drills (straight- and expanded-base forms); plano-convex adzes; rectangular gorgets; rolled-sheet-copper beads (large and small varieties); sheet-silver button cover with perforated edges; ground wolf mandible; and antler flaking tool of small diameter.

Of this group, the corner-notched points, gorgets, copper and silver articles, and ground wolf mandible are good Hopewellian traits, although everything else reported here has repeatedly been recovered from other Hopewell-related mounds of New York and Pennsylvania and apparently refers to the Hopewell-influenced complex.

Of especial interest in the Lewiston mound are the potsherds, also found randomly dispersed throughout the fill, therefore at least as old as this dated feature, and plausibly a part of the cultural assemblage of the builders. Most of the 150 odd sherds are thumbnail size or smaller, but seventy-one larger ones are susceptible of analysis, as follows: Vinette 1, two probable specimens, with interior cord imprints of unusually fine diameter; Geneseo Cord Marked, thirty, including six rims, one thickened, all slightly everted, three with narrow rounded lip, two with narrow flat-

tened lip and one with outflaring wedge-shaped lip; seventeen dentate-stamped; two rocker-dentate-stamped; nine St. Lawrence Pseudo Scallop Shell; seven incised or comb-marked; and four rim sherds of one pot with unique interior cross-hatching and possible basket-impressed exterior decoration. All interior surfaces (except for Vinette 1) are smooth or brushed, none is channeled. The probable chronological placement of this small group of sherds seems to be with the middle level of the Vinette site, in the latter part of the Early Point Peninsula sequence. No sherd of zone-decorated ware or of other characteristic Hopewellian styles was found here or in any reported New York mound.

The LeVesconte Mound

Of much interest and pertinence to the Hopewellian-influenced period in the Northeast is the LeVesconte mound, excavated in 1962 by Walter Kenyon for the Royal Ontario Museum, Toronto, and to be reported by him. The following brief account, included with the kind permission of Mr. Kenyon and the Royal Ontario Museum, is based upon a discussion and examination of the material by the writer in December 1962.

The mound, which lies on a promontory about forty feet above the Trent River, some six miles east of Campbellford, Northumberland County, Ontario, measured approximately forty by thirty by three to four feet. It evidently rested upon a prepared floor, as no sod line could be seen.

The numerous burials occurred in sub-mound pit graves and at various levels within the mound. Some of the latter occupied post-mound intrusive pits, but for the most part they seemed to represent accretion burials, each covered with a layer of clean clay. Single bones and burned bone fragments were randomly present throughout the fill.

A considerable proportion of the skeletons pertained to children, interred in a loosely flexed position, usually with grave offerings. Adults were, for the most part, represented by single or multiple bone bundles and by cremations, and mortuary goods were much less common.

Offerings generally occurred in clusters, each seemingly designed to serve a group of individuals. The well-diversified inventory is rich quantitatively and qualitatively, the following list covering only the most salient items: four copper and five silver Panpipe covers, a rectangular copper pendant, a cut square of biotite mica, an ovate conch-shell pendant, a perforated shark tooth, 194 *Marginella*-shell beads, four side-notched points of ground bone or antler, several copper and bone gorges, two barbed bone points, an antler toggle-head harpoon, four conical antler points, three antler-hafted beaver-incisor tools, and ten triangular stone objects, perhaps specialized abrading tools, which are so diagnostic of Hopewell-influenced sites in New York State (Plate 77, Figure 19).

The Cain Mound

Illustrative of the diversity presented in the burial mounds of New York State and the corresponding difficulty of attaining to a more precise cultural classification than has been attempted in this volume, is the Cain mound (Ctg. 5-2) (Figure 4, site number 52), located three and a half miles east of Gowanda, Erie County, on a gently sloping, northward-facing hillside, about a mile north of Cattaraugus Creek. Nearly circular in outline, with the usual diameter for mounds in New York State of approxi-

mately thirty feet, the downhill elevation measured around four and a half feet while the opposite perimeter merged into the hillside, whose sandy-loam soil composed the mound fabric.

In 1933 it was partially dug over by the owner and his sons, who found human bones and relics. Following a report to the Rochester Museum of Arts and Sciences in 1937, the site was visited by the writer, who observed bones of at least two adults and a child still in the possession of Mr. Cain. With the skeleton of the latter were said to have occurred some fifty partially interfused, short, cylindrical, rolled-copper beads and an oval, copper, boat-shaped object, about three inches in length, with perforated ends (like Figure 1, Plate 74). Near the adult skeletons, in two groups, about twenty-five leaf-shaped blades, between two and a half and six inches in length, are reported to have been found (Ritchie 1944, pp. 224, 227).

Permission was refused the Museum to further excavate the mound. However, in July 1954, following the owner's death, the site was visited by Messrs. A. C. Glamm, Sr. and Jr., and Jack Walsh, who obtained the consent of the family to dig the remaining portion of the feature. I am grateful to A. C. Glamm, Jr., for the following information, the loan of his notes and specimens for illustration, and for permission to publish these data, some of which have already appeared in print (Glamm, 1957).

On trenching the mound remnant, the central section was found to be virtually intact and to contain a multiple-bundle burial of at least five individuals, two adults and three children, with the following grave goods, most of them illustrated on Plates 74 and 75: seven leaf-shaped blades, a limestone elbow pipe, a second copper

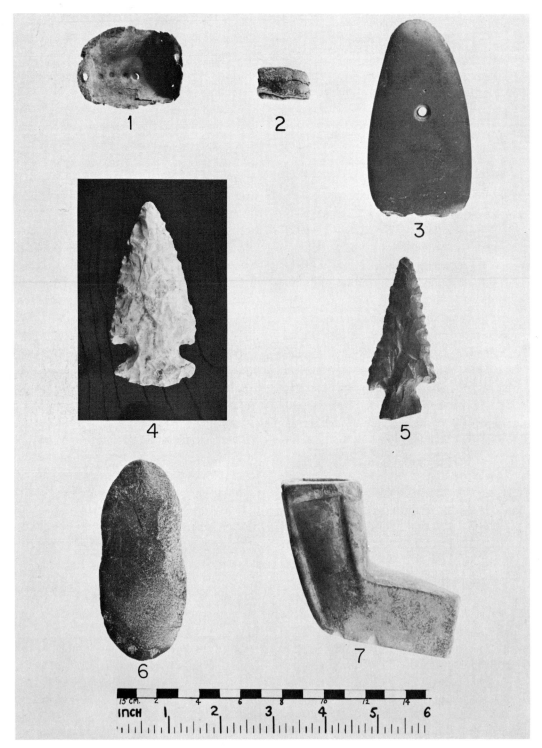

PLATE 74 Burial offerings from the Cain mound, Erie Co., N.Y. 1 dish-shaped copper artifact; 2 copper bead; 3 stone pendant; 4, 5 projectile points; 6 notched celt; 7 stone pipe. Collection of Arthur C. Glamm, Jr., Scotia, N.Y.

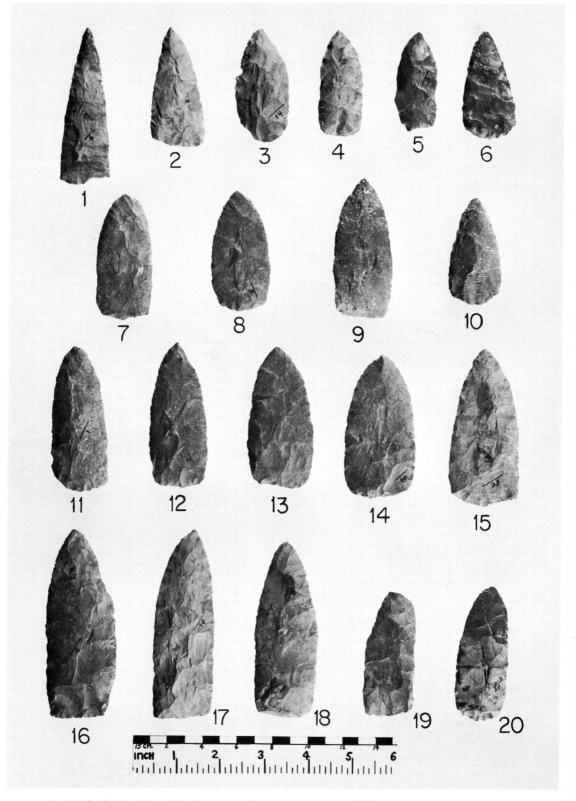

PLATE 75 Cache blades from the Cain mound, Erie Co., N.Y. Collection of Arthur C. Glamm, Jr., Scotia, N.Y.

boat-shaped object containing three quartz pebbles, two corner-notched points, a slate pendant, a notched celt, portions of a turtle carapace preserved by copper salts, and a cluster of eight quartz pebbles, probably from a decayed turtle-shell rattle. A large, rolled-sheet-copper bead was found some two feet away.

At a separate nearby locus lay a flexed adult skeleton, in very poor condition, like the other bones in the mound, with a crude celt and ten leaf-shaped blades in proximity (Plate 75).

In all cases, burial seems to have been made on the sloping ground surface of the hillside, and as no mention of a humus line is made, a prepared floor is suggested. It would seem that all the burials, primary and secondary, had been made at one time and the mound then constructed over them of the brown sandy loam of the surrounding area. Very little industrial material, chiefly flint chips, occurred in the fill; no potsherds were present. The related habitation site therefore would appear to have been situated elsewhere.

The artifacts accompanying the human remains correspond to some extent with those from other mound and non-mound burial sites in the New York area showing varying degrees of relationship to the Hopewell culture. The leaf-shaped blades (Plate 75) are, for the most part, of comparable form, but of prevailingly superior workmanship, to those recovered from Squawkie Hill mound 3 (Ritchie, 1938a, Plate 6, Figure c), the Geneseo mound (ibid., Plate 18, Figures cc, gg-ii), the Sea Breeze cemetery (Ritchie, 1944, Plate 56, Figures 1–4, 11, 12), and other sites. Similar projectile-point forms and materials are represented at Sea Breeze (Ritchie, 1944, Plate 56, Figures 26–28, 35, 36), Bluff Point (Plate 76, Figure 2), the Lewiston mound (page 217), and elsewhere. Cylindrical rolled-copper beads were present at Sea Breeze and at the Lewiston mound. A single-hole pendant, albeit of different shape, came from the Bluff Point mound (Plate 76, Figure 7), and another of oval form from the Irvine mound 2, in northwestern Pennsylvania (Carpenter, 1956, Plate 16).

The unique boat-shaped copper objects, which in one case contained pebbles, and which may have been sewed on the clothing as rattle ornaments, and the stone elbow pipe have no known parallels in a similar context in the Northeast, although a steatite pipe of this kind, with a conventionalized human figure incised on the front of the bowl, in the Rochester Museum of Arts and Sciences (catalogue number AR 1313), is stated to have been found in a mound on the Cornell University campus at Ithaca, New York. Except for their rectangular cross section, these pipes resemble the stone elbow pipes, round in cross section, from three sites of the Copena culture in northern Alabama (Webb, 1939, pp. 188–92, Plate 40, a; Webb and Wilder, 1951, p. 20, Plate 5, D).

The Cain mound cannot be identified with any well-defined cultural manifestation. It probably belongs to the late Hopewellian time period, sharing with certain other tumuli of western New York and northwestern Pennsylvania chipped-flint cache blades of a distinctive form, rolled-copper beads, and side-notched or corner-notched projectile points, mainly of Flint Ridge chalcedony or other exotic flint, having a general resemblance to the Snyders point.

The Rector Mound

The Rector mound, one and a half miles north of Savannah, on Lot 51 in the Township of Savannah, Wayne County (Figure

PLATE 76 Articles from the Bluff Point mound, Cayuga Co., N.Y. 1 cache blade; 2–5, 8 projectile points; 6 biotite mica; 7 slate pendant. Photograph courtesy of the Rochester Museum of Arts and Sciences.

4, site number 53), affords a good example of a component of the Hopewell-influenced period in central New York. A small feature, thirty to forty feet in diameter and about two feet in maximum height, this mound is situated on Crusoe Creek, where the stream leaves the marsh surrounding the shrunken vestige of Crusoe Lake. In Indian days the lake shore probably reached the hard land where the site is situated. Relics of a number of cultures occur at this attractive locus—Lamoka, Brewerton, Frost Island and Point Peninsula—in a shallow accumulation of dark "Indian dirt" covering some two acres. Stratigraphy, however, seems to be wanting, due probably to original lack of depth in the refuse and long cultivation of the land.

The fabric of the mound component consists mainly of the dark soil of the site, containing scattered relics of various earlier occupations as well as the contemporaneous culture. This soil appears to have been thrown over a group of some fifteen burials, placed in the flexed position either on the original submound surface or in shallow pits dug therein. Atop the primary fill was a clay-gravel cover, a few inches in thickness, light-colored and sterile, over which, as a final capping, more of the refuse-containing dark soil had been placed, to an indeterminate thickness, since surely some part of it has been eroded away through farming operations.

Several persons have dug into this feature during a period of many years. The writer's data come principally from the collection and records of Harold S. Secor of Savannah, with whom he has visited and tested the site in an effort to obtain additional, firsthand information. Five or six burials were found by Mr. Secor, all in very poor condition. A little grave goods accompanied about half of these flexed skeletons; most of the mortuary furniture, however, was discovered apart from the bones, in separate shallow pits or as clusters on the mound floor. In each case these groups of offerings had been sprinkled with red ocher, a treatment apparently not accorded to the corpses themselves.

An inventory of the principal artifact traits from this mound in the Secor collection, most of them illustrated on Plate 77, is as follows: side-notched projectile points, mostly rather broad and thick (Figure 12); large corner-notched points, some of exotic flint, generally conforming to the Snyders type (Figures 10, 11); large triangular points or knives, one or more of yellow jasper (Figure 13); cache blades of crude to fair workmanship, of local Onondaga flint, present in lots ranging in number from thirteen to ninety in several of the graves (Figures 20, 21); prismatic or lamellar flake knives of Flint Ridge chalcedony (Figures 14–16); partially worked quartz crystals; rectanguloid gorgets (Figure 17); rectanguloid celts (Figure 18); long, narrow, well-made adzes (Figure 22); pitted hammerstones; narrow, triangular artifacts of unknown use, probably specialized abrading stones (Figure 19); bone awls from ground splinters or whole long bones (Figures 1–3); unique artifacts of problematical function, made from the tarsal bones of some small mammal, with bifurcated end terminating in dual points (Figure 4); chisel-shaped and otherwise modified beaver incisors and unworked incisor teeth of this and other rodents (Figure 5); perforated dog canines (Figures 6, 7); and cut maxillary sections of the bear, probably representing animal headdresses (Figures 8, 9). The burial of a small dog was also found in one of the subfloor pits.

Additional artifact traits said to have been found in the Rector mound, and seen

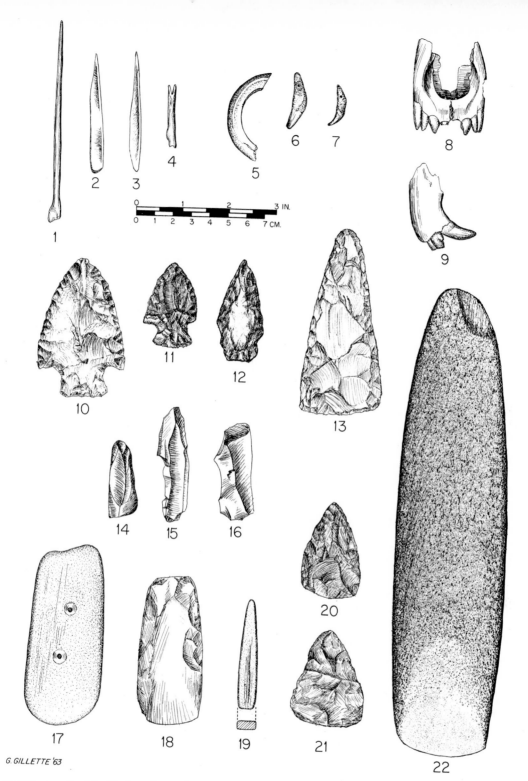

G. GILLETTE '63

PLATE 77 Burial offerings from the Rector mound, Wayne Co., N.Y. 1–3 bone awls; 4 bone object of unknown use; 5 modified beaver incisor; 6, 7 perforated dog canines; 8, 9 cut anterior jaw sections of a bear; 10–12 projectile points; 13 triangular knife; 14–16 prismatic flake knives; 17 gorget; 18 celt; 19 probably a specialized form of abrading stone; 20, 21 cache blades; 22 plano-convex adz. Collection of Harold S. Secor, Savannah, N.Y.

by the writer in other collections, comprise a large, uncut plaque of biotite mica; a rectanguloid pendant of dark-green slate; six bear canines ground flat on one face (like Figure 7, Plate 80); a group of some twenty long-bone awls from the deer metapodial, perforated near the base; several flat bone daggers (?) with incised crisscross designs, found with the awls under a scatter of red paint; eight thick, nugget-like rolled-sheet-copper beads; a bone-hafted copper awl (like Figure 6, Plate 80); a conical antler projectile point; a multiple, bilaterally weakly barbed bone point; a graphite paintstone; and a cylindrical conch-shell bead. From the fill of one of the graves came a rim sherd with the narrow, outflaring, rounded lip of the Early Point Peninsula stage in New York, decorated inside and out with dentate rocker-stamping.

Hopewellian infusions into the Rector site complex as represented by the burial mound are indicated by a group of artifact traits, some obviously actual trade goods, which are more distinctive of the Hopewellian than of any other culture within or outside of New York, viz., Snyders points, flake knives of Flint Ridge material, ground bear canines and anterior maxillary sections, antler-hafted copper awls, mica, rather roughly made flint blanks, and the specialized abrading stones (see for comparison, Shetrone, 1926, Figure 39 and pp. 114–16; cf. Ritchie, 1944, Plate 56, Figures 5–8, 15, 16).

Nuclear Mound, Burial and Artifact Traits

The nuclear traits of the Squawkie Hill phase in the Northeast are to be found in varying measure in the tumuli and cemetery sites referred to or described in this account. Probably the most important of the latter or non-mound components is the Sea Breeze site, on Irondequoit Bay, Monroe County (Roc. 20-2) (Figure 4, site number 54), several times referred to, which was excavated by the writer and described as affording "the best evidence thus far found in New York of Hopewellian influence on the Point Peninsula Focus" (Ritchie, 1944, pp. 128–32, Plates 56, 57).

Habitation sites of this manifestation seem to be indicated by surface finds of some of the characteristic artifacts from the mounds and graves, usually on multicomponent stations in western New York and the upper Ohio Valley area. The excavated Watson site in Hancock County, West Virginia (Dragoo, 1956), looks like an example of a large site of this kind.

The following is a summary listing of the mound features and burial and artifact traits of the Squawkie Hill phase, as presently known: Small earth mounds, approximately thirty feet in diameter and three to four feet in elevation. The largest reported New York mound, at Poland Center, Cattaraugus County, was around fifty feet in diameter and eight to nine feet high. The occasional use of slab rock, less so of boulders, in mound construction. There are a few examples of small primary mounds covered by a larger secondary tumulus. Preparation of the mound floor by scraping away the humus layer was common. A circumvallation of cobblestones about five feet in breadth occurs in a number of instances.

Individually prepared graves were the rule, with the central mound area holding the principal burial. In common use was a subfloor pit or stone cist grave, generally with heavy slab-rock sides and cover. Rarely the cover consists of boulders or cobblestones. A small clay basin with or for cremation is an occasional feature. Cremated burials, burned elsewhere, predominate in some mounds. Extended burials occur in some of the cists. Flexed and bundle burials are less common. Burial of a "trophy" skull or miscellaneous bones is a frequent element.

Grave goods, not abundant or highly diversified, include the following: plain, curved-base, platform pipes, usually of Ohio fireclay, and locally made copies thereof, together with small, straight-base, modifications of the platform pipe, sometimes with rude animal effigies; elongate, rectangular, two-holed slate gorgets; rectangular or pentagonal one-holed slate pendants; copper beads and crescent-shaped breast ornaments; copper- and/or silver-covered wooden breast ornaments and buttons; copper "double-cymbal"-type ear spools; copper or silver Panpipe covers; flat copper celts with expanded bits; copper awls; polished stone celts and adzes; prismatic flake knives, usually of Flint Ridge chalcedony; leaf-shaped cache blades of two basic forms, viz., moderately thin, symmetrical and well chipped, and thick, rudely chipped and asymmetric (quarry blanks?); side-notched, corner-notched and stemmed projectile points; drills; and simple, notched or stemmed end scrapers. The chipped-stone artifacts are quite often crudely and sloppily made. Many are nondescript or resemble forms common to the Laurentian and Susquehanna manifestations. Some of this material may have been made solely for mortuary purposes, some may represent older remains accidentally incorporated in the mound fill, as is surely the case with the beveled adzes found at Sugar Run, Pennsylvania. The striking exceptions to this rule comprise the handsomely chipped corner-notched or straight-stemmed projec-

tile points, usually of large size, the former mostly of the Snyders type (Bell, 1958, pp. 88–89; Ritchie, 1961, p. 49), and made from Flint Ridge chalcedony or other Ohio flint. Rough stone artifacts, commonest in the mound fill, include plain pebble and pitted hammerstones, anvilstones, multiple-pitted stones, notched pebble netsinkers, and steatite potsherds, the latter at least suggesting the fortuitous inclusion of more ancient cultural debris. However, chalcedony flake knives, gorget fragments, and other Hopewellian items also are present under these same circumstances, and there is still the problem of why the stone potsherds and Susquehanna-like points occur in several New York mounds.

Much use was made of red ocher, less of yellow ocher; graphite pigment is sometimes found; unmodified galena and quartz crystals are recorded, as are fire-making sets with iron pyrites (decomposed to limonite) and flint strikers. Mica is often present, but only rarely cut, and then chiefly into disks, with only one known exception, a radially symmetrical stellate design from the Caneadea mound.

Pottery vessels as grave goods have not been reported from mounds in New York State, and even potsherds are rare or absent on most components. In the fill of some of the mounds have been found sherds of Vinette 1 ware, but its probable derivative, Geneseo Cord Marked, seems to predominate (Ritchie and MacNeish, 1949, p. 121), followed by Point Peninsula Corded, Vinette Dentate, Point Peninsula Rocker-Stamped and St. Lawrence Pseudo Scallop Shell, in about that order of frequency. Zone-decorated sherds of classic Hopewell styles seem entirely lacking, although a few such sherds are noted for the Sugar Run mounds in Pennsylvania (Mayer-Oakes, 1955, p. 66). It is chiefly on the basis of the slender ceramic associations that the Hopewellian-influenced period in the Northeast has tentatively been correlated with the Early Point Peninsula horizon of early Middle Woodland times in this area.

As in other areas of the eastern United States, the gradual fade-out of Hopewellian religious ideology and its traditional material expressions can be traced, albeit more or less vaguely, in intergrading sequences of late Middle Woodland times. In New York, the Late Point Peninsula Kipp Island phase (page 234) had its basic roots in decadent Hopewell and its efflorescence from the post-Hopewellian Intrusive Mound culture of Ohio. In the terminal portion of the long, involved, Point Peninsula continuum, pale Hopewellian ghosts remain discernible in certain traits and articles of the Hunter's Home phase (page 253), but not beyond this stage, which leads by several recognizable developments that we shall trace later on, into the Owasco and ultimately the early Iroquois culture.

THE MIDDLE AND LATE POINT PENINSULA CULTURES

It may be said that cultural influences from outside the New York area, coming at various times and from sundry directions, produced modifications of different kinds and intensities, according to the locality affected, in the Point Peninsula continuum. Thus, a still rather obscure Middle Point Peninsula stage is postulated, with Hopewellian and later with Intrusive Mound connections. Finally, internal developments within the resulting Kipp Island phase produced the Hunter's Home phase, transitional from Late Point Peninsula to nascent Owasco.

In the early centuries of our era Hopewellian traits were diffused or carried northward via the Ohio and Allegheny rivers into western and central New York areas only lightly touched by the Adena, which had been more vigorously manifested to the east (page 201). These Late Hopewellian effulgences produced mound and non-mound burial sites in the western half of New York State, western Pennsylvania, and southern Ontario (page 215). They exerted also a marked impact on the locally developing Point Peninsula culture, as is evident by the fact that sites of this period usually contain a mixture of Point Peninsula and Hopewellian artifacts and other traits (page 226; Ritchie, 1944, pp. 123, 128–32).

Age and General Characteristics

At Kipp Island in central New York a radiocarbon date of A.D. 310±100 years (Y-1378), from charcoal in a hearth feature containing dentate rocker-stamped pottery, excavated by the writer in 1963 (page 234), seems to pertain to this earlier period of Hopewellian influence at the site (Kipp Island No. 2).

Continuing influences from the Ohio area on the post-Hopewellian time level likewise became deeply integrated into the Point Peninsula continuity, as previously pointed out by the writer (Ritchie, 1937). The Intrusive Mound culture of Ohio, in particular, shows the strongest relationship to the Kipp Island phase of New York and Ontario, which probably began around A.D. 500. A pit feature (Number 11) at Kipp Island (Kipp Island No. 3), with Point Peninsula Corded, Jack's Reef Corded and other pottery, small barbed bone points, and other implements diagnostic of the mature Kipp Island phase, also excavated by

PLATE 78 Point Peninsula pottery types. 1, 2 Vinette Dentate; 3 Vinette Complex Dentate; 4 Point Peninsula Corded; 5 Point Peninsula Rocker-Stamped (plain variety); 6 St. Lawrence Pseudo Scallop Shell; 7 Wickham Incised; 8 Point Peninsula Plain; 9, 12 Point Peninsula Rocker-Stamped (dentate variety); 10 Kipp Island Crisscross; 11 Wickham Corded; 13 Jack's Reef Dentate Collar; 14, 15 Jack's Reef Corded Collar; 16 Jack's Reef Corded; 17 channeled interior; 18, 19 Jack's Reef Corded Punctate; 20 net-impressed body sherd; 21 Carpenter Brook Cord-on-Cord (Early Owasco type).

the writer in 1963 (page 234), has been radiocarbon-dated on charcoal at A.D. 630 ±100 years (Y-1379) at Yale University Radiocarbon Laboratory.

Major artifact traits of this stage are the polished stone pendant of several forms, but not the gorget; several pipe styles, including stone tubular, straight-based platform, and slightly bent elbow forms (the latter also sometimes of clay); thick cache blades; corner-notched and triangular projectile points; large, decorated antler combs; large antler flaking tools; barbed bone points of several styles; and a variety of shell beads (Plates 79–81).

Middle and Late Point Peninsula ceramic development begins to be manifest in the upper levels of the Vinette site and in the Point Peninsula component at the Wickham site (Ritchie, 1946; Ritchie and MacNeish, 1949, p. 118). It reaches it apogee at the Jack's Reef and Kipp Island sites, both referred to below.

This pottery differs from its Early Point Peninsula prototypes in the generally larger size of vessels, perhaps indicative of increasing group sessility, and broader, more rounded to slightly flattened lips. Cord-malleated surface treatment becomes the rule, with the decoration, usually corded, applied over this cord-roughened surface in a cord-on-cord technique. There is a decrease in such decorative techniques of the earlier stage as dentate, and especially complex dentate, stamping, while pseudo-scallop-shell marking has wholly disappeared. There is a corresponding marked rise in the cord-decorated styles. Also, appliquéd-collar forms make their appearance, but these are not prototypic of Late Woodland varieties. Of the decorative motifs, platting comes sharply and enduringly to the fore, while a crisscross pattern shows a transitory popularity. After

reaching a crest in the early part of the Kipp Island phase, rocker-stamping also undergoes a sharp and rapid decline.

Many of these traits set the general trend for the development of Early Owasco ceramics of the succeeding Late Woodland period, a matter to which I shall later return in some detail on pages 254, 290.

There are other modifications and tendencies observable in the developmental Late Point Peninsula sequence which also point in the direction of the early Owasco configuration. Few suitable sites for filling in the details of the picture of the immediately post-Kipp Island continuity, are, however, known. The most illustrative examples, all from central New York, are the Hunter's Home site in Wayne County, the Kipp Island No. 4 component of the Kipp Island site in Seneca County, and the White site in Chenango County. The sum of the evidence suggests that without additional noticeable outside influence, the Point Peninsula culture of the Kipp Island phase underwent a gradual transition into what may with almost equal reason be regarded as a terminal Point Peninsula or a nascent Owasco stage, which I am calling the Hunter's Home phase (page 253). In the process of change were progressively lost most of the remaining traces of the mortuary ritualism which had been flourishing in the area since Early Woodland times. Cremation and the use of red ocher in burials all but disappeared, while grave offerings became fewer and more humble. Pots, pipes, barbed bone points of various styles, projectile points and other artifacts of stone and bone display this gradual transition. The use of stone pendants and platform pipes lingered until the early Owasco. The latter are of especial interest, for some of them appear to have been cherished as heirlooms. Reworked pieces

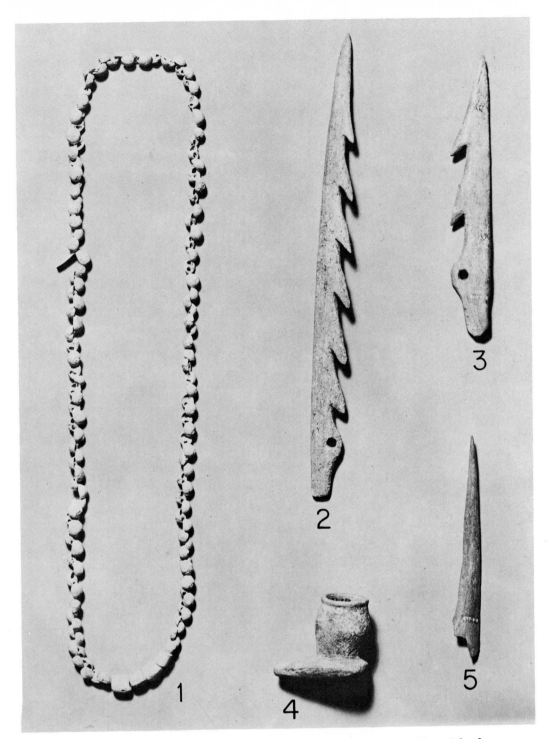

PLATE 79 Grave offerings from the Williams site, Kent Co., Ontario. Kipp Island phase. 1 necklace of *Anculosa* shells and cylindrical shell beads; 2, 3 barbed antler harpoon points; 4 straight-base platform pipe; 5 bone awl. Length of Figure 2 is 9$\frac{5}{16}$ inches. Photograph courtesy of the Royal Ontario Museum, University of Toronto.

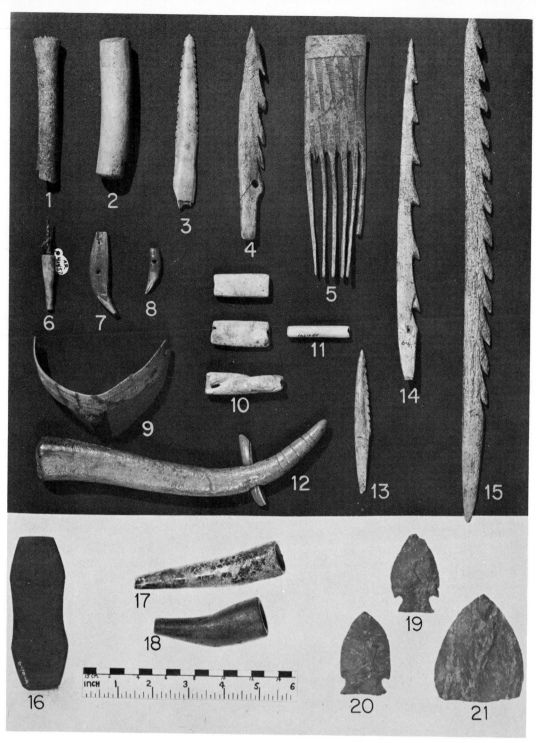

PLATE 80 Artifacts of the Kipp Island phase. 1 serrated bone tubular object of unknown use; 2 antler flaker; 3, 4, 13–15 varieties of barbed bone and antler points; 5 ornamented antler comb; 6 copper awl in antler handle; 7 ground and perforated bear canine; 8 perforated lynx canine; 9 ornamented antler armband; 10 flat, rectangular, shell beads; 11 cylindrical shell bead; 12 antler-hafted beaver-incisor wood-carving tool; 16 slate pendant; 17 stone pipe; 18 plain pottery pipe; 19, 20 projectile points of Jack's Reef Corner-Notched type; 21 triangular knife. Provenience: All from Kipp Island No. 3 site except 5 from Durkee site; 2, 7, 8, 12, 17, 18 from Menard Bridge No. 1 site.

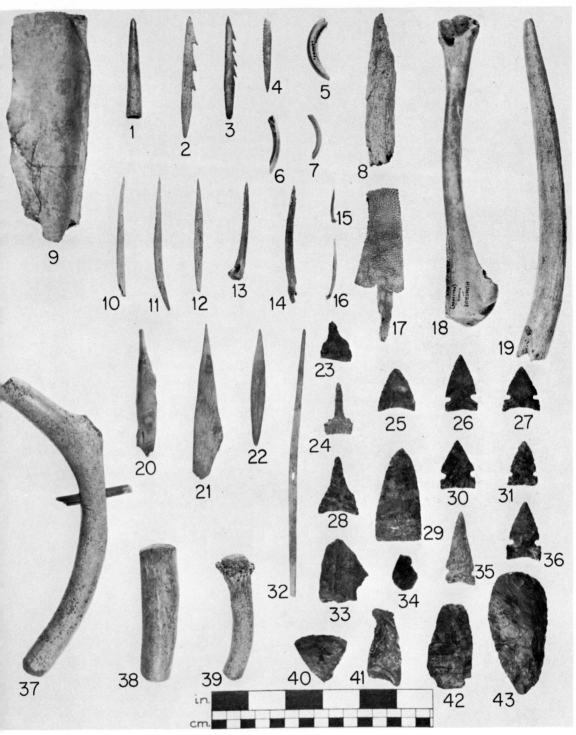

PLATE 81 Grave lot from child's burial, Port Maitland, Welland Co., Ontario. Kipp Island phase. 1 conical antler arrow point; 2–4 barbed antler points; 5, 6, 7 modified incisors of beaver, porcupine and woodchuck, respectively; 8, 19 antler "raw material"; 9 deer-scapula scraper; 10–12 possible bone leister points; 13–16 unworked fish spines; 17 unworked turtle-plastron fragment; 18 humerus of sandhill crane showing polish from unknown use; 20–22 bone awls; 23, 24, 28 flint drills; 25 triangular arrow point; 26, 27, 30, 31, 35, 36 thin, side-notched arrow points resembling "Raccoon Notched" type; 29 triangular knife; 32 bone mat-weaving needle; 33, 34 unworked flint flakes; 37 antler-hafted beaver-incisor wood-carving tool; 38, 39 antler flaking tools; 40 retouched flake knife; 41 retouched flake side scraper; 42 retouched flake end scraper; 43 triangular end scraper, bifacially chipped. Photograph courtesy of the Rochester Museum of Arts and Sciences.

233

and patched specimens, mainly fragments bearing drill holes for lacing the parts together, have been found in refuse and burials on sites of the Hunter's Home phase, one of the latter radiocarbon-dated to c. A.D. 905 (Plate 87, Figure 19, and page 255).

THE KIPP ISLAND PHASE

Distribution

This phase embraces essentially the Point Peninsula manifestation I have earlier termed the Point Peninsula 3 Focus of the Middle Woodland II period (Ritchie, 1951). It has been named from the largest known site of this culture, situated on Kipp Island (Aub. 13-1) in the Seneca River, surrounded by the great Montezuma Marsh, in Seneca County, New York (Figure 4, site number 55). Several futile attempts to obtain permission for excavations by the Rochester Museum of Arts and Sciences on this key site, which gravediggers had molested off and on over a period of many years, were made by the writer in the early 1930s. When the land changed hands suddenly several years later, local collectors immediately seized the opportunity to virtually demolish the remainder of the site. The writer's account of the grave finds made here at that time is all that will ever be known about this unhappy episode of the site's history (Ritchie, 1944, pp. 132–43, 354–64). Still later, the New York State Thruway appropriated for fill the entire northern two thirds of the island, which had contained the burial plots.

Phenomenally, in the fall of 1962, the writer, searching the island remnant for settlement-pattern potentials, suspected because a thin, much dug-over refuse mantle was known to have existed there, discovered a new group of burials near the south end of the inland. This cemetery, Kipp Island No. 4 (Aub. 12-1), excavated by a New York State Museum party in charge of the writer in July 1963, has provided most of what is known of the burial customs of the Hunter's Home phase. Work done by the same group on the adjacent habitation area of the island and on refuse middens in the bordering marsh produced settlement-pattern and other data pertaining to both the Kipp Island and the Hunter's Home phases, which will be described in subsequent pages.

Kipp Island, with its surface mantle of refuse; extensive middens over the low, marshy ground extending westward from the southern third of the island to near the former bed of the Clyde River, the Indians' main approach to the island; several cemeteries; and one low mound, was obviously, over a considerable period, a favorite place of residence or sojourn for a number of prehistoric peoples. Except for minor Archaic and Late Woodland traces, however, it was the long-occupied major center or base camp of Middle and Late Point Peninsula groups who inhabited the central New York region. The same or closely related groups also frequented Bluff Point, a similar glacial drumlin island in the Montezuma Marsh, in the Seneca River, only five miles to the north of Kipp Island, in Cayuga County, where they left side-hill and marsh refuse middens and burial clusters on the high ground, all greatly ransacked by the ubiquitous collectors.

At Jack's Reef, a favorite fishing place on the Seneca River into historic days, further extensive remains of the Kipp Island people came to light, and one sizable midden, found and excavated by the writer, is described below.

Apart from these principal components, and several small camp sites also along the Seneca River or the margins of the big Montezuma Marsh, the known surviving evidences of the Kipp Island phase consist of widely distributed burials in central, northern and western New York, and in southern Ontario, from the Bay of Quinté west to the vicinity of the Detroit River (Figure 4, sites number 55–64). The relationships of the culture lie still farther west, in Michigan, northern Indiana and Ohio (Mills, 1922, pp. 563–84; Hinsdale, 1930, pp. 127–35; Ritchie, 1937, pp. 188–93; 1944, p. 118; Faulkner, 1960, pp. 123–36).

The east-west connections apparently involve the north shore of Lake Erie and both the north and south shores of Lake Ontario, close to, or within some twenty-three miles of, these great water bodies, suggesting dissemination by water travel. Although the Kipp Island phase is not recognizable as a complex east of central New York, a number of its diagnostic traits have a far wider range, occurring sporadically even into Maine. These traits, which include the straight-based platform pipe, several styles of the stone pendant, Jack's Reef Corner-Notched and Jack's Reef Pentagonal-type projectile points, have evidently been assimilated to local cultural assemblages of late Middle Woodland age, as is further attested by their association, in some cases with pottery identifiable with Kipp Island forms.

The discovery, however, of an apparently cremated burial on Minisink Island in the upper Delaware Valley in northern New Jersey, accompanied by the calcined remains of a large, decorated comb of classic Kipp Island style, two perforated shark teeth, and a fragmentary straight-based

platform pipe, all index markers for this phase, emphasizes the tentative nature of this statement (Ritchie, 1949a, p. 160; Carpenter, 1950, p. 313).

As eight of the eleven sites shown on the map, Figure 4, have previously been described and their materials illustrated in whole or part, and inventoried in trait tables (Ritchie, 1944, pp. 124–25, 132–46, 148–50, 166–75, 178–81, 354–64), and as no significant further descriptive data can be added, the following brief account will concentrate upon the newer discoveries of Kipp Island cultural provenience.

Four of the total of eleven components listed for this culture on the map, Figure 4 (Brock Street, Jack's Reef, Durkee, Plum Orchard), consisted, insofar as known, of but a single burial; in one other instance (Bay of Quinté) the single grave held a multiple burial; two others (Williams, Port Maitland) comprised two separate graves; while three components (Point Peninsula, Kipp Island, Menard Bridge No. 1) can properly be referred to as cemeteries. Only three were directly related to a habitation site (Williams, Kipp Island, Jack's Reef), suggesting that in a fairly large number of cases the burial was made at some distance from the principal settlement site. Most of the skeletons are identifiable as adult males, probably individuals of some prominence in the group, as judged by their careful, well-accoutered burials.

Save for one cremation (Jack's Reef), with both curved-base and straight-base platform pipes, probably referable to the earlier part of this phase, most heavily influenced by the Hopewellian culture, all the burials were inhumations in the flesh, in a flexed posture, or actually sitting or semi-erect in one definite (Durkee) and two probable instances (Port Maitland, Bay of Quinté). As indicated by the published accounts and by those that follow, the lavish use of red ocher was customary, and mortuary furnishings of weapons, tools, ornaments and pipes, but *not* pottery, were the rule.

The Williams Site
(Beyond the map limits of Figure 4)

Located on the farm of H. D. Williams, Concession 1, Lot 11, Township of Howard, Kent County, Ontario, this accidentally discovered component was investigated in August 1949 by Neil Coppieters and Stanley Wortner, both of nearby Chatham. I am indebted to Mr. Coppieters for permission to publish this brief account, based upon the data he kindly sent me, and to the Royal Ontario Museum at Toronto, and its Curator of Ethnology, Kenneth E. Kidd, for the illustration.

Apparently the sand-pit workers uncovered two skeletons, referable to an adult and a child which had been interred in a sand knoll overlooking the Thames River Valley, near Thamesville, some eighteen miles north of the Lake Erie shore. Presumably these burials were related to a small camp site, the burned stone, chipping debris, deer bones and other vestiges of which occurred in the surrounding sand.

All of the artifacts, some of which are illustrated on Plate 79, were present with the adult skeleton, probably a male, which had been heavily sprinkled with red ocher. Other grave goods not shown comprised the following: a double-pointed copper awl, square in cross section; a second string of *Anculosa*-shell beads (the total number of such beads found is estimated by Mr. Coppieters at approximately seven hundred); a small flint drill; three corner-notched projectile points; three crude flint cache blades; two or more flint strike-

a-lights and two iron-pyrites nodules; two large, flint, trianguloid knives; an end scraper; a double-bitted plano-convex adz; and an abrading stone. The small whole shell beads were identified at the Smithsonian Institution as *Anculosa subglobosa* (Say). They are pierced for suspension by grinding obliquely from the end opposite the spire. They have their exact counterpart in the Intrusive Mound culture in Ohio.

The Williams component has close parallels with the Kipp Island site, especially in barbed-antler-point and projectile-point types (compare Plate 79, Figures 2, 3, with Plate 80, Figures 4, 14, 15). Rude cache blades and plano-convex adzes are also found on both sites. So are the bead forms, except for the different genera of the small shells. Only the platform pipe is missing at Kipp Island, but this trait is present at four other components of this phase (Port Maitland, Point Peninsula, Jack's Reef, Felix).

The Brock Street Burial
(Figure 4, site number 63)

In December 1960 a workman digging a parking-meter hole in the city of Peterborough, Peterborough County, Ontario, struck this burial, which was promptly investigated by Walter Kenyon of the Royal Ontario Museum. It was found to consist of a single adult male skeleton, tightly flexed on the back, head to the north, at a depth of between two and three feet below the present surface. The usual red ocher was absent, but as in so many other instances, the numerous offerings formed a "pillow" under the head, or lay at the shoulder and hip.

These mortuary furnishings, described and illustrated in the site report by Kenyon and Cameron (1961, pp. 41–55, Plates I–

III), comprise in the main the familiar objects of this culture, viz., eight crude flint cache blades, two polished slate pendants, two small antler flaking tools, two unmodified beaver incisors, seven thin side-notched points, a polished greenstone celt, and four barbed antler points. Two of the latter have multiple, unilateral barbs, and long tapering bases, like, but in one example much larger than, two from the child's grave at Port Maitland (Plate 81, Figures 2, 3).

The unusual articles from this grave include one complete (nearly nine inches long) and one basal fragment of antler harpoons, having bold angular barbs along one edge, and a recurved barb, rather than a line-hole at the base. The antler-hafted beaver-incisor tool, present in nearly every component of this culture, occurred here as a unique variant in possessing a handle-extremity cut to resemble a comb with six rudimentary teeth, a modification of obscure function. Finally, this grave produced two unique disks, believed to be of human skull bone, measuring about one and a half inches in diameter, imperforate and with bilaterally beveled edges.

The Plum Orchard Burial
(Roc. 26-2) (Figure 4, site number 60)

As in nearly all discoveries pertaining to the Kipp Island phase, this find was accidental, resulting from sand-removal at the western summit of a steep hill, 125 feet above Irondequoit Bay, near Float Bridge, Township of Penfield, Monroe County, New York.

Charles F. Hayes III, of the Rochester Museum of Arts and Sciences, and associates, who investigated, report this as the probably isolated burial of a male, about forty-five years of age (Hayes, 1963, and personal communications).

The mode of interment and arrangement of the customary large assortment of offerings were indeterminate, since everything was recovered by sifting the sand talus into which the burial had fallen. Red ocher covered the skeleton and artifacts, many of which have a near identity in the Kipp Island burial goods illustrated on Plate 80. There are three large barbed antler points, like Figure 15 of that plate; a hafted beaver-incisor carving tool, like Figure 12; three large antler chipping tools, similar to Figure 2; three flat rectangular shell beads, like Figure 10; a small discoidal shell bead; two side-notched, fossil shark's-tooth arrowheads; two rude flint cache blades; two incomplete celts and an adz of polished stone; and a number of unworked or partially shaped pieces of bone and antler.

The Felix Site
(Bwv. 1-3) (Figure 4, site number 57)

This important component, one of the few known habitation sites of the Kipp Island culture, is situated on a low, level strip of brush-covered land, bordering the south side of the Seneca River at the hamlet of Jack's Reef, on the John W. Felix farm, Lot 35, Township of Elbridge, Onondaga County, New York. It consists of a riverbank midden approximately fifty feet long and more than sixteen feet in breadth, the full width being undetermined in our excavations because the northern portion of the midden, which occupies the steep riverbank, is deeply covered with a tough clay-and-stone overburden, the spoil heap from the construction here in 1857 of a navigation channel through the shallow river bed.

Prior to this construction, a considerable

stretch of the river below the site consisted of a series of rocky rifts or shallow rapids, locally called "reefs," which, with intervening pools, afforded such ideal waters for spearing, netting and hook-and-line fishing as to have attracted Indian groups of all periods from the Archaic to the Late Woodland. Later references will be made to some of these sites. Extensive midden deposits here, pertaining to the Late Point Peninsula and Early Owasco cultures, were dug over during the 1930s by local collectors, one of whom found, in a subsoil grave beneath a midden, an important cremation burial which evidently belonged to the early part of the Kipp Island phase (Figure 4, site number 56) (Ritchie, 1944, pp. 83–86, 148–50).

Excavations were made by the writer in the riverbank midden, in 1947, under the auspices of the Rochester Museum of Arts and Sciences, and in 1951 for the New York State Museum and Science Service, exploring *in toto* more than thirty-five feet of its length to a maximum width of sixteen feet, beyond which the drop-off was so steep as to require the removal of four to five feet of indurated fill overburden, a task beyond our manpower resources. The work, carefully done by troweling five-foot sections, disclosed a consistent stratigraphy, with, however, a considerable variation in the thickness of individual strata. This stratigraphy comprised:

1) The topsoil, a brown loam, overlaid by the hard mixture of stones (ranging in size from gravel to small boulders) and clay dug from the river channel and piled along the bank, as already mentioned. The topsoil complex varied in thickness from six inches along the southern edge of the midden to nearly five feet at the northern terminus of the excavations.

2) A dark brown to black loamy stratum, containing some gravel and larger stones, occasional shell refuse, and a very few artifacts from near the base, and deepening progressively northward from about four to fifteen inches. This level apparently represented an old topsoil of forest humus (A soil).

3) A compact layer of fresh-water mussel shell and black dirt, the shell being for the most part fragmentary, but not trampled into small pieces, with whole valves not infrequent. The granular black dirt occurred intermixed with the shell, as well as in streaks, lenses and small layers within the more or less solid shell accumulation. Only two to six inches in thickness, this stratum, represented solely by the black dirt in some portions of the deposit, constituted a true midden horizon, built up by periodic additions of shell and other refuse, and accumulating forest mold. Artifacts were numerous in this layer.

4) Also a true midden deposit built up along the riverbank at the camp edge, in a forested environment, this basal layer consisted of a very dark brown sandy soil with some fine gravel, turning black near the bottom. Considerable fine gray ash was present in thin spreads under, within, and in some places overlying the dark stratum, which varied in thickness from about two to twenty inches, deepening toward the north, where, however, it was less productive, being farthest away from the actual living area of the site.

The industrial remains in this stratum constituted a high percentage (about 66 per cent) of the total artifacts found on the site, plus chipping debitage; also numerous shell fragments and the bones of fish, mammals and birds, in descending order of frequency.

5) Below the productive dark basement layer came the sterile brown sand and gravel subsoil.

The midden as a whole, comprising strata 3 and 4, pertained to the Late Point Peninsula complex. Omitting from consideration the group of sherds derived from at least three pots of Owasco Corded Collar type, obviously intrusive in one section in the base of stratum 2 and top of stratum 3, the ceramic content from strata 3 and 4 show both qualitative and quantitative differences of some interest. The following analysis is based upon a sample of four hundred rim sherds obtained in the 1951 excavations only, for which we have more detailed data. This material occurred in the proportions of three sherds in stratum 4 to one in stratum 3. The typological differences indicate a general trend in the direction of Early Owasco ceramic types, when this new Jack's Reef sample is seriated with the Owasco sequence published in 1949 (Ritchie and MacNeish, p. 118). Thus, progressing upward in time from stratum 4 to stratum 3, the incidence of Vinette Dentate declines from 19.3 per cent to 5.9 per cent, of Point Peninsula Rocker-Stamped from 43 per cent to 9.8 per cent, and of Jack's Reef Corded from 9.3 per cent to 2 per cent. Point Peninsula Corded, on the other hand, continues about constant at 20 per cent to 20.6 per cent, suggesting that it was through this form, rather than through the unembellished Jack's Reef Corded type, that the later Owasco corded types developed. This probability is further strengthened by the fact that the Point Peninsula Corded type foreshadows in rim and lip form, and in decorative technique and motifs, the full Owasco series of cord-ornamented, horizontal, oblique, herringbone and platted types. At the Felix site, however, the transitional Hunter's Home phase (page 253) was apparently not yet developed.

This same 1951 Jack's Reef ceramic spectrum, when compared with the upper levels of the Vinette site (Ritchie and Mac-Neish, 1949, p. 118), further emphasizes this trend. Thus there are marked increases in the Point Peninsula Corded and Jack's Reef Corded categories, and decreases in the following types which, with one exception (Point Peninsula Plain), lack all continuity with the Owasco: Vinette Dentate, Vinette Complex Dentate, Point Peninsula Rocker-Stamped and Point Peninsula Plain. (See Plates 78, 85 for ceramic type illustrations.)

The appliquéd-collar forms (Jack's Reef Dentate Collar, Jack's Reef Corded Collar), however, increase slightly from this late Vinette level into stratum 4 of the Felix site, where they terminate, insofar as the sequence at this site is concerned. (Parenthetically, the appliquéd-collar forms of the Late Point Peninsula are *not* the foretypes of the much later Owasco collared varieties, in which the morphologically different collar was formed by molding not by appliqué.) The presence of these collared styles in the lower level of the Felix site, although in minor amounts (less than 2 per cent of each), together with Kipp Island Crisscross (only 2.5 per cent), helps to place this component definitely within the Kipp Island phase. (These types are portrayed on Plate 78.)

Fuller support for this attribution comes from the typologies of the chipped-stone, polished-stone, bone and antler inventories of the Felix site, which will be described in some detail in the succeeding account of the Kipp Island phase, according to the general outline followed in this work (Plate 82).

The People of the Kipp Island Phase

Concerning the physical characteristics of the people responsible for the Kipp Island phase of culture, current data are far

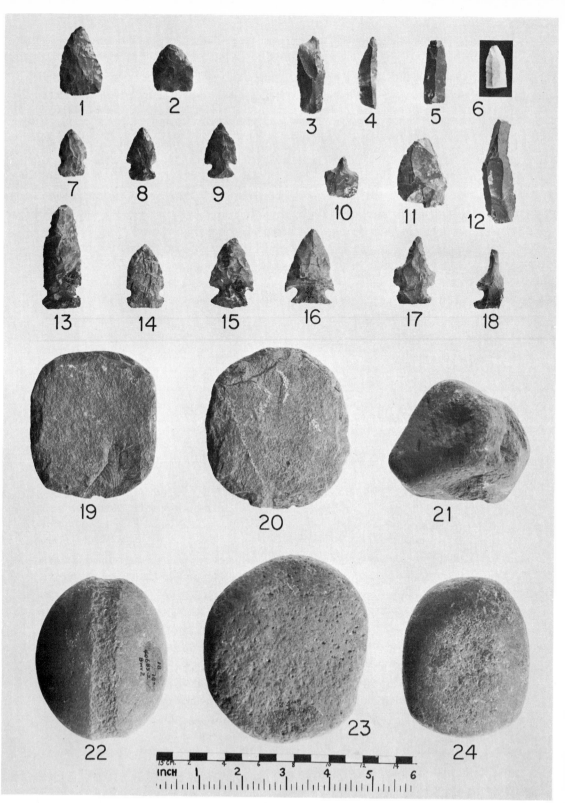

PLATE 82 Implements from a midden on the Felix site, Onondaga Co., N.Y. Kipp Island phase. 1, 2 arrow points of Jack's Reef Pentagonal type; 3–6, 12 prismatic flake knives, some showing fine marginal chipping from use; 7, 8, 13, 14 untyped arrow points of thin, side-notched form; 9, 15, 16 arrow points of Jack's Reef Corner-Notched type; 10, 17, 18 drills with expanded, and expanded side-notched and corner-notched bases, respectively; 11 knife from retouched flake; 19, 20 disciform objects with chipped periphery, use unknown; 21 multiple-pitted stone; 22 grooved pebble sinker; 23, 24 unpitted hammerstones.

too limited to be of more than suggestive value. The little available evidence hints at a heterogeneous population involving essentially two physical types, one already long familiar to the area, the second perhaps of recent introduction.

Our best data come from only four male skeletons, in fair to good condition, representing individuals between about forty and fifty years of age. Three of these skeletons pertain to, apparently, a new long-headed variety of Indian in the New York area, not to be confused with the dolichocranial Lamoka people (page 46). These remains, derived from the Kipp Island, Durkee, and Brock Street (Kenyon and Cameron, 1961, pp. 44–46) sites, depict persons of approximately five feet eight inches in stature; relatively light body build; long, oval heads of medium height; relatively long and narrow faces with medium to high orbits, and medium-broad noses. The skulls lack the marked rugosity of muscular attachments and the heaviness which are associated features of the second type.

It seems likely that a more generous sample of this group would establish its relationship to the "Lenapid" variety (Neumann, 1952, pp. 23–25). Its introduction into the eastern Ontario and New York area may have been correlative with the Hopewellian culture, and been followed by the interaction both of this culture and the genetic combination of its carriers on the regional Late Point Peninsula manifestation. The indisputable occurrence in New York State of the "Lenapid" variety, in association with the Late Woodland Owasco and Iroquois cultural assemblages, would suggest that the physical type continued here, *pari passu* with cultural developments from the Late Point Peninsula.

The second physical variety is represented by the skeleton from the Plum Orchard site (Cornwell, n.d.). This ruggedly built, middle-aged man, about five feet seven inches tall, had the heavy, broad and high skull of the "Walcolid" variety already described as a type long resident in the New York area since Late Archaic times (pages 46, 92).

Both the Brock Street and Plum Orchard skeletons show evidence of mild osteoarthritis, chiefly as marginal lipping of the vertebral bodies. All exhibit slight dental pathology involving loss of one to a few teeth in life, due to periodontal disease and apical abscesses, evidently contingent upon attrition of the crown; but caries is uniformly absent. These facts link the subjects more closely to the Archaic hunters than to the known agriculturists of Late Woodland times.

The Subsistence Basis of the Kipp Island Culture

On a theoretical basis the subsistence economy of the Late Point Peninsula people included some use of horticultural products, since there is now reliable archaeological evidence for corn production in Hopewellian (Griffin, 1960; Prufer, 1964), one of the interacting cultures with the middle phase of the Point Peninsula. However, no plant remains were reported for the earlier digging on Kipp Island, a not surprising fact considering the agents and methods employed. A small quantity of carbonized vegetable material resulting from our 1963 excavations on this site, among which seeds of *Chenopodium* (goosefoot) have tentatively been identified, has been submitted for expert paleobotanical analysis. Close watch at the Felix midden for carbonized plant remains yielded negative results, but this was doubtless only a sporadically inhabited fishing-camp site.

Of hunting and fishing pursuits there is ample testimony, both in weapons and other equipment, and in food-animal refuse. The latter, as found at the Felix site, includes a large volume of mussel shells taken from the adjacent river, and small amounts of fish, turtle, bird and mammal bone. Following is an analysis of the non-molluscan material, which indicates that, although the Indians were probably in summer residence along the river rifts, feeding heavily on mussels, fish and turtles, their aquatic diet was relieved by venison, beaver and other "red meat." The presence throughout the midden of projectile points argues in the same direction.

The list comprises deer (57 per cent), fish, all species (18 per cent), beaver (9 per cent), bear (7.6 per cent), turtles, all species (4 per cent), and woodchuck, muskrat, mink, bobcat, and various unspecified birds (less than 2 per cent each). The fishbones have been identified by John E. Guilday, Associate Curator of Comparative Anatomy at the Carnegie Museum, as channel catfish (*Ictalurus* sp.), bullhead (*Ictalurus* sp.), and pike-perch (*Stizostedion vitreum*); the turtles by Dr. Edgar J. Reilly, Associate Curator of Zoology, New York State Museum, as the snapping turtle (*Chelydra serpentina*), painted turtle (*Chrysemys picta*), and wood turtle (*Clemmys insculpta*).

In the Kipp Island site excavations of 1963 animal bone was carefully collected from the pits and hearths of the habitation area and from middens in the adjacent marsh. The artifact associations of this refuse material demonstrated that the features and dumps had accumulated over some period of time, during which the Kipp Island phase was developing and changing into the Hunter's Home phase.

Charcoal samples from features in the village area containing the typical pottery of each phase are in process of carbon-14 analysis. Two samples have thus far been dated, one (Y-1378) at A.D. 310±100 years apparently denotes the Hopewellian-influenced beginnings of the Kipp Island phase, (Kipp Island No. 2) the other (Y-1379), at A.D. 630±100 years, is clearly related to its later, fully mature, post-Hopewellian aspect (Kipp Island No. 3) (page 234). The food debris, therefore, pertains to the Middle and Late Point Peninsula stages at this site, rather than to any particular phase. It was submitted for expert study to John E. Guilday of the Carnegie Museum, Pittsburgh, whose report follows.

Vertebrate Remains from the Kipp Island Site

by John E. Guilday and Donald P. Tanner
Carnegie Museum

The Kipp Island people made extensive use of the aquatic resources about them. In terms of actual pounds of usable meat, deer was the primary source, but in terms of numbers of individual animals, fish, and most especially small bullheads, were by far the most abundant. Of the 30 species of wild animals represented, 15 were aquatic. These 15 accounted for 85 per cent of the total individual animals. Minimum number of individuals were: 56 mammals, 3 birds, 9 turtles, 6 amphibians and 425 fish.

Deer bones, especially those marked as being from the "marsh," were too poorly preserved to provide any observations as to skinning and butchering techniques.

Deer, elk, and bear bones were much commoner in the "marsh" area. If this was once swamp, it might reflect upon the relative effects of dog scavenging at the site.

One upper molar and the humerus of a young domestic sheep were recovered from the topsoil.

All the bullheads were of uniform size, possibly adult *Ictalurus nebulosus,* weighing about 1.5 pounds apiece. Four channel catfish, probably *I. punctatus,* were an estimated 10 pounds live weight, a fifth possibly 25 pounds. Fish, therefore, accounted for an estimated 694 pounds of meat, as against 2200 pounds for deer. This is extremely high and indicated extensive utilization of fish and other marsh resources.

Note the complete lack of box turtle (*Terrapene carolina*) remains. This may become significant when more archaeofaunas from varying time horizons in New York State are examined.

FAUNAL LIST

		Items	Indiv.	Est. lbs. meat
Odocoileus virginianus	whited-tailed deer	741	22	2200
Cervus canadensis	elk	9	1	400
Ursus americanus	bear	37	3	600
Canis familiaris	dog	3	2	
	fox species	1	1	
Procyon lotor	raccoon	6	2	10
Lynx sp.	bobcat or lynx	1	1	15
Lutra canadensis	otter	2	1	10
Martes pennanti	fisher	3	2	10
Mephitis mephitis	striped skunk	1	1	2
Marmota monax	woodchuck	4	1	2
Tamias striatus	chipmunk	5	1	
Sciurus sp.	gray or fox squirrel	5	1	1
Tamiasciurus hudsonicus	red squirrel	1	1	
Ondatra zibethicus	muskrat	121	11	1
Castor canadensis	beaver	22	3	30
Sylvilagus sp.	rabbit	1	1	
Ovis aries	sheep	2	1	
	mammal, unidentified	1239		
Meleagris gallopavo	turkey	7	1	5
Branta canadensis	Canada goose	1	1	5
Mergus sp.	merganser duck	3	1	
	bird, unidentified	8		
Chelydra serpentina	snapping turtle	49	3	30
Sternotherus odoratus	musk turtle	12	5	
Chrysemys picta	painted turtle	4	1	
	turtle, unidentified	75		
Rana catesbiana	bullfrog	8	4	
Rana cf. *clamitans*	green (?) frog	2	2	
	frog/toad, unidentified	19		
Ictalurus sp.	bullhead	1100	411	600
Ictalurus sp.	channel cat		4	55
Stizostedion cf. *vitreum*	walleyed pike	10	3	15
Esox lucius	northern pike	6	4	20
Micropterus sp.	bass	4	2	4
Catostomus sp.	sucker	1	1	
	fish, unidentified	1100		

Hunting and Fishing Gear

Weapon typologies of the Kipp Island phase are limited to projectile points of chipped stone, bone and antler, all seemingly suitable by their size and lightness for use as arrow points. This is particularly true of the broad, thin triangular point which makes its initial appearance in central New York in this level of culture, and continues, beyond doubt as an arrowhead, with slight modifications in size and shape, through the cultures of the Late Woodland period.

The triangular point of Levanna type (Ritchie, 1961, pp. 31–32) (Plate 81, Figure 25), is, however, relatively rare. The index points of the Kipp Island phase are rather the broad, thin, Jack's Reef Corner-Notched variety (ibid., pp. 26–27) (Plate 82, Figures 9, 15, 16), the Jack's Reef Pentagonal (ibid., p. 28) (Plate 82, Figures 1, 2), and a generally thin, well-made, side-notched form, apparently a holdover from Early Point Peninsula times (page 212) (Plate 82, Figures 7, 8, 13, 14). Some of these points show morphological resemblances to the "Raccoon Notched" point, ascribed to the Middle Woodland period in the Beaver and Ohio valleys of western Pennsylvania and adjacent Ohio (Mayer-Oakes, 1955, pp. 84–87) (Plate 81, Figures 26, 27, 30, 31, 35, 36).

On a few sites of the Kipp Island phase, conical antler-tip missiles, and points made from fossil sharks' teeth, have been found (Plate 81, Figure 1). It is clear that both varieties, which were also probably for tipping arrows, were intrinsic constituents of this culture.

Certain of the numerous, small, barbed bone and antler points may also have served as armament for arrows, for taking large fish and perhaps other animals (Plate 81, Figures 2–4). It is also not improbable that the longer, heavier barbed antler points, seemingly overmassive for fish-spearing in local waters, served at least an alternate function in spearing beaver in their winter houses (Plate 80, Figures 14, 15). This practice is attested for several northern Algonkian tribes, including the Penobscot of Maine (Speck, 1940, pp. 36–44), who also netted beaver under the ice and killed them by clubbing.

Other hunting and/or war weapons comprise the large, hilted, bone dagger, with engraved blade, believed to have been made from the femur of a moose (Ritchie, 1944, Plate 76, Figure 20; Plate 77, Figure 14), and club spikes (?) of antler from the same sites.

The ownership of dogs by the Kipp Island people, and their apparent regard for this animal, is indicated by our recent discovery of a careful burial of an immature individual in a partially refuse-filled pit on the Kipp Island site (Plate 83). Perforated canine teeth from one of the Kipp Island burials constituted the only previous evidence for the dog in this culture.

The important role of fishing in the diversified economy of these people is demonstrated by the prevalence of fishbones and the abundance and assortment of fishing tackle, both in the burial and living places, attesting to the use of nets and spear, gorge and hook-and-line angling. Fish traps and weirs, probably known and employed, have left no trace, and of nets we have only the indirect evidence furnished by the common side- or end-notched, flat pebble sinker, the longitudinally grooved pebble sinker (Plate 82, Figure 22), and net impressions on pot bodies (Plate 78, Figure 20). At the Felix site also occurred flat sandstone disks with chipped

PLATE 83   Dog burial on the Kipp Island No. 3 site, Seneca Co., N.Y.

periphery, sometimes side-notched, believed to be a special kind of netsinker, which is better known from the succeeding Owasco culture (Plate 82, figures 19, 20), where, however, it has been regarded by some as a hoe (page 279).

Fish spears of several styles seem to be represented in the surviving material, which includes a variety of barbed bone and antler points, embracing unilaterally and bilaterally barbed forms, the former in the great majority, and both fixed and detachable heads. The conical antler toggle-head harpoon has not been reported for this culture.

There is a great length range in the barbed points, from about two to fourteen inches, with two distinguishable broad groupings, large and small. The large points, from six inches up, exhibit less variability than those in the other group. Virtually all are made of antler and have prominent multiple unilateral barbs, which may be closely or widely spaced and sharply hooked or trapeziform in shape. The shanks are usually long and tapering to a blunt point, but in some cases they are short and truncated, and carry a drilled or gouged-out line hole either through the middle or in a lateral lobate projection. These perforated weapons are probably to be regarded as the detachable heads of true harpoons, the fish (or aquatic mammal?) being played on a line held in the spearman's hand. Illustrations of the large varieties are given on Plate 79, Figures 2, 3; Plate 80, Figures 4, 14, 15.

In the category of the much more numerous shorter points, made of bone and antler, the following styles can be recognized as standard forms appearing over a broad territorial range:

1) Unilaterally barbed with from one (rarely) to ten (rarely), usually two to six, triangular- or trapeziform-shaped barbs; shank fairly long and tapered to a blunt point or rounded base, never pierced (Plate 81, Figures 2, 3). A variant of similar over-all shape and size differs in having ten or more very weak "barbs," little more than serrations, in fact (Plate 80, Figure 13; Plate 81, Figure 4). Although extremely small, such "barbs" would probably remain firmly imbedded in the body of an animal, since the traumatised muscle tissue would tend to expand and fill the spaces between them.

2) Bilaterally barbed points, in the minority, as already remarked, generally duplicate the just described group in most respects; they do, however, show a marked tendency to be longer; for the shank to be broader, flatter, and more truncated at the base; and for the barbs to be sharp and triangular, rather than trapeziform (Plate 80, Figure 3). This form persisted with little change into the Owasco and later Iroquois cultures.

There may well have been functional explanations for this heterogeneity of barbed bone points in the Kipp Island culture. As already surmised, smaller examples might have performed as arrow points, especially for taking fish, the light fishline being attached to the arrow shaft. Long slender points, with or without a row of sharp barbs on one or both edges (Plate 81, Figures 10–

12), might also have done duty as leisters for the spearing of fish, especially eels, of which the Indians were notably fond, and waterfowl, particularly during the period of molt.

For hook-and-line capture two types of the bone fishhook were employed, one a simple barbless hook with round and knobbed shank, essentially like the kind in use in the area since Lamoka times (Ritchie, 1944, Plate 61, Figure 1); the second a well-barbed hook. This form appeared for the first time during the Kipp Island phase; it continued in use into the early Owasco culture, but only in central New York (page 278 and Plate 92, Figure 14), and even, in a limited and local way, into the prehistoric Iroquois culture of this area and in northern New York. It would seem to depict the transfer of the barb device from the heavily employed barbed fish spears just described.

The bone gorge, whose function has already been discussed (page 48), is represented by numerous examples from three sites (Port Maitland, Point Peninsula, Felix). It was likely an important fishing contrivance, particularly when used in numbers, each bone spike tied to a dropper-line, on a trot-line for "coarse fish," such as bullheads, catfish and eels, all favorites, as shown by the predominance of their remains among the fishbones at the habitation sites. Night-feeding fish, like those enumerated, are exceptionally easy to capture on a trot-line.

No cultivated-plant remains are as yet demonstrated for the Kipp Island culture, and wild vegetal foods are represented only by a few carbonized hickory and butternut shells and possible *Chenopodium* seeds found in our Kipp Island excavations of 1963. Moreover, food-processing equipment is limited to our recovery at the Felix site of a single cylindrical pestle, of a reported shallow mortar at the Menard Bridge No. 1 site, and a muller from Kipp Island. Possible food-storage pits occurred in fair number (approximately twenty-two) in the habitation area of Kipp Island explored in 1963. Most of them were round, two and a half to three feet in diameter, and dug from ten to twenty-one inches deep in the subsoil (Figure 7). A few of oval shape measured as much as six feet in length by four feet wide. Despite this body of equivocal evidence, it must be supposed that wild plant foods were significantly utilized and that cultigens were probably known.

Housing

Very little is known about the housing and settlement-pattern aspects of the Kipp Island phase. The 1963 excavations of the New York State Museum in the habitation area of the Kipp Island site disclosed a very large number of post molds, testifying to a long and intensive occupation, with much overlapping of house floors, resulting in obscurity of the pattern molds of individual structures. Moreover, ceramic remains found in the pit and hearth features, and scattered in the ground midden, most of which was included in the plow zone, pertained to the Kipp Island-Hunter's Home continuum, rather than exclusively to either phase. Consequently, such house data as it seems possible to extract should be thus broadly attributed.

As shown in Figure 7, three house-floor outlines were tentatively traced in whole or part, the most convincing being nearly round, eighteen to twenty feet in diameter, with a short entrance corridor opening to the south. Small central and large peripheral hearth pits (Features 32, 31), and pos-

sible storage pits (Features 11, 26, 30), one (Feature 11) showing heavy traces of fire, have no convincing direct relationship to this structure, for which no close parallels have so far been found in any archaeological assemblage of the New York State area. It is surmised, however, that this house had pertained to the Kipp Island phase of occupation.

The less well defined rectanguloid outline with rounded corners and end doorway facing the southeast, measuring approximately nineteen by ten feet, is reminiscent of the slightly larger Owasco houses (page 281 and Figure 9). It, too, contains unattributable pit features (Numbers 23, 24).

The most hypothetical structure, partially outlined to the right in Figure 7, suggests a large oblong dwelling, forty or more feet in length, like those found on the Maxon-Derby and Bates sites, of early and middle Owasco provenience, respectively (pages 282, 285 and Figures 9, 10). This, and its smaller possible prototype, just described, may signalize the appearance of a major Owasco house form on the Hunter's Home level of cultural development.

Dress and Ornament

For the dress and personal ornamentation of these Indians some indirect and more direct evidence exists. The former consists of such assumed skin-working tools as bone awls, manufactured from splinters and sections with attached condyles, of various mammal and bird long bones (Plate 81, Figures 20–22); copper awls, some still in antler handles, like those found in the Hopewell culture (Plate 80, Figure 6); beaming or dehairing tools fashioned from the metapodial bone of the deer; deer-scapula scrapers (Plate 81, Figure 9); ovate and triangular end scrapers, the latter bi-

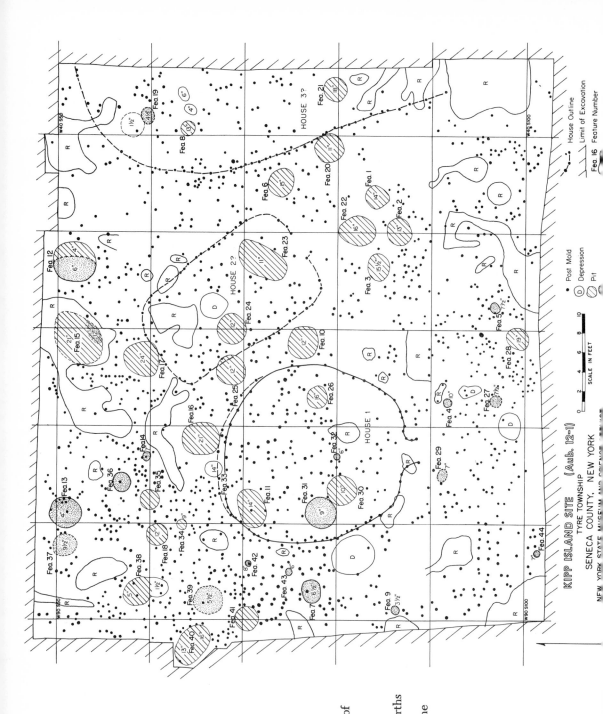

Figure 7 Excavated portion of habitation area at the Kipp Island No. 4 site. Features include definite and possible house floor outlines, pits, hearths and unattributed post molds. Kipp Island and Hunter's Home phases represented.

248

facially chipped (Plate 81, Figure 43); and short flat needles, perforated near one end or the center, probably actually mat-sewing implements (Plate 81, Figure 32).

For body decoration and other purposes, we have ample testimony for the use of powdered red hematite or ocher paint. Personal embellishments also included shell beads in large quantities and in considerable variety. The small, thin, discoidal form was apparently less favored than tubular styles of lengths ranging from approximately one half inch to over six inches, and in diameters from about one fourth to one inch (Plate 79, Figure 1; Plate 80, Figure 11). Oblate-spheroidal and flat, rectangular beads are present on some sites of this culture (Plate 80, Figure 10). These sundry varieties were all fabricated from the columella of the conch *Busycon,* two large species of which are available along the Atlantic coast from Cape Cod southward.

The popularity of whole small shells, worn as necklaces and bracelets and sewed on the clothing, as surmised from their positions relative to the skeletons, is affirmed by their presence in at least half the sites. Shells of the genus—*Marginella,* modified for stringing or sewing by having the spire ground away, are the commonest. Another gastropod shell similarly treated and used was the *Olivella.* Both genera occur along the South Atlantic coast from Florida to the Carolinas. At the Williams site some seven hundred shells of the gastropod *Anculosa subglobosa* (Say) were found, pierced for suspension by grinding obliquely from the end opposite the spire (Plate 79, Figure 1). One circular pendant, perforated near the edge, and cut from a whelk whorl, has been reported from the Menard Bridge No. 1 site. It, and much of the other shell material from this culture, is illustrated in Ritchie, 1944, Plates 59,

66–69. On Plate 67 of the same work are also illustrated copper beads of two styles, both short and tubular, one of small diameter and thin rolled metal, the other of larger caliber and thick sheet copper. Only the Menard Bridge No. 1 site has produced copper beads, insofar as is known. A short tubular bone bead came from a Kipp Island No. 3 site grave; also two long-bone pins, one with carved head.

The prevalence of animal teeth for ornamental purposes, and perhaps as charms, is denoted by such finds as bear canines with drilled apex, or ground flat and perforated through the inner wall into the root canal, a good Hopewellian trait (Plate 80, Figure 7); lynx canines, similarly perforated (Figure 8); and drilled fossilized sharks' teeth. The source of the fossilized sharks' teeth used for arrow points (page 237) and decorative elements was doubtless the geological exposures of the Tertiary period of the Middle Atlantic coast. The same area would have yielded much of the sea-shell material.

Stone pendants (one perforation), of at least four styles, all generally well made and polished, often of striped slate foreign to the New York area, were a significant element of the Kipp Island culture. It should be restated for emphasis that the gorget (two or more perforations), in any form, was *not,* on current knowledge, used by these later Point Peninsula people (or by their Owasco descendants). The four pendant varieties, all illustrated on Plate 84, are as follows: 1) a long, narrow, isosceles trapezoid (Figure 1); 2) rectangulate (Figure 4); 3) similar, but with partially incurving sides (Figure 2); and 4) rhomboidal, with truncated ends (Figure 3).

The long, narrow, pentagonoid form, shown as Figure 5 of the same Plate, although not reported from any of the Kipp

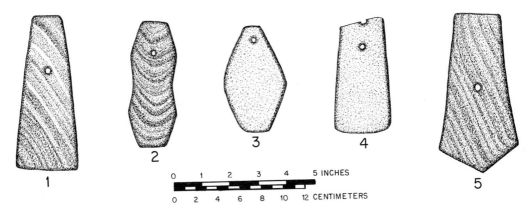

PLATE 84 Stone pendant forms of the Kipp Island phase.

Island sites, will prove, I believe, to be a trait of this culture, as well as a Late Hopewellian form (Plate 76, Figure 7).

On Plate 80, Figure 9, is depicted one of a pair of remarkable antler armbands found at Kipp Island. A rather neatly incised design of parallel ladder motifs covers the exterior surface, and the ends have holes gouged out for tying. These ornaments, unique for New York State, have their almost exact counterpart in the Laurel culture of the northern Minnesota area.

The most impressive items of personal ornamentation known from the Kipp Island culture are the extraordinary combs, fashioned with remarkable skill from the palmate portion of moose antler, which have been found in five of the listed sites (Port Maitland, Bay of Quinté, Jack's Reef, Kipp Island, Durkee). All are of large size, up to about fifteen inches in length and to five inches in maximum breadth, and bear from four to eight long, carefully delineated teeth. There is some individual variability both in the shape of the comb top and in its embellishment. In all cases, however, the latter consists of an incised design or pattern of triangles, usually filled in part with parallel vertical or horizontal lines (Plate 80, Figure 5; cf. Ritchie, 1944, Plate 87).

Figures 10 and 11 of the latter illustration depict two large combs of precisely the same kind, found as burial goods in the Bowman mound, near Linville, Rockingham County, Virginia, by Gerard Fowke (Fowke, 1894, pp. 37–44). Associated objects in this very important component included stone and clay elbow pipes, stone pendants, flint arrowheads, shell ornaments, and certain bone and antler artifacts, all of which correspond so closely with Kipp Island forms as to render certain some still obscure connection. Plausibly this hypothesized relationship might involve diffusions into the Southeast in late Middle Woodland times of post-Hopewellian cultural developments in the Ohio area, parallel to the situation postulated for the Northeast. (See discussion in Ritchie, 1944, pp. 120–21; Carpenter, 1950, pp. 308–11. The latter illustrates much of the material from this mound.)

Register of Tools

The people of the Kipp Island phase made fire by the already ancient method in their area of percussion with iron-pyrites anvil and flint strikers.

They cut and worked wood with the

familiar ungrooved ax or celt, trianguloid or rectanguloid in outline; and with plano-convex adzes, ranging in length from around two to eight inches, occasionally double-bitted. Adzes are about three times as prevalent as celts in this culture.

A very distinctive index trait of the culture is the antler-hafted beaver incisor, presumably a wood-carving tool, present at a majority of sites of the Kipp Island phase. The use of this distinctive implement in the New York area goes back to Meadowood times (page 193) and it has a wide range of distribution in cultures of the Middle (and Late?) Woodland period in the Upper Great Lakes area, e.g., the Laurel culture of northern Minnesota and adjacent parts of Canada. In New York it does not continue into the Late Woodland Owasco culture.

The usual style has the beaver incisor, with ground chisel-shaped incisal edge, set at right angles to the handle, through a slot cut for the purpose. Evidently a resin gum was employed for fastening, traces of which remain in some specimens (Plate 80, Figure 12; Plate 81, Figure 37). Occasionally the same handle holds, in parallel arrangement, a pair of such teeth (Ritchie, 1944, Plate 55, Figure 7).

A less common style has a similarly adapted beaver incisor mounted perpendicularly in a hollowed antler handle.

Unmounted incisors of the beaver, porcupine and woodchuck occur with fair abundance on most sites of this phase; the former with chisel- or gouge-shaped incisal edge, or split lengthwise and with the long enamel edges ground sharp, the others chisel-edged only (Plate 81, Figures 5–7).

For splitting wood or peeling bark the antler-tine wedges or chisels found rarely in this culture would doubtless have been useful implements.

Multipurpose tools recorded for the Kipp Island complex include the following: unpitted pebble hammerstones (Plate 82, Figure 24); thick discoidal hammerstones (Plate 82, Figure 23); abrading stones of flat tabular form, rubbed on one or more surfaces to produce trough-shaped hollows, narrow channels, or flat planes, and of rounded elongate form, rarely with weak grooves or "sinewstone" markings on the edge; knives from large retouched flakes (Plate 82, Figure 11) or thin, unretouched, prismatic flakes, as in the Hopewellian (Plate 82, Figures 3–6, 12); ovate and triangular, bifacially chipped knives (Plate 80, Figure 21; Plate 81, Figure 29); simple end scrapers (Plate 81, Figure 42); rare side scrapers from retouched flakes (Plate 81, Figure 41); and drills of several varieties, listed in descending order of frequency: with expanded rounded or rectangular base (Plate 82, Figure 10); expanded side-notched base (one corner-notched example) (Plate 82, Figures 17, 18); base crudely finished (Plate 81, Figure 23); triangular, concave base (Plate 81, Figure 28); straight and T-shaped base (Plate 81, Figure 24).

Chipped-flint artifact blanks, or "cache blades," are of frequent occurrence with burials of this culture. They are the crude, thick, "quarry blank" variety of the Hopewellian in New York (page 227), and totally unlike the fine, thin, leaf-shaped "mortuary blades" of the Meadowood phase (page 183), which occurred on only one of the eleven sites (Menard Bridge No. 1). Unworked flint chips, sometimes in small heaps, are also present in some graves of this culture (Plate 81, Figures 33, 34).

Cylindrical chipping tools of antler abound, some of small size, but the great majority large and characteristic of this culture. Some of the larger ones may have been hafted as chipping mallets (Plate 80, Figure 2; Plate 81, Figures 38, 39).

In addition to the flint blanks and chips used as grave goods, most of the burials of this culture contain quantities of "raw" or partially modified bone and antler, rodent teeth and jaws, and, in at least one case, the pectoral fin spines of fish, evidently to provide ready source materials for artifact manufacture for the deceased in the spirit realm, which likely was conceived as a continuation of earthly existence requiring the same necessities (Plate 81, Figures 8, 13–17, 19).

A bone device of problematical significance but apparently of some importance, and a prime diagnostic of the Kipp Island culture, is illustrated on Plate 80, Figure 1. It was fashioned from the humerus of some large bird, probably an eagle, and has one or both ends finely serrated with short teeth (suggesting the fur comb of the Eskimo). One specimen, from the Point Peninsula site, has a small drilled hole through one wall near the small end, as though for suspension. Several from Kipp Island are ornamented with incised designs.

Smoking Pipes

The number and variety of pipes found in sites of the Kipp Island culture testify to the popularity of smoking, but whether the substance or substances smoked included "Indian tobacco" (*Nicotiana rustica*) cannot be determined. Seven of the eleven sites listed in Figure 4 produced one or more pipes (Williams, Port Maitland, Point Peninsula, Jack's Reef, Felix, Kipp Island, Menard Bridge No. 1), and on three sites (Port Maitland, Jack's Reef, Felix) two styles of pipes occurred in the same burial or level of refuse.

There are essentially three categories of pipes: 1) platform, 2) right-angle elbow, and 3) obtuse-angle elbow. Pipes of the platform group, all of stone, apparently soapstone or related talcose rocks, are further divisible into two classes, viz., with curved base, of Hopewellian style (Point Peninsula and Jack's Reef sites, see Ritchie, 1944, Plate 69, Figures 1, 3; Plate 76, Figure 48), and with straight base and usually ridged stem from bowl to mouthpiece, like the Intrusive Mound type (from the Williams, Port Maitland, Jack's Reef and Felix sites; Plate 79, Figure 4; cf. Ritchie, 1944, Plate 78).

The right-angle elbow type, of stone or clay, is a rarer form, and its flat base seems to relate it, as a modification, to the flat-base platform type, rather than to the obtuse-angle elbow variety. Present on only one of the sites (Port Maitland), it has close parallels in certain pipes found in Michigan, in Lapeer County, and in Montmorency County, the latter find occurring in a mound together with hafted beaver-incisor tools, large barbed antler points with basal line-hole, and thin side-notched and triangular arrow points, all typical of the Kipp Island complex, and an undecorated pottery vessel with cord-malleated exterior, suggesting the Jack's Reef Corded type, another Kipp Island element (Hinsdale, 1930, Plates 32, 33).

The obtuse-angle elbow variety, illustrated on Plate 80, Figures 17, 18, occurs in plain pottery, with one example (Figure 17) made of polished limestone, on three sites of this culture (Kipp Island, Menard Bridge No. 1, Felix), all in central New York. Some of the pipes of the Kipp Island phase are nearly straight (Plate 80, Figure 17). It should be noted that the straight pipe, as defined by the writer, differs from the tubular form, in that the former has a discrete bowl chamber which constricts abruptly into a stem passage of narrow gauge.

The straight and obtuse-angle elbow pipes persist from late Kipp Island times through the Hunter's Home phase, into the Owasco culture, where further evolution can readily be traced through progressively more angular forms, until the virtually right-angle pipe of the latest stage is achieved. The decorative treatment of this pipe variety progresses *pari passu* with its formal modifications, from simple beginnings in the Carpenter Brook phase to the finely stamped and even effigy bowl treatment of the Castle Creek phase (page 294 and Plate 100). Some of the later styles appear to be directly ancestral to certain early Iroquoian pipes of the Oak Hill phase (pages 296, 303 and Plates 100, 107).

There is a small but intriguing group of objects from two of the Kipp Island sites which seem to pertain to the recreational and/or ceremonial aspects of life in the New York area during late Middle Woodland times. Unique among these are the thin, biconvex, elliptical or pumpkin-seed-shaped, antler "gaming pieces," about one and a half inches in length, found with burials at the Jack's Reef and Kipp Island sites (see for illustrations Ritchie, 1944, Plate 62, Figures 2–5; Plate 69, Figure 13). To me, at least, these are strongly reminiscent of the bone, antler or peachstone gaming dice of the Iroquois bowl and deer-button games.

Rattles of box-turtle shell, bearing perforations evidently for the attachment of a handle, are represented by fragmentary parts from two of the sites (Kipp Island, Felix). As a probably ceremonial object, this style of rattle seems not to have undergone any significant change in design from Archaic to Late Woodland times in the same region, since it has been found in complexes ranging from the Lamoka to the early historic Seneca (see discussion of this subject in Ritchie, 1954, pp. 63–65).

The magical or ritualistic usage of other animal bones, exhibiting a polish or wear from much handling, is suggested by the following objects: two bird humeri from the Port Maitland site, viz., a left wing bone from a sandhill crane (Plate 81, Figure 18), and a right wing bone from a Canada goose; two radii of the black bear from Kipp Island; and two disks of human skull bone from the Brock Street site, in each case found together in the same grave.

In the lingering aura of the Hopewellian tradition which seems to have invested the Kipp Island culture, aesthetic craftsmanship in media which have succumbed to dissolution may have been comparatively high for the New York area. This is suggested, for instance, by the superior quality of the antler combs, the extraordinary hilted bone dagger, and the antler armbands, all previously described.

Rather wide trade connections outside the area are indicated, another apparent surviving trait from earlier Middle Woodland times. These involve such distant regions as the Middle Atlantic coast for shell materials and fossil shark teeth; probably the Gulf of Mexico for some of the shell employed; eastern Pennsylvania for jasper, rhyolite and argillite; and presumably the Lake Superior district for copper and banded slate. Very little copper occurs, however, in the Kipp Island phase, where it was used for small tools and ornaments, as already mentioned. By late Middle Woodland times the influx of copper, begun with the tools of the Late Archaic and continued with the tools and ornaments of the Early and Middle Woodland cultures, was reduced to a mere trickle which ceased altogether during the Late Woodland stage.

THE HUNTER'S HOME PHASE

As previously remarked (page 228), the Hunter's Home phase represents the terminal development, in the late Middle Woodland period, of the Point Peninsula cultural continuum in central and eastern New York. It is a vague stage of transition into inchoate Owasco culture, and difficult to explicitly define. The concept of a Hunter's Home phase seems, however, to be justified by the obvious distinctions observable between the Kipp Island climax and the differentiated Carpenter Brook, or initial, phase of Owasco, which is taken as the commencement of the Late Woodland period in the same area (page 272).

The progressive shift from late Kipp Island, through Hunter's Home, into the Owasco pattern, involved both material and mortuary aspects. In the ceramic category, cord decoration on a cord-malleated surface rapidly succeeded the older dentate, rocker-stamped, and other styles which had been in vogue from Early Point Peninsula into early Kipp Island times. Corded horizontal, corded oblique, corded punctate, and platted motifs prevailed. Appliquéd collars went out of fashion, and pot-lip shapes gradually changed from rounded to flattened (Plates 78, 85, 86). Certain of these stylistic modifications (corded horizontal and platted designs and flat lips) were to endure throughout the life of the Owasco culture.

In pipes, the straight or slightly bent obtuse-angle elbow form, of clay or stone, and usually undecorated, which were rare in the Kipp Island phase, increased in number during the Hunter's Home phase (Plate 87, Figures 10–13). This would seem to mark the period when pipe smoking attained its first general popularity, perhaps with the introduction into the Northeast of *Nicotiana rustica* as a domesticate rather than a trade commodity. In the succeeding Owasco culture, as we shall see, this trend was continued with emphasis, accompanied

by the further evolution of the smoking pipe. A particular index of this continuity is found in a singular mammillary art motif (Plate 87, Figure 22) which makes its first appearance on pipes of the Hunter's Home phase and persists through early Owasco times (Plate 100, Figure 4).

However, in other classes of chipped-stone tools—knives, drills, and scrapers—a converse tendency toward greater diversification, as well as number, seems to have taken place on the Hunter's Home level (Plate 88, Figures 1–29). This short-lived evanescence was largely over by middle Owasco times.

The elaboration of the so-called sinew-stone (Plate 87, Figures 29, 30) from a simpler form, which has been noted for some of the Kipp Island burial sites (page 251), is another feature of the Hunter's Home-Owasco continuum.

The commonest of the pendant styles of Kipp Island lineage persisted through the Hunter's Home phase (Plate 87, Figures 14, 16–18, 24, 25) and well into the Owasco. New ornamental forms emerged, including a small discoidal pendant and, on certain sites, crude maskette-like objects which may provide the earliest clue to the employment of the false face (Plate 87, Figures 15, 23).

During the Hunter's Home phase the broad triangular arrow point of the Levanna type (Ritchie, 1961, pp. 31–32) rapidly achieved ascendancy over the Jack's Reef and other styles of the Kipp Island complex (Plate 88, Figures 30–70).

In the category of barbed bone points, too, a simplification was taking place, the "Christmas tree" form, with its triangular barbs, coming to the fore (Plate 87, Figure 2) and the large Kipp Island point (Figure 1 of the same plate) going out of use. Thus, both the predominant stone and

PLATE 85 Rim of pottery vessel of Point Peninsula Corded type from the Wickham 2 component, Oswego Co., N.Y. Kipp Island phase.

bone point forms of the Hunter's Home phase directly foreshadow weapon styles which were to characterize the whole sequence of Owasco development.

The retention of the shark's-tooth pendant (Plate 87, Figure 4); the straight-based, stone platform pipe, virtually as an heirloom (Plate 87, Figure 19); and the bone-hafted copper awl, by now exceedingly rare (Plate 87, Figure 21), provide additional links between the Kipp Island and Hunter's Home phases. None of these traits is known to survive into the Owasco culture.

The burial customs of the Hunter's Home phase afford a directional trend paralleling that outlined for the material culture. Most of the elements of the old mortuary ritualism, some part of which had endured into the Kipp Island phase, suffered extinction during Hunter's Home times, a helpful fact in the more or less arbitrary differentiation

PLATE 86 Potsherds from the White site, Chenango Co., N.Y. Hunter's Home phase. Collections of Stanford Gibson, Norwich, N.Y., and Theodore Whitney, New Berlin, N.Y.

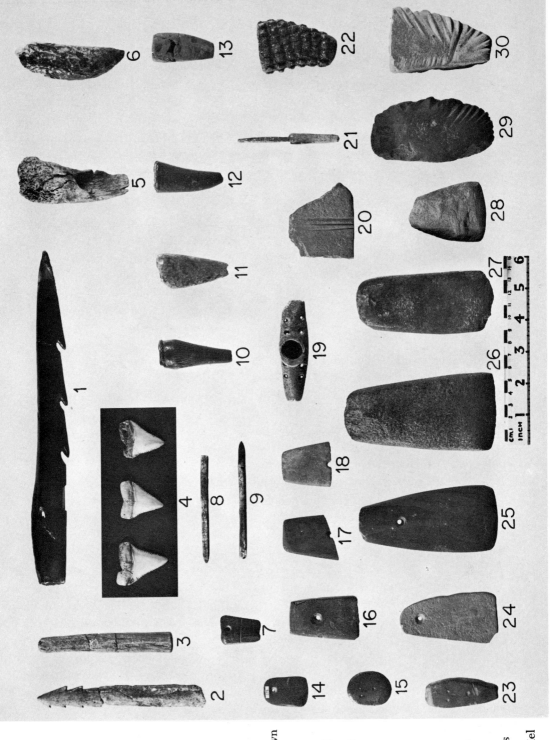

PLATE 87   Artifacts from the White site, Chenango Co., N.Y. Hunter's Home phase. 1, 2 barbed antler points; 3 antler chipping tool; 4 shark teeth; 5, 6 antler articles of unknown use, possibly war-club spikes; 7, 14, 16–18, 24, 25 stone pendants; 8, 9 bone or antler pins (?); 10, 11 straight pipes of stone; 12, 13 pottery pipes showing slight bend; 15, 23 stone maskette-like objects; 19 straight-base platform pipe of stone, broken in two places, showing lacing holes for repairs; 20 whetstone; 21 antler-hafted copper awl; 22 pottery pipe with mammillary decoration; 26–28 celts; 29, 30 sinewstones. Collections of Theodore Whitney, Stanford Gibson and Daniel Noble.

of this terminal Point Peninsula phase from the succeeding early Owasco manifestation.

The use of red ocher, lavish grave furniture, intentional destruction of grave offerings, and other significant mortuary ceremonial traits of Early and Middle Woodland cultures had about run its course with the waning of the Kipp Island phase. The Hunters' Home stage saw, with rare exceptions, a more commonplace treatment of the dead, with few if any provisions for the afterworld, as is best illustrated by our recent discoveries at the Kipp Island No. 4 site (page 261).

The Hunter's Home Site

Few components of the Hunter's Home phase have been found and excavated. The type station, locally known as "Hunter's Home," is situated on a level sand terrace some ten feet above the present mean water level of the Montezuma Marsh, five miles east of Savannah, Wayne County, New York (Figure 4, site number 65). A mile to the southeast, across the Seneca River, Bluff Point rises as an island in the marshland (page 234) (Figure 4, site number 66). Both earlier and later components occur on both these sites, and in the immediate vicinity of Hunter's Home, the locality being very favorable as a camping ground, especially for food-gathering peoples. The materials referable to the Hunter's Home phase of occupation were obtained from refuse pits and about eighteen shallow graves by Harold S. Secor of Savannah, who had kindly made his notes and collection available to me.

In 1960, with the cooperation of Mr. Secor and Elwood Malone, the landowner, a State Museum party in my charge opened a trench encompassing 268 square feet in a nearby refuse midden (designated Wpt. 3-3) formed by the disposal of trash over the low bank of the then shallow lake which filled the basin of the Montezuma Marsh, a remnant of proglacial Lake Iroquois (page 14), until drained by the Erie Canal and later the Barge Canal system.

Below a sterile eighteen-inch overburden of recent wash was found an eight-inch layer of dark sand which yielded a large number of early Owasco styles of potsherds, and several decorated pipe fragments. Directly beneath this level, but especially between thirty-five and forty inches from the surface, in virtually black sand, the abundant potsherds pertained to styles attributed to the Hunter's Home phase, or they represented intergrades with the stratigraphically superior Owasco varieties (Plate 78, Figures 18, 19, 21). Broad triangular points, but no pipe fragments, occurred in this lower level.

The White Site

The largest known component of the Hunter's Home phase is the White site (Nbn. 2-3) near Norwich, Chenango County, New York (Figure 4, site number 67). Originally listed with early Owasco sites (Ritchie, 1944, p. 89), it was, ten years later, referred to by the writer in connection with a radiocarbon sample from the site (page 261) as "very early Owasco with marked transitional features from Point Peninsula and is highly significant from the point of view of cultural continuity" (Crane, 1956, p. 668). Now, with fuller knowledge and the postulation of a Hunter's Home transitional phase, this would seem to be its valid taxonomic status.

The site covers about two thirds of an acre of level ground bordered by a brook draining a small marsh, on the high wooded divide, around 1725 feet above sea level, separating, at a point of closest conjunction, the Unadilla and Chenango rivers.

Since its discovery more than seventy years ago it has been extensively and randomly dug over by relic collectors who have, for the most part widely dispersed their numerous finds. More recently, in an attempt to understand the site's significance, systematic re-excavation work was undertaken by Stanford Gibson of Norwich and Theodore Whitney of New Berlin, aided by various members of the Chenango Chapter, New York State Archeological Association. The writer, who has several times visited the site and has participated briefly in this organized search, is indebted to the current investigators for most of his data, and for all of his illustrations (Plates 86–89), which were made from their generously loaned collections.

The subject of intensive search, post molds have only recently been found, but there is as yet no evidence of any sort of fortification. Apparently White's was an open village, with oblong communal houses like one partially traced at the Kipp Island site (page 247) and like some found on Owasco sites to be described later in this report. Small pits, probably cooking features, abound. These measure approximately two feet in diameter and fifteen inches in depth and contain fire traces, refuse and artifacts. A close watch for carbonized corn or other evidence of cultivated plants has proved negative to date. Mammal bone has, however, been collected for subsequent study.

While no cemetery has been disclosed by extensive searching, four burials have been uncovered, three individually scattered on the site's periphery, one near the center, all relating beyond cavil to its occupation.

Data are lacking for two, said to have been previously disturbed and fragmentary, while the others, of much interest, have been described by the finders (Whitney, 1962, pp. 3–4; Noble, 1962, p. 2). The first, opened in 1947, lay in a shallow oval pit, measuring approximately three by two by one and a half feet, in a tightly flexed position, facing east. The bones were heavily carbonized from *in situ* cremation in the flesh, with the preservation by charring, near the skull, of scraps of textile material, an exceedingly rare event on archaeological sites in the Northeast. The fire had destroyed some of the human bone, had damaged a large, antler harpoon head, of good Kipp Island type (Plate 87, Figure 1), and two or more bone or antler "pins" (Plate 87, Figures 8, 9), and shattered several Levanna-type arrow points, all burial accompaniments.

The textile remnants suggest that they may have been derived from a shroud or large bag, perhaps from more than one article. They depict a coarse twined fabric, in a simple over-and-under weave, with soft warp and weft bundles of the same material, quite possibly basswood-bark fiber (Plate 89).

In 1950 the Nobles uncovered a poorly preserved, uncremated skeleton, seemingly of a large male, flexed and facing west, whose burial offerings consisted of eleven Levanna points (Plate 88, Figures 63, 65, 69, 70), a side-notched point, a polished slate pendant (Plate 87, Figure 25) and, beneath the jaw, as though worn on a necklace, five shark teeth, one having a small root perforation (Plate 87, Figure 4).

Age of the Hunter's Home Phase

Fortunately, some of the carbonized sticks from the cremated burial of 1947

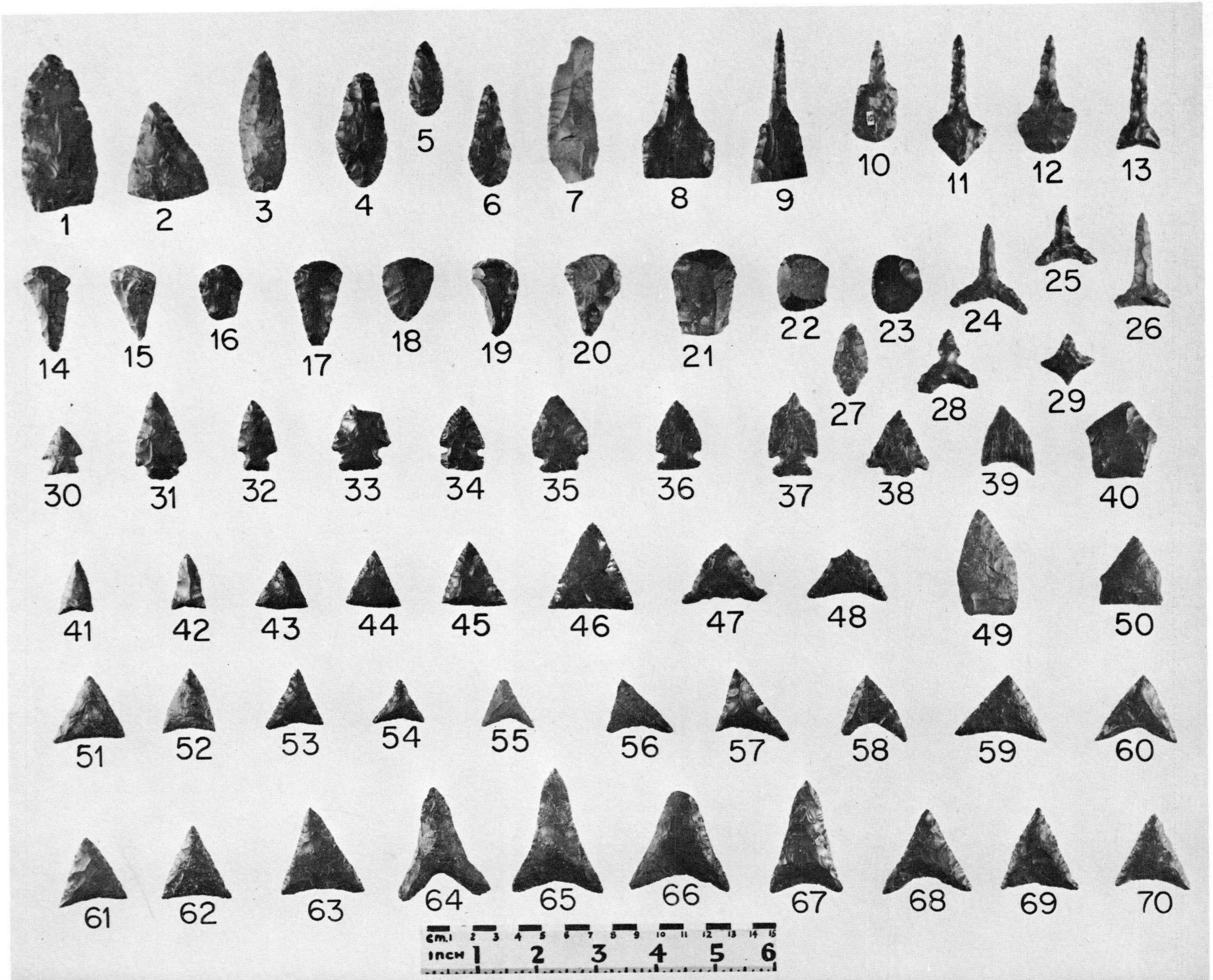

PLATE 88 Chipped-flint implements from the White site, Chenango Co., N.Y. Hunter's Home phase. 1–6 trianguloid, lanceolate and ovate knives; 7 knife from retouched flake; 8–13, 24–26, 28 drills with expanded, Y-shaped and T-shaped bases; 29 cruciform drill; 14–16 strike-a-lights; 17–23 end scrapers; 27 lobate stemmed point; 30–34, 36 side-notched arrow points; 35, 37, 38 (?) arrow points of Jack's Reef Corner-Notched type; 39, 40, 49, 50 arrow points of Jack's Reef Pentagonal type; 41, 42 arrow points resembling Madison type; 43–46, 51–53, 61–63, 65–70 arrow points of Levanna type; all others untyped aberrants.
Collections of Stanford Gibson, Theodore Whitney and Daniel Noble.

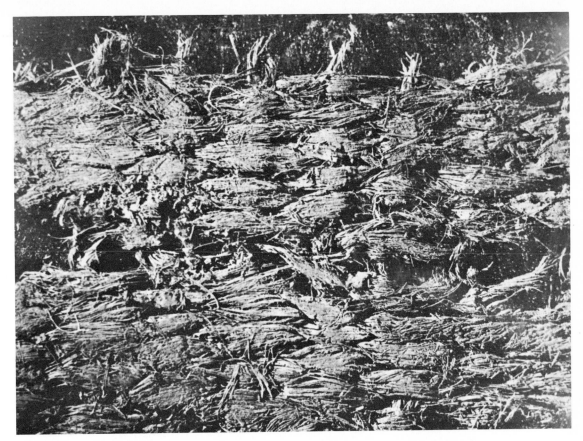

PLATE 89 Textile fragment from burial on White site, Chenango Co., N.Y. Hunter's Home phase. Photomicrograph by Vincent J. Schaefer, Schenectady, N.Y. Collection of Daniel Noble, Norwich, N.Y.

were collected by Theodore Whitney and these were later submitted by the writer for radiocarbon assay to the University of Michigan. The resulting date, A.D. 905± 250 years (M-176) (Crane, 1956, p. 668), which fits well into the general sequence (Figure 1), constitutes one of the few dates for this phase, although a sample collected in our 1963 excavations at Kipp Island No. 4, referable to the Hunter's Home phase, has been submitted for analysis. [This date is A.D. 895±100 years (I-3441.)]

In eastern New York there are several sites which appear to represent the transitional Hunter's Home phase. Two of them, the Turnbull site (Ams. 3-6) and the Willow Tree component (Las. 10-7) (Figure 4, sites number 68, 69), are situated in the Mohawk Valley and are the subjects of published reports (Ritchie, Lenig and Miller, 1953, pp. 22–40). The younger of the two on typological evidence, the Willow Tree site, has been radiocarbon-dated at A.D. 955±250 years (M-177) (Crane, 1956, p. 668), or approximately half a century later than the White site. The most recent date of A.D. 1000±75 years (M-1163) applies to the Portage site in western New York, attributed to this phase.

The Kipp Island No. 4 Component

Passing references have been made to the State Museum's excavations of 1963, under the writer's direction, on the Kipp

Island No. 4 component (Aub. 12-1), to which we owe the most comprehensive data on the burial customs of the Hunter's Home phase. The burial area, which I had discovered in the previous fall, lay on nearly level ground near the southeastern end of Kipp Island (page 234). It was covered by a shallow refuse mantle that became deeper toward the west, where the principal habitation area with pits, hearths, post molds, and other features, belonging both to the Kipp Island and the Hunter's Home phases of occupation, was explored during the same season by the Museum group (Figure 7), through the courtesy of Mr. John K. Jackson of Savannah, the land-owner.

The twenty-nine closely clustered graves, some overlapping or actually overlying one another, were distributed over an area of only nine hundred square feet, but additional burials, found by testing and left unexcavated for want of time, are known to extend the boundaries of the cemetery (Figure 8). All the evidence strongly indicated a single cultural provenience, the Hunter's Home phase, for this component, which will be reported in more detail in a subsequent publication.

The topsoil covering the cemetery, many times plowed, consisted of compact dark-brown gravel and sandy loam, eleven to twelve inches deep, with a pH of 6.0 to 6.5. Grave outlines were of course obliterated in this horizon. Grave fossae had been extended into the similar, but lighter colored (from lack of refuse and humus) subsoil, from a few to about fifteen inches in depth, consequently all graves were shallow, which fact, together with poor drainage and the slightly acid soil medium, had resulted in a very defective state of bone preservation.

The twenty-nine grave pits excavated contained the remains of approximately 120 individuals of both sexes and all ages, as nearly as could be determined, chief reliance being placed on dental age and the size and degree of robusticity of the skull and postcranial parts. Grave offerings were present in only three graves, as noted below.

The burial mode was surprisingly diversified, considering the lateness of the period and the recorded occurrence of only single flexed and bundle burials at the Hunter's Home site. The following modes were present at Kipp Island No. 4:

1) Single flexed interment—burials 3, 9, 10, 12, 16, 17, 28. These graves held collectively the remains of two adult males, one (number 28) accompanied by a decorated (with annular punctations), slightly bent elbow pipe, a fragmentary rectanguloid pendant and a nodule of iron pyrites, probably for fire making; two adult females; three adults, sex indeterminate; and an infant loosely flexed on its back (number 12) (Figure 8).

2) Single bundle burial—numbers 2, 15, 18; containing two adults, one probably female, and a child.

3) Single cremation burial—number 7, bones of a young adult, not burned in situ.

4) Multiple flexed disposal—numbers 8 (five individuals—an adult male, two adult females, a child and an infant); 13 (an adult female and young infant); and 20 (two adult males and a child) (Plate 90).

5) Multiple bundle burial—numbers 1 (five adults); 4 (at least fourteen individuals, mostly adults, some immature); 6 (three adult individuals, accompanied by a plain elbow pipe); 21 (four adults, at least two of them females, one child); 23 (ten closely packed individuals—three adult males, two adult females, two unidentified adults, two children, one infant); 24 (four adults—two of each sex); 25 (four adults—

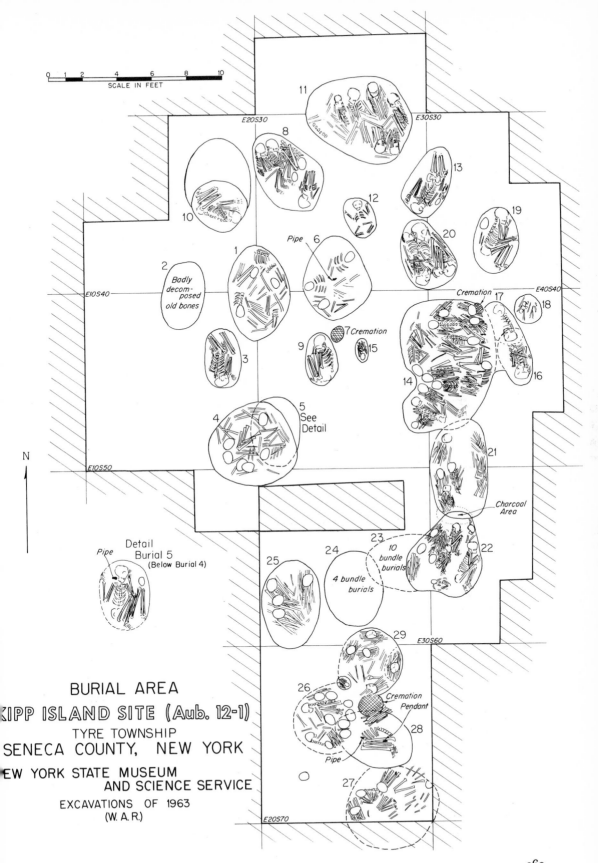

Figure 8 Burial area at the Kipp Island No. 4 site. Hunter's Home phase.

PLATE 90 Multiple flexed burial of five individuals on Kipp Island No. 4 site, Seneca Co., N.Y. Hunter's Home phase.

a male, a female, two indeterminate); 27 (two each adult male and female, one each child and infant).

6) Multiple bundle and cremation—number 29 (three adult males, two adult females, an infant, and an adult male not cremated at this place).

7) Multiple flexed and bundle—numbers

5 (adult male, plain elbow-type pipe at right shoulder [Plate 91] and bundle of infant bones over left tibia); 11 (six flexed, two bundled skeletons, representing three adult males, an adult female, a child, an indeterminate); 19 (a flexed adult male and a bundle of child's bones); 22 (nine individuals, four flexed, five bundled—re-

PLATE 91 Flexed burial of adult male with plain pottery pipe over right shoulder, on Kipp Island No. 4 site, Seneca Co., N.Y. Hunter's Home phase.

solvable into three adult males, an adult female, two children, one infant, two indeterminate); 26 (nine individuals, two flexed, overlying seven closely packed bone bundles, apparently derived from two adult males, five adult females, two children).

8) Multiple flexed, bundle and cremation—number 14, with twelve individuals— three flexed, eight bundled, one cremated, comprising four adult males, three adult females, three adults, sex indeterminate, and a child's bones cremated elsewhere.

The population of 120 individuals represented by the excavations in this cemetery

therefore consisted of thirty-one adult males (25.8 per cent), twenty-seven adult females (22.5 per cent), thirty-one adults of indeterminate sex (25.8 per cent), eighteen children, about four to sixteen years of age (15.0 per cent), eight infants (6.6 per cent), and five individuals whose bones were too much disintegrated for either sex or age analysis (4.1 per cent).

The predominance of secondary burials, and especially of multiple interments involving bone bundles, points unequivocally toward mortuary customs retaining the corpse above ground, perhaps in a charnel house, for a considerable period between death and inhumation in the ground. A very marked proportion of the remains, even some identified as flexed burials in the flesh, seem to have been partially, if not completely, skeletonized individuals, whose bones were still held together by hardened and shrunken ligaments. In many cases the anatomical order of the bones was disrupted, a leg, arm, foot or hand, for example, being out of place in the grave, which showed no rodent or other disturbances as the causative agent.

The extreme shallowness of the grave fossae, and the large number of skeletons deposited in some, also argues that most or all of the flesh had disappeared before the tightly wrapped corpses or bundles of denuded bones were pressed into the pits. Certain of these multiple burials, in fact, could probably correctly be described as miniature ossuaries.

It would seem that, directly after death, the still-relaxed body was closely enveloped in a shroud and deposited in a mortuary or charnel house, and that periodically—perhaps seasonally or in connection with a ceremonial calendar, some form of a "feast of the dead"—the bundles, new and old, certain of the latter reduced by decay to near mummies or loose bones, were laid in a shallow, saucer-shaped grave fossa, together with an occasional flexed body still in the flesh, or more rarely a cremation. If the site was seasonally occupied by this group, the interval of burial may have been on such a basis. If not, a ceremonial periodicity is hinted at, an echo of the long past reaching far back, as we have seen, at least to Orient times (page 175). It may thus be the only archaeologically ascertainable remnant of the ages-old "cult of the dead" in the New York area.

THE SEBONAC PHASE OF THE WINDSOR TRADITION

This Late Woodland cultural manifestation on eastern Long Island was named and described by Smith (1950, pp. 133–34) on the basis of data supplied by published excavations on the Sebonac site in New York (Harrington, 1924), the Old Lyme and South Woodstock sites in Connecticut (Praus, 1942, 1945), and on unpublished collections from two other New York sites, Soak Hides and Squaw Cove (Figure 4, sites number 90, 91). Additional data have come from the Conklin site at Aquebogue, excavated by Charles F. Goddard between 1933 and 1936 (field notes on loan to the writer), the Wells site near Aquebogue, also excavated by Mr. Goddard in the 1930s (field notes on loan to the writer) and by the writer in 1961, the Old Field A component on the north fork of Long Island, and several others (Smith, 1950, pp. 178–82) (Figure 4, sites number 89–95). At several of the New York sites and on all the Connecticut stations, both Sebonac and Niantic[1] materials occur, but it has been possible in some cases to determine, stratigraphically or otherwise, the precedence of at least the major part of the Sebonac remains (Rouse, 1947, pp. 19–20; Smith, 1950, p. 144).

Except for some inland sites in Connecticut, the Sebonac components, large for the most part, typically occupy well-drained locations on bays and tidal streams, close to available sources of marine shellfish. Shell detritus occurs in midden masses and in pits scattered over areas of from one to

[1] The tentatively defined Niantic Focus of Smith (1950, pp. 132–33) is too little known to be included in this account.

three or more acres. The evidence attests to stable communities of perhaps one hundred or more people, who dwelt in circular wigwams, ten to twenty feet in diameter, thatched with grass or rushes, and who were dependent not only upon the immense shellfish reserves, but also upon agriculture, combined with fishing and the taking of deer and lesser mammals.

While the food remains from these still undated stations have never been expertly studied either qualitatively or quantitatively, it is certain that they included the oyster, quahog or hard clam, long clam, scallop, mussel, whelk, crab, deer, turkey, raccoon, muskrat, various species of ducks and turtles, the sea sturgeon, sundry other fish, and possibly the whale, whose bones have been reported from the type station, where also carbonized corn was found (Harrington, 1924, pp. 249–53).

Pits, numerous on all Sebonac sites, are broad and basin-shaped, about six feet across and two to three feet deep, or U-shaped, three to five feet in diameter and three to four or more feet in depth. The first type especially appears to have served as baking ovens for shellfish, the heat being retained by stones placed on the bottom; food storage and cooking seem the principal functions of the second type; both kinds were sometimes employed as graves for the human and dog population, and regularly as trash depositories.

Hunting equipment is common enough on Sebonac sites to show, in connection with bone refuse, that even at this late time, estimated as post A.D. 1000, deer and other game was available on Long Island. Most of the hunting was probably done with the bow and arrow, tipped predominantly with the broad, triangular, Levanna-type point. With rare exceptions, the arrow points were fashioned, often skillfully and neatly, from the local, refractory, white-quartz pebbles. Hammer- and anvil-stones and antler flaking tools occur on the sites, which yield abundantly of workshop debris. Conical antler arrow points are also recorded for this culture.

Fishing, probably done in large part from dugout boats, utilized the single-piece barbless bone hook, the compound hook with bone, antler or wooden shank and bone point, the large bone or antler harpoon with single or multiple unilateral barbs and line-hole, and nets, as inferred from notched or grooved pebble sinkers. It is not known whether the Sebonac people pursued the whale or used his stranded carcass, or if they were capable of pelagic fishing. The large size of some of the fishing tackle suggests, however, deep water angling.

In the preparation of vegetable foods, which are known to have included the acorn as well as maize, cylindrical stone pestles and probably wooden mortars and pestles were the grinding devices. Food was prepared by baking in pits, boiling in clay pots, and doubtless by roasting. Utensils for personal use included cups, bowls and spoons of turtle shell and wood.

The recovery at the Sebonac site of a twined woven textile fragment of twisted bast fibers raises the possibility that clothing, as well as bags and other articles, were fashioned of such material (Harrington, 1924, p. 272).

Personal adornments, as archaeologically witnessed, were few and simple, consisting of circular or rectanguloid stone pendants, drilled through center or edge, some with crudely incised designs; rare tubular bone and shell beads; and paint ground from pieces of hematite, limonite and graphite.

For felling trees and shaping wood the technology of the Sebonac culture supplied the fully grooved ax, notched ax, celt, plano-convex adz, chipped end and side scrapers, and graving and scraping tools from modified beaver incisors.

In the general tool kit were chipped-stone knives of several varieties—triangular, ovate, lanceolate, stemmed; drills, some with expanded triangular or T-shaped base; pebble hammerstones, with or without pits; anvilstones; and sinewstones.

As in most of the sedentary cultures of the Late Woodland stage, pottery outranks in amount and variety all other industrial vestiges. Sebonac pots were in shape prevailingly elongate, with conoidal or semiconoidal base, and straight or in-sloping collarless rim. The paste was tempered with crushed shell, or rarely in New York, more frequently in Connecticut, with crushed stone aplastic. The external surface was brushed or wiped, apparently with the back of a scallop shell, fabric or cord marked, or plain. The interior was smoothed, brushed or scraped, leaving channels or striae, suggesting use of a scallop-shell edge.

Decoration, applied from shoulder to lip, in many instances involved the further use of a scallop shell to produce trailed, combed or stamped impressions of simple linear, crisscross or rectangular designs (Plate 103). Triangular or circular punctations, occasionally raising interior rim bosses, also occur.

Smoking pipes of stone and clay are present in this culture. Straight and obtuse angular forms occur in both media. Pottery pipes are plain or decorated with stamped or occasionally incised designs and sometimes have a flaring mouthpiece. The much rarer steatite pipes usually lack embellishment.

The mortuary customs of the Sebonac people stand in sharp contrast to those of their Orient predecessors of the same region (page 175). Here on Long Island, as elsewhere in New York and the Northeast, the dead received in Late Woodland times such commonplace treatment as to suggest the loss or decline of the older and widespread concept of athanasia, as inferred from the burial traits we have described. Sebonac folk, like their unrelated Owasco contemporaries upstate, seem most often to have laid their dead, folded or flexed, and probably clothed and shrouded, in a convenient cache or cooking pit, very rarely with any parting gift or equipment for a supermundane destiny. At the Conklin site, Goddard has recorded in his field journal the multiple burial of thirteen individuals, one a child, in a veritable ossuary of jumbled bones. This find hints at the possible survival, as a trait of Sebonac culture, of the use of the charnel house, postulated for much earlier times in the same district (page 177).

While the Sebonac culture, the product of a group or groups of people whose physical anthropology is still to be studied from their available scanty skeletal remains, persisted almost, if not to, European contact, evidence for their precise identification with any historic Algonkian group is unsatisfactory, although Harrington may have been correct in attributing the key station to the Shinnecock tribe (Harrington, 1924, p. 246).

THE BOWMANS BROOK PHASE OF THE EAST RIVER TRADITION

In the earlier part of the Late Woodland stage the Bowmans Brook culture apparently entered the southern subarea of New

York from New Jersey via Staten Island, where the type site is located. Eventually its range came to include western Long Island, Manhattan Island, and the lower Hudson Valley in Westchester and Rockland counties.

On western Long Island and adjacent Manhattan Island the Bowmans Brook phase is said to have been immediately preceded by the Clearview Focus (phase), which had ceramic types linking it to Middle Woodland cultures farther north. Clearview is believed by Smith to overlie the Early Woodland North Beach Focus. Nothing can be added to Smith's description of these manifestations pending the discovery and excavation of additional components (Smith, 1950, pp. 134–135).

From the Bowman's Brook site at Mariners' Harbor on the northwestern shore of Staten Island, superficially investigated by Skinner in 1906 (Skinner, 1909, pp. 5–9; Smith, 1950, pp. 176–77) (Figure 4, site number 96), and from two other components, Wilkins and Grantville B, both on western Long Island, Smith has named and defined the Bowmans Brook Focus (phase) (Smith, 1950, pp. 177–78; 122–23) (Figure 4, sites number 97, 98).

The large Abbott Farm site on the Delaware River near Trenton, New Jersey, produced a pot and several sherds of Bowmans Brook Incised type, and the close relationship of this to the Abbott Zoned Incised type of New Jersey has been remarked by Cross (1956, p. 155 and Plate 37, a). Relationship to the Overpeck Incised type farther west in Pennsylvania is also suspected.

Sites of the Bowmans Brook culture are situated on tidal streams or coves, the type site being described as a large village with fifty to one hundred pits. Shell spreads from a few inches to a foot or more in thickness and pits filled with shell and other refuse mark these apparently semipermanent dwelling places. Pits vary greatly in size and depth; at the type site they are said to have ranged from four to six feet in diameter and from three to six feet in depth. Probably they served several purposes—as earth ovens for shellfish and other food, for food storage, and secondarily as refuse dumps and occasionally as graves.

None of the sites has been radiocarbon-dated, but a beginning date for the culture of around A.D. 1100 has been estimated, probably correctly, by Smith (1950, p. 107), making it approximately coterminous with the Canandaigua phase of Owasco culture in upstate New York (Figure 1).

Marine shellfish appear to have furnished the main support, other animal protein coming from game and fish. Corn and perhaps other cultivars, while not reported, seem probable dietary items of this as of the synchronous Sebonac and Owasco cultures. Shallow stone mortars and a rectanguloid stone pestle are the known food-grinding implements, but wooden tree-trunk mortars and pestles are likely elements of the culture, as are wooden utensils. Box-turtle-carapace receptacles have been found.

The hunting activity employed the bow and arrow tipped with broad triangular points of quartz, flint and other stone, or hollowed, conical, antler tines. Antler and bone flaking tools are present. Grooved and notched pebble sinkers are the only units of fishing tackle reported.

Nothing is known concerning the housing, clothing or personal decoration of the Bowmans Brook people beyond the fact that a bone pin with carved head, a fragmentary rectangular pendant and a hematite paintstone have been collected on their sites. The cut and apex-drilled deer pha-langeal or toe bones may have been fringe ornaments on skin clothing, elements of the cup-and-pin game, or both. Bone awls are relatively plentiful, as are hammer- and anvilstones; the fully grooved ax, but not the celt or adz, is known, and there are a few tabular abrading stones and worked-beaver-incisor cutting or scraping tools.

Potsherds, vastly outnumbering all other items, fall into two main groups—stamped and incised ware. Bowmans Brook Stamped is described as pertaining to grit-tempered vessels with elongate body, co-noidal base, straight or flaring rim, cord-malleated exterior and smooth interior sur-faces, and cord-wrapped stick decorations in simple linear, chiefly horizontal, patterns (Smith, 1950, pp. 191–92).

Bowmans Brook Incised vessels differ in sometimes having an in-sloping rim, occa-sionally shell tempering, smooth exterior surface for the most part, and broad line-incising in bold triangular or rectangular plats arranged around the rim and extend-ing well down on the shoulder. The her-ringbone motif is common and a few ves-sels of this type have stylized human faces formed by three punctates placed on raised nodes about the rim. This trait may have been adopted through contact with Sebonac groups adjacent to the east on Long Island (Lopez and Latham, 1960).

Similar in shape to these types, but with-out decoration, is the East River Cord Marked type also present in this culture. It takes its name from the fact that the whole exterior surface is cord roughened, sometimes partially smoothed over.

Pottery pipes, straight and unorna-mented, or with stamped decoration, are represented by a few fragments on the sites.

As among the coexistent Sebonac and Owasco peoples, the Bowmans Brook In-dians were little concerned with mortuary matters. Their dead were interred, appar-ently sans ceremony and without offerings, in flexed or folded posture, in a convenient cache or cooking pit or, as at the type site, in a cemetery on a knoll adjacent to the vil-lage. A few secondary or bone-bundle bur-ials are noted. Dog burials also occur in some of the village pits.

The ethnic identity of the Bowmans Brook folk is unknown, but they may have been some division of the Lenni Lenapé or Delaware of New Jersey.

THE CLASONS POINT PHASE OF THE EAST RIVER TRADITION

Succeeding the Bowmans Brook phase in the same area and evidently developing from it, with probable influences from out-side, was the Clasons Point phase, named from the type site on Clasons Point on the north side of the East River in the Borough of the Bronx, which was excavated by Skinner in 1918 (Skinner, 1919, pp. 75–124; Smith, 1950, pp. 168–69) (Figure 4, site number 99). Smith, who has described the culture, states that its range extended beyond that of the former Bowmans Brook phase to include a larger portion of western Long Island and the mainland district be-tween the Hudson and Housatonic rivers north to or beyond the Hudson Highlands (Smith, 1950, pp. 120–22).

Twelve components are recognized, in-cluding two rockshelters, the Finch Rock House and Helicker's Cave, both in West-chester County (Harrington, 1909, pp. 125–30, 132–34; Smith, 1950, pp. 163–64, 171) (Figure 4, sites number 100, 101).

Estimated to have attained its character-istic conformation by approximately A.D.

1300 (there are no carbon-14 dates), the Clasons Point development paralleled that of the final Owasco and early Iroquois elsewhere in New York and survived to the period of European contact in the first quarter of the seventeenth century.

Most of the sites are situated on the second rise of ground above high-water level on tidal inlets and they approximate an acre in extent. Refuse, occurring as a surface veneer and in pits, consists of profuse remains of marine shellfish and much lesser amounts of mammal, bird, amphibian and fishbones. Fresh-water clam shells were found in the inland rock shelters, indicating a well-developed taste for shellfish, along with more ample debris of hunting, especially the deer.

Pits, similar to those on Bowman's Brook sites, are numerous, some being of larger size, but all probably serving the same functions of storage and cooking, and later trash bins and graves for the human and canine inhabitants.

Hunters continued to favor the wide Levanna type triangular stone arrowhead, but also employed projectile points of antler and bone. A long-bone dagger with serrated edges occurred on one of the sites. Fish were captured in nets weighted with notched flat or grooved ovate pebbles and with single-piece, barbless bone hooks. The food resources of the Clasons Point people on the type site, described by Skinner in some detail, included corn, hickory nuts, walnuts and sweet-flag roots (Skinner, 1919, pp. 117–19).

Stone hoes, elongate stone pestles, shallow mortars, mullers, and bowls and dishes from the box-turtle carapace have all been archaeologically recovered, while historical accounts for Algonkian groups of this area supply such items as wooden grinding gear and personal utensils.

No data on housing have come from the ground, but not improbably dwelling forms included a variety of the longhouse, sheltering a multiple-family group, of a kind observed and described by two Dutch travelers in 1679 among the neighboring Canarsee at the southwestern end of Long Island (Murphy, 1867, pp. 124–27, quoted by Smith, 1950, pp. 104–5).

For felling trees and other manipulation of wood, the three-quarter-grooved ax and celt or ungrooved hatchet constituted the heavy tools. Antler-tine wedges or chisels, beaver-incisor scrapers, gravers and chisels, and retouched flake scrapers served the finer needs of shaping. Dugout log canoes, as well as wooden utensils, shafts, handles, etc., were manufactured, as historically recorded for this area.

In keeping with most earlier cultures one finds here a variety of chipped and rough stone implements, including trianguloid, stemmed and lanceolate knife forms; drills; unpitted and bipitted hammerstones; anvilstones; sinewstones; bone awls; perforated mat needles; antler tool handles and lesser items.

Personal vanity was served by tubular bone beads, probable dress jinglers of deer-toe bone, shell pendants and, on later sites of European contact, shell wampum beads. It seems clear that, properly speaking, wampum was a European-trade-inspired commodity, developed from rather crude and rare shell-bead prototypes after metal tools had become available and when a need for currency arose through extensive trade relationships with white men and other Indian groups.

The very common potsherds of this phase belonged to vessels of medium size—one to two gallons—showing a considerable variation in form and decoration through the life of the culture. Earlier pots have a more elongate body and semiconoidal or semi-globular base, more are shell- than grit-tempered, straight or flaring rims predominate, collars are uncommon, the body-surface treatment has been applied with a cord-wrapped paddle, and the decoration is, in the main, cord-impressed.

Later, the vessel form becomes globular with rounded base, everted and collared rim. Shell-tempering prevails. Body surface is smooth and, in addition to cord-imprinted embellishment, a new technique —incising—is used on rim and collar. The chief cord-decorated type of this late stage, the Van Cortland Stamped of Smith (Smith, 1950, p. 191; Lopez, 1958) conforms very closely with our Owasco Corded Collar type (Ritchie and MacNeish, 1949, pp. 112, 114), while the popular incised collar style, Eastern Incised (Smith, 1950, p. 190), has its match in our Chance Incised and Deowongo Incised early Iroquois types in upstate New York (Ritchie, 1952a).

Elbow-shaped smoking pipes of baked clay, with stamped or incised embellishment, were in use in this culture.

In keeping with the burial practices of this time throughout the New York State area, the Clasons Point Indians disposed of their deceased without apparent ritualistic observances, by simply placing the flexed corpse, unaccompanied by grave goods, in a convenient storage or cooking pit, or in a shallow grave dug in a midden. There is some evidence for secondary or bone burial.

The Clasons Point phase endured into historic times as proved by the presence of European trade materials in the superior level of several sites. Historic records connect the cultural range with the territory of sundry members of the western Metoac on Long Island, with Wappinger groups on Manhattan Island and northward, and perhaps with certain Delaware groups on northern Staten Island. Skinner assigned, probably correctly, the type site to the Siwanoy, and identified it as their village of "Snakapins," "which was in full life from late prehistoric times, say about 1575, until the early Dutch Colonial period, say 1625–43" (Skinner, 1919, p. 120).

THE OWASCO CULTURE

Because of the relative abundance in relation to sites of earlier cultures, the Owasco is the best-known of the pre-Iroquoian occupations of New York State. Excavations of varying extent have been conducted by the writer on twenty-three components representing apparently the full range of Owasco cultural development from its immediately ancestral Hunter's Home phase to its transition in the Oak Hill phase into nascent eastern Iroquois culture. Besides numerous site reports covering much of this work, a concise general descriptive account of the Owasco culture has appeared (Ritchie, 1951c).

The Owasco culture takes its name from the first reported site, located in Lakeside (now Emerson) Park on the outlet of Owasco Lake, at Auburn, Cayuga County (Aub. 7–2) (Figure 4, site number 71). Here in 1915 E. H. Gohl, a local resident, discovered pottery and other artifacts which he called to the attention of Arthur C. Parker at the New York State Museum, who made a brief investigation (Parker, 1922, pp. 340–43; Ritchie, 1944, pp. 80, 83). The distinctiveness of the assemblage from other cultures known at that time was recognized by Parker, who attributed the site to his "Third Algonkian Period" (Parker, 1922, p. 49).

This designation was retained following excavations, first by Parker in 1923, then by the writer in 1927, on the similar Levanna site in the same county (Ritchie, 1928) (Figure 4, site number 72), but following the writer's exploration in 1934 of the Sackett site at Canandaigua, Ontario County (Can. 1) (Figure 4, site number 73) (Ritchie, 1936a), and the formulation and adoption of the Midwestern Taxonomic Method of classification in 1935, the cultural designation was changed to the "Owasco Aspect," and two foci were differentiated, an early or Canandaigua Focus and a late or Castle Creek Focus (Ritchie, 1936a, p. 4). This assessment was based upon the field work of the Rochester Museum of Arts and Sciences, conducted by the writer, mostly in the early 1930s, at the Levanna, Clark, Wilbur Lake, St. Helena, Hilltop, Sackett, Castle Creek and Bainbridge sites (Ritchie, 1928, 1934, 1936a, 1938b, 1939, 1944, pp. 29–96). With subsequent excavations two additional foci were postulated, the Carpenter Brook and the Snell (Ritchie, 1946, 1951; Ritchie, Lenig and Miller, 1953).

These several "foci," now called "phases" (page xxviii), still seem in the main to be generally applicable to the development of Owasco culture as currently comprehended. However, it must be emphasized that as the culture represents a developmental continuum through time and space, it becomes exceedingly difficult, if not impossible, narrowly and specifically to define and characterize separable and distinctive phases. One might more readily and validly discern earlier, intermediate and later stages, based mainly upon ceramic criteria, the first having closest affinities with the Hunter's Home phase, which we regard as terminal Point Peninsula, the last hardly distinguishable from the Oak Hill phase, arbitrarily assumed to represent inchoate Iroquoian culture in the New York area. Therefore, the following comprehensive description of the Owasco culture will be given in terms of an early, formative, or Carpenter Brook phase; a middle, mature, or Canandaigua phase; and a late, efflorescent, or Castle Creek phase (Figure 1). A fuller picture of each may be drawn from the pertinent site reports and other references.

Geographic Range

Sites of the Owasco culture have their major distribution in central and eastern New York (Figure 4, sites number 71–87). Available evidence indicates that western New York during the whole of Owasco times was inhabited by a group or groups continuous into southwestern Ontario. The Canadian sequence, from the Late Point Peninsula Glen Meyer and Pickering foci into the early western Iroquoian Uren and Middleport foci, constitutes a parallel development to that outlined for central New York phases from Hunter's Home to Oak Hill, and radiocarbon dates for Ontario sites demonstrate the contemporaneity of both sequences. Certain sites of this period in western New York yield some ceramic materials—pottery and pipes—of Owasco typology, in contrast to prevailing non-Owasco forms, which would seem to reflect cultural contact with central New York rather than an aberrant, regional, Owasco development.

In the Hudson Valley and southward a congruent situation appears to have prevailed. Resident Late Woodland groups, probably ancestral to the historic Algonkian tribes of this area, and as yet little known from archaeological remains, seem effectively to have barred Owasco settlement, but not influences, again primarily of ceramic character. These facts suggest the possibility of hostile relationships between the Owasco groups and their neighbors to west and east, with the capture of women potters, and an explanation of the fortified settlements of middle and late Owasco times in New York and southern Ontario.

Owasco occupation was slight and deviant in northern New York. Indeed, the Pillar Point site in Jefferson County (Skh. 1-1) (Figure 4, site number 70) shows a closer relationship in most traits to the Pickering Focus in Ontario than to any known Owasco site in New York. To the south of the state, however, the Owasco province extended well down the Susquehanna Valley, apparently as far as the West Branch Valley, and in the Delaware Valley to the vicinity of the Water Gap. All phases of Owasco culture are represented to some degree in this region.

In the Susquehanna Valley from near Binghamton, New York, down at least to the Wyoming Valley of Pennsylvania, early Owasco development had some still unanalyzed relationship with the little-known Clemson's Island culture, apparently the temporal equivalent in this area of the Hunter's Home phase and the beginning of the Carpenter Brook phase in upper New York State. Later Owasco phases were in touch with late prehistoric Delaware and proto-Iroquoian groups in the upper Susquehanna-Delaware Valley region of Pennsylvania and New Jersey.

Site Locations

The geographic range of the Owasco reveals a partiality toward the rugged country of the Glaciated Allegheny Plateau (endpaper map and Figure 4), where the sites occupy a variety of situations. The more numerous camp sites lie mainly along river rifts and the margins of large marshes or lake shallows, like the Wickham 3, Jack's Reef No. 2 and Hunter's Home No. 2 components, and ready access to fishing grounds seems to have been the primary concern. Hamlets and villages were frequently built upon the second terrace of large streams, next above the flood plain on which the planting was done, like the Bates, Castle Creek, Roundtop, Nahrwold No. 1 and Bainbridge sites. Settlement directly on the flood plain, subject to inundation, was also practiced, as shown by numerous sites of small to medium size in the Genesee, Susquehanna and Delaware valleys. The many cache or food-storage pits on these components, which are usually masked by accumulated alluvium, denote, together with the scarcity of artifacts other than pottery, emphasis upon agriculture. Some sites, however, like Levanna, Maxon-Derby and Sackett, were located a considerable distance from any waterway. The relics from these sites testify to a mixed economy, with varying stress. Thus, for example, the Maxon-Derby site appears to have been the agricultural village for the group which spent the summer at the Jack's Reef fishing camp, about three miles distant on the Seneca River.

Chronology

The radiocarbon established recency of the Owasco culture, and the nature of its faunal and floral remains, denote an ecological and climatic environment corresponding to that glimpsed through early historic records, and prevailing into modern times.

A radiocarbon chronological framework for the Owasco culture has been obtained on hearth charcoal samples from eight of the sites (Figure 1). The earliest date from the Roundtop site, A.D. 1070±60 (Y-1534) (page xxiv), closely approximates that from the Maxon-Derby site, which seems securely founded upon the corresponding results of two assays by different laboratories of two samples from separate features, at A.D. 1100 (A.D. 1100±150 years, M-1077, Crane and Griffin, 1962, p. 192; A.D. 1100±100 years, Y-1173, Stuiver, *et al.*, 1963, p. 332). Currently there seems to be an unfilled temporal gap of only 70 years between the Roundtop date and the youngest figure yet obtained for a site of the ancestral Hunter's Home phase, viz., the Portage site, dated at A.D. 1000±75 years. This hiatus, however, is readily bridged by the standard deviation in the two dates.

Sites of the middle Owasco stage show more variation (Figure 1), but the following figures seem the most consistent and agreeable in relation to the whole sequence: Sackett—A.D. 1130±150 years (M-1076) (Crane and Griffin, 1962, p. 192); Snell—A.D. 1156±200 years (M-492) (Crane and Griffin, 1958, p. 1100); O'Neil 4—A.D. 1160±80 years (Y-1278); Bates—A.D. 1190±100 years (Y-1174); (Stuiver, *et al.*, 1963, p. 332).

Only two late Owasco sites, Castle Creek and Nahrwold No. 1, have been radiocarbon-dated. The two Castle Creek site dates conflict mutually and with the Owasco series, being, respectively, it would seem, too early—A.D. 1196±200 years (M-493) (Crane and Griffin, 1958, p. 1100)—and too late—A.D. 1435±200 years (M-179) (Crane, 1956, p. 668). I would guess that the true date for this site lies somewhere between A.D. 1200 and 1300, or within the span of the standard deviations. The Nahrwold No. 1 site date of 1310±95 (I-2399) tends to confirm this estimate (page xxvi).

The chronology of the Owasco developmental sequence, from its roots in late Middle Woodland, Point Peninula and perhaps other cultures, including the Clemson's Island, to the general and widespread stage of its transition into what is usually accepted as the initial stage of eastern Iroquoian culture, viz., the Oak Hill phase, seems therefore to have spanned a period of some 300 years, or between about A.D. 1000 and 1300.

The Owasco People

In determining the physical appearance of the people responsible for the Owasco culture, we are dependent upon a rather small series of some forty skeletons, most of them not especially well preserved. Burials were discovered on only about half the sites, where with one exception, the Sackett village with cemetery areas, they occurred sporadically, in cache pits for the most part. The metrical data (Ritchie, 1936a, pp. 74–75; 1944, pp. 74, 100–1; Ritchie, Lenig and Miller, 1953, p. 15) and the still unpublished results of morphological studies made on the same series by Georg K. Neumann and the writer, indicate a quite consistent group of the Lenapid variety (Neumann, 1952, pp. 23–25), having its closest approximation in our area to the prehistoric Iroquois.

As previously described by the writer, the typical Owasco Indian, man or woman, was of medium stature; had a relatively long, narrow and fairly high skull; a face of medium height and breadth, with medium-high orbits and a moderately broad nose. The bones offer no suggestion of a robust body build; indeed, there is often a marked gracility throughout the skeleton, especially in the case of women (Ritchie, 1951c, p. 137) (Plate 102).

The diseases and injuries suffered by the

Owasco people, as registered on their bones, while not excessive for a primitive group of this kind, include some very rare disorders.

The commonest lesions are those affecting the teeth, and they include caries, which occurred even among young children, root abscesses and alveoloclasia or pyorrhea. Nearly every person was afflicted with dental troubles, chiefly tooth decay, but whether or not this high incidence of caries can be attributed to a diet heavy on starch, is indeterminate, although an etiological relationship is suggested by the relative and absolute rarity of this disease among earlier, non-agricultural groups of the same area.

The pathology of the postcranial skeleton is less extensive, comprising a few mild to moderate cases of osteoarthritis of the spine and joints in older adults of both sexes and two instances in children of a diffuse periostitis or osteoperiostitis suggesting rickets, a nutritional disorder not yet established in prehistoric America.

Of much interest are the skeletons bearing advanced lesions of apparently rare and fatal ailments. At the Clark site on Willow Point, Broome County (Figure 4, site number 76), our excavations unearthed the flexed skeleton of a senile male, evidently of the late Castle Creek phase, with advanced perforating lesions believed to represent the first reported prehistoric instance of multiple myeloma or bone-marrow tumor (Ritchie and Warren, 1932).

A probable case of Pott's disease or tuberculosis of the spine was unearthed by Charles F. Wray from a grave on the Rapp site at Golah, Monroe County (Figure 4, site number 74), pertaining to the early Canandaigua phase. The kyphotic or hunchbacked subject was a male of about forty years of age (Ritchie, 1952, pp. 307–8).

One of the bony plaques found in our Sackett-site explorations has been attributed, again on expert medical authority, to advanced arteriosclerosis affecting the wall of the aorta (Ritchie, 1036a, pp. 67–70).

Minor ossifications, as of costal cartilages, and healed fractures of ribs and long bones, have also been found in the physical remains of Owasco people.

Subsistence Basis

The Owasco is the earliest culture in New York State for which the cultivation of corn, beans, and squash can positively be asserted. Corn has been found on the village sites of every phase; beans and squash are only recently known from the early or Carpenter Brook horizon of this culture, which marks the beginning, so far as we are presently aware, of a diversified economy wherein an accelerating emphasis was accorded hoe tillage of garden crops. This was essentially the Iroquois pattern, and it is abundantly clear that it preceded recognized Iroquois culture by several centuries in our area.

Hunting, fishing and the collecting of wild vegetable foods retained importance in the food quest down to historic times. Earlier Owasco stations yield more hunting equipment than do later ones, and certain contemporaneous camp sites on fishing waters produce most of the angling tackle.

Hunting and Fishing Equipment

Throughout the whole of Owasco times the standard hunting weapon seems to have been the bow and arrow, tipped with a broad, triangular flint point. Earlier specimens are generally the largest and most equilateral, and have a concave or straight base (Plate 92, Figures 1–6, 9), resembling

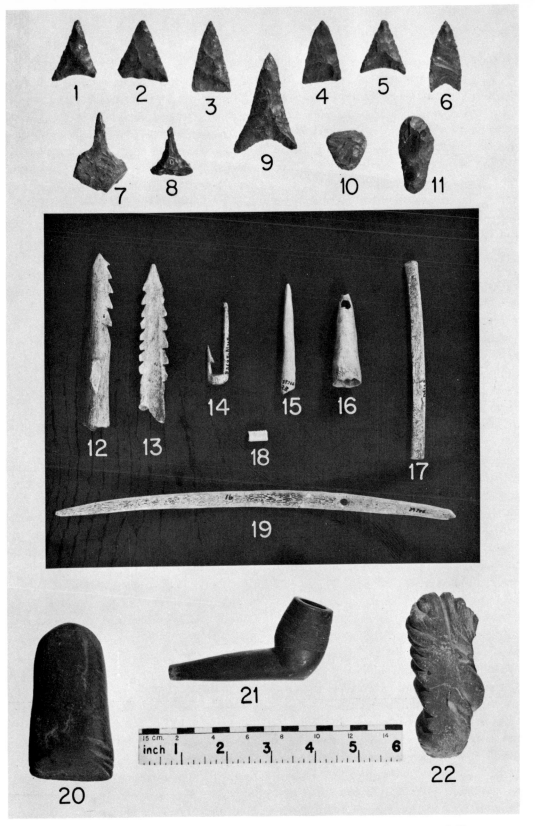

PLATE 92 Artifacts of the Owasco culture. 1–6, 9 Levanna-type arrow points; 7 drill;
8 graver; 10 end scraper; 11 strike-a-light; 12, 13 barbed bone points; 14 barbed
bone fishhook; 15 conical antler arrow point; 16 conized deer phalangeal bone;
17 antler flaker; 18 tubular bone bead; 19 mat-weaving needle made from deer rib;
20 celt, showing some secondary use as a sinewstone; 21 pottery pipe; 22 sinewstone.

a Late Point Peninsula form (Plate 81, Figure 25). The principal modifications of later Owasco times are a decrease in size and a shift toward an isosceles shape, both trends which ultimately transpose the point from the Levanna type of the Owasco (Ritchie, 1961, pp. 31–32) to the Madison type of the Iroquois (ibid., pp. 33–34). Both styles have a very wide distribution over eastern North America in Late Woodland times.

For chipping such flint points, slender, cylindrical, antler tools, some having an expanded top like those of the Iroquois, have been found on most Owasco sites (Plate 92, Figure 17). They suggest indirect percussion as an employed technique. Bone flakers, showing no bruising from the stone hammer, may have served in pressure flaking.

Much less common in the Owasco culture were conical antler and flat bone points, some of the latter barbed or side-notched (Plate 92, Figure 15). Nothing definitely a spear point has been recognized. Some references to the animals hunted appear below.

Dogs of a small breed have been found buried on several of the sites and this animal was no doubt an aid and ally of the hunter.

Fishing, which may have been the work of women, older children and old men, as among the Iroquois, was followed more extensively in earlier than in later times, as judged by the diminishing numbers of appropriate artifacts, except netsinkers, found on sites of different phases.

Fish were captured by spearing with a barbed bone point, fixed to the shaft, and prevailingly of multiple bilateral form with sharp triangular barbs—the "Christmas tree" variety (Plate 92, Figures 12, 13). The multipronged leister may also have

been used, as long, slender, double-pointed bone artifacts occur on most of the sites. Both types of spear were of greatest service in the rifts or rapids of the rivers, along which most of are found in such sites as Wickham and Jack's Reef.

Angling with hook and line is attested by barbless and barbed fishhooks, manufactured from curved pieces of hollow bird bone or from flat sections of mammal long bone, and having a plain, grooved or knobbed shank. The rarer barbed variety is known only from sites of the Carpenter Brook phase in central New York (Plate 92, Figure 14). Like the major barbed bone-point style, the barbed hook has its prototype in the Kipp Island phase of the same region.

The bone gorge, likely a trot-line appurtenance, was not used, but a remarkable trot-line was preserved by carbonization at the Castle Creek site. This unique object consists of a hank of two-strand twisted fishline of Indian-hemp fiber (*Apocynum cannabinum*), equipped with nineteen dropper lines (at indeterminate intervals due to the fragility of the specimen), each carrying a compound hook ingeniously contrived from two hawthorn spines, each measuring about one inch in length (Plate 93, Figures 4, 5). Baited, weighted with a flat sinker, and left overnight on a favorable bottom, such a device could produce a good catch of bullheads, eels, suckers and other coarse fish, of which Indians of all our cultures seemed exceedingly fond, to judge from the bone refuse.

Net fishing, probably with a variety of types which included the seine and set nets anchored in the stream or lake with flat notched pebble sinkers, was practiced throughout Owasco times, indeed, apparently over the entire span of Indian occupation from Lamoka to Iroquois. Unfortu-

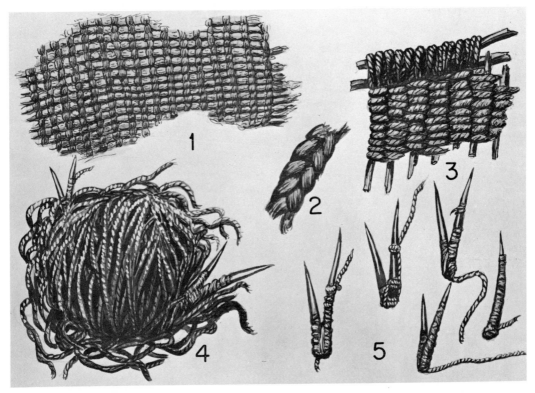

PLATE 93 Carbonized specimens from the Castle Creek site, Broome Co., N.Y. Owasco culture. 1 probable fragment of bag of twined woven basswood bast; 2 braided selvage of the same material; 3 portion of very unusual twined basketry with split-twig foundation and twisted-cord weft of Indian-hemp fiber; 4 trot-line of Indian-hemp fiber with dropper lines and fishhooks; 5 compound fishhooks made from hawthorn spines tied to dropper lines. Photograph courtesy of Foster Disinger, Binghamton, N.Y.

nately, we have no clue, not even a pottery imprint, to the character of Owasco nets.

Vegetable Foods and Their Storage

The dietary of the Owasco folk included both wild and cultivated vegetal foods, some vestiges of which are preserved to us by charring. In the first category were acorns, hickory nuts, butternuts, walnuts, hazelnuts, hawthorn apples, cherries and plums. There were doubtless many others. Cultigens, so far found and identified, com-

prised maize of both flour (*Zea mays amylacea*) and flint (*Zea mays indurata*) types, found on some sites of all phases, and beans (*Phaseolus vulgaris*), squash (*Cucurbita pepo*) and gourds (*C. pepo*, var. *ovifera*).

Surviving implements of hoe tillage include stone hoes probably of two varieties, much the rarer one of elongate, true hoe-shape; the other disciform, with chipped or ground notches. Variously known as net sinkers and "pot covers," this tool with worn edges is thought by some archaeologists to

279

have been hafted as a hoe. We have also found, on the later sites, hoes made from the palmate sections of elk antler. Antler picks from the Castle Creek site may have been agricultural or pit-digging tools.

Food-storage or cache pits are a common feature of many, but not all, Owasco sites, and they are present in every phase of the culture, although they increase in frequency and size with time. There are two prevalent forms, U-shaped and bell- or bottle-shaped, the latter being more plentiful on the more recent sites. Size range for both is similar, from about three to six and a half feet in depth and three to four feet in oral diameter. The majority measure around three and a half feet in diameter at the top and four to four and a half feet in depth, and usually terminate in a porous level of sand or gravel to insure good drainage. Carbonized traces of a grass and/or bark lining are often found, and it is probable that a bark roofing further protected the contents, stored in the shelled state if corn or beans. The bark has tentatively been identified as hemlock, the grass positively as bluestem (*Andropogon furcatus*, now *A. Gerardi*), which is said to be mold resistant and much used by corn-raising tribes of the Eastern Plains.

When abandoned for storage purposes, presumably because of mold, rodent or insect infestation, these pits provided the convenient and customary receptacles for refuse of all kinds—garbage, ashes from cleaned-out hearths and probably human excreta. They also served quite often as graves, perhaps for winter burial.

Food Preparation

In the preparation of their food the Owasco Indians employed the cylindrical stone pestle, also the flat muller or mealing stone. The former was almost certainly used in the hollow wooden mortar, along with the wooden pestle; the latter on flat to slightly concave stone mortars. Most of the mortars, however, show unmistakable scarring, resulting from crushing, with the stone hammer, burned crystalline rocks to obtain grit tempering for pottery paste.

Spoons made from deer skulls or turkey sternums have been found, also bowls fashioned by smoothing all surfaces of the box-turtle carapace. That wooden bowls and spoons were in common use, as among the Iroquois, cannot be doubted.

Cooking was accomplished by roasting or baking over beds of heated stones and by boiling in clay pots, described below (page 290).

Fire was created at will by means of that old device, several times referred to, the flint striker and iron-pyrites anvil. A specialized strike-a-light of trianguloid form is common on many Owasco sites (Plate 92, Figure 11).

Settlement Pattern

Chiefly as the result of our recent settlement-pattern studies, considerable data on this aspect of Owasco life are now in hand, and they will constitute an important part of the final detailed report on these investigations, currently in preparation. Very succinctly, Owasco habitation sites consist of camp, hamlet and village components, the first ranging in area from less than one thousand square feet to more than half an acre, in the case of much frequented fishing spots, for example, Jack's Reef on the Seneca River, and the Wickham and adjacent components along the Oneida River at Brewerton. The Jack's Reef site was almost certainly related, as a summer fishing camp, to the large inland Maxon-Derby site presently to be described (page 281).

Camp sites, some buried under the silt,

are also known from alluvial river flats, on the margins of large marshes, and in improbable places high in the rugged hill country of the Allegheny Plateau Province. One, at least, of the latter seems to represent a workshop of extraordinary character (Ritchie, 1938b; 1944, pp. 90, 94). Others were used by fishing, hunting or food collecting parties from the larger, more permanent settlements.

Post-mold patterns of dwellings or other structures are unknown for camp sites, not for want of searching, but likely due to use there of temporary flimsy shelters.

Village sites also exhibit a considerable size range from approximately one to three acres, and unlike most camp sites, their situation is on relatively high, well-drained ground, often a sand-and-gravel knoll, either along a stream or a mile or more distant from a major waterway. Cache pits, hearths, burned stone platforms, post-mold imprints of houses and sometimes stockade lines and burials are present on these sites.

Hamlets, less well known through excavation, resemble village sites in miniature. The Bates component, outlined below on page 285, is a classic example.

The house form of the Owasco culture shows considerable variation both in size and shape, and it seems evident that there was less uniformity in this regard than can be adduced from our limited evidence for any other culture in New York State. The reasons behind this variability are not yet clear, but the forms themselves will receive summary description in the following pages.

Like their immediate predecessors of the Hunter's Home phase, early Owasco village sites were not palisaded, according to current evidence. Levanna and Maxon-Derby were open towns, and as such sharply contrast with the later settlements. It would look as though the onset of hostilities, either between Owasco communities or with alien neighbors, or perhaps both, did not develop in our area until middle Owasco times, and could be correlated with the larger and more numerous components, reflecting a rapidly multiplying population, known now to depend heavily on horticulture for their subsistence.

According to an ingenious hypothesis by Witthoft, this situation may have its explanation in the shift of emphasis in the basic economy from the hunting activities, dominated by men, to horticulture, the role of women. When the latter became the main food producers, men were released from hunting game and turned, as an extension of the probably ages-old blood feud, to the greater predation of warfare (Witthoft, 1959a, pp. 32–34).

An alternative explanation might be found in the more conventional argument of felt pressures developing from accelerating demographic demands upon available land, tillable with existing technological equipment, and, especially, game resources, necessary not only for protein food but for hides, furs, bones and antlers used in clothing and implements. The natural increase in game supply may well not have kept pace with human reproduction.

A more comprehensive picture of Owasco village communities may be formed from the following vignettes of the sites most recently excavated under the settlement-pattern project already referred to, and the subject of a subsequent major report.

The Maxon-Derby Site
(Bwv. 13-3) (Figure 4, site number 83)

This site, the largest known village of the early or Carpenter Brook phase, is located a mile east of Jordan, Onondaga County, on a farm owned by Carroll and Elwyn Maxon and operated by John Derby. Excavations by the New York State Museum and Science Service were conducted there by the writer in 1959 and 1960, through the kind permission of these gentlemen.

An area of two acres on the gentle south slope of a low ridge, bordered on the south by a small spring-fed brook, is dark with a veneer of midden material eight to fifteen inches in depth. No evidence of fortification could be found. Charred corn was present in hearths and small storage pits.

Seven house floors were uncovered in whole or part, representing essentially one model in greatly varying sizes. The floor outline can best be described as oblong with rounded corners. The smallest examples were nearly square. House C, measuring twenty by twenty-three feet, with a doorway facing west, appeared to have been partitioned into four trapezoidal-shaped sections, each with a hearth and other features.

In the next size category were two structures, thirty-four feet in length by twenty-three and twenty-five feet in breadth, respectively. Doorway openings faced various directions (Plate 94). Both these features either underlay or were superimposed upon (the relative ages were indeterminate from the evidence) the two largest houses, with dimensions of sixty-one by twenty-five feet for house A and sixty by twenty-seven feet for house E. Both had doorway openings at the east end (Figure 9).

All four of the major houses seem to have been several times repaired and enlarged, and house A may also have had one or more vestibules in the doorway area, presumably for the storage of firewood, food and gear, as in some of the Iroquois longhouses.

In contrast to the latter, however, the fireplaces, small basin-shaped depressions, were arranged along one or both long sides of the Maxon-Derby houses, rather than down the center, and the usual Iroquois bed-lines could not be traced in these otherwise prototypic Iroquois longhouses of early Owasco provenience.

The Maxon-Derby site shows evidence of occupation over a number of years, with considerable shifting, as well as modification, of the dwelling units. These were probably arbor-roofed structures of bark, with a pole supporting framework, imprints of which varied from two and a half to three inches in diameter and from four to nine inches in depth below plow-line (Plate 95). The bluntly pointed saplings, spaced six to ten inches apart, must have been "screwed" into the ground in the spring of the year when abundant moisture softened the otherwise compact clay-and-gravel glacial soil. There was, as usual, no evidence that any poles had been set into dug holes.

At least ten houses had been erected on the site, and our estimate of the probable total population at any one time approximates 200 to 250 people.

The food remains, consisting of carbonized corn, wild plants, fish, birds and mammals, will be reported on in the full account of the excavations.

The Maxon-Derby site, occupied around A.D. 1100 (page 275), has a close parallel in most respects in the Miller site near Toronto, Ontario, Canada, excavated by Walter Kenyon of the Royal Ontario Museum, and to be described by him. Radiocarbon-dated at approximately A.D. 1127, this component of the Pickering Focus contained five oblong houses, ranging in size from thirty-eight by twenty feet to sixty by twenty-three feet, nearly identical with the two larger varieties at the Maxon-

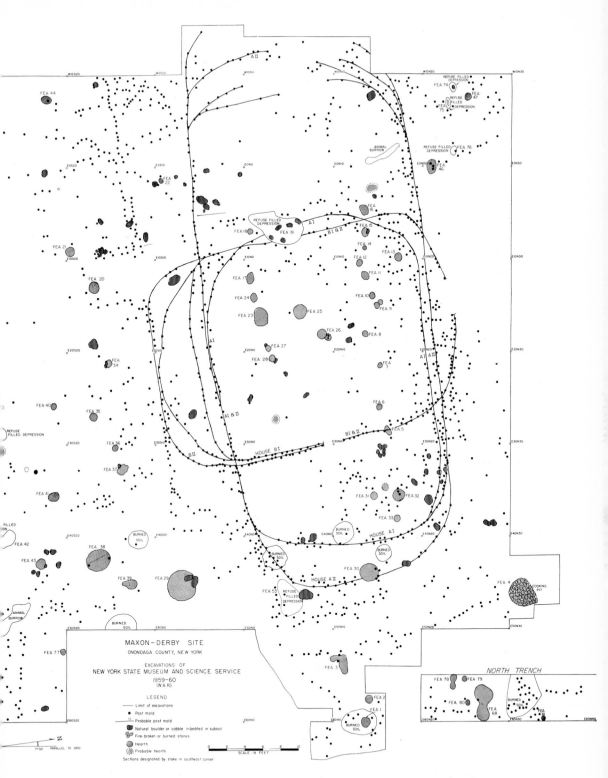

Figure 9 Portion of excavated area at the Maxon-Derby site, showing overlapping house floors A and B, hearths and other features. Note evidence of several stages of construction in both houses. Carpenter Brook phase, Owasco culture.

PLATE 94 Excavation of small rectanguloid house floor on the Maxon-Derby site, Onondaga Co., N.Y. See plan on Figure 9, house B.

PLATE 95 Pole framework of arbor-roofed longhouse, the medicine lodge of the Seine River band of Chippewa or Ojibway of the Rainy River district of Ontario, 1934. Photograph courtesy of the National Museum of Canada.

Derby village. The Miller site, however, only about half the size of its New York counterpart, or one acre in extent, was encompassed within a roughly circular, single wall of palisades. In this respect it corresponded with the Bates site, now to be described.

The Bates Site
(Grn. 1) (Figure 4, site number 85)

On the broad, level, sandy terrace of glacial outwash, between the mouth of Genegantslet Creek and the Chenango River, about thirty feet above the water, is situated an instructive component of the late middle stage of development of the Owasco culture, radiocarbon-dated to around A.D. 1190. The spot is some two miles south of Greene, Chenango County, on the farm of the late Melvin Bates, who generously allowed our excavations of 1957 and 1958, despite a new seeding of alfalfa.

An area of less than half an acre was involved in the habitation complex, which consisted of an oval enclosure ninety-five by fifty feet, containing a large dwelling structure, a single burial, and numerous pits and hearths, which continued outside along the terrace front facing the river (Figure 10).

The stockade had consisted of a single line of posts, of indeterminate height, about three inches in diameter, set five to ten inches deep below plowline and three to eighteen inches apart. In these respects it closely resembled the somewhat earlier Miller-site feature in Ontario and the Iroquois fortifications on the Kelso and Getman sites of the early prehistoric Iroquois period in New York (pages 305, 314). To become effective as a barrier against man, and most other predatory mammals, the wall posts would require uniting, probably

by means of interwoven withes or sheets of bark, into a tight, fence-like wall. Vines and bast ropes were also probably employed in holding the units together. This type of palisade differs materially from that usually envisioned and described, but our evidence from the several sites mentioned unequivocally denotes it the prevailing form until very late prehistoric and historic times in our area. The introduction of the iron trade ax in the early seventeenth century made possible the felling and shaping of the larger tree trunks.

The single dwelling protected by the stockade at the Bates site resembled, in outline and the character of the revealing post molds, the oblong house type of the Maxon-Derby site of about a century earlier. From a primary unit measuring thirty-eight by twenty-two feet, it seems to have grown by four successive extensions, into a final longhouse-like habitation seventy-three feet long by twenty-five feet wide (Figure 10). In every stage of expansion the doorways opened to the southwest upon a street-like corridor. A similar open lane lay to the rear. No interior appurtenances can with assurance be attributed to this multiple feature, although hearths, cache pits, and puzzling small arcs of post molds are numerous in the interior area.

This hamlet, the best-known representative of its kind, was probably founded by a small group burgeoning from some larger settlement in this region. Growth obviously took place, and the approximately eighty large food-storage pits (sixty-one were excavated, an unknown number destroyed, together with several graves, by bulldozing the terrace face) attest to a residency of at least several years for a maximum population that could scarcely have exceeded fifty individuals.

Studies of the animal-food remains, in

285

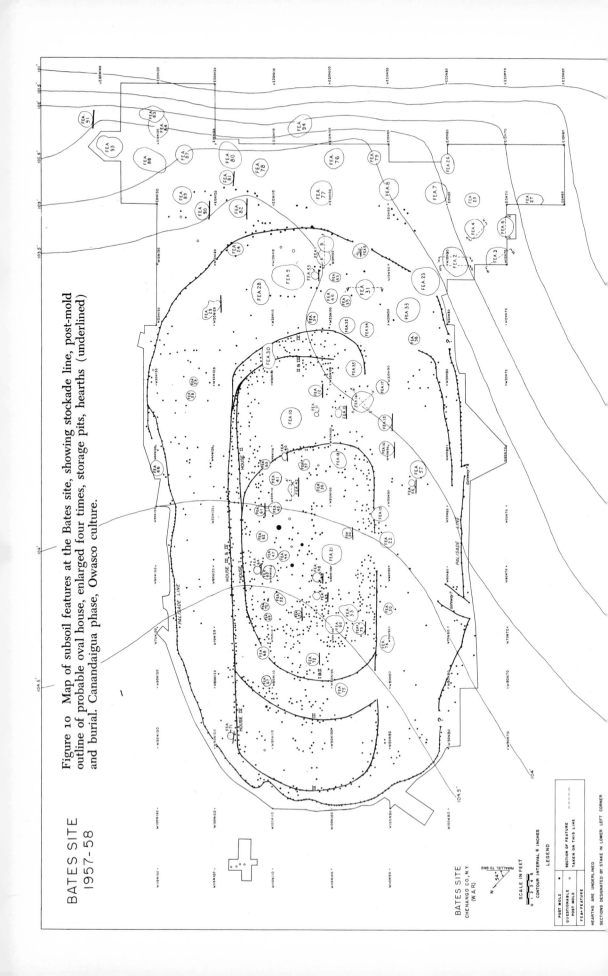

BATES SITE
1957-58

Figure 10 Map of subsoil features at the Bates site, showing stockade line, post-mold outline of probable oval house, enlarged four times, storage pits, hearths (underlined) and burial. Canandaigua phase, Owasco culture.

which bones of the white-tailed deer greatly predominate, point to a year-round settlement—the bucks being fall and winter kills, the fawns taken in summer, the shad netted in the spring.

The Sackett Site
(Can. 1) (Figure 4, site number 73)

To study further the small circular house type of the Owasco culture which had been found there in his original excavations (Ritchie, 1936a, pp. 41, 43), the writer returned in 1959 to the Sackett site with a small field party from the New York State Museum and Science Service. Three previously unexamined areas totaling twenty-six hundred square feet were explored through the courtesy of Dr. and Mrs. James O. Ault.

Located on Arsenal Hill, on the western limits of the city of Canandaigua, about one and a half miles northwest of the foot of Canandaigua Lake, the area of occupation covers over three acres, making the Sackett site one of the largest known Owasco villages. The heaviest refuse mantle invests the portion which had been enclosed within a roughly ellipsoidal ditch, 343 by 202 feet, triangular in cross section, seven to eleven feet in breadth and two to three feet in depth, dug by the Indians as part of the village defenses. Earth from the ditch was probably used to support a row of interior stockade posts, set upon but not into the ground. A series of outlying ditches suggests that the Sackett village had been expanded at least once with the growth of population.

As in the first excavation, a large and confusing number of post molds was uncovered, resoluble in part into four reasonably distinct and an equal number of indefinite house patterns, pertaining to circu-

lar or oval structures, twelve to fourteen feet across. Near-central hearths in shallow basin-shaped depressions were found in all, while in some an inner ring of post molds showed, probably, that a narrow bench had extended around the interior (Figure 11).

This newly acquired evidence confirms our earlier findings at the site of small, wigwam-like, single-family dwellings (Plate 96). Insubstantial and frequently replaced, these probably mat- or bark-covered lodges have left their overlapping pole prints in every portion of the site examined. Calculations, based upon evidence to be discussed in the final settlement-pattern report, suggest a maximum population for this village at any one time of 300 to 350 persons, the largest figure yet postulated for an Owasco town.

This population was sustained primarily by an abundance of corn and beans. Fish and game animals, especially the deer, were still of much importance, as attested by the artifacts and bones, the analysis of which will be included in the above-mentioned report.

Clothing and Personal Decoration

While there are no direct clues to the manner of dress of the Owasco Indians, we may suppose that, as among their predecessors who have left us similar artifacts, the clothing was of tanned leather and peltry. Tools for the preparation of skins and hides include bone scrapers or "beaming" tools for the dehairing of deer hides, made from deer metapodial and innominate bones and the tibia of the bear; simple flint end scrapers in a variety of shapes— round, ovate, trianguloid (Plate 92, Figure 10); side scrapers from retouched flakes; and sinewstones with single or multiple grooves, presumably for preparing sinew

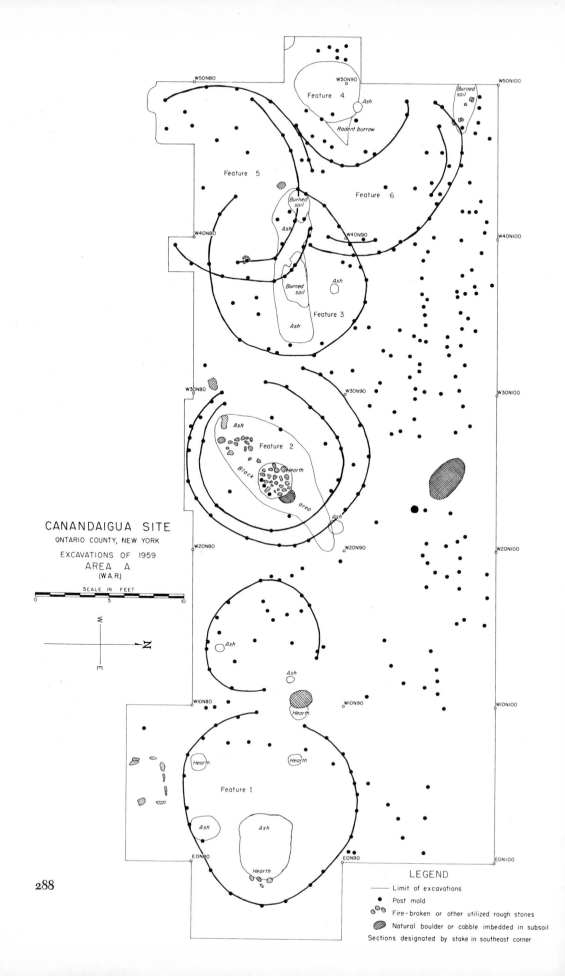

CANANDAIGUA SITE

ONTARIO COUNTY, NEW YORK

EXCAVATIONS OF 1959
AREA A
(W.A.R.)

SCALE IN FEET

0   5   10

W
N
E

Feature 4

Feature 5

Feature 6

Feature 3

Feature 2

Feature 1

Burned soil

Burned soil

Burned soil

Ash

Ash

Ash

Ash

Ash

Ash

Ash

Ash

Ash

Ash

Hearth

Hearth

Hearth

Hearth

Hearth

Hearth

Black area

Rodent burrow

LEGEND

—— Limit of excavations
•   Post mold
🌀   Fire-broken or other utilized rough stones
▨   Natural boulder or cobble imbedded in subsoil
Sections designated by stake in southeast corner

288

PLATE 96 Summer wigwam of Seine River band of Chippewa or Ojibway of the Rainy River district of Ontario, 1934. Covering is elm bark. Photograph courtesy of the National Museum of Canada.

thread (Plate 92, Figure 22). No bone needles have been found, save for the flat, curved type probably for sewing rush mats (Plate 92, Figure 19), but bone awls of some twenty-four varieties are known (Ritchie, 1944, pp. 343–44).

Personal ornaments were simple and relatively few, except that on certain sites (e.g., Sackett and Castle Creek) there was an abundance of deer phalangeal bones, with detached base and apex perforated by drilling or notching, some ground to cone shape, and thought to represent fringe bangles for the deerskin garments (Plate 92,

Figure 16). Certain of these, particularly the line-ornamented or nicked-edge specimens, may have been elements of the cup-and-pin game.

Necklace components consist of short, tubular, bird-bone beads (Plate 92, Figure 18); longer tubes, often with incised decoration, from sections of mammal long bone; grooved or perforated canine teeth of bear, wolf and dog; and small, round, oval or rectanguloid, flat, stone or fresh-water clam-shell pendants, variously perforated, some having incised radial lines.

Rather handsome, long-bone pins with

Figure 11 Portion of excavated area of 1959 on the Sackett or Canandaigua site, showing circular house floor patterns. Canandaigua phase, Owasco culture.

engraved expanded heads have been found on the Castle Creek site. Two crude three-tooth bone or antler combs, forerunners of an early Iroquois type, have been dug up, and there are equally rare examples of human bone ornaments cut from femoral head, skull or mandible; and ground hematite paintstones.

Tools, Textiles and Basketry

For felling trees and hewing, shaping and finishing wood, doubtless widely employed for bows, arrows, tool handles, utensils, and many other purposes, including perhaps dugout boats, the Owasco culture contains a variety of stone and bone implements. These embrace rectanguloid and trianguloid celts (Plate 92, Figure 20) and plano-convex adzes, usually well made and polished from hard rocks; bar and chisel forms, closely resembling Iroquois styles (some of these may have been weapons); antler sleeves or sockets, presumably for small celts, and diagnostic for the Owasco culture; antler chisels and wedges; and beaver incisors with gouge- or chisel-shaped incisal edge.

Serving a wider category of purposes were chipped-flint drills of several styles—with trianguloid, T-shaped or Y-shaped base; boring or more likely graving tools with very delicate, fine points, about one-quarter to three-quarters inch in length, chipped on a rough flake (Plate 92, Figures 7, 8), and characteristic of all phases of Owasco culture; a good assortment of hammerstones—unpitted pebble with battered ends or used over the whole surface to produce a roughly spherical or faceted exterior, disciform with beveled edge, and simple oval bipitted or rectanguloid with multiple (four to six) bold depressions, another characteristic Owasco tool form;

anvilstones; and abrading stones of tabular shape with incised or rubbed faces, apparently for shaping and sharpening awls and other bone tools, and of stationary boulder type with grooved cavities, probably for grinding and sharpening stone cutting tools.

Through the rare accident of carbonization, a few remnants of textiles and basketry were preserved on the Castle Creek site. These exceptionally instructive items include fragments, probably of bags, of twined woven bast, provisionally identified as basswood fiber (Plate 93, Figure 1); a braided selvage fragment of the same material (Plate 93, Figure 2); bits of very unusual twined basketry having a split-twig foundation and twisted-cord weft of Indian-hemp fiber (*Apocynum cannabinum*) (Plate 93, Figure 3); and a section of coiled basketry with stiff twig foundation and cord-binding thread of Indian hemp.

Pottery

While doubtless the artistic sensibilities of the Owasco people were expressed in basketry, leather, wood and other perishables, our best index of their aesthetic craftsmanship is preserved in the ceramics —pottery and pipes. Pottery, as the most abundant relic, is present in varying amounts on all camp as well as village components. Sherds exhibit in their fracture planes no evidence of coil or fillet construction, such as characterizes the pottery of the Point Peninsula tradition. Rather, Owasco vessels appear to have been modeled by the paddle-and-anvil method. The paste is always grit-tempered, becoming finer with the passage of time. The interior surface is smooth, the exterior cord, sometimes fabric-impressed, or check-stamped in the later phases. The surface treatment was applied by malleation with a cord-wrapped, fabric-wrapped, or carved wooden paddle. The lip shape is flat, and in the earlier vessels often wide or thickened, in the later ones sometimes sharply splayed outward. Owasco vessels are prevailingly large, having capacities of from two to twelve gallons. Caldrons or soup kettles of this size suggest a numerous and sedentary people.

In the Carpenter Brook phase the pot bodies were elongate, the bases conoidal and the rims slightly everted (Plate 97). While this form persisted during the Canandaigua phase (Plate 98), there was a tendency for the vessel form to become progressively more globular, the base semiconoidal, and the rim more outflaring; and the first straight, and even channeled, collars, some with weak rim points, appeared. In the Castle Creek phase the vessel shape, while still usually higher than wide, had a rounded base and a well-differentiated rim area, often collared and castellated (Plate 99, Figures 1–3).

It should again be remarked that Owasco collars were not appliquéd and were not genetically related to the collared forms of the Late Point Peninsula (pages 230, 239).

In Owasco pottery the decorations are confined to the shoulder, rim, collar if pres-

PLATE 97 Restored pottery vessel from the Angel site, Mt. Upton, Otsego Co., N.Y. Early Owasco culture. Horizontal and platted designs in cord-on-cord technique. Photograph courtesy of the Rochester Museum of Arts and Sciences.

PLATE 98 Restored pottery
vessel from the Lakeside Park
site, Auburn, Cayuga Co., N.Y.
Canandaigua phase, Owasco
culture. Wickham Corded
Punctate type.

ent, lip, and upper inner-rim area, and they are almost invariably executed with a cord-wrapped stick or paddle edge. The impressed technique dominated throughout the life span of Owasco ceramics, being continuous from Point Peninsula into the Oak Hill phase of Iroquois. Decorative designs consist, for the most part, of simple linear motifs—plats, herringbones, and horizontal, vertical and oblique arrangements.

In the early or Carpenter Brook phase the decoration is characteristically laid over the cord malleation, which extends upward to the lip, to continue a Late Point Peninsula cord-on-cord technique (Plate 78, Figure 21; Plate 97). In subsequent developments the shoulder and rim areas were smoothed to receive the embellishment (Plate 98). This ornamentation, in the Cas-

tle Creek phase, includes use of appliquéd rim beading, nodes and bosses, and there is one example of the use of highly stylized human figures (Ritchie, 1944, Plate 15). In this late phase also, incising is present on the rim, but not the collar, principally of two types (Castle Creek Incised Neck and Bainbridge Collared Incised). A new category, the Bainbridge Notched Lip, makes its appearance toward the close of the phase. Most of the ceramic traits of this phase foreshadow those of the following Oak Hill phase of early Iroquois.

Typological descriptions of Owasco pottery and seriation charts for the major sites excavated by the writer up to 1948 are given in Ritchie and MacNeish, 1949, pp. 107–20. Similar data for later excavated components are presented in the site re-

1

2

3

4

PLATE 99 Pottery vessels and antler maskette of the Owasco culture. 1 intact vessel of Castle Creek Punctate type, height 3¾ inches; 2 restored pot of Owasco Corded Collar type; 3 restored jar of Castle Creek Beaded type, check-stamped malleated body, height 21 inches; 4 antler maskette, length 1¼ inches. 1–3 from Castle Creek site, Broome Co., N.Y., Castle Creek phase; 4 from Snell site, Montgomery Co., N.Y., Canandaigua phase. Photographs 1 and 3 courtesy of Foster Disinger, Binghamton, N.Y.; photograph 2 courtesy of the Rochester Museum of Arts and Sciences.

ports. Four aberrant types found on the Snell site in eastern New York are also described elsewhere (Ritchie, Lenig and Miller, 1953, pp. 18–21; Ritchie, n.d.).

Travel and Trade

The location of a number of the Owasco villages at quite some distance from navigable waterways suggests that, in addition to such transportation, possibly by this time including the bark canoe, overland woods trails had become established, linking sites frequented by the group at various seasons of the year, as well as neighboring communities. This seems to have been the beginning of the well-known Iroquois travel pattern, so foreign to the earlier cultural groups of our region who made the water routes their travel and trade channels.

With respect to trade, too, the Owasco Indians stand apart from most of their predecessors and closer to the prehistoric Iroquois, in manifesting little interest or activity in trade. The general impression conveyed by archaeology is of a very provincial, self-sufficient and locally orientated people, primarily concerned with the day-by-day routine of securing a living by means already discussed, with ever greater dependence on farming, hence a more stable village life.

Warfare

The rather idyllic vision of peace and plenty evoked by this description is not entirely sustained by some of the evidence, indirect, as afforded by the growing tendency from middle Owasco times onward toward stronger fortifications, and directly by the mute testimony of the arrow-riddled corpses found at the Sackett site (Ritchie,

1936a, pp. 56–61). The physical characteristics of these six adult men, ranging in age from about nineteen to fifty, and bearing from one to eleven arrow points, many imbedded in the bones, indicated, along with the type of points which slew them, probable relationship to the Owasco group. Although other possible explanations have been considered—criminals executed by their own people, human sacrifice in connection with some esoteric rite, etc. (Ritchie, 1936a, pp. 62–65)—the war-victim explanation is perhaps the most cogent.

Games

Besides the game of war, which in the next, Iroquoian, epoch was to assume such sinister proportions, first of an internecine, later of an intertribal or international character, the Owasco villagers seem to have found amusement in the more innocent pastimes of playing the cup-and-pin game, with perforated deer phalanges and bone or wooden awl-like pins, and of dancing to the chink of the turtle-shell rattle. Both the box and painted turtle yielded shells for the only known musical instrument of this culture.

Smoking Pipes

As a form of relaxation and enjoyment, smoking must have figured largely in the customary manners of the Owasco people. In their pipes, too, as in their pottery, this folk expressed an artistry of form and decoration of a fairly high order among the prehistoric groups of the Northeast.

Pipes were created in two media, clay and stone, the latter quite rare and confined to the early phase. Made from steatite or chlorite schist, in obtuse-angle

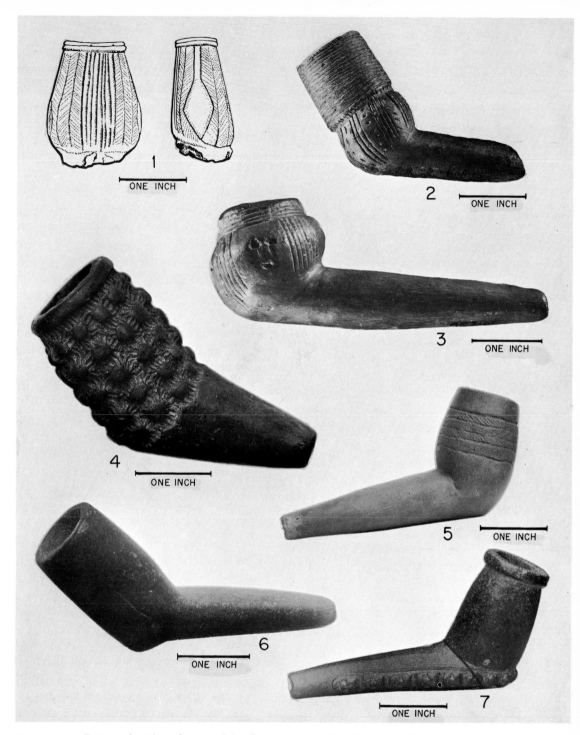

PLATE 100 Pottery (1–6) and stone (7) elbow pipes of the Owasco culture. 1 bowl decorated in *pointillé* work; 2, 3 incised and punctate ornamentation; 4 decorated with mammillary bosses; 5 *pointillé* work; 6 plain; 7 of steatite with row of human faces on either side of stem. 1–3 Castle Creek phase; 4, 7 Carpenter Brook phase; 5, 6 Canandaigua phase. Provenience: 1 Castle Creek site, Broom Co.; 2 Throop, Cayuga Co.; 3 Bainbridge site, Chenango Co.; 4 Hilltop site, Delaware Co.; 5, 6 Lakeside Park site, Cayuga Co.; 7 Bettysburg, near Afton, Chenango Co.

295

form, most stone pipes were plain, but at least one example has been found carrying a row of human-face effigies along either side of the stem (Plate 100, Figure 7).

Pipe forms in clay range from straight (not tubular, see page 252) to nearly right-angular. As a whole, the group may be assigned to the obtuse-angle elbow category. Straight and slightly bent varieties characterize the Carpenter Brook phase and have their prototypes in the Hunter's Home manifestation. They are plain for the most part, but one notable exception, of which both straight and bent examples exist, is ornamented with mammillary bosses, depicting, perhaps, an ear of corn (Plate 100, Figure 4; cf. Plate 87, Figure 22). Stem shapes of the early period are frequently oval, rectanguloid or subtriangular in cross section; some are round.

For the middle or Canandaigua phase, a much larger variety of decorations is known, although plain pipes are still common. Some of the ornate bowls seem to reproduce miniature pots, with their prevailing ceramic styles. Now also occur climbing effigies of the tree frog and salamander. Stems are sometimes short and thick, and by now, frequently round in section (Plate 100, Figures 5, 6).

Pipes of the Castle Creek phase portray much imagination. New bowl shapes appear and new decorations, including use of the human face and extremely fine *pointillé* work (Plate 100, Figures 1–3). There is both in pipe and pot styling an efflorescence signifying an obvious break with tradition in the industrial products presumed to pertain, respectively, to men and women. Development in this phase attained its climax for Owasco culture. This was to pass into a post-climactic or epigenous stage of transition into the Oak Hill phase, next to be described.

Burial Customs

It has been stated that the final elements of the mortuary ritualism of the Early and Middle Woodland cultures disappeared from our area during the Hunter's Home phase (page 230). Owasco burial customs, as far as known, mark a return to the secularism of Archaic times, and set the pattern for Iroquois practices up to the historic period, when change again occurred.

Regular cemeteries are the exception on Owasco sites, most burials being randomly dispersed in old cache pits scattered over the site. At the Sackett site, however, two well-separated cemetery areas were found and others probably exist. These may reflect family or even clan separation, as in the Iroquois towns. It should be added that, since several of the Owasco sites have yielded no graves, and the numbers found in cache pits on others seem too few for the size of the site, we may still be due for some surprises in this aspect of Owasco culture.

Burials, with few exceptions, were simple flexed interments in the flesh, without definite orientation (Plate 101, Figures 1, 2, 4). One sitting and one semiseated burial were found at Castle Creek (Plate 101, Figure 3). Young infants were as a rule extended. Grave goods were the rare exception, consisting of an occasional pottery vessel with a child, or a pipe with an adult. Personal ornaments found with some skeletons support the belief that the body was buried fully clothed, wrapped and tied in a robe or mat.

Social and Political Organization

In groping for clues to the nature of the socio-political organization of Owasco com-

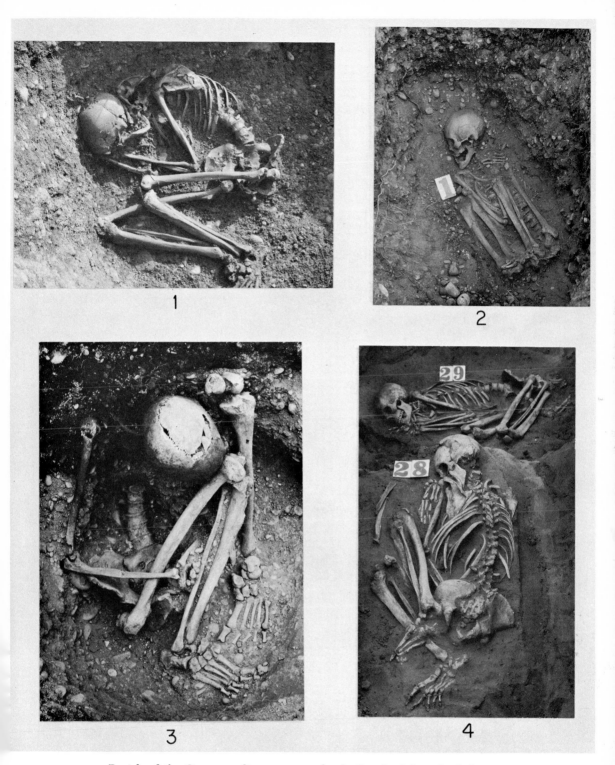

PLATE 101   Burials of the Owasco culture. 1, 2, 4 closely flexed adult male skeletons; 3 burial in sitting posture of adult male. Provenience: 1, 3 Castle Creek site, Broome Co.; 2 Palmer site, Willow Point, Broome Co.; 4 Sackett site, Ontario Co. Photographs 1 and 3 courtesy of Foster Disinger, Binghamton, N.Y.; photographs 2 and 4 courtesy of the Rochester Museum of Arts and Sciences.

munities, we find a dimly lit vista. Further planned field investigations under the settlement-plan program may provide some illumination. The data so far gathered and analyzed will be discussed in the forthcoming report already referred to. Very briefly, it is now amply perspicuous that in the New York State area the inception and growth of sedentary community life based primarily upon an agricultural economy, accompanied, *pari passu,* the development of Owasco culture. We have demonstrated that this culture contained all the essential elements of the succeeding Iroquois culture in the same area, wherein the latter largely emerged from the former. The social and political aspects of Iroquois culture at the dawn of the historic period are known, and by inference from archaeological data, some of which will presently be adduced, may be projected backward into prehistoric stages of this culture.

Since these stages, in respect to economy, settlement patterns and other primary characteristics, are closely paralleled by their obvious antetypes in Owasco culture, it would seem reasonable, by extrapolation, to suspect similar correlatives in social organization, at least. We may therefore hypothesize an Owasco society in which the influence of women as the cardinal food producers had resulted in matrilineal descent and, in certain of the villages, in matriolocal residence, perhaps already in clan groups, in communal dwellings of longhouse type.

Extensions to political structuring are more difficult to infer. Iroquois tribalism may well have been foreshadowed in the Owasco villages, but tribal federation probably lay in the future, although some of its etiological factors—rapid population expansion, accelerating sessility, pressures of various kinds both from within and without

—seem to have had their genesis in Owasco times.

Religious Concepts

While the mortuary aspects of Owasco culture may have been freed from the religio-magical traditions of earlier cultures and brought under secular control, it is likely that other religious ideologies flourished in the culture. Evidence in support of this assumption is admittedly meager and equivocal.

The most intriguing find of this character was made by the writer on Carpenter Brook, Onondaga County (Figure 4, site number 81), in 1946, where a unique, apparently ceremonial, pottery dump was uncovered along the bank. Among the sherds of some two hundred vessels of the early phase were a very few associated artifacts, one of singular character being a virtually anatomically perfect, modeled clay phallic effigy; all were intermixed with animal bones; predominantly of the black bear. The total circumstances of the find seem best explained on the hypothesis that the Owasco group here had practiced the ancient and widely diffused institution among boreal hunting peoples of bear ceremonialism (Ritchie, 1947, 1947a). The attitude of reverence or great respect accorded the bear, requiring a prescribed ritualism in the killing, eating and disposal of the remains, emanates from the belief that this animal was under the spiritual control of a supernatural power which regulated the supply of this and perhaps other game to the hunters. To avoid offense to this spiritual keeper of the game, thus assuring a continued food resource, was the object of the ritualized behavior (Hallowell, 1926).

The occurrence among the Munsee-Mahican people of our general area of bear

This process of "upstreaming" or the application of the "direct historical approach" to archaeological data is of very limited service in our area, particularly with regard to the Algonkian-speaking peoples of eastern and southern New York, because of the rapidity of their acculturation following European contacts in the early seventeenth century, and since so much of the region involved in these first contacts has been intensively settled by modern civilization with consequent loss of the archaeological record (Ritchie, 1958, pp. 7–8).

Iroquois culture, as portrayed to us by archaeology, ethnohistory and ethnology, affords a number of distinguishing criteria, some surviving from prehistoric times in the ground, among which the ceramic category of pottery and smoking pipes is a particularly sensitive register of the events of cultural change and contact.

Some characteristic traits of Iroquois culture have long been recognized, others postulated and widely accepted (Parker, 1922, pp. 98–151; Wintemberg, 1931, pp. 65–125). With the growth of knowledge of the archaeology of Iroquoia, however, it has become increasingly difficult to delineate the beginnings of a specifically Iroquois cultural horizon, either in the western nucleus of southeastern Ontario or in the eastern center in New York, on which attention will be focused in the following account. In the latter area, as previously remarked (pages 272, 273), the Oak Hill phase has more or less arbitrarily been considered to depict nascent Iroquois culture.

In Situ *Theory*

Until rather recently it has been customary to regard the Iroquois people and their culture as intrusive into the Northeast from a center or centers situated south or southwest of our area (Parker, 1916). Under this hypothesis, agricultural economy, village life, and their related socio-political organization, as found historically among the Iroquois, were traits introduced by these invaders into territory long held by Algonkian-speaking hunting groups (Fenton, 1940, pp. 164–65; Speck, 1945, p. 38). The various migration theories (discussed in Ritchie, 1961a, pp. 27–30) have suffered from the failure of archaeologists to discover any convincing evidence of the postulated group movements into Iroquoia, and, conversely, from the recovery within this area of much new archaeological data which fill in large part the former cultural hiatus by providing intermediary and transitional expressions of culture serving to integrate conventional Iroquois manifestations with antecedent phases. The occurrence in New York and Ontario of the essential elements of Iroquois maize economy and settlement patterns in the Owasco and Pickering phases, respectively, radiocarbon-dated to around A.D. 1100, has unequivocally been demonstrated.

As a result of these determinations, the alternative view of an *in situ* development of Iroquois culture, in its several regional guises, which was propounded by Dr. Richard S. MacNeish (MacNeish, 1952), has found increasing support both in New York and southeastern Ontario. In the latter region, a developmental sequence has been traced through the probably concurrent Glen Meyer and Pickering phases to Uren, Middleport and prehistoric tribal subdivisions of the Neutral-Erie and Huron-Petun (Wright, 1966), and with variations on this basic theme by other investigators (MacNeish, 1952; Ridley, 1954, 1958; Emerson, n.d.).

Extensions from this Canadian nuclear center of developing Iroquois culture took place on the Uren and probably the Middleport horizons, resulting, in my opinion,

PLATE 103 Restored pottery vessel of Sebonac Stamped type from the Conklin site at Aquebogue, Long Island. Height approximately 15 inches. Collected by Charles F. Goddard, Mattituck, N.Y.

in the Oakfield phase of western New York (Plate 104). This phase, and subsequent Iroquoian developments in this subarea of the state, are still under investigation by Dr. Marian E. White of the University of Buffalo (White, 1961, 1967).

THE OAK HILL PHASE

Ceramics

East of the Genesee Valley, in the central, eastern and northern subareas of the state, a synchronous developmental se-

quence, with its roots in the Hunter's Home phase, passed through the Owasco succession, apparently missing from the western part of New York and adjacent Canada, into the Oak Hill phase, as already recounted (pages 272, 301). This phase, the subject of an intensive comparative analysis by Donald Lenig (1965), is predicated upon a horizon having a high predominance of corded-collar vessels, mainly of the Owasco Corded Collar type (Plate 99, Figure 2) and its derivative type, Oak Hill Corded (Plate 105; Plate 106, Figure 1), a pottery spectrum much constricted from the just-preceding ancestral late Castle

PLATE 104 Restored Iroquois pottery vessel from the Oakfield Fort site, Genesee County, N.Y. Oakfield phase. Photograph courtesy of the Rochester Museum of Arts and Sciences.

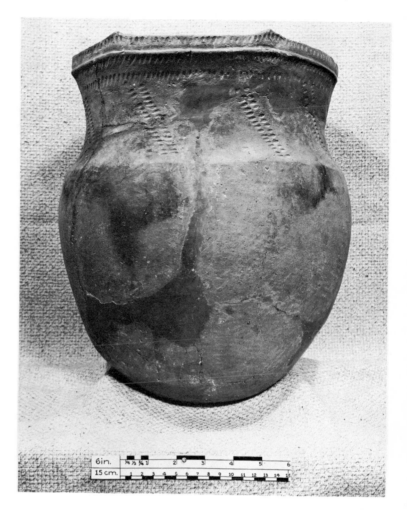

Creek phase. Conversely, Oak Hill pipe styles show an expanded stylistic range, including mostly new varieties, but continuing the development of the Willow Point style of the Castle Creek phase (Plate 100, Figures 2, 3; Plate 107, Figures 1, 2).

The novel pipe styles, nearly all represented only by fragments, include straight-sided, slight to moderately flaring, and barrel-shaped bowls. Decoration, done by incising and punctation, as in the later Iroquois styles, but not by the traditional cord impression of the Owasco pipe-makers, consists of plats composed of parallel horizontal, oblique or vertical lines and dots; chevron, herringbone and rectangular designs. Modeled on the bowl and stem of a few specimens are effigies of the tree frog and salamander, reminiscent of Owasco pipes from the Sackett site.

From the Oak Hill phase, shown by radiocarbon dating to have flourished between approximately A.D. 1300 and 1390, emerged the Chance phase, next to be considered, in which incising as a pottery technique came to replace cord impressing, to produce the same design motifs. It is of some interest to note that the ancient tradition of cord imprinting persisted longer on the pottery, supposedly the product of

6in.
15 cm.

PLATE 105 Restored Iroquois pottery vessel of Oak Hill Corded type from the Clark site, Willow Point, Broome Co., N.Y. Oak Hill phase. Photograph courtesy of the Rochester Museum of Arts and Sciences.

women's work, than on the pipes, which are generally attributed to male creators.

Sites

Iroquois sites of the Oak Hill and Chance horizons are generally small, encompassing less than a quarter of an acre, but exceptions covering one to two acres will presently be described. Their locations maintain the preference begun in Owasco times for upland country, remote from large waterways, and continued among the later Iroquois, who were essentially a woodsloving people, intercommunicating much more by means of foot trails through the forest than by canoe routes. Two fairly large village sites, the Kelso component of the Oak Hill phase and the Getman component of the Chance phase, have been excavated by New York State Museum and Science Service parties in the writer's charge, as part of a major settlement-pattern study, and a brief description of each will afford insight into the essential configuration of early Iroquois culture in the eastern nuclear center. (See page xxvi for recent data.)

The Kelso Site
(Bwv. 12) (Figure 4, site number 103)

This largest and earliest-known component of the Oak Hill phase, explored in 1963 by a State Museum party directed by the writer and Robert E. Funk, is situated on a low ridge of Palmyra gravelly-silt loam, on the Joseph Szablock farm, one mile south of the village of Elbridge, Onondaga County, New York, and some six hundred feet east of a small stream, Skaneateles Creek.

Excavations revealed two overlapping, stockaded villages, each of two acres, shown in Figure 12. Most of the western area was in rough, brushy pasture, had apparently never been plowed, and was heavily disturbed by the bulldozing of hawthorn bushes. Consequently it afforded poor prospects for settlement-pattern work and, also for lack of time, received minor attention beyond the tracing out of the stockade outlines and the excavation of many small, thin patches of refuse which seemed to have been used to level off shallow, natural depressions, including several deeper tree-fall hollows.

The eastern village area, long in pasture, but frequently cultivated in past years, had a nine-inch tilth zone, and fewer refuse deposits sufficiently deep to have escaped the plow. More than ten thousand square feet were completely uncovered to the subsoil level, which was minutely investigated and mapped. These detailed maps, showing individual post molds and all other

features, will be published in the settlement-pattern report, but are omitted from this volume. The excavations did not unequivocally disclose the relative ages of the two components, but some data, to be fully adduced in the final report, suggest the priority of the western village. It can, however, be confidently asserted from the archaeological remains that both settlements were produced by people of one culture, most probably by a single group, who used the same ceramic and other items, built identical longhouses, and returned to a favorable locus after a sojourn elsewhere.

Since no evidence was found of destruction by fire, one may speculate that the exhaustion of local supplies of firewood, game, and perhaps soil fertility resulted in the removal of the village for a decade or so, or until adequate natural restitution had been accomplished. There may even have occurred non-material reasons for such a move; the Iroquois are known to have left their towns for seemingly irrational reasons arising from dream phenomena. One thing is clear, neither community departed in haste, for the occupants took with them virtually everything of value which they possessed, leaving few whole items, and a scant quantity of broken discards.

Fortification

The fortification features of the site are of considerable interest, being the earliest known for the eastern Iroquois. Each community had protected itself behind a double-, in places treble-walled enclosure, roughly ovate in shape, composed of sapling poles set into the ground, apparently by a screwing or oscillatory twisting motion, not by digging, the power probably being provided by two strong men, one on either side, and doubtless done in the

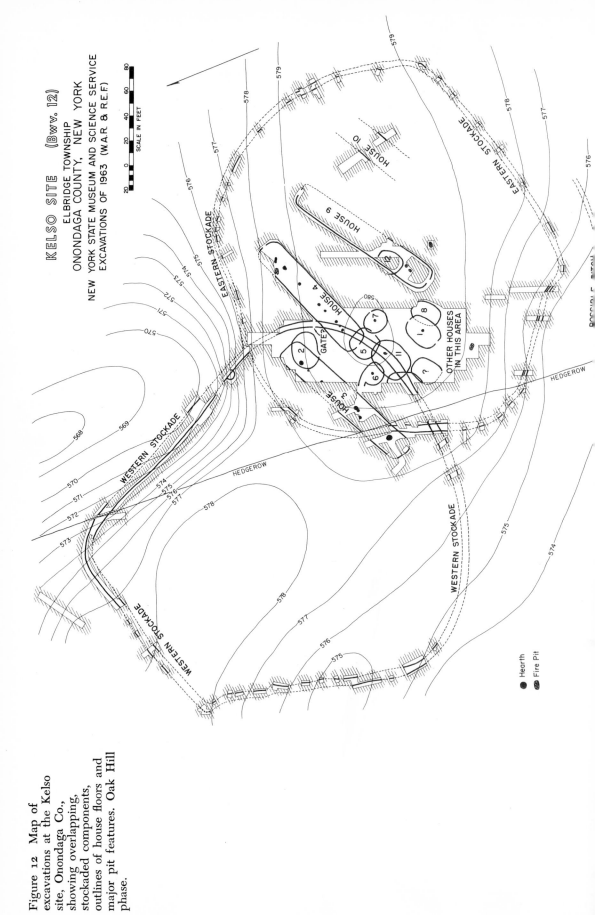

Figure 12 Map of excavations at the Kelso site, Onondaga Co., showing overlapping, stockaded components, outlines of house floors and major pit features. Oak Hill phase.

KELSO SITE (Bwv. 12)
ELBRIDGE TOWNSHIP
ONONDAGA COUNTY, NEW YORK
NEW YORK STATE MUSEUM AND SCIENCE SERVICE
EXCAVATIONS OF 1963 (W.A.R. & R.E.F.)

SCALE IN FEET

● Hearth
⬤ Fire Pit

spring when the ground was soft enough for this purpose. As shown by the post molds, these stockade elements ranged from three to six inches in diameter, three to four inches for most, penetrated into the light-colored subsoil for from eight to seventeen inches, were individually spaced six to eight inches apart, and from the sectioned profiles, had bluntly pointed bases, such as might have been produced by felling with the stone celt, a few whole and broken examples of which were recovered (Plate 106, Figure 22). A possible, much eroded, stockade-post remnant, thirteen inches long, has tentatively been identified as either white or red cedar by Dr. Eugene C. Ogden, State Botanist, New York State Museum and Science Service.

The, in general, two lines of palisades were spaced between four and six and a half feet apart (Plate 108), except for the northern segment of the western village which ran along the base of the rise, and here the interspace broadened to around ten feet.

At one locus on the southwestern side of the eastern enclosure, a series of large post molds, up to eight inches in diameter and twenty-six inches in depth, formed a clear line of oblique buttress molds which had served to brace the outer wall along the slope. A little experimentation indicated that posts set here at this angle of incidence would intersect a vertical wall at a minimum elevation of around twelve feet. Since we may assume that the palisade poles projected above this junction, the wall lines may have been at least fifteen feet high.

As already described for the Bates site, where a single stockade line of this kind was found (page 285), the Kelso "fort," and that at the Getman site still to be discussed (page 314), was essentially a double fence of saplings, each line doubtless interlaced with withes to create a tight wall, and probably having an access corridor between them. Something of this kind seems to have been indicated by Champlain in his 1615 encounter with the Iroquois of central New York (Biggar, 1929, p. 70). Want of adequate time and manpower prevented the full uncovering of the Kelso stockades, most of which were traced by trenching, as shown on Figure 12, and so such significant details as the size and placement of the gateways largely remain enigmatic. In the southeast walls of the western stockade a possible gateway two and a half feet wide was discovered (see map), the only example of this kind found. The aperture favorably compares in size with the eyewitness description given for a Mohawk town of 1634 (Jameson, 1909, p. 148). The site was being prepared for plowing during the final stages of our work.

Houses

While, for the same reason, the interior area of the eastern village could not be fully cleared, it is believed that the location, size and character of the most important houses in this community can be assessed. Floor plans of two forms of structures, both apparently dwellings, as judged from the included hearths and refuse, were traceable with much clarity and less confusion than existed on some of the sites we have explored (pages 247, 285). There seem to be neither cultural nor temporal differences to account for these.

The smaller houses, which may have sheltered minor clan groups, can be described as oval to oblong; they measure between nineteen by sixteen feet for number 7 and thirty-two by twenty-six feet for number 11 (Figure 12). These features resemble the smaller dwelling units at the

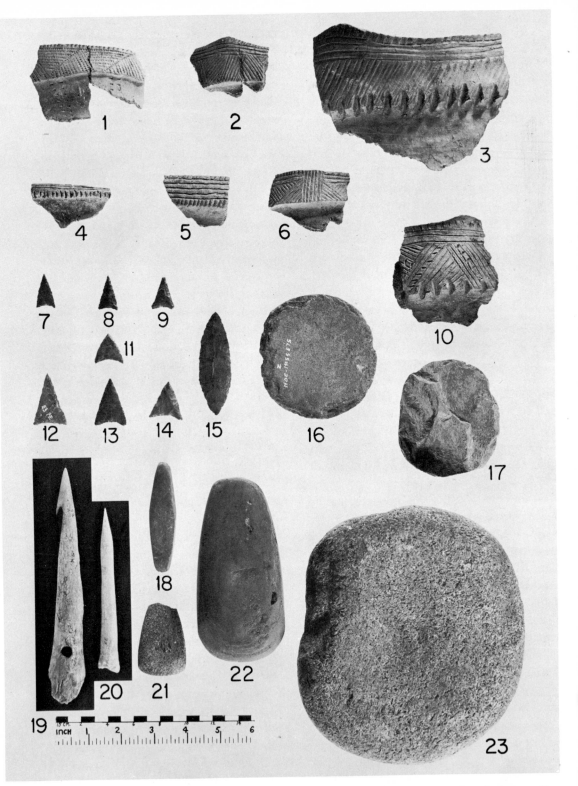

PLATE 106 Artifacts of early and late Iroquois culture in central and eastern New York. 1 rim sherd of Oak Hill Corded type; 2, 6 rim sherds of Chance Incised type; 3, 10 rim sherds of Cayadutta Incised type; 4 rim sherd of Bainbridge Notched Lip type; 5 rim sherd of Iroquois Linear type; 7–9 Madison-type arrow points; 11–14 arrow points of Levanna type; 15 willow-leaf-shaped knife; 16, 17 stone hoes (?); 18 stone chisel; 19 antler harpoon head; 20 bone awl; 21 stone adz; 22 stone celt; 23 biconcave mortar. Provenience: 1 Chance site; 2, 4–6 Deowongo Island; 3, 7, 8, 10, 15, 19, 20 Garoga site; 9, 11–14, 16–18, 21–23 Kelso site.

Maxon-Derby site (page 282, Figure 9 and Plate 94) and the assumed primary unit at the Bates component (page 285, Figure 10).

The second type of lodge is a true longhouse, corresponding in shape with the large rectanguloid structures of the Maxon-Derby and Bates sites, which have similar rounded ends (Figures 9, 10). They differ from these, however, in the possession of a central linear arrangement of hearths and in having had, apparently, bed platforms, five or six feet wide, along either wall. The Kelso longhouses are surprisingly large for this early period, measuring respectively, 128 feet (house 3), 112 feet (house 4) and 128.5 feet (house 9) in length. A uniform width of 22 feet prevails.

The Kelso site houses of whatever form were constructed of poles which produced molds around three inches in diameter and five to eight inches in depth in the subsoil. Spacing was quite irregular, ranging from three to eighteen inches, but for the most part between five and eight inches apart. Some larger molds, five to fourteen inches across and seven to twenty-two inches deep, were uncovered at infrequent and irregular intervals in the wall and midline of the longhouses, where they seemed to signify major support posts, set in dug holes, rather than twisted into the ground, as was the apparent case with the smaller ones.

Hearths or fireplaces, found in most of the houses, single and central in the smaller units, multiple in the midline of the larger ones (Figure 12), consisted mainly of indurated, fire-reddened subsoil patches, some two to three feet in diameter, with overlying accumulations of charcoal-flecked ash. In a few cases the fire had occupied a shallow, basin-shaped depression dug into the subsoil. This kind of fireplace occurred much more frequently outside the confines of the houses, suggesting that a great deal of the summer cooking took place out of doors. Bone refuse, potsherds, and more rarely other artifacts were taken from, or in the close vicinity of, these cooking features.

Charcoal from one of these small hearths with associated potsherds (Feature 6) has been radiocarbon-dated at the Yale Radiocarbon Laboratory at A.D. 1390±100 years (Y-1380). The true age is believed to fall within the minus range of the standard deviation, or approximately A.D. 1300.

The cooking of food on the Kelso site involved not only boiling in pottery vessels, but apparently baking on hot stones in large pits. Three such features were uncovered, all oval, bathtub-shaped pits with steep sides and flat bottoms, which are heavily oxidized by heat to a brick-red color. Feature 12, pictured in process of excavation on Plate 109, will illustrate the type, which has some unusual characteristics. It measured ninety-three inches in length, sixty inches in breadth and eighteen inches in depth, and the bottom was covered several inches deep with charcoal, most of it in the form of small logs. Fire-cracked cobbles and boulders of crystalline rocks, chiefly gneisses, covered the charcoal and were in turn invested with a clean, tan, compact soil, evidently subsoil, discolored by heat like the walls and base. A few scraps of pottery and a bone fragment occurred in this layer.

Seemingly, each of these features had been used intensively but once, creating the suspicion of some esoteric function, as, for instance, in a bear-ceremonial feast.

Perhaps largely because we were unable to accomplish the complete excavation of the twin villages, some difficulty has been experienced in the interpretation of the data. It would seem, however, that long-houses 4, 9 and 10, the latter indicated only by wall-line sections exposed in a final exploratory trench, had belonged to the eastern component, along with probably all of the smaller structures. Longhouse 3 likely pertained to the western community (Figure 12). A northeast-southwest orientation holds for all the longhouses and for several of the smaller houses (numbers 1, 8, 11).

For reasons and calculations to be published in the full site account, we believe that, in the eastern village, three long-houses (numbers 4, 9, 10) probably coexisted with three of the smaller units (1, 2 and 11, or 1, 2 and 6, or 2, 8 and 11, or 2, 6 and 8), and that the population of this settlement approximated 225 persons.

Subsistence

Sustenance was dependent upon a mixed economy, which included maize, wild plants, large and small mammals, birds and fish. Other cultivars were probably used but were not found. Analysis of the foods will appear in the site report.

The inventory of hunting and fishing gear is indeed small, comprising only twenty-three flint arrow points, twenty of Levanna type (Plate 106, Figures 11–14), the remainder referable to the Madison type (Figure 9 of the same plate), and a single notched netsinker.

Possible stone hoes, roughly chipped disks with or without ground notches (Plate 106, Figures 16, 17), numbered thirty-five, indicating, perhaps, an emphasis on tillage. There were, however, no storage pits on the site. Food must therefore have been stored above ground in the houses or in special granaries. Some of the smaller structures may have been devoted to this purpose.

Food-grinding devices consisted of a few mullers; a cylindrical pestle; a shallow, bi-concave mortar (Plate 106, Figure 23), perhaps also used in pulverizing burned crystalline rocks for pottery temper; and a circular, flat milling stone.

Tools

Woodworking tools embraced, besides the celt, already mentioned (Plate 106, Figure 22), a small plano-convex adz (Plate 106, Figure 21) and two narrow chisels, one very small (Plate 106, Figure 18). The scarcity of such tools (a total of nine) is indeed surprising on a site where so much wood cutting had obviously taken place.

A trivial amount of worked bone was present, reflecting both the meagerness of midden deposits and a general cultural tendency in this direction among late Owasco and eastern Iroquois groups, for whom a major industry in wooden artifacts is suspected. Tubular bird-bone beads; a few splinter awls; a deer-scapula flaking tool; and a curved, thin, eyed, mat-weaving needle, like that illustrated on Plate 92, Figure 19, constitute the range of discovered traits.

Somewhat more numerous were the rough stone tools, viz., unpitted and bi-pitted hammerstones (six of each), anvil-stones (twenty-one), and combination tools —hammer-anvil, anvil-muller, and hammer-anvil-muller (fourteen).

Pottery

Pottery on the Kelso site, while by far the commonest of the artifactual remains, totals only 425 rim sherds, 930 neck sherds, and 2769 body sherds. Analysis of this material by components shows no appreciable differences, as already noted (page 305), between the eastern and the western villages. Sixty-nine per cent of the rims are indistinguishable from the late Owasco Corded Collar type (Plate 99, Figure 2), and only 2.6 per cent show the oblique-line and chevron-collar designs which distinguish the Oak Hill Corded type from this form (Plate 105; Plate 106, Figure 1). Also present, in minor amounts (between 0.3 and 1.7 per cent) are Chance Incised (Plate 106, Figures 2, 6), Goodyear Lipped, Bainbridge Notched Lip (Plate 106, Figure 4), Owasco Platted and Owasco Corded Horizontal (see Ritchie and MacNeish, 1949, for formal descriptions of these types). Of the total rim sherds, 21 per cent were too small to be validly typable.

Most of the neck sherds (83.6 per cent) were cord embellished, only 8 per cent bore incising, the remainder were plain.

The body sherds were very instructive with 91 per cent check-stamped or smoothed-over check-stamped, only 5.9 per cent corded or smoothed-over corded, and the small remainder smooth. Check-stamping as a surface treatment was replacing cord malleation in late Owasco times, occurring on 20 per cent of the pots at the Castle Creek site (Plate 99, Figure 3), and 36 per cent of those at the Bainbridge component (Ritchie and MacNeish, 1949, Figure 43). Corded-collar types had also risen to 60 per cent of the total at the latter station (ibid., Figure 42).

In comparing the Kelso site with the Oak Hill site in the Mohawk Valley (Cnj. 40-2) (Figure 4, site number 104), it will be seen that 43.5 per cent of the latter's rim sherds pertain to the Oak Hill Corded type (Plate 106, Figure 1), 18.8 per cent to Iroquois Linear (Plate 106, Figure 5), 18.8 per cent to Durfee Underlined, 7.2 per cent to Goodyear Lipped, and minor amounts to other early Iroquois styles, including

Chance Incised (5.8 per cent) (Plate 106, Figures 2, 6). Most of the body sherds are smooth, as in all later Iroquois ware (94.2 per cent), check-stamping accounting for only 5.8 per cent (Ritchie, 1952a, p. 6 and Figures 2, 4). This site, formerly regarded as the type station of the early Iroquois Oak Hill horizon, is now seen to seriate into the later part of this phase, while Kelso occupies typologically an intermediate position, close to the stage of emergence from the late Castle Creek phase.

Burials

No burials could be located on or in the vicinity of the Kelso site and very little information is presently available on either the burial customs or the physical characteristics of the Oak Hill Indians, who seem to have resembled their probable Owasco forebears (page 275). A few graves attributable to this phase, excavated by the writer on the Clark site, Willow Point, Chenango County, New York (Figure 4, site number 76) (Ritchie, 1944, p. 61), held simple flexed burials. With one of these, believed at that time to belong to the Castle Creek component at the site, was a pottery pipe, of the now classic Willow Point style pictured on Plate 107, Figure 1. One of the associated nearby pits produced the sherds of the fine Oak Hill Corded pot shown on Plate 105.

On the El Rancho site in the Mohawk Valley, near Palatine Bridge, Montgomery County, attributed by Lenig to the Oak Hill phase, a flexed burial accompanied by a very beautifully modeled, human-face effigy pipe was uncovered by the late Edward J. Sheehan of Fultonville (Plate 107, Figure 3).

Sites of the Oak Hill phase offer no evidence of trade or outside contacts. They

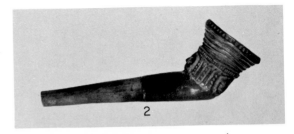

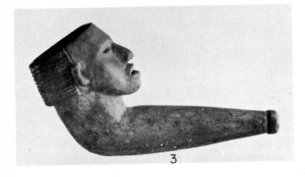

PLATE 107 Early Iroquois pipe styles. Oak Hill phase (1, 3), Chance phase (2). 1 Clark site, Willow Point, Broome Co.; 2 Second Woods site, Montgomery Co.; 3 El Rancho site, Montgomery Co. Figure 1 courtesy of the Rochester Museum of Arts and Sciences, Figures 2, 3 courtesy of the Mohawk-Caughnawaga Museum.

seem to have continued the late Owasco tradition of self-contained communities, sometimes secured against potential danger by walls of poles and withes, orientated rather toward the forest than toward the waterways, and dependent in considerable part on agricultural crops. The larger sites, like Kelso, were semipermanent in character, with communal longhouse life. This combination of traits, all actually developed in the preceding Owasco phase (page 298), points toward a matrilineally related, matrilocally resident, clan-structured society, like that of the historic Iroquois.

THE CHANCE PHASE

Ceramics

The Chance phase developed progressively out of the Oak Hill complex throughout the approximate territory of the lat-

ter. For reasons and through specific avenues still undetermined, the incising technique came to replace, by the end of the phase, the long-established cord-impression method of pottery adornment. Incising, which requires a different set of motor habits from those employed in stamping, occurred rarely in middle Owasco times; more extensively on such Castle Creek ceramics as the Castle Creek Incised Neck and Bainbridge Collared Incised types (Ritchie and MacNeish, 1949, pp. 114–15). Here, however, it was always confined to the neck of the vessel, and was executed in a careless, experimental manner, in sharp contrast to the complete mastery exhibited by the rim and collar designs done in the traditional corded technique (Ritchie, 1934, p. 50).

It has been suggested that the change in technique from impressing to incising was effected through a transitional method of application known as the push-pull or interrupted linear technique, in which the two motor habits of stamping and drawing are combined alternately in the same process. This technique, already present in a minor way in the Bainbridge Linear type of the late Castle Creek phase (Ritchie and MacNeish, 1949, pp. 115–16), characterizes the Iroquois Linear type (MacNeish, 1952, pp. 18–19), which was absent from the Kelso site and present in small amounts on only a few components of the Oak Hill phase.

Whatever the explanation of its rise in popularity, the replacement of Oak Hill Corded pottery by the Chance Incised variety took place during the course of emergence of the Chance phase. Both types

utilized the same fine-grit-tempered paste, semiglobular vessel shape, and collar and neck designs (Plate 106, Figures 1, 2, 6). During this phase, too, check-stamping and cord malleation, as body-surface treatments, were largely replaced by smooth surfacing (Ritchie, 1952a, Figure 4).

The artistic quality of Iroquois pottery in the eastern area attained its zenith in the Chance phase, particularly in the developmental stage represented by the late Oak Hill-early Chance horizon.

The inventory of pipe styles was modified during the Chance phase by the addition of new "trumpet" bowl forms, carrying trailed or beaded bars or bands of dec-

PLATE 108   Eastern segment of the double stockade line of the western component at the Kelso site, Onondaga Co., N.Y. Oak Hill phase.

oration, and by a number of new effigy varieties portraying the human face and figure, as well as sundry bird and mammal heads, always facing toward the smoker.

The remainder of the artifact typology continued that of the Oak Hill phase, insofar as we are aware, and will be detailed in site reports. One significant distinction is the appearance of the conventional Iroquois longhouse form of historic times, as discovered at the Getman site. This square-ended, rectangular form was doubtless descended from the round-ended type of the Kelso site.

Chronology

Two radiocarbon dates place the Chance phase within the fourteenth century. The earlier date of A.D. 1325±75 years (M-1185) (Crane and Griffin, 1963, p. 243) was derived from a very small component in the Mohawk Vally (Oak Hill No. 7) assigned by Lenig to the beginning of the phase on the basis of associated pottery; the later and overlapping date of A.D. 1398 ±150 years (M-763) (Crane and Griffin, 1959, p. 184) from the Getman site clearly applies, on the same considerations, to the upper part of the Chance phase.

The Getman Site
(Cnj. 25) (Figure 4, site number 106)

The Getman site, the largest-known and most intensively explored station of the Chance phase, was the first site to be excavated under our settlement-pattern investigation, begun in 1957. The work was supervised by the writer and James V. Wright and is described in full in a manuscript report by the former as part of the final report.

The Getman component lies on a long, low ridge of Nellis and Amelia calcareous loam, on the farm of George Russell Getman, four and a half miles north of the Mohawk River, in Palatine Township, Montgomery County. Like the Kelso site, in a similar location, and lacking natural protective topography, it was enclosed within an oval, double-walled stockade, surrounding slightly over one acre, somewhat over half the size of the Kelso components. The wall lines, spaced from two and a half to five feet apart, provided a guarded interior corridor of sufficient width for passage if desired. This double line may have been bridged at the top for a fighting platform, with the outer line taller to shield the defenders, as was the case with some early historic Iroquois towns (Biggar, 1929, p. 70).

Individual post molds varied from three to four and a half inches in diameter, four and a half to nine and a half inches in depth in the subsoil, and were spaced four to nine inches apart. This double barricade was probably constructed like those already described for the Kelso and Bates sites (pages 305, 285).

The Getman village had comprised from four to six longhouses, ranging up to 114 feet in length by twenty-two feet in breadth, only one of which could be entirely excavated (Plate 110). This apparently typical example measured eighty-six feet in length by twenty-two feet in breadth, and had a rectangular floor plan delineated by double rows of wall lines, close together, each composed of post molds approximately three inches in diameter and eight to fifteen inches in depth below subsoil level. Vertical walls of overlapping, horizontally placed sheets of bark had doubtless been supported between these sapling wall poles. Occasional larger molds, four to six inches in diameter in

PLATE 109 Large cooking pit, Feature 12, partially excavated on the Kelso site, Onondaga Co. Oak Hill phase.

these lines, and even larger ones of some ten inches across in the interior, are believed to have indicated roof supports.

Interior features were marked by apparent post-mold patterns, included bench-beds five to six feet in breadth ranged along the walls, partitions at ten- to twelve-foot intervals separating the sleeping compartments, and tranverse walls crossing the house at either end to create subdivisions or "rooms" twenty feet in length.

Nine hearths were rather irregularly spaced along the center of the eight-foot-wide corridor. Each occupied a shallow, basin-shaped depression in the burned subsoil and still contained ashes and bits of charcoal. Some overlapping and crowding

of these fireplaces suggests, however, that the locus was occasionally shifted, so that fewer than the total number were in use at any one time.

Novel appurtenances were two large, U-shaped storage pits, situated, respectively, in the northwest corner and in an east-central position in the corridor. Both of these features, especially the latter, had doubtless been provided with stout bark covers. A few similar cache pits occurred elsewhere on the site.

Charred corn was the only cultivated plant represented, but surely the full range of Iroquois cultigens—corn, beans, squashes, pumpkins and tobacco—were in use at this late site.

PLATE 110 Excavated floor of longhouse number 1 at the Getman site, Montgomery Co., N.Y. Length is 86 feet, breadth 22 feet. Storage pits near lower left-hand corner and at range pole. Series of hearths outlined in string along center. Chance phase.

Of the animal food, 98 per cent pertained to mammals; 75.6 per cent of these were deer, 9.4 per cent a large breed of dog which seems to have been eaten.

Population estimates for the Getman site are based on the reasonable assumption (discussed in the site report) that no more than three of the houses could have been in simultaneous use. Ethnohistorical data for the Mohawk Iroquois going back to 1634 (Jameson, 1909, pp. 137–80) provide a helpful guide which, with other information, chiefly from the *Jesuit Relations* (Kenyon, 1927), lead to the supposition of an approximate average occupancy by 160 people of the Getman site, which was a direct precursor of the large town type of the Iroquois of the succeeding late prehistoric phase in New York.

The Late Prehistoric Iroquois

The florescence of native Iroquois culture occurred between approximately A.D. 1450 and 1600, during which century and a half it attained to its classic form. The tribalism and localism of the early historic era were certainly accomplished well before the end of this period and seem to have been associated with the regional developments and specializations in culture pertaining to this time, but not readily apparent on the preceding horizon in New York and Ontario. During this interval also

316

some still vaguely comprehended major group movements took place. Chief among these is the historically supported exodus from the St. Lawrence Valley of the so-called Laurentian Iroquois (Fenton, 1940, pp. 167–77), who may have contributed to the ancestry of the composite Huron people. Ethnic and cultural elements from western New York seem likewise to have been added during this late time to the Seneca group, which had been undergoing in the Genesee country the modifications we have been tracing from early Owasco antecedents (Ritchie, 1954, pp. 30–55). Mohawk, or Mohawk-Oneida and Onondaga, have, perhaps, the strongest claim to a wholly autonomous development, with little outside influence, in their historic localities.

Other characteristics of the late Iroquois period include a major population expansion throughout Iroquoia, as determined from the increasing number and size of the communities, and an acceleration of intercommunication among the tribal units, as judged by the distribution of certain pottery and pipe varieties. This activity probably prepared the immediate way for some of the channels of the opening phase of European trade, both indirectly through intertribal agencies and directly by European and native contacts (Ritchie, 1954, pp. 70–74). Its attendant hostilities may also have contributed to the formation of the League of the Iroquois in the latter part of the same period.

THE GAROGA PHASE

In eastern New York the final, specialized, prehistoric stage of Iroquois cultural growth and change is being termed the Garoga phase. It has its approximate tem-

poral and cultural equivalents throughout Iroquoia, a subject far too large for the present volume, which will tersely utilize some of the Mohawk data as illustrative of this level of Iroquois culture.

Settlements

The Mohawk at this period were inhabiting a few large villages and a larger number of small settlements or hamlets located in the middle Mohawk Valley on terrain often far inland, north or south of the river, selected with cardinal reference to the natural protective topography. Thus virtually all known sites are on tongues or ridges of high land with precipitous slopes into ravines on at least two sides, the easily accessible approach being barred by palisades. Some sites of this and the following early historic period were fully stockaded. While the chief subsistence for these villages came from hoe tillage, the produce being stored in pit granaries and storehouses above ground, as well as in the large bark longhouses, hunting, fishing, and gathering were still important activities.

Some insight into the way of life of a typical Iroquois village of the late prehistoric period may probably be had from the "Narrative of a Journey into the Mohawk and Oneida Country, 1634–1635," attributed to Harmen Meyndertsz van den Bogaert (Jameson, 1909, pp. 137–62).

This journey from Fort Orange (Albany) took place in late December and early January. Villages, hamlets and hunters' lodges in the woods were visited. In the hilltop villages, most of them protected by two or three lines of palisades, stood bark-covered longhouses, some at least with flat roofs, arranged in rows like streets. Settlements with sixteen, thirty-two, fifty-five and sixty-six houses are specifically mentioned, each house from fifty to one hundred paces long and twenty-two to twenty-three feet in height (breadth ?).

Foods

Foods seen or eaten in these communities comprised venison, fresh and dried, the favorite meat; bear (captive bears were kept for fattening); beaver; white hare (snowshoe hare), cooked with walnuts; turkey; fresh and dried salmon (?); corn; beans; baked pumpkins; dried strawberries; beans and maize cooked with deer or turkey fat; and bread (cornbread) baked with beans, nuts, cherries, dry blueberries and sunflower seeds. Fire was made with flint strike-a-lights.

Our excavations, at the late prehistoric Mohawk Garoga site, throw considerable light upon the final stage of aboriginal existence in eastern New York just prior to European discovery.

The Garoga Site
(Las. 7–4) (Figure 4, site number 109)

The Garoga site in the Township of Ephratah, Fulton County, some six miles north of the Mohawk River, is one of the three largest-known late prehistoric Mohawk components. The two others, Cayadutta (Figure 4, site number 107) and Otstungo (Figure 4, site number 108), have almost completely been dug over by relic collectors since their discovery in the latter part of the last century. It may still be possible, however, to obtain settlement-pattern data from these stations by careful excavations on the subsoil level.

Garoga, too, has suffered damage from the same cause and the side-hill dumps are virtually exhausted. In 1905 M. R. Harring-ton conducted limited excavations on the site for the Peabody Museum of Harvard University and has left us a manuscript record of his work. For many years thereafter the site was owned and protected as well as possible against vandalism by Wilford E. Sanderson of Loudonville, New York, who in 1960 generously extended the privilege of excavation to the New York State Museum and Science Service. Following a thorough reconnaissance in the fall of that year by the writer and Robert E. Funk, Junior Archaeologist at the Museum, the site was partially cleared of brush, surveyed and mapped. Intensive excavations were conducted in 1961, 1962 and 1964, under the field supervision of Mr. Funk.

Houses and Palisades

The Garoga village of two and a half acres is typically sited, covering the nearly level summit of a peninsula-like ridge composed of laminated sands and gravels of glacial origin. From an elevation of 920 feet above sea level and 180 feet over its immediate surroundings, the ridge slopes precipitously on three sides into gulleys, the northern one carrying Caroga Creek on its course from the Adirondack Mountains to the Mohawk River. Only on the west, over a narrow neck of gently sloping land, was easy approach possible.

Some sixty thousand square feet or about one third of the occupied area has been thoroughly explored and mapped.

Fully uncovered was the anticipated multiple-stockade line across the narrow access route, comprising two rows of large post molds, each of approximately ninety feet, bow-shaped, with the inward-curving extremities extending over the slopes toward the site proper. Near the middle, the rows stood fifteen feet apart, the distance gradually decreasing to six feet at either end. Individually spaced between twelve and fifteen inches apart, the molds were very much larger than those involved in defensive construction on any of the earlier settlements we have described, being fifteen to twenty inches in diameter, and sunk three feet or so into the ground. Gaps of twenty-seven and thirty-three inches near the south end, in the outer and inner lines, respectively, were interpreted as marking the probable gateway.

House-wall alignments of small post molds, two and a half to three inches across, penetrating four to twelve inches into the yellow subsoil, were present over the greater part of the exposed area, their profusion indicating a considerable relocation of the dwellings as well as extensive repairs to existing walls, the latter shown in particular by clustered molds. Most of the apparently seven houses seem to have been oriented roughly parallel to the long axis of the site, or east and west.

Two parallel wall lines, twenty feet apart, pertained to a completely uncovered longhouse floor 210 feet in length. Large, apparently roof-support molds of a six- to ten-inch diameter and twelve- to twenty-eight-inch depth were irregularly interspersed among the smaller molds, whose dark outlines stood out boldly against the clear yellow sand. Fairly evenly spaced along the central line were some twenty hearths in basin-shaped hollows one and a half to three feet across and two to ten inches in depth, filled with ash, charcoal, burned stones and dark sand. Along either side, seemingly beneath bench-beds, occurred a row of storage pits. Interior adjuncts of this sort, absent at the Kelso site,

were beginning to be utilized on the Getman-site stage (page 315).

Food and Storage

Most storage or cache pits seem to have been located inside the lodges. They were U-shaped or bell-shaped and very like those already described, especially for late Owasco sites (page 280). The 380 examples found in our excavations (fifty-one others were reported by Harrington) ranged from two to ten feet in diameter and two to eight feet in depth, with usual dimensions of approximately three by five feet.

Traces of a carbonized bark and grass lining were infrequently present and small quantities of the doubtless stored foods—corn, beans, hickory nuts, walnuts and acorns—occurred in some. In many examples also, to complete the correspondence with earlier pits of this kind, a secondary use as trash bins is attested by the ashes, charcoal and burned stones, probably fireplace debris; black dirt with animal bones, potsherds, etc., the probable lodge sweepings and garbage; and layers or patches of clean sand, either washed in by rain or more likely scattered over offal, excrement and such mephitic matter. From the pits, too, came most of the artifacts, whole, fragmentary and in process, found in our excavations. They were not, except for potsherds, numerous. Most of the refuse on this, as on similar Iroquois sites, had been thrown over the banks, and the artifact content of the hillside middens on such stations is generally much higher per unit volume than the pit fill, a fact in part accounting for the popularity of the former as relic-collecting grounds and their early exhaustion.

Artifact Categories

The artifact forms, as well as the house typology, fortifications, storage pits and other features at the Garoga site are typical not alone of the late prehistoric Mohawk, but with some significant ceramic exceptions, of the New York Iroquois of this period as a whole, insofar as known. Moreover, in large part, again with ceramic (pottery and pipes) exceptions, the inventory of material goods, mainly the weapons, tools and other equipment, underwent little modification from the preceding Chance phase. Hunting and fishing gear comprised the bow and arrow tipped with the small Madison-type triangle of flint (Plate 106, Figures 7, 8); barbed bone or antler points with single or multiple, usually bilateral barbs, some true harpoons with line-hole, (Plate 106, Figure 19); the conical toggle-head harpoon form of antler with single basal barb or spur and lateral line-hole; the bone fishhook, rarely barbed; and the flat, notched pebble netsinker.

Stone celts, adzes and chisels, mostly thick-polled, well made and polished, were the tree-felling and wood-cutting tools.

Flint drills and scrapers were minor traits, but ovate, trianguloid, and willow-leaf-shaped, chipped-flint knives occur on most of the sites (Plate 106, Figure 15); as do bone awls (Plate 106, Figure 20); long, cylindrical, antler flaking tools; and bone mat-sewing needles.

Large, caldron-like pots of several gallons' capacity are heavily represented by the sherds. Doubtless stew kettles, always on the fire, they denote a numerous and sedentary people. The pottery of this final prehistoric stage of Iroquois culture, although well made (by the paddle-and-an-vil method), carefully fired, and tastefully adorned, is artistically inferior to that of the preceding Chance phase, which it resembles in technique and motif of decoration. The incised linear patterns, mainly composed of oblique lines, generally chevrons, are coarser and more carelessly applied than in their Chance antetypes. (Compare Plate 106, Figures 2, 6, with Plate 111 and Plate 106, Figures 3, 10.) Rim castellations and bold base-of-collar notches are the rule. Among the Oneida, Onondaga and Susquehannock, conventionalized human face and figure effigies are of common occurrence. Body-surface treatment is nearly always smooth. A rapid decline in pottery making followed the introduction of the brass or copper trade kettle in the early seventeenth century.

Smoking pipes, conversely, proliferated in style and improved in artistic quality during late prehistoric times. This is particularly true for the Onondaga of northern New York who specialized in the effigy and so-called "escutcheon" forms of the trumpet pipe, which they modeled in clay or, much more rarely, carved from the local steatite or talc. Human faces and figures, mammal heads—apparently depicting for the most part the bear, wolf and deer (clan symbols ?)—and bird heads—chiefly the owl, crow and passenger pigeon —are represented, nearly always facing the smoker, with high fidelity, skill and aesthetic excellence.

A comparative analytical study of Iroquois pipes from the Oak Hill phase in New York and the comparable Uren phase in Ontario to the full historic period in both areas would throw much light on Iroquois developmental history and intertribal contacts and relations, and suggests itself as an admirable topic for a doctoral dissertation.

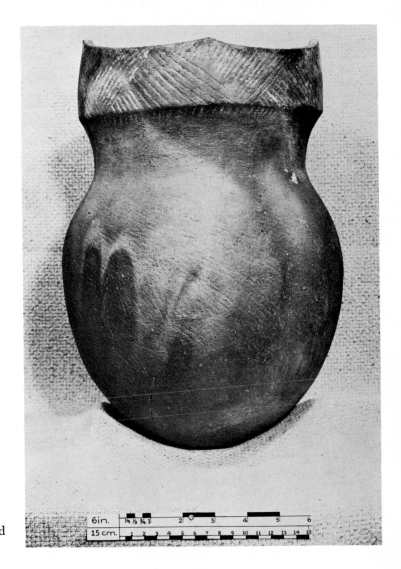

PLATE 111 Late prehistoric Iroquois pottery vessel, found intact under rock ledge near Windsor, Broome Co., N.Y. Photograph courtesy of the Rochester Museum of Arts and Sciences.

Burial Traits

The burial customs of the late prehistoric Iroquois are not well known. The cemeteries seem often to have been located quite a distance from the villages, a trait traceable backward into Owasco times and maintained into the contact period (Jameson, 1909, p. 148); consequently most of them have so far escaped discovery. Flexed burial without mortuary goods was the rule in the graves that have been found.

Following European contact and the opening of trade relations a dramatic change in this custom took place, the dead being attended by an increasingly sizable and varied assortment of the new wealth, along with aboriginal-made articles, which diminished in ratio to the others as time passed (Plate 112). Weapons, tools, utensils, ornaments, pipes, ceremonial objects,

321

PLATE 112 Loosely flexed burial of male Seneca Indian, about twenty-four years of age, on the Dutch Hollow site, Livingston Co., N.Y. Early historic period (*c.* 1590–1615). Note large iron knife in right hand, effigy antler comb beside head, triangular arrow points on opposite side of head, and near left arm the following principal grave goods: an iron bracelet, antler flaking tool, unmodified beaver and dog teeth, whetstones, graphite paintstone, 3 Iroquois triangular points and 3 notched Archaic points, the latter probably regarded as hunting charms. Photograph courtesy of the Rochester Museum of Arts and Sciences.

and even dogs and items of food were often lavished on the dead, children as well as adults (Wray and Schoff, 1953; Ritchie, 1954). Not surprisingly the custom reached its zenith at the height of the fur trade. The rationale involved in this major change from prehistoric custom remains obscure. By the early part of the eighteenth century the flexed-burial mode of prior times was supplanted by extended burial, often in wooden coffins.

Soon after the close of the American Revolution, or around 1785, bark longhouses began to be superseded by single-family log cabins of European introduction and by about 1800 this change had probably been completed. Longhouses of logs with bark roofs persisted, however, in ceremonial usage for at least another fifty years.

With the reservation period following the Pickering Treaty of 1794, communalism

REFERENCES

AGOGINO, GEORGE A.
  1963 The Paleo-Indian relative age and cultural sequence. Great Plains Journal, Fall 3-1, pp. 17–24.

ALLEN, GLOVER M.
  1920 Dogs of the American aborigines. Bulletin of the Museum of Comparative Zoology, Harvard College, Vol. LXIII, No. 9. Cambridge.

ANONYMOUS
  1943 Report on the first archaeological conference on the Woodland pattern. American Antiquity, Vol. VIII, No. 4, pp. 393–400. Menasha.

ANONYMOUS
  1951 Soil survey manual. U. S. Department of Agriculture, Handbook No. 18. Washington.

ARNOLD, J. R., AND LIBBY, W. F.
  1951 Radiocarbon dates. Science, Vol. 113, No. 2927, pp. 111–20. Lancaster.

BABY, RAYMOND S.
  1954 Hopewell cremation practices. Ohio State Historical Society, Papers in Archaeology, No. 1. Columbus.

BAERREIS, DAVID A., et al.
  1954 The burial complex of the Reigh site, Winnebago County, Wis. The Wisconsin Archeologist, Vol. 35, No. 1, pp. 1–36. Lake Mills.

BAILEY, JOHN H.
  1939 A ground slate producing site near Vergennes, Vermont. Bulletin of the Champlain Valley Archaeological Society, Vol. I, No. 2. Fort Ticonderoga, N.Y.

———
  1939a Archeology in Vermont in 1938. The Vermont Alumnus (unpaginated reprint). Burlington.

BEARDSLEY, RICHARD K.; HOLDER, PRESTON; KRIEGER, ALEX D.; MEGGERS, BETTY J.; RINALDO, JOHN B., and KUTSCHE, PAUL
  1956 Functional and evolutionary implications of community patterning. In, Seminars in Archaeology: 1955, edited by Robert Wauchope, pp. 129–57. Memoirs of the Society for American Archaeology, No. 11. Salt Lake City.

BEAUBIEN, PAUL L.
  1953 Cultural variation within two Woodland mound groups of northeastern Iowa. American Antiquity, Vol. XIX, No. 1, pp. 56–66. Salt Lake City.

BEAUCHAMP, WILLIAM M.
  1902 Metallic implements of the New York Indians. New York State Museum, Bulletin 55. Albany.

BEETHAM, NELLIE, and NIERING, WILLIAM A.
  1961 A pollen diagram from southeastern Connecticut. American Journal of Science, Vol. 259, No. 1, pp. 69–75. New Haven.

BELL, ROBERT E.
  1958 Guide to the identification of certain American Indian projectile points. Special Bulletin No. 1, Oklahoma Anthropological Society. Oklahoma City.

BENT, ARTHUR C.
  1932 Life histories of North American gallinaceous birds. Bulletin of the U. S. National Museum, No. 162. Washington.

BIGGAR, H. P. (editor)

1929 The works of Samuel de Champlain. The Champlain Society. Vol. III. Toronto.

BINFORD, LEWIS R.

1963 The Hodges site, a Late Archaic burial station. *In,* White, Anita M.; Binford, Lewis R., and Papworth, Mark L., Miscellaneous studies in typology and classification. Anthropological Papers, Museum of Anthropology, University of Michigan, No. 19, pp. 124-48. Ann Arbor.

——

1963a The Pomranky site, a Late Archaic burial station. *In,* White, Anita M.; Binford, Lewis R., and Papworth, Mark L., Miscellaneous studies in typology and classification. Anthropological Papers, Museum of Anthropology, University of Michigan, No. 19, pp. 149-92. Ann Arbor.

BLEAKNEY, SHERMAN

1958 The significance of turtle bones from archaeological sites in southern Ontario and Quebec. The Canadian Field Naturalist, Vol. 27, No. 1, pp. 1-5. Ottawa.

BLISS, WESLEY

1942 Archaeological field activity of the Pennsylvania Historical Commission in 1941. Pennsylvania Archaeologist, Vol. 12, No. 2, pp. 35-38. Milton.

BLOOM, ARTHUR L., and STUIVER, MINZE

1963 Submergence of the Connecticut coast. Science, Vol. 139, No. 3552, pp. 332-34. Washington.

BRAUN, E. LUCY

1950 Deciduous forests of eastern North America. Blakiston Co. Philadelphia.

BRAY, WILLIAM L.

1930 The development of the vegetation of New York State. Second edition. New York State College of Forestry, Technical Publication No. 29. Syracuse.

BRENNAN, LOUIS A.

1962 A beginning in chronology for the Croton River area. Pennsylvania Archaeologist, Vol. XXXII, Nos. 3-4, pp. 138-56.

——

1963 A short evaluation of the current state of knowledge of New York prehistory stated in terms of the problems raised by it. The Bulletin, New York State Archeological Association, No. 26, pp. 6-15. Ossining.

——

1967 The Taconic tradition and the Coe axiom, The Bulletin, New York State Archeological Association, Number 39, pp. 1-14. Ann Arbor.

BULLEN, RIPLEY P.

1949 Excavations in northeastern Massachusetts. Papers of the Robert S. Peabody Foundation for Archaeology, Vol. 1, No. 3. Andover.

BURGER, VALERIE

1953 Indian camp sites on Kempt and Manowan lakes in the Province of Quebec. Pennsylvania Archaeologist, Vol. 23, No. 1, pp. 32-45. Milton.

BUTLER, PATRICK

1959 Palynological studies of the Barnstable Marsh, Cape Cod, Massachusetts. Ecology, Vol. 40, No. 4, pp. 735-37. Durham.

BYERS, DOUGLAS S.

1954 Bull Brook—a fluted point site in Ipswich, Massachusetts. American Antiquity, Vol. 19, No. 4, pp. 343-51. Salt Lake City.

——

1955 Additional information on the Bull Brook site, Massachusetts. American Antiquity, Vol. 20, No. 3, pp. 274-76. Salt Lake City.

——

1956 Ipswich B.C. Essex Institute Historical Collections, Vol. 92, pp. 252-64. Salem.

——

1959 An introduction to five papers on the Archaic stage. American Antiquity, Vol. 24, No. 3, pp. 229-32. Salt Lake City.

——

1959a The eastern Archaic: some problems and hypotheses. American Antiquity, Vol. 24, No. 3, pp. 233-56. Salt Lake City.

1959b Radiocarbon dates for the Bull Brook site, Massachusetts. American Antiquity, Vol. 24, No. 4, Pt. 1, pp. 427–29. Salt Lake City.

——— 1960 The rape of Wayland. American Antiquity, Vol. 25, No. 3, p. 420. Salt Lake City.

——— 1961 Second comment on William A. Ritchie's "Iroquois archeology and settlement patterns." *In,* Symposium on Cherokee and Iroquois culture, edited by William N. Fenton and John Gulick. Smithsonian Institution, Bureau of American Ethnology, Bulletin 180, pp. 47–50. Washington.

——— 1966 The Debert Paleo-Indian site. A guide for stop no. 11, field trip no. 4, Geological Association of Canada, Mineralogical Association of Canada.

CALDWELL, JOSEPH R.
1952 The archeology of eastern Georgia and South Carolina. *In,* Archeology of eastern United States, edited by James B. Griffin, pp. 312–21. University of Chicago Press. Chicago.

——— 1954 The Old Quartz industry of Piedmont Georgia and South Carolina. Southern Indian Studies, Vol. 5, pp. 37–39. Chapel Hill.

——— 1958 Trend and tradition in the prehistory of the eastern United States. American Anthropological Association, Memoir No. 88. Menasha.

CARPENTER, EDMUND S.
1950 Five sites of the Intermediate period. American Antiquity, Vol. 15, No. 4, pp. 298–314. Menasha.

——— 1950a Four Hopewellian tumuli in western New York. Journal of the Washington Academy of Sciences, Vol. 40, No. 7, pp. 209–16. Washington.

——— 1956 The Irvine, Cornplanter and Corydon mounds, Warren County, Pennsylvania. Pennsylvania Archaeologist, Vol. 26, No. 2, pp. 89–115.

———, and SCHOFF, HARRY L.
1951 The Nelson mound, Crawford County, Pennsylvania. Pennsylvania Archaeologist, Vol. 21, Nos. 3–4, pp. 57–59. Gettysburg.

CLAFLIN, WILLIAM H., JR.
1931 The Stalling's Island mound, Columbia County, Georgia. Papers of the Peabody Museum of American Archaeology and Ethnology, Harvard University, Vol. 14, No. 1. Cambridge.

CLARK, GRAHAME
1957 Archaeology and society. Harvard University Press. Cambridge.

CLARK, NEIL A.; LANZT, STANLEY W., and ROBINSON, WILLIAM J.
1960 The Danner mound. Pennsylvania Archaeologist, Vol. 30, No. 2, pp. 37–45. Gettysburg.

COE, JOFFRE L.
1964 Formative cultures of the Carolina Piedmont. Transactions of the American Philosophical Society, Vol. 54, No. 3. Philadelphia.

COLEMAN, A. P.
1936 Lake Iroquois. Forty-fifth annual report of the Ontario Department of Mines, Vol. 45, Pt. 7, pp. 1–36. Toronto.

CORNWELL, WILLIAM S.
n.d. Late Point Peninsula burial at Plum Orchard site (Roc. 26-2) Penfield, Monroe County, New York.

COX, DONALD D.
1959 Some postglacial forests in central and eastern New York State as determined by the method of pollen analysis. New York State Museum and Science Service, Bulletin No. 377. Albany.

CRANE, H. R.
1956 University of Michigan radiocarbon dates I. Science, Vol. 124, No. 3224, pp. 664–72. Washington, D.C.

———, and GRIFFIN, JAMES B.

1958 University of Michigan radiocarbon dates II. Science, Vol. 127, No. 3306, pp. 1098–1105. Washington, D.C.

———

1959 University of Michigan radiocarbon dates IV. American Journal of Science Radiocarbon Supplement, Vol. 1, pp. 173–98. New Haven.

———

1960 University of Michigan radiocarbon dates V. American Journal of Science Radiocarbon Supplement, Vol. 2, pp. 31–48. New Haven.

———

1961 University of Michigan radiocarbon dates VI. American Journal of Science, Radiocarbon, Vol. 3, pp. 105–25. New Haven.

———

1962 University of Michigan radiocarbon dates VII. American Journal of Science, Radiocarbon, Vol. 4, pp. 183–203. New Haven.

———

1963 University of Michigan radiocarbon dates VIII. American Journal of Science, Radiocarbon, Vol. 5, pp. 228–53. New Haven.

CROSS, DOROTHY

1941 Archaeology of New Jersey, Volume One. Archaeological Society of New Jersey and New Jersey State Museum. Trenton.

———

1956 Archaeology of New Jersey, Volume Two. Archaeological Society of New Jersey and New Jersey State Museum. Trenton.

CROZIER, A.

1939 The steatite quarry near Christiana, Lancaster County, Pennsylvania. Bulletin of the Archaeological Society of Delaware, Vol. 3, No. 2, pp. 12–15. Wilmington.

CUNNINGHAM, WILBUR M.

1948 A study of the Glacial Kame culture in Michigan, Ohio, and Indiana. Occasional Contributions from the Museum of Anthropology of the University of Michigan, No. 12. Ann Arbor.

DAVIS, MARGARET BRYAN

1958 Three pollen diagrams from central Massachusetts. American Journal of Science, Vol. 256, No. 8, pp. 540–70. New Haven.

DEEVEY, EDWARD S., JR.

1943 Additional pollen analyses from southern New England. American Journal of Science, Vol. 241, No. 12, pp. 717–52. New Haven.

———

1951 Late-glacial and postglacial pollen diagrams from Maine. American Journal of Science, Vol. 249, pp. 177–207. New Haven.

———, and FLINT, R. F.

1957 Postglacial hypsithermal interval. Science, Vol. 125, No. 3240, pp. 182–84. Lancaster.

———, GRALENSKI, L. J., and HOFFREN, VÄINÖ

1959 Yale natural radiocarbon measurements IV. American Journal of Science Radiocarbon Supplement, Vol. 1, pp. 144–72. New Haven.

DINCAUZE, DINA

1968 Cremation cemeteries in eastern Massachusetts. Papers of the Peabody Museum of Archaeology and Ethnology, Harvard University, Vol. 59, No. 1. Cambridge, Mass.

DRAGOO, DON W.

1956 Excavation at the Watson site, 46Hk34, Hancock County, West Virginia. Pennsylvania Archaeologist, Vol. 26, No. 2, pp. 59–88. Gettysburg.

———

1959 Archaic hunters of the upper Ohio Valley. Carnegie Museum, Anthropological Series, No. 3. Pittsburgh.

———

1961 An Adena burial site in Delaware. Bulletin of the Eastern States Archeological Federation, No. 20, p. 12. Trenton.

———

1963 Mounds for the dead: an analysis of the Adena culture. Annals of Carnegie Museum, Vol. 37. Pittsburgh.

DROSTE, JOHN B.; RUBIN, MEYER, and WHITE, GEORGE W.

1959 Age of marginal Wisconsin drift at Corry, northwestern Pennsylvania. Science, Vol. 130, No. 3391, p. 1760. Washington, D.C.

DUNN, GERALD C.

1945 The Oaklawn soapstone quarry. Bulletin of the Massachusetts Archaeological Society, Vol. 6, No. 4, pp. 49–52. Attleboro.

EISELEY, LOREN C.

1955 The Paleo-Indians: Their survival and diffusion. *In*, New interpretations of aboriginal American culture history, edited by Betty J. Meggers and Clifford Evans. 75th Anniversary Volume of the Anthropological Society of Washington, D.C., pp. 1–11. Washington, D.C.

ELLIS, H. HOLMES

1940 Flint-working techniques of the American Indians: an experimental study. Ohio State Archeological and Historical Society. Columbus. (Mimeographed.)

EMERSON, J. N.

1955 The Kant site: a Point Peninsula manifestation in Renfrew County, Ontario. Transactions of the Royal Canadian Institute, Vol. XXXI. Pt. I.

———

n.d. The archaeology of the Ontario Iroquois. Unpublished Ph.D. dissertation, University of Chicago, 1954.

EVANS, CLIFFORD

1955 A ceramic study of Virginia archeology. Smithsonian Institution, Bureau of American Ethnology, Bulletin 160. Washington.

FAIRBANKS, CHARLES H.

1942 The taxonomic position of Stalling's Island, Georgia. American Antiquity, Vol. 7, No. 3, pp. 223–31. Menasha.

FAIRBRIDGE, RHODES W.

1958 Dating the latest movements of the Quaternary sea level. Transactions of the New York Academy of Sciences. Ser. II, Vol. 20, No. 6, pp. 471–82. New York.

———

1960 The changing level of the sea. Scientific American, Vol. 202, No. 5, pp. 70–79. New York.

———

1960a Recent world-wide sea level changes. Bulletin of the Massachusetts Archaeological Society, Vol. 21, Nos. 3, 4, pp. 49–51. Attleboro.

FAIRCHILD, H. L.

1909 Glacial waters in central New York. New York State Museum, Bulletin 127. Albany.

———

1928 Geologic story of the Genesee Valley and western New York. Published by the author. Rochester.

FAULKNER, CHARLES H.

1960 Walkerton: a Point Peninsula-like focus in Indiana. Indiana History Bulletin, Vol. 37, No. 10, pp. 123–36. Indianapolis.

FENNEMAN, N. M.

1938 Physiography of eastern United States. McGraw-Hill. New York.

FENTON, WILLIAM N.

1940 Problems arising from the historic northeastern position of the Iroquois. *In*, Essays in historical anthropology of North America. Smithsonian Miscellaneous Collections, Vol. 100, pp. 159–251. Washington.

FISHER, DONALD W.

1955 Prehistoric mammals of New York. New York State Conservationist, February–March, pp. 18–22. New York State Conservation Department. Albany.

FLINT, RICHARD FOSTER

1953 Probable Wisconsin substages and late-Wisconsin events in northeastern United States and southeastern Canada. Bulletin of the Geological Society of America, Vol. 64, pp. 897–919. Baltimore.

———

1956 New radiocarbon dates and late-Pleistocene stratigraphy. American Journal of Science, Vol. 254, pp. 265–87. New Haven.

1957 Glacial and Pleistocene geology. John Wiley and Sons. New York.

———, *et al.*
1959 Glacial map of the United States east of the Rocky Mountains. Geological Society of American. New York.

FOWKE, GERARD
1894 Archaeological investigations in James and Potomac valleys. Bureau of American Ethnology, Smithsonian Institution. Washington.

FOWLER, MELVIN L.
1959 Modoc Rock Shelter: an Early Archaic site in southern Illinois. American Antiquity, Vol. 24, No. 3, pp. 257–70. Salt Lake City.

FOWLER, WILLIAM S.
1961 Projectile points and their cultural significance. Bulletin of the Massachusetts Archaeological Society, Vol. 23, No. 1, pp. 5–13. Attleboro.

FUNK, ROBERT E.
1965 The Archaic of the Hudson Valley— new evidence and new interpretations. Pennsylvania Archaeologist, Vol. XXXV, Nos. 3–4, pp. 139–160. Gettysburg. (Issued June, 1967.)

1966 An Archaic framework for the Hudson Valley. Unpublished Ph.D. dissertation, Columbia University. New York.

GIFFORD, E. W.
1936 California balanophagy. *In,* Essays in Anthropology Presented to A. L. Kroeber, pp. 87–98. University of California Press. Berkeley.

GLAMM, A. C., JR.
1957 The Cain Mound (Ctg. 5-2), Erie County, New York. The Bulletin, New York State Archeological Association, No. 9, pp. 8–10. Rochester.

GREENMAN, E. F., and STANLEY, G. M.
1943 The archeology and geology of two early sites near Killarney, Ontario. Papers of the Michigan Academy of Sciences, Arts and Letters, Vol. 28, pp. 505–30. Ann Arbor.

GRIFFIN, JAMES B.
1960 Climatic change: a contributory cause of the growth and decline of northern Hopewellian culture. The Wisconsin Archeologist, June, unpaginated reprint.

——— (editor)
1961 Lake Superior copper and the Indians: Miscellaneous studies of Great Lakes prehistory. Anthropological Papers, Museum of Anthropology, University of Michigan, No. 17. Ann Arbor.

GUILDAY, JOHN E.
1961 Prehistoric record of *Scalopus* from western Pennsylvania. Journal of Mammalogy, Vol. 42, No. 1, pp. 117–18. Lawrence, Kan.

———
n.d A possible caribou-Paleo Indian association from Dutchess Quarry Cave, Orange County, New York.

———, PARMALEE, PAUL W., and TANNER, DONALD P.
1962 Aboriginal butchering techniques at the Eschelman Site (36 La 12), Lancaster County, Pennsylvania. Pennsylvania Archaeologist, Vol. 32. No. 2, pp. 59–83. Gettysburg.

GUTHE, ALFRED K.
1951 The Williams mound, a manifestation of the Hopewellian culture. Eastern States Archeological Federation, Bulletin No. 10, pp. 4–5. Milton.

———
1959 Filling out the story through cooperation. Rochester Museum of Arts and Sciences, Museum Service, Vol. 32, No. 1, pp. 174–75. Rochester.

HALLOWELL, A. IRVING
1926 Bear ceremonialism in the northern hemisphere. American Anthropologist, Vol. 28, No. 1, pp. 1–175. Menasha.

HAMILTON, WILLIAM J., JR.
1963 Distribution of the fox squirrel in New York. Journal of Mammalogy, Vol. 44, No. 1, pp. 124–25. Lawrence, Kan.

HARRINGTON, M. R.
1909   Rock-shelters of Armonk, New York. *In,* The Indians of greater New York and the lower Hudson, edited by Clark Wissler. Anthropological Papers of the American Museum of Natural History, Vol. III, pp. 125–38. New York.

———

1924   An Ancient village site of the Shinnecock Indians. Anthropological Papers of the American Museum of Natural History, Vol. XXII, Pt. V. New York.

———

1933   Gypsum Cave, Nevada. Southwest Museum Papers, No. 8. Los Angeles.

HARTNAGEL, CHRIS, and BISHOP, SHERMAN
1922   The mastodons, mammoths, and other Pleistocene mammals of New York State. New York State Museum, Bulletin 241–242. Albany.

HAURY, EMIL W.; RANDS, ROBERT L.; SPAULDING, ALBERT C.; TAYLOR, WALTER W.; THOMPSON, RAYMOND H.; WAUCHOPE, ROBERT, and WHITE, MARIAN E.
1956   An archaeological approach to the study of cultural stability. *In,* Seminars in Archaeology: 1955, edited by Robert Wauchope, pp. 31–57. Memoirs of the Society for American Archaeology, No. 11. Salt Lake City.

HAY, OLIVER P.
1923   The Pleistocene of North America and its vertebrated animals from the states east of the Mississippi River and from the Canadian provinces east of longitude 95°. Carnegie Institute of Washington, Publication 322. Washington, D.C.

HAYES, CHARLES F., III
1963   A Point Peninsula burial. Museum Service, Bulletin of the Rochester Museum of Arts and Sciences, Vol. 36, No. 1, pp. 6–7. Rochester.

———

1967   The longhouse at the Cornish site. In Iroquois culture, history, and prehistory, ed. by Elisabeth Tooker, pp. 91–97. New York State Museum and Science Service, Albany.

HAYNES, VANCE, and AGOGINO, GEORGE
1960   Geological significance of a new radiocarbon date from the Lindenmeier site. Denver Museum of Natural History, Proceedings No. 9. Denver.

HEIZER, ROBERT F.
1958   Prehistoric central California: a problem in historical developmental classification. *In,* Papers on California Archaeology: 63–69, Paper 66, pp. 19–23. University of California Archaeological Survey, University of California. Berkeley.

HESTER, JIM J.
1960   Late Pleistocene extinction and radiocarbon dating. American Antiquity, Vol. 26, No. 1, pp. 58–77. Salt Lake City.

HEUBUSCH, CAROL A.
1959   Mastodons and mammoths in western New York. Science on the March. Buffalo Museum of Science, Vol. 40, No. 1, pp. 3–9. Buffalo.

HINSDALE, WILBERT B.
1930   Reports of archaeological field work in the summer of 1928 in Montmorency, Newaygo and Lake Counties, Michigan. Papers of the Michigan Academy of Science, Arts and Letters, Vol. 12, 1929, pp. 127–35. Ann Arbor.

HOLMES, WILLIAM HENRY
1897   Stone implements of the Potomac-Chesapeake tidewater province. Fifteenth Annual Report of the Bureau of Ethnology, pp. 13–152. Washington.

HOUGH, JACK L.
1958   Geology of the Greak Lakes. University of Illinois Press. Urbana.

HOWE, FRANK B.
1935   Classification and agricultural value of New York soils. Cornell University Agricultural Experiment Station, Bulletin 619. Ithaca.

HUNTINGTON, E. GALE
1959   An archaeological study from Martha's Vineyard. The Dukes County Intelligencer, Dukes County Historical Society, Vol. 1, No. 2. Edgartown.

JAMESON, J. FRANKLIN
1909 Narratives of New Netherland, 1609–1664. Charles Scribner's Sons. New York.

JOHNSON, FREDERICK, and RAUP, HUGH M.
1947 Grassy Island. Papers of the Robert S. Peabody Foundation for Archaeology, Vol. 1, No. 2. Andover.

JOHNSTON, RICHARD B.
1958 The Serpent Mounds site, 1957. Royal Ontario Museum Bulletin of the Division of Art and Archaeology, No. 27, pp. 3–7. Toronto.

1958a The findings after two years of work at Serpent Mounds site, Rice Lake, Ontario. Proceedings of the Indiana Academy of Science, Vol. 67, pp. 96–97. Indianapolis.

1959 The 1958 interim report on the Serpent Mound site. Royal Ontario Museum, Art and Archaeology Division. Toronto.

1960 More findings at the Serpent Mounds site, Rice Lake, Ontario. Proceedings of the Indiana Academy of Science for 1959, Vol. 69, pp. 73–77. Indianapolis.

JURY, WILFRED, and JURY, ELSIE
1952 The Burley site. University of Western Ontario, Bulletin No. 9. London.

KARROW, P. F.; CLARK, J. R., and TERASMAE, J.
1961 The age of Lake Iroquois and Lake Ontario. Journal of Geology, Vol. 69, No. 6, pp. 659–67. Chicago.

KELLY, A. R.
1938 A preliminary report on archaeological explorations at Macon, Georgia. Smithsonian Institution, Bureau of American Ethnology, Anthropological Papers, No. 1, Bulletin 119, pp. 1–68. Washington.

KENNEDY, CLYDE C.
1966 Preliminary report on the Morrison's Island-6 site. National Museum of Canada, Bulletin No. 206, pp. 100–124. Ottawa.

KENYON, EDNA (editor)
1927 The Indians of North America. From the Jesuit Relations and allied documents. 2 volumes. Harcourt, Brace and Company. New York.

KENYON, WALTER
1957 The Inverhuron site. Royal Ontario Museum, Occasional Paper 1. Toronto.

1961 The Swan Lake site. Occasional Paper 3, Art and Archaeology Division Royal Ontario Museum, University of Toronto, pp. 1–37. Toronto.

———, and CAMERON, NANCY S.
1961 The Brock Street burial. Occasional Paper 3, Art and Archaeology Division Royal Ontario Museum, University of Toronto, pp. 41–55. Toronto.

KINSEY, W. FRED, III
1959 Recent excavations on Bare Island in Pennsylvania: the Kent-Hally site. Pennsylvania Archaeologist, Vol. 29, Nos. 3–4, pp. 109–33. Gettysburg.

KOCHAN, EDWARD
1961 Riverhaven sites #1 and #2, Grand Island, New York. The Bulletin, New York State Archeological Association, No. 22, pp. 13–14. Rochester.

n.d. A possible mortuary blade factory site.

KREMP, FRANK
1961 The Coburn site: a burial complex on Cape Cod. Bulletin of the Massachusetts Archaeological Society, Vol. 22, Nos. 3, 4, pp. 33–42. Attleboro.

KRIEGER, ALEX D.
1954 A comment on "fluted point relationships" by John Witthoft. American Antiquity, Vol. 19, No. 3, pp. 273–75. Salt Lake City.

LATHAM, ROY
1953 Notes on the Orient focus of eastern Long Island, New York. Pennsylvania Archaeologist, Vol. 23, Nos. 3–4, pp. 108–10. Milton.

LEE, THOMAS E.

1954   The first Sheguiandah expedition, Manitoulin Island, Ontario. American Antiquity, Vol. 20, No. 2, pp. 101–11. Salt Lake City.

——   1955   The second Sheguiandah expedition, Manitoulin Island, Ontario. American Antiquity, Vol. 21, No. 1, pp. 63–72. Salt Lake City.

——   1957   The antiquity of the Sheguiandah site. Canadian Field Naturalist, Vol. 71, No. 3, pp. 117–37. Ottawa.

LENIG, DONALD

1965   The Oak Hill horizon and its relation to the development of Five Nations Iroquois culture. Researches and Transactions of the New York State Archeological Association, Vol. XV, No. 1. Buffalo.

LIBBY, W. F.

1954   Chicago radiocarbon dates IV. Science, Vol. 119, No. 3083, pp. 135–40. Lancaster.

——   1954a   Chicago radiocarbon dates V. Science, Vol. 120, No. 3123, pp. 733–42. Lancaster.

——   1955   Radiocarbon dating. Second edition. University of Chicago Press. Chicago.

LOGAN, WILFRED D.

1952   Graham Cave, an Archaic site in Montgomery County, Missouri. Missouri Archaeological Society, Memoir No. 2. Columbia.

LOPEZ, JULIUS

1958   The Milo rock site, Pelham Bay Park, Bronx County, N.Y. Pennsylvania Archaeologist, Vol. XXVIII, Nos. 3–4, pp. 3–18.

——, and LATHAM, ROY

1960   Faces on Sebonac pottery from eastern Long Island. Pennsylvania Archaeologist, Vol. XXX, No. 2, pp. 58–62. Gettysburg.

LORD, ARTHUR C., SR.

1962   The Hawes site: a burial stone bowl complex. Bulletin of the Massachusetts Archaeological Society, Vol. 23, Nos. 3, 4, pp. 21–23. Attleboro.

MACCLINTOCK, PAUL, and TERASMAE, J.

1960   Glacial history of Covey Hill. Journal of Geology, Vol. 68, No. 2, pp. 232–41. Chicago.

MACNEISH, RICHARD S.

1952   Iroquois pottery types, a technique for the study of Iroquois prehistory. National Museum of Canada, Bulletin No. 124. Ottawa.

MANSFIELD, J. ALFRED

1961   The Mansion Inn site—Wayland. Bulletin of the Massachusetts Archaeological Society, Vol. 23, No. 1, pp. 1–5. Attleboro.

MANSON, CARL

1948   Marcey Creek site: an early manifestation in the Potomac Valley. American Antiquity, Vol. 13, No. 3, pp. 223–27. Menasha.

MARTIN, PAUL S.

1958   Taiga-tundra and the full-glacial period in Chester County, Pennsylvania. American Journal of Science, Vol. 256, No. 7, pp. 470–502. New Haven.

MASON, CAROL IRWIN, and MASON, RONALD J.

1961   The age of the Old Copper culture. The Wisconsin Archeologist, Vol. 42, No. 4, pp. 143–55. Lake Mills.

MASON, RONALD J.

1958   Late Pleistocene geochronology and the Paleo-Indian penetration into the lower Michigan Peninsula. Anthropological Papers, Museum of Anthropology, University of Michigan, No. 11. Ann Arbor.

——   1960   Early man and the age of the Champlain Sea. Journal of Geology, Vol. 68, No. 4, pp. 366–76. Chicago.

——   1962   The Paleo-Indian tradition in eastern North America. Current Anthropology, Vol. 3, No. 3, pp. 227–83. Chicago.

MAYER-OAKES, WILLIAM J.
1955   Prehistory of the upper Ohio Valley; an introductory archaeological study. Anthropological Series, No. 2, Carnegie Museum. Pittsburgh.

MCCANN, CATHERINE
1962   The Wilson site, Bradford County, Pennsylvania. Pennsylvania Archaeologist, Vol. 32, No. 2, pp. 43–55.

MCCARY, B. C.
1951   A workshop site of early man in Dinwiddie County, Virginia. American Antiquity, Vol. 17, No. 1, Pt. 1, pp. 9–17. Salt Lake City.

MCKERN, W. C.
1939   The midwestern taxonomic method as an aid to archaeological culture study. American Antiquity, Vol. 4, No. 4, pp. 310–13. Menasha.

MILES, SUZANNA W.
1951   A revaluation of the Old Copper industry. American Antiquity, Vol. 16, No. 3, pp. 240–47. Salt Lake City.

MILLER, CARL F.
1957   Radiocarbon dates from an Early Archaic deposit in Russell Cave, Alabama. American Antiquity, Vol. 23, No. 1, p. 84. Salt Lake City.

MILLS, WILLIAM C.
1922   Exploration of the Mound City group. Ohio Archaeological and Historical Quarterly, Vol. 31, No. 4, pp. 423–584. Columbus.

MITCHELL, B. M.
1963   Occurrence of overall corded pottery in the upper Ottawa Valley, Canada. American Antiquity, Vol. 29, No. 1, pp. 114–15. Salt Lake City.

MOOREHEAD, WARREN K.
1922   A report on the archaeology of Maine. Department of Archaeology, Phillips Academy. Andover.

MULLER, E. H.
1957   Physiography and glacial geology of Allegany County, N.Y., and vicinity. Guidebook for 29th annual meeting of the N.Y. State Geological Association, May 1957. Syracuse.

———
1957a   Glacial geology of western and central New York. Geological Society of America, Bulletin 68, p. 1897 (abstract). Baltimore.

———
1960   Glacial geology of Cattaraugus County, New York. Friends of Pleistocene Geology, Eastern Section. 23rd Reunion, May 21 and 22, 1960, Dunkirk, N.Y. Department of Geology, Syracuse University. (Mimeographed.) Syracuse.

MURPHY, HENRY C. (editor)
1867   Journal of a voyage to New York and a tour in several of the American colonies in 1679–80, by Jaspar Dankers and Peter Sluyter of Wiewerd in Friesland. Memoir Long Island Historical Society, Vol. 1. Brooklyn.

NEUMANN, GEORG K.
1952   Archeology and race in the American Indian. In, Archeology of the Eastern United States, edited by James B. Griffin. University of Chicago Press. Chicago.

NICHOLS, JOHN B.
1928   Notes on rock crevice burials in Jefferson County at Point Peninsula. Researches and Transactions of the New York State Archeological Association, Vol. 5, No. 4. Rochester.

NOBLE, DANIEL A., SR.
1962   An Owasco burial from "Whites" (Nbn. 2). Chenango Chapter, N.Y.S.A.A., Vol. 4, No. 3, p. 2. (Mimeographed.) Norwich.

OSTBERG, NEIL J.
1957   Report on the Reigh site. The Wisconsin Archeologist, Vol. 38, pp. 282–87. Lake Mills.

PARKER, ARTHUR C.
1916   The origin of the Iroquois as suggested by their archeology. American Anthropologist, Vol. 18, pp. 479–507.

———
1922   The archeological history of New York. New York State Museum, Bulletin Nos. 235–238. Albany.

——

1924 The great Algonkin flint mines at Coxsackie. Researches and Transactions of the New York State Archeological Association, Vol. IV, No. 4. Rochester.

PARMALEE, PAUL W.

1959 Animal remains from the Raddatz Rockshelter, Sk. 5, Wisconsin. The Wisconsin Archeologist, Vol. 40, No. 2, pp. 83–90. Lake Mills.

——

1960 Animal Remains from the Durst Rockshelter, Sauk County, Wisconsin. The Wisconsin Archeologist, Vol. 41, No. 1, pp. 11–17. Lake Mills.

PATTERSON, EDWARD D.

1955 Garvie Point—Nas. site 1. Bulletin of the Nassau Archeological Society, Vol. 1, No. 1, pp. 1–3. Sea Cliff, N.Y.

PHILLIPS, PHILIP, and WILLEY, GORDON R.

1953 Method and theory in American archeology: an operational basis for culture-historical integration. American Anthropologist, Vol. 55, No. 5, Pt. 1, pp. 615–33. Menasha.

POTZGER, J. E.

1951 The fossil record near the glacial border. Ohio Journal of Sciences, Vol. 51, No. 3, pp. 126–33. Columbus.

——, and OTTO, JAMES H.

1943 Postglacial forest succession in northern New Jersey as shown by pollen records from five bogs. American Journal of Botany, Vol. 30, No. 2, pp. 83–87. Baltimore.

PRAUS, ALEXIS A.

1942 Excavations at the Old Lyme shell heap. Bulletin of the Archaeological Society of Connecticut, No. 13, pp. 3–66. New Haven.

——

1945 The South Woodstock site. Bulletin of the Archaeological Society of Connecticut, No. 17, pp. 1–52. New Haven.

PRUFER, OLAF H.

1960 Early man east of the Mississippi. Sonderdruck aus Festschrift für Lothar Zotz. Steinzeit fragen der Alten und Neuen Welt. Bonn.

——

1964 The McGraw site: a Middle Woodland site near Chillicothe, Ross County, Ohio. Abstracts of Papers, Twenty-ninth Annual Meeting, Society for American Archaeology, The University of North Carolina at Chapel Hill, pp. 36–37. Chapel Hill.

——, and BABY, RAYMOND S.

1963 Palaeo-Indians of Ohio. Ohio Historical Society. Columbus.

PUTNAM, F. W.

1878 The manufacture of soapstone pots by the Indians of New England. 11th Report, Peabody Museum of American Archaeology and Ethnology, Vol. II, No. 2, pp. 273–76. Cambridge.

QUIMBY, GEORGE I.

1954 Cultural and natural areas before Kroeber. American Antiquity, Vol. 19, No. 4, pp. 317–31. Salt Lake City.

——

1958 Fluted points and geochronology of the Lake Michigan basin. American Antiquity, Vol. 23, No. 3, pp. 247–54. Salt Lake City.

——

1959 Lanceolate points and fossil beaches in the Upper Great Lakes region. American Antiquity, Vol. 24, No. 4, pp. 424–26. Salt Lake City.

——

1960 Indian life in the Upper Great Lakes, 11,000 B.C. to A.D. 1800. University of Chicago Press. Chicago.

——

1962 The age of the Oconto site. Wisconsin Archeologist, Vol. 43, No. 1. (Unpaginated reprint.)

RICE, T. D., and ALEXANDER, L. T.

1938 The physical nature of soil. In, Soils and men. U. S. Department of Agriculture, Yearbook of Agriculture 1938. Washington.

RIDLEY, FRANK

1954   The Frank Bay site, Lake Nipissing, Ontario. American Antiquity, Vol. 20, No. 1, pp. 40–50. Salt Lake City.

——

1958   The Boys and Barrie sites. Ontario Archaeological Society, Publication No. 4, pp. 18–42. Toronto.

RITCHIE, WILLIAM A.

1928   An Algonkian village site near Levanna, N.Y. Research Records of the Rochester Municipal Museum, No. 1. Rochester.

——

1929   Hammerstones, anvils and certain pitted stones. Researches and Transactions of the New York State Archeological Association, Vol. 7, No. 2. Rochester.

——

1932   The Lamoka Lake site. Researches and Transactions of the New York State Archeological Association, Vol. 7, No. 4. Rochester.

——

1934   An Algonkin-Iroquois contact site on Castle Creek, Broome County, N.Y. Research Records of the Rochester Municipal Museum, No. 2. Rochester.

——

1936   New evidence relating to the Archaic occupation of New York. Researches and Transactions of the New York State Archeological Association, Vol. 8, No. 1. Rochester.

——

1936a   A prehistoric fortified village site at Canandaigua, Ontario County, New York. Research Records of the Rochester Museum of Arts and Sciences, No. 3. Rochester.

——

1937   Culture influences from Ohio in New York archaeology. American Antiquity, Vol. 2, No. 3, pp. 182–94. Menasha.

——

1938   A perspective of northeastern archaeology. American Antiquity, Vol. 4, No. 2, pp. 94–112. Menasha.

1938a   Certain recently explored New York mounds and their probable relation to the Hopewell culture. Research Records of the Rochester Museum of Arts and Sciences, No. 4. Rochester.

——

1938b   A unique prehistoric workshop site. Museum Service, April, pp. 1–6, Rochester Museum of Arts and Sciences. Rochester.

——

1939   Excavations in a prehistoric village site near Bainbridge, New York. Museum Service, April–May, pp. 86–90, Rochester Museum of Arts and Sciences. Rochester.

——

1940   Two prehistoric village sites at Brewerton, New York. Research Records of the Rochester Museum of Arts and Sciences, No. 5. Rochester.

——

1944   The pre-Iroquoian occupations of New York State. Rochester Museum of Arts and Sciences, Memoir No. 1. Rochester.

——

1945   An early site in Cayuga County, New York. Research Records of the Rochester Museum of Arts and Sciences, No. 7. Rochester.

——

1946   A stratified prehistoric site at Brewerton, New York. Research Records of the Rochester Museum of Arts and Sciences, No. 8. Rochester.

——

1947   Archaeological evidence for ceremonialism in the Owasco culture. Researches and Transactions of the New York State Archeological Association, Vol. XI, No. 2. Rochester.

——

1947a   A prehistoric ceremony of sacrifice in New York State. New York History, Vol. XXVIII, pp. 458–65. New York State Historical Association. Cooperstown.

—— 1949 An Archaeological survey of the Trent waterway in Ontario, Canada. Researches and Transactions of the New York State Archeological Association, Vol. 12, No. 1. Rochester.

—— 1949a The Bell-Philhower site, Sussex County, New Jersey. Indiana Historical Society, Prehistory Research Series, Vol. 3, No. 2. Indianapolis.

—— 1950 Another probable case of prehistoric bear ceremonialism in New York. American Antiquity, Vol. 15, No. 3, pp. 247–49. Menasha.

—— 1951 A current synthesis of New York prehistory. American Antiquity, Vol. 17, No. 2, pp. 130–36. Salt Lake City.

—— 1951a Ground slates: Eskimo or Indian? Pennsylvania Archaeologist, Vol. 21, Nos. 3–4, pp. 46–52. Milton.

—— 1951b Radiocarbon dates on samples from New York State. In, Radiocarbon Dating. Assembled by Frederick Johnson. Memoirs of the Society for American Archaeology, No. 8, pp. 30–31. Salt Lake City.

—— 1951c Their mouths are stopped with dust. Archaeology, Vol. 4, No. 3, pp. 136–44. Archaeological Institute of America. Brattleboro, Vt.

—— 1952 Paleopathological evidence suggesting pre-Columbian tuberculosis in New York State. American Journal of Physical Anthropology, n.s., Vol. 10, No. 3, pp. 305–18. Philadelphia.

—— 1952a The Chance horizon, an early stage of Mohawk Iroquois cultural development. New York State Museum, Circular 29. Albany.

—— 1953 A probable Paleo-Indian site in Vermont. American Antiquity, Vol. 18, No. 3, pp. 249–58. Salt Lake City.

—— 1954 Dutch Hollow, an early historic period Seneca site in Livingston County, New York. Researches and Transactions of the New York State Archeological Association, Vol. 13, No. 1. Rochester.

—— 1955 Recent discoveries suggesting an Early Woodland burial cult in the northeast. New York State Museum and Science Service, Circular 40. Albany.

—— 1955a The northeastern Archaic—a review. (Mimeographed.) Albany.

—— 1956 Prehistoric settlement patterns in northeastern North America. In, Prehistoric settlement patterns in the New World, edited by Gordon R. Willey. Viking Fund Publications in Anthropology, No. 23, pp. 72–80. New York.

—— 1957 Traces of early man in the northeast. New York State Museum and Science Service. Bulletin No. 358. Albany.

—— 1958 An introduction to Hudson Valley prehistory. New York State Museum and Science Service, Bulletin No. 367. Albany.

—— 1959 The Stony Brook site and its relation to Archaic and Transitional cultures on Long Island. New York State Museum and Science Service, Bulletin No. 372. Albany.

—— 1961 A typology and nomenclature for New York projectile points. New York State Museum and Science Service, Bulletin No. 384. Albany.

———

1961a Iroquois archeology and settlement patterns. *In,* Symposium on Cherokee and Iroquois culture, edited by William N. Fenton and John Gulick. Smithsonian Institution, Bureau of American Ethnology, Bulletin 180, pp. 27–38. Washington.

———

1962 The antiquity of pottery in the northeast. American Antiquity, Vol. 27, No. 4, pp. 583–84. Salt Lake City.

———

1962a Northeastern crossties with the Arctic. *In,* Prehistoric cultural relations between the Arctic and temperate zones of North America, edited by John M. Campbell. Arctic Institute of North America. Technical Paper No. 11, pp. 96–99. Montreal.

———

1965a The "small stemmed point" in New England. Pennsylvania Archaeologist, Vol. XXXV, Nos. 3–4, pp. 134–138. Gettysburg. (Issued June, 1967.)

———

1969 The archaeology of Martha's Vineyard: a framework for the prehistory of southern New England. Natural History Press. New York. (In press.)

———

n.d. Four new Owasco pottery types in New York. *In,* Prehistoric pottery of the eastern U.S., edited by James B. Griffin. No pagination. University of Michigan, Museum of Anthropology. Ann Arbor.

———, and WARREN, STAFFORD L.

1932 The occurrence of multiple bony lesions suggesting myeloma in the skeleton of a pre-Columbian Indian. The American Journal of Roentgenology and Radium Therapy, Vol. XXVIII, No. 5, pp. 622–28. Springfield, Ill.

———, and MACNEISH, RICHARD S.

1949 The pre-Iroquoian pottery of New York State. American Antiquity, Vol. 15, No. 2, pp. 97–124. Menasha.

———, LENIG, DONALD, and MILLER, P. SCHUYLER

1953 An early Owasco sequence in eastern New York. New York State Museum, Circular 32. Albany.

———, and DRAGOO, DON W.

1959 The eastern dispersal of Adena. American Antiquity, Vol. 25, No. 1, pp. 43–50. Salt Lake City.

———, and DRAGOO, DON W.

1960 The eastern dispersal of Adena. New York State Museum and Science Service, Bulletin No. 379. Albany.

RITZENTHALER, ROBERT E.

1946 The Osceola site, an "Old Copper" site near Potosi, Wisconsin. The Wisconsin Archeologist, Vol. 27, No. 3, pp. 53–70. Milwaukee.

———

1958 Some carbon-14 dates for the Wisconsin Old Copper culture. The Wisconsin Archeologist, Vol. 39, No. 3, pp. 173–74. Lake Mills.

———, and WITTRY, WARREN L.

1952 The Oconto site—an Old Copper manifestation. The Wisconsin Archeologist, Vol. 33, No. 4, pp. 199–223. Milwaukee.

———, and QUIMBY, GEORGE I.

1962 The Red Ocher culture of the Upper Great Lakes and adjacent areas. Fieldiana, Anthropology, Vol. 36, No. 11, pp. 243–75. Chicago.

ROBBINS, MAURICE

1960 Wapanucket No. 6, an Archaic village in Middleboro, Massachusetts. Cohannet Chapter, Massachusetts Archaeological Society, Inc. Attleboro.

———

1963 Secondary cremation burial no. 2, the Hawes site. Bulletin of the Massachusetts Archaeological Society, Vol. 24, No. 2, pp. 30–33. Attleboro.

ROBBINS, MAURICE, and AGOGINO, GEORGE A.

1964 The Wapanucket no. 8 site: a Clovis-Archaic site in Massachusetts. American Antiquity, Vol. 29, No. 4, pp. 509–13. Salt Lake City.

ROECKER, ROBERT

1953–54 Waneta and Lamoka Lakes. New York State Conservationist, December–January, p. 25. State of New York Conservation Department. Albany.

ROGERS, E. S., and ROGERS, M. H.

1948 Archaeologcal reconnaissance of Lakes Mistassini and Albanel, Province of Quebec, 1947. American Antiquity, Vol. 14, No. 2, pp. 81–90. Menasha.

——

1950 Archaeological investigations in the region about Lakes Mistassini and Albanel, Province of Quebec, 1948. American Antiquity, Vol. 15, No. 4, pp. 322–37. Menasha.

——, and JEAN, H.

1959 The yearly cycle of the Mistassini Indians. Arctic, Vol. 12, No. 3, pp. 131–38. Montreal.

ROSE, EDWARD F.

1953 Five unusual caches at the Boats site. Bulletin of the Massachusetts Archaeological Society, Vol. 14, No. 4, pp. 109–11. Attleboro.

ROUSE, IRVING

1947 Ceramic traditions and sequences in Connecticut. Bulletin of the Archaeological Society of Connecticut, No. 21, pp. 10–25. New Haven.

RUBIN, MEYER, and ALEXANDER, CORRINNE

1960 U. S. Geological Survey radiocarbon dates V. American Journal of Science Radiocarbon Supplement, Vol. 2, pp. 129–85. New Haven.

——, and BERTHOLD, SARAH M.

1961 U. S. Geological radiocarbon dates VI. American Journal of Science, Radiocarbon, Vol. 3, pp. 86–98. New Haven.

SALWEN, BERT

1962 Sea levels and archeology in the Long Island Sound area. American Antiquity, Vol. 28, No. 1, pp. 46–55. Salt Lake City.

SARGENT, HOWARD R.

1952 A preliminary report on the excavations at Grannis Island. Bulletin of the Archaeological Society of Connecticut, No. 26, pp. 30–50. New Haven.

SCHMITT, KARL

1952 Archeological chronology of the middle Atlantic states. In, Archeology of eastern United States, edited by James B. Griffin, pp. 59–70. University of Chicago Press. Chicago.

SEARS, PAUL B.

1948 Forest sequence and climatic change in northeastern North America since early Wisconsin time. Ecology, Vol. 29, No. 3, pp. 326–33. Durham.

——

1963 Vegetation, climate, and coastal submergence in Connecticut. Science, Vol. 140, No. 3562, pp. 59–60. Washington.

SEARS, WILLIAM H.

1954 A late Archaic horizon on the Atlantic coastal plain. Southern Indian Studies, Vol. V, pp. 28–36. Archaeological Society of North Carolina and Research Laboratories of Anthropology, University of North Carolina. Chapel Hill.

SHEPARD, FRANCIS P.

1964 Sea level changes in the past 6000 years: possible archeological significance. Science, Vol. 143, No. 3606, pp. 574–76. Washington, D.C.

SHETRONE, H. C.

1926 Explorations of the Hopewell group of prehistoric earth works. Ohio Archaeological and Historical Quarterly, Vol. XXXV, No. 1, pp. 1–227. Columbus.

SKINNER, ALANSON

1903 Recent excavations in Indian camp sites at Mariners' Harbor. Proceedings of the Natural Science Association of Staten Island, Vol. 8, p. 58. Staten Island.

—— 1903a List of Indian villages and camp sites on Staten Island. Proceedings of the Natural Science Association of Staten Island, Vol. 8, pp. 59–60. Staten Island.

—— 1906 A list of collections of Staten Island archeologic material now extant. Proceedings of the Staten Island Association of Arts and Sciences, Vol. 1, pp. 89–91. Staten Island.

—— 1909 The Lenapé Indians of Staten Island. Anthropological Papers of the American Museum of Natural History, Vol. 3, pp. 3–62. New York.

—— 1909a Archaeology of the New York Coastal Algonkian. Anthropological Papers of the American Museum of Natural History, Vol. 3, pp. 213–35. New York.

—— 1912 Indian camp or village sites in the southern part of Staten Island and adjacent parts of New Jersey. Proceedings of the Staten Island Association of Arts and Sciences, Vol. 4, pp. 90–98. Staten Island.

—— 1919 Exploration of aboriginal sites at Throgs Neck and Clasons Point, New York City. Contribution from the Museum of the American Indian, Heye Foundation, Vol. V, No. 4. New York.

SLATTERY, RICHARD G.
1946 A prehistoric Indian site on Selden Island, Montgomery County, Md. Journal of the Washington Academy of Sciences, No. 8, pp. 262–66. Menasha.

SMITH, B. L.
1948 An analysis of the Maine cemetery complex. Massachusetts Archaeological Society Bulletin, Vol. 9, Nos. 2–3, pp. 17–72. Attleboro.

SMITH, CARLYLE SHREEVE
1950 The Archaeology of coastal New York. Anthropological Papers of the American Museum of Natural History, Vol. 43, Pt. 2. New York.

SMITH, PHILIP W.
1957 An analysis of Post-Wisconsin biogeography of the Prairie Peninsula region based on distributional phenomena among terrestrial vertebrate populations. Ecology, Vol. 38, No. 2, pp. 205, 218. Durham, N.C.

SMITH, RALPH H.
1954 A history and definition of game ranges in New York State. Division of Fish and Game, State of New York Conservation Department. Albany.

SOLECKI, RALPH
1950 The archeological position of historic Fort Corchaug, L.I., and its relation to contemporary forts. Bulletin of the Archaeological Society of Connecticut, No. 24, pp. 3–40. New Haven.

SPAULDING, ALBERT C.
1946 Northeastern archaeology and general trends in the northern forest zone. In, Man in northeastern North America. Papers of the Robert S. Peabody Foundation for Archaeology, Vol. 3, pp. 143–67. Andover.

—— 1955 Prehistoric cultural development in the eastern United States. In, New interpretations of aboriginal American culture history, pp. 12–27. Anthropological Society of Washington. Washington, D.C.

SPECK, FRANK G.
1926 Culture problems in northeastern North America. American Philosophical Society Proceedings, Vol. 65, No. 4, pp. 272–311. Philadelphia.

—— 1935 Naskapi. University of Oklahoma Press. Norman.

—— 1940 Penobscot man. University of Pennsylvania Press. Philadelphia.

1945 The Iroquois, a study in cultural evolution. Cranbrook Institute of Science, Bulletin No. 23. Bloomfield Hills, Mich.

1945a The celestial bear comes down to earth. Reading Public Museum and Art Gallery, Scientific Publications, No. 7. Reading, Pa.

SQUIER, E. G.
1851 Antiquities of the State of New York. Geo. H. Derby and Co. Buffalo.

STRONG, WILLIAM DUNCAN
1930 A stone culture from northern Labrador and its relation to the Eskimo-like cultures of the Northeast. American Anthropologist, Vol. 32, No. 1, pp. 126–44. Menasha.

STUIVER, MINZE, and DEEVEY, EDWARD S.
1962 Yale natural radiocarbon measurements VII. American Journal of Science, Radiocarbon, Vol. 4, pp. 250–62. New Haven.

———, and ROUSE, IRVING
1963 Yale natural radiocarbon measurements VIII. American Journal of Science, Radiocarbon, Vol. 5, Yale University, pp. 312–41. New Haven.

TAGGART, DAVID W.
n.d. The Late Archaic period in Michigan as seen from the Saginaw Valley.

TAYLOR, WALTER W.
1948 A study of archeology. American Anthropologist, Vol. 50, No. 3, Pt. 2, Memoir No. 69. Menasha.

TERASMAE, J.
1959 Notes on the Champlain Sea episode in the St. Lawrence lowlands, Quebec. Science, Vol. 130, No. 3371, pp. 334–36. Washington, D.C.

1960 Contributions to Canadian palynology, No. 2, Pt. 1. Geological Survey of Canada, Bulletin 56, pp. 1–22. Ottawa.

THOMAS, CYRUS
1894 Report on the mound explorations of the Bureau of Ethnology. Twelfth Annual Report of the Bureau of Ethnology, Smithsonian Institution, Washington.

TRAUTMAN, MILTON A.
1963 Isotopes, Inc. Radiocarbon measurements III. American Journal of Science, Radiocarbon, Vol. 5, Yale University, pp. 62–79. New Haven.

TUCK, JAMES A.
1967 The Howlett Hill site: an early Iroquois village in central New York. In, Iroquois culture, history and prehistory, ed. by Elisabeth Tooker, pp. 75–79. New York State Museum and Science Service. Albany.

WEAVER, JOHN E., and CLEMENTS, FREDERIC E.
1938 Plant ecology. McGraw-Hill. New York.

WEBB, WILLIAM S.
1939 An archaeological survey of Wheeler Basin on the Tennessee River in northern Alabama. Smithsonian Institution, Bureau of American Ethnology, Bulletin 122. Washington.

1946 Indian Knoll, site Oh 2, Ohio County, Kentucky. Reports in Archaeology and Anthropology, University of Kentucky, Vol. 4, No. 3. Lexington.

1950 The Carlson Annis mound, site 5, Butler County, Kentucky. Reports in Archaeology and Anthropology, University of Kentucky, Vol. 7, No. 4. Lexington.

———, and HAAG, W. G.
1940 The Cypress Creek villages, sites 11 and 12, McLean County, Kentucky. Reports in Archaeology and Anthropology, University of Kentucky, Vol. 4, No. 2. Lexington.

———, and SNOW, CHARLES E.
1945 The Adena people. Reports in Anthropology and Archaeology, University of Kentucky, Vol. VI. Lexington.

———, and WILDER, CHARLES G.

1951 An archaeological survey of Guntersville Basin on the Tennessee River in northern Alabama. University of Kentucky Press. Lexington.

———, and BABY, RAYMOND S.

1957 The Adena people—No. 2. Ohio Historical Society. Columbus.

WEST, GEORGE A.

1929 Copper: its mining and use by the aborigines of the Lake Superior region. Bulletin of the Public Museum of the City of Milwaukee, Vol. 10, No. 1. Milwaukee.

———

1932 Exceptional prehistoric copper implements. Bulletin of the Public Museum of the City of Milwaukee, Vol. 10, No. 4. Milwaukee.

WHITE, MARIAN E.

1961 Iroquois culture history in the Niagara frontier area of New York State. Anthropological Papers, Museum of Anthropology, University of Michigan, No. 16. Ann Arbor.

———

1967 1965 excavations at the Simmons site: a Niagara frontier Iroquois village. In, Iroquois culture, history, and prehistory, ed. by Elisabeth Tooker, pp. 85–89. New York State Museum and Science Service. Albany.

WHITNEY, TED

1962 Description of a burial from "Whites" (Nbn. 2). Chenango Chapter, N.Y.S.A.A., Vol. 4, No. 3, pp. 3–4. (Mimeographed.) Norwich.

WILLEY, GORDON R.; DI PESO, CHARLES C.; RITCHIE, WILLIAM A.; ROUSE, IRVING; ROWE, JOHN H., and LATHROP, DONALD W.

1956 An archeological classification of culture contact situations. In, Seminars in Archaeology: 1955, edited by Robert Wauchope, pp. 1–30. Memoirs of the Society for American Archaeology, No. 11. Salt Lake City.

———, and PHILLIPS, PHILIP

1958 Method and theory in American archaeology. University of Chicago Press. Chicago.

WILLOUGHBY, CHARLES C.

1922 The Turner group of earthworks, Hamilton County, Ohio. Papers of the Peabody Museum of American Archaeology and Ethnology, Harvard University, Vol. 8, No. 3. Cambridge.

———

1935 Antiquities of the New England Indians. Peabody Museum of American Archaeology and Ethnology, Harvard University. Cambridge.

———

WINTEMBERG, W. J.

1931 Distinguishing characteristics of Algonkian and Iroquoian cultures. National Museum of Canada, Annual Report for 1929, Bulletin No. 67, pp. 65–125. Ottawa.

WITTHOFT, JOHN

1949 An outline of Pennsylvania Indian history. Pennsylvania History. Quarterly Journal of the Pennsylvania Historical Association, Vol. 16, No. 3, pp. 3–15. Harrisburg.

———

1952 A Paleo-Indian site in eastern Pennsylvania: an early hunting culture. Proceedings of the American Philosophical Society. Vol. 96, No. 4, pp. 464–95. Philadelphia.

———

1953 Broad spearpoints and the transitional period cultures. Pennsylvania Archaeologist, Vol. 23, No. 1, pp. 4–31. Milton.

———

1954 A brief history of the Indian hunter. Pennsylvania Game News, Vol. 25, Nos. 6, 7, 8, 9, June, July, August, September. Harrisburg.

———
1959 Notes on the Archaic of the Appalachian region. American Antiquity, Vol. 25, No. 1, pp. 79–85. Salt Lake City.

———
1959a Ancestry of the Susquehannocks. *In,* Susquehannock miscellany, edited by John Witthoft and W. Fred Kinsey III. Pennsylvania Historical and Museum Commission, pp. 19–60. Harrisburg.

WORMINGTON, H. M.
1957 Ancient man in North America. Fourth edition. Denver Museum of Natural History, Popular Series No. 4. Denver.

WRAY, CHARLES FOSTER
1948 Varieties and sources of flint found in New York State. Pennsylvania Archaeologist, Vol. 18, Nos. 1–2, pp. 25–45. Milton.

———
1965 An Early Woodland site near Cuylerville, New York. Morgan Chapter Newsletter, Vol. V, pp. 3–7. Rochester.

———, and SCHOFF, HARRY L.
1953 A preliminary report on the Seneca sequence in western New York, 1550–1687. Pennsylvania Archaeologist, Vol. XXIII, No. 2, pp. 53–63. Milton.

WRIGHT, JAMES V.
1962 A distributional study of some Archaic traits in southern Ontario. National Museum of Canada, Bulletin No. 180, pp. 124–42. Ottawa.

———
1966 The Ontario Iroquois tradition. National Museum of Canada. Bulletin 210. Ottawa.

———
1967 The Laurel tradition and the Middle Woodland period. National Museum of Canada, Bulletin 217. Ottawa.

———
n.d. The archaeology of Ontario.

———, and ANDERSON, J. E.
1963 The Donaldson site. National Museum of Canada, Bulletin No. 184. Ottawa.

INDEX

Abbott Farm site (N.J.), 269
Adena culture
  infiltration of, 202, 204–5
  link with Middlesex phase of, 201
Anderson, Albert J., 140, 145
Andrews site (Mich.), 201
Archaic stage (*c.* 3500–1300 B.C.), 31–149
  archaeological specimens of, 20, 21
  Brewerton phase of (*see* Brewerton phase)
  coastal New York sequence of (*see* Coastal New York sequence)
  culture characteristics of, 31–33
    community patterning, 34
    seminomadic life, 33–34
  dated span of, 19, 32
  definition of, 31
  Frontenac phase of (*see* Frontenac phase)
  Glacial Kame culture in (*see* Glacial Kame culture)
  Lamoka phase of (*see* Lamoka phase)
  Late, xvi, 35
    breakthrough in study of, xix
    link between Woodland stage and, 150
  Laurentian tradition in (*see* Laurentian tradition)
  radiocarbon dating of, 19, 32
  River phase of (*see* River phase)
  site locations of, 40
  Snook Kill phase of (*see* Snook Kill phase)
  Staten Island sequence of (*see* Staten Island sequence)
  Vergennes phase of (*see* Vergennes phase)
  Vosburg phase of (*see* Vosburg phase)
Arrow points
  Levanna type
    of Hunter's Home phase, 254, 259
    of Iroquois culture, 308
    of Oak Hill phase, 310
    of Owasco culture, 277, 278
    of Sebonac phase, 267
  Madison type, 308
Artifacts. *See* Basketry; Ornaments; Pottery; Textiles; Tools
Ault, Dr. James O., 287

Bailey, John H., 84
Bannerman site (N.Y.), 84
Basketry
  of Meadowood phase, 194–96
  of Owasco culture, 279, 290
Bates site (N.Y.), 285–87
  animal skeletal remains at, 287
  fortification features at, 307
  house structures at, 285, 309
  subsoil features of, 286
Baxter, William J., 169

Baxter site (L.I.), 165–70
  geographical location of, 169
  mammal bones found at, 170
  nature of soil layers at, 169–70
  related to Solecki site, 175
  shellfish remains at, 166, 169
Bent site (N.Y.), 125–32
  as central settlement in River phase, 132
  nature of soil at, 125–26
  radiocarbon dating of, 127
  skeletal remains at, 129
Bloom, Arthur L., on submergence of Connecticut coast, 169
Bluff Point site (N.Y.), 222–23
Bodnar, Joseph, xvii, xviii
Bogaert, Harmen M. van den, 317
Borst, Roger, 21
Bowmans Brook A site (N.Y.), 146–47, 269
Bowmans Brook phase, 268–70
  distribution of, 268–69
  mortuary customs in, 270
  ornaments of, 269–70
  subsistence activities in, 269
Brammer, Mauk, 144
Brennan Louis A., 144
Brewerton phase, 35, 83, 89–104
  burial ritualism of, 103–4
  compared with Vosburg phase, 84
  discoveries of sites of, 89
  distribution and ecology of, 91
  linked to Laurentian tradition, 89, 91
  ornaments of, 99, 100
  people of, 92
  radiocarbon dating of, 91–92
  settlement patterns during, 96–99
    cyclical travels in, 98–99
    ecological reasons for, 98
    proximity of water in, 96–97
  subsistence activities during, 92–96
    bone and stone tools used in, 94–97
    firemaking, 96
    hunting as major, 92
    role of fishing in, 94, 98
    types of points used for, 92–94
  tools of
    bone and stone tools, 94–97
    characteristics of, 99
    for woodworking, 99, 101–2
  trade connections during, 101–3
  utilitarianism in, 104
Broad points
  Brewerton type, xx, 92–94
  of Kipp Island phase, 233, 244
  Lehigh type, 142, 153
  Snook Kill type, 137
    as ancestor to Lehigh Broad point, 142
    distribution of, 140–41, 147

WILLIAM A. RITCHIE is State Archaeologist for the New York State Museum and Science Service. He received his B.S. and M.S. degrees in archaeology from the University of Rochester, and his Ph.D. degree in anthropology from Columbia University. He also holds an honorary Sc.D. degree from Waynesburg College. He was formerly Curator of Anthropology at the Rochester Museum of Arts and Sciences, and has taught at the University of Rochester, and at Syracuse University and Harpur College as Visiting and Adjunct Professor of Anthropology. He is currently a Visiting Professor of Anthropology at the State University of New York at Albany. He is a member of Phi Beta Kappa and Sigma Xi.

Dr. Ritchie has conducted field researches on more than 100 major archaeological sites in the eastern United States and Canada, and has written more than 150 articles on the archaeology and paleopathology of the Indians of the Northeast. He is the author of *The Pre-Iroquoian Occupations of New York State,* which was awarded an A. Cressy Morrison Prize by the New York Academy of Sciences, and in 1964 he presented a paper at the 36th International Congress of Americanists in Spain. Member and past president of the Society for American Archaeology, he is also a Fellow of the American Anthropological Association, the American Association for the Advancement of Science, and the New York State Archeological Association. Dr. Ritchie presently lives in Delmar, New York.

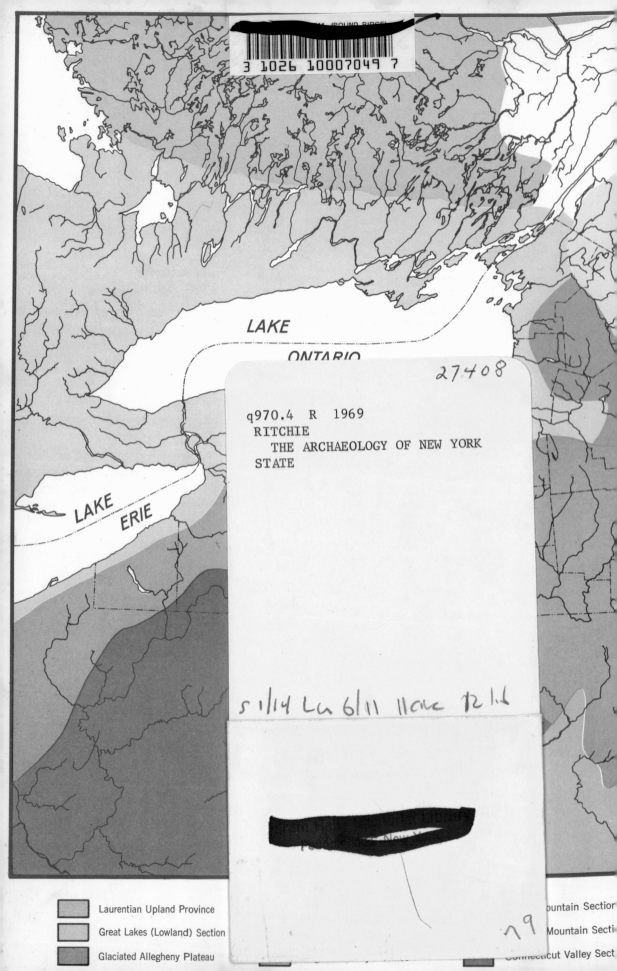

LAKE

ONTARIO

LAKE ERIE

27408

q970.4 R 1969
RITCHIE
    THE ARCHAEOLOGY OF NEW YORK
STATE

5 1/14 La 6/11 llavie 12 l.l

Laurentian Upland Province

Great Lakes (Lowland) Section

Glaciated Allegheny Plateau

ountain Section

Mountain Secti

Connecticut Valley Sect